THE UNIVERSITY OF WINCHESTER

'A
As

Bl   of
'th   ory
asj   nd
to   ers.
                                                                      in
th   ies,
an   o a
flc   ary.

•
•
•
•
•
•   Mustapha Matura
•   Dark and Light Theatre   •   Tamasha
•   The Keskidee Centre   •   Talawa.

Black and Asian Theatre in Britain is an enlightening and immensely readable resource and represents a major new study of theatre history and British history as a whole.

Colin Chambers was Kingston University's first Professor of Drama. Formerly a journalist and theatre critic, he was Literary Manager of the Royal Shakespeare Company from 1981 to 1997. His books include *The Story of Unity Theatre* (1989), the award-winning biogra   (1997), *The Continuum Companion*   he Royal *Shakespeare Company* (200

Black and Asian Theatre in Britain

A History

Colin Chambers

Routledge
Taylor & Francis Group

LONDON AND NEW YORK

First published 2011
by Routledge
2 Park Square, Milton Park, Abingdon, Oxon OX14 4RN

Simultaneously published in the USA and Canada
by Routledge
711 Third Avenue New York, NY 10017

Routledge is an imprint of the Taylor & Francis Group, an informa business

British Library Cataloguing in Publication Data
A catalogue record for this book is available from the British Library

Library of Congress Cataloging-in-Publication Data
Chambers, Colin.
  Black and Asian theatre in Britain: A history/Colin Chambers.
    p. cm.
  Includes bibliographical references and index.
  1. Black theater–Great Britain–History. 2. Theater, South Asian–
  Great Britain–History. 3. English drama–South Asian authors–
  History and criticism. 4. English drama–Black authors–History
  and criticism. 5. Blacks in literature. 6. South Asians in literature. I. Title.
  PN2595.13.B34C43 2011   2010038421
  792.089'96041–dc22

ISBN: 978-0-415-36513-0 (hbk)
ISBN: 978-0-415-37598-6 (pbk)

Typeset in Bembo by
HWA Text and Data Management, London

Printed and bound in Great Britain by
CPI Antony Rowe, Chippenham, Wiltshire

For my grandchildren, Alfie, Mia and Louis

CONTENTS

FIGURES

Every effort has been made to seek permission to reproduce copyright material before the book went to press. If any proper acknowledgement has not been made, we would invite copyright holders to inform us of the oversight.

ACKNOWLEDGEMENTS

I thank the following for their help:

Mustafa Abdelwahid, Michael Abbensetts, Hakim Adi, Yemi Ajibade, June Baden Semper, Martin Banham, Jeremy Barlow, Jane Bernal, Rustom Bharucha, Colin Blumenau, Stephen Bourne, David Boxer, Yvonne Brewster, Ian Brown, and Martin Brown.

Conrad Brunstrom, Suman Buchar, Tess Buckland, John Burgess, Margaret Busby, Gilli Bush-Bailey, Earl Cameron, Malcolm Chase, Geraldine Connor, Karen S. Cook, Chris Cooper, Sean Creighton, Andy Croft, Sarah Dadswell, John Davis, Alan Dein, Rachel Douglas, Ian Duffield, Clare DuVergier, John Faulkner, Margaret Ferguson, Anne Fletcher, Tony Flood, Peter Fraser, Sophie Fuller, Dimple Godiwala, Christopher Gordon, Tony Graves, Jeff Green, John Greene, Trevor Griffiths, Jagdish Gundara, Simelia Hodge-Dallaway, Christian Hogsbjerg, Peter Holland, Isobel Howson, Mark Howell, Robert Hutchison, Paul Iles, Alby James, Stephen Johnson, Nesta Jones, Raminder Kaur Kahlon, Rashid Karapiet, Farah Karim-Cooper, Naseem Khan, Nicolas Kent, David Killingray, Kaylan Kundu, Shompa Lahiri, Ananda Lal, Bernth Lindfors, Joyce MacDonald, Rob Marx, Joan-Ann Maynard, Isha Mckenzie-Mavinga, and Peter Millington.

Sara Moore, Chris Morash, Gregory Mosher, Hugh Murray, Norma Myers, Alistair Niven, Max Novak, Marian O'Connor, Susan D. Pennybacker, Thelma Perkins, Anton Phillips, Richard Pilbrow, Daphne Power, William Radice, Ahmad Rahman, Amalia Ribi, Brian Roberts, Andrew Robinson, Lawrence Rodgers, Alaknanda Samarth, Jonathan Schneer, Stephen Solley, Pat Stone, SuAndi, Michael Tadman, Alda Terracciano, Peter Thomson, Joanna van Gyseghem, Virginia Vaughan, Jatinder Verma, Rozina Visram, Tony Walton, Hazel Waters, Lisa Whistlecroft, Karina Williamson, Steve Wilmer, Val Wilmer, and Peter Woodford.

Archivists, administrators, librarians, and registrars of the various collections, libraries, and organisations I contacted and/or visited:

BBC Radio 7, BBC Wales South West, Bernie Grant Archives (Middlesex University).

Bodleian Library of Commonwealth and African Studies, Boughton Trust, Bournemouth Library, British Council Archive (National Archives), British Library, British Sociological Association, Camden Local Studies and Archives Centre, City of Westminster Archives Centre, East Sussex Libraries, and Eastbourne Local History Society.

George Padmore Institute, Gray's Inn Library, Guildhall School of Music and Drama, Haringey Local History Library and Archives, Housman Society, and Howard University.

Inner Temple Archives, Institute of Race Relations, Kali Theatre Company, Lancashire Records Office, Leverhulme Family Archive, Lewisham Local Studies, Lincoln's Inn Library, London Metropolitan Archive, Marx Memorial Library, National Theatre Archive, New York Public Library, Oval House, Oxford Dictionary of National Biography, People's History Museum, Royal Academy of Dramatic Art, Royal Albert Hall Archive, Samuel French, Schomburg Center for Research in Black Culture, Somerset Studies Library, Strode Theatre, Theatre Royal Margate, Theatres Trust, Universities of: Bristol (Theatre Collection), Kansas (Spencer Research Library), Nottingham (Manuscripts and Special Collections), Pennsylvania Library, Sussex (Special Collections), the West Indies (West Indiana and Special Collections, Victoria and Albert Museum (Theatre Collections), Westminster Library, Wigmore Hall, and Women in Jazz.

Funding for research visits came from the British Academy (small grant) and Kingston University.

INTRODUCTION

If there is no struggle, there is no progress … Power concedes nothing without a demand. It never did and it never will.

Frederick Douglass, former slave and emancipation leader, 1857

In aiming to chart the history of black and Asian theatre in Britain, this book is attempting to recover a history that has been downgraded, ignored, or suppressed.[1] It is a long and complicated history of a struggle for self-definition, of a struggle in an often-hostile culture to create spaces for self-assertion and self-expression. It is a history that, because of its subject, the nature of the society in which it took place, and the available sources, focuses at the outset on individuals and groups of individuals. It then moves beyond the achievements of such individuals in the last decades of the twentieth century when the black and Asian presence in British theatre, however disputed, fraught, and fragile, acquired a level of organization, dynamism, and reach that made it recognizable as a distinct and autonomous phenomenon. In this process of becoming, British theatre was rethought. New performance aesthetics shaped by diasporic customs reinvigorated the traditional repertoire and introduced countervailing images and new verbal and visual vocabularies that challenged British preconceptions.

Such a history is necessarily part of a wider story, of the presence in Britain of peoples from the African, Asian, and Caribbean diaspora, and of their struggles against racism and for national independence, justice, and equality. Their presence can be traced back possibly before – but certainly since – Roman times and, from the mid-1550s, in an unbroken line through to the more familiar migrations and settlings that followed World War 2. Globalization, propelled by imperialism, brought large non-white populations to transform the cultures and languages of continental Europe and Britain. In consequence, globalization highlighted hybridity as the defining trait of what might be called post-colonial times, and hybridity is embodied by black and Asian theatre: it is British and not British, diasporic and not diasporic, drawing on and producing a culture both of exile and belonging, and of neither. As such, black and Asian theatre stands at the heart of the debate about the identity and direction of Britain and what it means to be British in the twenty-first century.

The scholarly context for this history is both theatre-specific and much broader, joining the growing number of studies exploring the black or Asian presence in Britain. Although Kenneth Little's *Negroes in Britain* was published in 1948, the momentum of such publications did not gather pace until the 1970s, with books such as James Walvin's *Black Presence* (1971), Edward Scobie's *Black Britannia* (1972), Folarin Shyllon's *Black People in Britain 1555–1833* (1974), and Peter Fryer's *Staying Power* (1984).[2] Though there were books at the same time on postwar migration from South Asia, similar books about the longer Asian presence came a little later, with Rozina Visram's *Ayahs, Lascars, and Princes: Indians in Britain 1700–1947* (1986), Chandau Amarjit's *Indians in Britain* (1986), Roger Ballard's (ed.), *Desh Pardesh: The South Asian Presence in Britain* (1994), and Shompa Lahiri's *Indians in Britain* (2000).[3] These have since been supplemented by many other titles, and educational curricula have embraced their subject matter.

Beginning in the last decades of the twentieth century, black studies became a recognizable academic discipline that overlapped with developments in other related fields, such as identity studies (notably concerning the meaning of race and ethnicity), post-colonial studies and, in the examination and theorising of outsider or marginal practice, deconstruction, cultural, and border theory (across the spectrum from the works of Bhabha, Bourdieu, Brah, Deleuze, and Derrida to Foucault, Hall, and Spivak). Scholars progressed beyond the need to prove there existed a distinct and worthy field of study to demonstrating that the subjects of this study had made, and continued to make, significant contributions on their own terms – terms that were not necessarily (though could be) the same as the terms employed in white discourse but which were certainly of equal value. In the process, the vocabulary of both discourses was changed.

One strand of this wider account is the exploration of the black and Asian contribution in theatre and linked areas, such as dance, radio, film, and television. This book owes a particular debt to those who have undertaken such research. A pioneering biography of Ira Aldridge by Herbert Marshall and Mildred Stock appeared in 1958, but it was a rare case and not widely known.[4] In 1989, my book, *The Story of Unity Theatre*, identified black involvement in a left-wing theatre group and hinted at the beginnings of a black theatre history. Jim Pines edited a series of important interviews in *Black and White in Colour* (1992), which, though focused on television, featured artists who were central to the black theatre movement. This is also true of Stephen Bourne's *Black in the British Frame: Black People in British Film and Television 1896–1996* (2001). *Fringe First* (1992) by Roland Rees (ed.) contains an important section on black theatre; Ruth Tompsett (ed.), *Black Theatre in Britain* (1996), reports from a conference on black theatre; and in chapters, essays, and articles, others look at important aspects of black and Asian theatre in their social and artistic contexts. These authors include Tyrone Huggins, Raminder Kaur, Bruce King, Michael McMillan, Kwesi Owusu, Malcolm Page, D. Keith Peacock, SuAndi, and Alda Terracciano, as well as others listed in notes and the bibliography.[5] Theatre was covered in volumes such as Alison Donnell (ed.), *Companion to Contemporary Black British Culture* (2002), whereas major and broader contributions were made in 2006 by two more edited volumes: Geoffrey V. Davis and Anne Fuchs (eds), *Staging New Britain* (2006), and Dimple Godiwala (ed.), *Alternatives Within the Mainstream* (2006).[6] Meanwhile, interest in specific areas has grown, most notably in relation to women, through work by (among others) Elaine Aston, Susan Croft, Mary Karen Dahl, Lynette Goddard, Dimple Godiwala, Liz Goodman, Gabrielle Griffin, Valerie Kaneko Lucas, Meenakshi Ponnuswami, and Katherine Starck.[7] The University of Exeter won grant money in 2004 for a four-year project on British Asian Theatre that resulted in a conference in 2008 and promises two books on the subject. In 2010, Dominic Hingorani's *British Asian Theatre* was published, offering an examination of companies and writers from the 1970s on.[8]

In the foregoing, however, there is little of detail on the history of black and Asian theatre in Britain before the 1970s, and much in that decade is left uncovered. The aspiration of this book is to fill this conspicuous gap. It aims to construct a continuous – though not teleological – theatre history and to present a multivalent account that recognizes and validates different, diverse, and even contradictory aspects of that history, the scope and rhythms of which change over the centuries. The chronologically earlier and larger part of the history (in terms of time span) focuses on representation by white theatre of those perceived to be the Other, a characteristic that has been central not only to British theatre since the sixteenth century but to the formation of notions of British national identity.

For much of the period covered by this book, the difference between an imagined image of the non-white Other and the physical representation in theatre was personified in blackface. The signs associated with blackface – makeup, costume, use of language and physicality – accrued a set of meanings that became recognizable and accepted. These meanings were renewed through repetition and modification in changing historical circumstances and provided continuity for the construction and representation of racialized difference. Such a process is not exclusive to Britain, though its characteristics are, because the strands that comprise this representation follow the specific contours of the expansion of British capital and culture into colonialism, imperialism, and post-colonialism. It would be wrong, however, to read the images produced in this process in simple terms, as can happen in accounts that rely on the binary of victim and oppressor. As Mita Choudhury says, 'Resistance to, appropriation and acculturation of the other follows haphazard even disconnected trajectories of intention, instigation, purpose and desire.'[9]

The interlacing strands of representation, of repeated, familiarizing mimicry, could be intricate and crude, and formed part of a complex ideological matrix in which gender, class, nationality, ethnicity, and colour were intermixed. These strands were not always homogenized and were frequently contested, containing much that was subversive and more that was conservative. Nevertheless, it is striking how constant the chief anxieties regarding the Other – sex, religion, morality, status – remain throughout their different historical manifestations as white theatre promulgated white dominion over the representation of non-white peoples. Whatever the reasons for the peculiar persistence and longevity of Britain's Othering (its small size and being an island as well as its imperial project), in British theatre, the overwhelming idea of control and containment of the Other and of the superiority of British civilization was rarely challenged with any determination or thoroughness.

Performers from the African, Asian, and Caribbean diaspora do appear in this first part of the history, but they are relatively few in number and, until the arrival of African-American actor Ira Aldridge in the 1820s, make little impact, being mostly anonymous and un-, or under-, reported. Writers arrive, in extremely small numbers, only at the turn of the Victorian era into the Edwardian era when modern Pan-Africanism was being born. With a couple of exceptions, they do not begin to exert significant influence until much later.

The second part of the history, covering primarily the twentieth century, initially explores the achievements of the early years, achievements which – piecemeal, uneven, and marginalized as they were – begin to open up spaces to challenge dominant perceptions and enact an agenda determined by non-white diasporic practitioners themselves. Against the backdrop of community activism in Britain and anti-colonial struggle abroad, this trajectory is carried through to the flourishing of black and Asian theatre in the last quarter of the twentieth century, when extreme right-wing attacks on 'ethnic communities' and aggressively racist policing drew a concerted riposte from besieged communities.

The two parts of the history are inseparably linked. The accumulation of images of difference produced by white theatre significantly shaped the environment of ignorance and prejudice in which diasporic theatre practitioners had to work. Identities, after all, are formed in and through, not outside, systems of representation, which are themselves connected to power relations and the spread of, or resistance to, dominance. White theatre was for much of this history a major and popular cultural force in Britain that helped sustain hegemony across the empire. Theatre was not alone in this, but it made a signal contribution alongside other artistic and social phenomena to the ideological predispositions underpinning colonialism and imperialism while, at the same time, being a potent site to explore their contradictions.

Challenges

Writing such a history inevitably brings with it many problems. Indeed, the words 'history,' 'black,' 'Asian,' 'theatre,' and 'Britain' in the title are all contested terms. Starting with theatre, as this is a theatre history, its definition can be wide or narrow and its capture inherently awkward. Theatre performance is ephemeral and particular to its own time, place, and conditions of production and reception. The various elements of performance – for instance, music, makeup, gesture, dance, costume, setting, and lighting – all have their own codes, as do the spaces in which performance takes place. The interplay between the codes affects the realization of intentions and the audience's interpretations of those intentions. Non-white diasporic theatre questioned the dominant codes by drawing on performance customs and codes that are different from those of Britain and Europe, customs of ritual and orality and of social function, customs that do not divide art from entertainment or dance from drama.

Carrying multiple meanings and being read in multiple ways means theatre, whether white or non-white, can be both traditional and/or transgressive. It is a topic of constant debate as to whether, or to what degree, theatre can undermine dominant authority and even pose an alternative rather than confirm or extend dominance or act as an incorporator. Performance can emphasize agency, which can undermine the rigidity of stereotypes that commonly nurture drama. However, performance can also deepen and renew those stereotypes. A production can simultaneously present contradictory views, but how do audiences deal with this concurrent challenge and confirmation? Issues of reality and authenticity come into play here; corporeal theatre, after all, speaks to the imagination, the world of 'might be' or 'what if', even when pretending to present the world 'as is'. In, for example, the use, role, and interpretation of stereotype (which features regularly in this history), to what extent do audiences distinguish between the representation of reality and the reality being represented? Even if audiences do make the distinction, to what extent do they apply in their lives outside the theatre the values of those systems of representation they encounter in the theatre that embody discrimination?

Such questions, which are hard enough to handle in contemporary situations, are even more troubling when dealing with the past. Just because the first Elizabethans, for example, did not think of race or skin colour in ways that became common in the nineteenth or twentieth centuries does not mean that prejudices or discriminatory practices were not active, but how to assess this centuries later? Or, to take another example, how to evaluate the theatre that the anti-slavery movement mobilized on its behalf, using depictions later generations would consider overtly racist? It is hard to identify historical specificity, let alone capture it, yet a major concern must be to balance the past and the present and to avoid judging the past by the standards of the present without accepting the past on its own terms or denying the connections.

A further issue in considering the significance of the un-empowered and marginalized who have often been invisible is the weight that should be given to visibility. When does presence turn into visibility and power? The presence of black or Asian actors or plays does not necessarily alter white theatre – indeed, it may reinforce it – but it has been a precondition for any change. Similarly, the achievements of individuals may not constitute black or Asian theatre, but they are an integral part of the process through which collective accomplishments have been realized.

Theatre history also faces the dilemma of the archive and its absences.[10] Recuperation of theatre that was produced before photographic and sound recording poses particular problems, though technology brings its own issues of selection. The traces performance leaves in texts, associated memorabilia, recordings, and commentary are of different kinds and hermeneutic value. Many are lost.

Compared to the number of plays performed, for example, few were published, and those that survive (often in the repository of censors) may have differed significantly in performance. Scholarship was slow to regard theatre as important, despite its richness as a location for investigation and cultural reflection. Theatre was overlooked in favour of more seemingly fixed and tangible forms such as painting or literature, and this bias influenced the keeping of documents and artifacts, resulting in unevenness of preservation.

In Britain, what was kept or recorded showed a predisposition toward London, mainstream venues, and their stars. Furthermore, just as in conventional histories of British theatre where black and Asian involvement has been neglected, theatre has tended to be marginalized in books on the cultural contribution of the non-white diaspora.[11] Archiving British black and Asian theatre began in earnest at the end of the twentieth and beginning of the twenty-first centuries, and the records of important companies are stored in various locations such as the Theatre Collections at the Victoria and Albert Museum; Middlesex University's Future Histories Collection; London Metropolitan Archives; and the George Padmore Institute. Such holdings are supplemented by publications such as the Theatre Museum's *Black and Asian Performance at the Theatre Museum* (2003) and the creation in 2010 of the Black Theatre Archive at the National Theatre Studio.[12]

Alongside theatre-specific problems come more general ones that, in relation to history and inequity, are well rehearsed but require noting nonetheless. They include recognizing similarities between oppressions without falling into relativism by eliding discriminations and losing their specificity and minimizing the disadvantages of having to use – and being implicated by – a necessarily imperfect methodological apparatus and its terminology. Examples of this latter issue are the use of the system of periodization that deploys terms such as *post-colonial*, which universalizes an imperial Eurocentric perspective even though simultaneously inscribing its demise, and the use of terms such as *black*, *white*, *Asian*, and *the Other*, which are inevitably imprecise and fluid and with a homogenizing tendency to essentialism.

Any writing that explores the heritage of empire has to grapple with a panoply of volatile practices (e.g., biology, philosophy, phenomenology, psychology) and their unstable vocabularies, which will have been used to determine social inclusion and exclusion by way of racial and ethnic signification. Demarcations of difference, such as colour or race, and their relationship to human features such as skin colour or facial characteristics change over time and place; they may be arbitrary and slippery, but they are nevertheless real in their implementation and consequences. As is the case with labels such as black and white, they assume a transcendent and emblematic force even when manifestly inaccurate.

The key concept of the Other, which has a psychological dimension that muddies its metaphorical use, implies an 'us' at the centre but does not deal with the process by which the Other, 'them', can become 'us' or can transform who 'us' is. Also problematic is determining who the Other is. Dubious ethnographic categorization has a long history; the term 'blackamoor', for instance, was applied in Elizabethan times to a vast range of disparate peoples and, in the twentieth century, a succession of competing descriptors unfurled with the shifting political situation (e.g., *negro* gave way to *coloured*, *ethnic* to *black*). The term *Asian* appears late in this process (seemingly with Indian and Pakistani independence). What it attempts to describe was often subsumed in the loose and plastic notion of the Orient or the East. Using *South Asian* and *East Asian* was an attempt to be more precise, as was *Anglo-Asian*, *BrAsian* or, in a different context, *black British*.

As applied to black and Asian theatre, terminology remains awkward not only for commentators. Rejecting the notion of ethnic arts deployed by state funding agencies in the 1970s and 1980s, practitioners briefly preferred the term *Black theatre*. It connected the lived experience of racism, which was marked by colour, with challenges to the dominant system of representation deployed by non-whites in white theatre. The capital *B* indicated a political idea that embraced common strands of experience and resistance among the former colonized peoples and their British-born successors. The capital *B* also implied a unity that attempted to overcome a sense of superiority fuelled by imperialism among those of Indian descent over those of African background. Black theatre, however, became more associated with African and Caribbean heritage than with South Asian and, in its political sense, Black theatre did not survive long.[13] It was replaced by black (lower case *b*) and Asian to reflect the dominant heritage strands (African, Caribbean, and Asian), though *black* was still used as a convenient shorthand. With the state's adopting a diversity agenda in the 1990s came increasing specificity – South Asian and East Asian, for example, as mentioned earlier – accompanied by use of generic descriptors such as BME (Black and Minority Ethnic), BAME (Black and Asian Minority Ethnic), or diasporic. Diasporic, however, can lack the focus of heritage strands, imply singularity of heritage cultures, and can remove their relationship to colour. Diasporic is also problematic for successive generations of the British-born for whom the diasporic is increasingly only one element among many that constitute their identities.[14] The 2006 *Whose Theatre…?* report into diversity abandoned heritage-based labels and talked instead of The Sector.[15] This industrial term also hides the role of colour in discrimination while being positive in recognizing the attainments of non-white practitioners and avoiding the separatism that the labels *black* and *Asian* imply.

Playwright Winsome Pinnock considers the term *black theatre* – and, by extension, *Asian theatre* – to be double-edged because it denotes both autonomy and exclusion: 'it reflects and articulates the reality of a division within theatrical institutions in which black or "other" performers are viewed solely in relation to their supposed difference'.[16] In common with other artists defined as belonging to a marginalized group – women, for example, or Jews, the Irish, gays and lesbians – Pinnock expresses a continuing anxiety about, and reluctance to be stuck with, any socio-political label, even if others classify this way. Like other artists, she looks toward a time when such labels can be dropped but recognizes this is some way off. This perspective was symptomatic of a late-twentieth-century struggle to change the system of representation on a non-racialized basis without losing the values drawn from heritage or denying the consequences of difference defined by colour. If white theatre were considered simply theatre, which it is, black and Asian theatre should be, too.

Such an approach is very different from that which masks racism in the theatre when declaring 'there is only theatre' or argues against the existence of black or Asian theatre on the grounds that the bulk of theatre is not called *white* theatre. *White* has no need to bring notice to itself because white has made itself the norm, the often unconscious, apparently colourless, and non-racialized benchmark that obscures the realities of power. Non-white theatre in Britain did not at first seek its distinctive status; this was conferred by empire. With the decline of empire and changes in the patterns and sources of migration, that distinctive status is being transformed into a different kind of presence altogether.

Choices

A few points about several of the choices that inform the book, which is written by an outsider, a white theatre historian brought up in south London in the 1950s when there was no black in the Union Jack – but there was on the streets.[17] As the title of the book shows, I have stayed with the terms *Britain*, *black*, and *Asian*, which, as I noted earlier, are all contentious. Although the bulk of the book deals with England and the English, the spread and impact of black and Asian theatre and its importance to debates around identity entail a British dimension. I have used *black* and *Asian* (as well as *white*) because they reflect the terminology of the key period in the late twentieth century when black and Asian theatre achieved its distinctive presence. They retain the crucial aspect of colour and, for the reader, are less clumsy than alternatives and are relatively clear in their meaning. In looking in the earlier chapters at the centuries in which the templates of white representation were laid down, I necessarily offer a selective and representative rather than comprehensive account. I am indebted to the specialists in the areas I cover and who are mentioned in the notes and bibliography and who, I hope, will understand, if not forgive, the level of generalization employed. In different ways, the problem of simplification also applies to the later periods of the book when massive and complex issues, such as funding, marketing, audience development, repertoire, language, the tensions within the black and Asian theatre (of gender and national identity, for instance), and the contribution of black British theatre to Caribbean theatre are touched upon but cannot be dealt with in the detail that their importance might command in other studies.

In the earlier chapters, the book also takes a wider view of performers and entertainment before narrowing as black and Asian activity makes its mark in the British theatre of the twentieth century. The history becomes less concerned with white representation at this juncture, not because such representation ceases to be important but because it is not the primary subject of the book. The focus is black and Asian practitioners in the British theatre they struggled to enter and transform. For this reason, own-language theatre, though mentioned, is not examined in detail. Use of English is one of the main differences between black and Asian theatre and theatre of other diasporas – Yiddish, for instance – which have also been marked by historic discrimination and form part of British theatre history.

On a practical note, pressure of space and a desire to avoid information overload has meant not always providing complete details of plays, such as dates (which are sometimes disputed) or full titles, especially pre-twentieth-century ones that habitually had long subtitles. Enough has been cited to allow plays to be placed and traced, and more information is given where it might be difficult to find elsewhere. Individuals and groups are included regardless of the degree to which they identified with a particular version of diasporic identity, itself a changing, contradictory, and complex reality. Despite the understandable demand exerted particularly by histories of the marginalized to find 'firsts,' I have tried to use the appellation judiciously and with adequate qualification, being aware that subsequent research frequently requires such claims to be rewritten. I accept that some of the 'firsts' I have identified and other claims will have to be revised. I also accept that in such a broad history, errors will appear, though I hope none so heinous as to undermine the points being registered or the passage of history being told.

The nature of the history has also meant an emphasis on companies and their landscape rather than the work of individual playwrights, actors, or directors. As mentioned earlier, there is a focus on certain individuals earlier in the history before collective activity becomes the driving force and, though individuals remain the cornerstone of any enterprise, the density of activity in the latter part of the twentieth century and beyond makes fair coverage or consideration of individuals impossible. The significant figures of this later period are also the ones more extensively studied elsewhere.

Together, however, individuals and the collective activity of which they are a part form the backbone of this history. Together, the individuals and the companies that comprise black and Asian theatre in Britain challenged those who saw themselves as the hosts to question their assumptions about the Other and their assumptions about themselves. They did this through theatre, in what might be called a *theatre of trespass*, a theatre too often confined to the margins of conventional history. This book is, therefore, a celebration of a particular culture of the marginalized and of its ability not only to survive and thrive but to redefine ideas of the periphery and the centre. As part of this reclamation, the customary models of configuring history – them (the Other)/us, mainstream/fringe – can be challenged, and the idea of being on the edge can recover its metaphorical association of vibrant innovation.

1

THE EARLY ERA

Representation of 'them' – the Other – has a long history in British theatre, linked to shifting notions of who constitutes 'us'. The portrayal of the non-white Other is a central strand of this history, a strand frequently associated with the use of the colour black. Unpicking the meanings over different historical periods of this complex, confused, and confusing tradition of representation is extremely difficult, especially as theatrical customs continually interact with extra-theatrical ones, which inevitably are always changing.

Colour was not always the chief index of difference, but its role is fundamental and deep-rooted. Blackening the face, for instance, appears to have been common in medieval village life, from poaching and protest to seasonal activities such as plough-witching and pace-egging. Although Morris dancing probably took its name from the Moors and some dancers wore blackface, whether, or in what ways, the early history of popular blackface practice is connected to people of African or Asian descent is not clear.[1] Black carried several connotations: it could signify sorrow or mourning and even constant and unrequited love. The dominant meaning, however – which was not exclusive to Christianity but which Christianity did most to promote – was black as the colour of evil. The early-mid-fifteenth-century morality play, *The Castle of Perseverance*, features Satan as 'Belial the blake', but the vernacular text does not otherwise show signs of racialized intent.[2] With religious change in Britain triggered by Henry VIII, such plays were suppressed at the same time as mutual exchange with other cultures boomed through war, trade, diplomacy, and exploration. Blackface customs continued in folk culture, at court and in theatrical presentations, such as pageants, where 'damned souls' would have their faces blackened, or interludes, in which sin was symbolized by a blackened face.[3] By the late sixteenth century, at the beginning of the modern professional playhouse tradition, black is often negative and has become firmly, though not solely, associated with the Other. Black is also a site for definitions of class and gender as well as the racialized Other. Moral attributes, both desirable and damaging, are cast onto the external Other while also being recognized as intrinsic (for example, blackness standing for sexual promiscuity). Accumulated and contradictory perceptions of what blackness signifies become ascribed to black characters who, with few exceptions, are portrayed until the twentieth century by white actors in plays by white writers written primarily for white audiences.

The theatrical use of blackface and related body decoration has to be interpreted not only in terms of social context, as part of the parade of blackness on display at a given moment in a given society (in paintings, literature, or fashion, for instance) but in terms of the complete vocabulary of theatrical signification employed at any one time, itself a highly intricate, often contradictory, and competing set of codes, inconsistently practised. The iconography of the blackface actors' external signals – makeup, costume, gesture – is multifaceted and does not offer an unequivocal connection to race.[4] Indeed, not all black roles were played in blackface. Nevertheless, blackface forms part of an increasingly racial and racist interpretation of humanity in the context of the transformation of England from a relatively minor entity, trying to establish its Protestant place in the face of European Catholic and Dutch competition, to an internationally powerful slave-trading nation in the eighteenth century and the heart of the supreme global power in the nineteenth.

During this transformation, there was little non-white presence within drama, either as artists or audience, and what presence there was has been found mainly in musical or nonspeaking entertainments and displays. From at least the thirteenth century, there had been a European court tradition of black musicians and entertainers, which carried over into England under the Tudors, if not before. Court records show that both Henry VII and Henry VIII employed a black trumpeter, John Blanke (a.k.a. Blanc), who possibly came with Catherine of Aragon from Spain in 1501. A tapestry of him at a 1511 royal jousting tournament is regarded as one of the first images of a black person in Britain in English art. The Scottish court of Stuart King James IV employed a small number of black Africans, including a minstrel, Peter the Moor, a drummer and a choreographer, and a female, 'Elen More', who may have participated as the black Queen of Beauty in a tournament of the black lady and the black (or wild) knight played by the king. Queen Elizabeth I, an icon of whiteness who ordered the expulsion of 'blackamoors' from England twice during her reign, had black African entertainers at court and a page. Having a black page was a fashion symbol for the nobility as reflected by Shakespeare in *A Midsummer Night's Dream* in the dispute between Oberon and Titania over a beautiful Indian servant boy who conjures up images of spice and barter as well as servitude. Shakespeare probably knew at least one black performer, Lucy Negro, a courtesan who took part in the 1594 Gray's Inn Christmas revels.[5] James VI of Scotland/James I of England, himself an outsider in England, employed at least one black performer. During his reign, some Asians, brought to England by way of the East India Company, joined a small number of Africans who had been arriving since the mid-sixteenth century as performers in civic and guild pageants. Such pageants had represented Moors since the early sixteenth century; mostly, it seems, but not always, they were played by whites.

FIGURE 1.1 Black musician in the procession from a Westminster tournament, 1511, thought to be John Blanke or Blanc ('Westminster Tournament Roll'. Courtesy of The College of Arms)

A mix of white and non-white performers in pageants continued through the seventeenth century when such pageants were used to laud the merits of colonialism and later of slavery itself.[6]

The court of James I, which was said to be more outward looking than Elizabeth's, has gained a reputation for its use of black as indicative of its love of oddity; when James's wife, Queen Anne of Denmark, asked Ben Jonson to write her first court masque, she requested that she and her ladies appear as 'blackamoors'.[7] He obliged, and in *The Masque of Blackness* (1605), they abandoned the customary black masks and blackened their skin with paint to promote the virtues of female beauty, which, at the time, was represented as white. Jonson plays with notions of blackness, which here is strongly gendered with a sexual undertow. There are echoes of the proverbial expression regarding the impossibility of washing an Ethiope white, which connects to a long tradition of an Ethiopian Satan alluded to in *The Castle of Perseverance*. According to Andrea Stevens, Jonson's masque was not well received because the women were not transformed back into white, possibly because no paint was available that could be removed quickly enough for the transformation to occur within the time frame of the masque.[8] Jonson could only conclude his story of the River Niger's search to change his black daughters back to their original white colour in a separate piece, *The Masque of Beauty* (1608). Technology seemingly had come to Jonson's aid by the time he wrote *The Gypsies Metamorphosed* (1621), as the masquers, who are disguised as tawny, are cleansed before the masque is finished.

The playwrights who authored masques and pageants were busy peopling all the public and private theatres with 'foreigners', whether contemporary or historical, from near or far. Alongside the Irish, Scots, Welsh, Spanish, French, Italian, Scandinavian, and Jewish (the traditional bogey) can be found ancient Romans and Greeks, Moroccans, Moors, Turks, Persians, and a host of other Others. They would appear in lurid reconstructions of notable events, in fantastic adventures unfettered by the straitjacket of fact, and in metaphorical stories usefully helping to bypass censorship and punishment when their authors were addressing sensitive topical issues. Marlowe, for example, consistently looked to the Other to write about his times. In his popular renderings of the central Asian conqueror Timur the Lame, a.k.a. Tamerlaine or Tamburlaine, he writes of the European tussle between England and Spain, of the conflict between Protestant and Catholic Christianity, and of the wider battle between papal Christendom and Islam.

Representation of the Other was central to the development of drama in this innovative phase, especially in the playhouses, which themselves were novel, exotic, and dangerous. London was the dynamo of the fast-expanding economy and of the newly emerging professional theatre. Although precise figures are unavailable because many texts have been lost, the sheer volume of plays of the Elizabethan/ Jacobean and first Caroline period that are known to feature the Other is remarkable. Louis Wann lists forty-seven plays from 1579 (the year of *The Blacksmith's Daughter*, which portrays the treachery of the Turks) to 1642 (closure of theatres) in which at least one character from Turkey, north Africa, Malta, Arabia, Persia, and Tartary appears in the cast list.[9] Turkish characters and settings figure the most, followed by North African Moors. Ottoman Sultan Suleiman I, probably the most powerful ruler of the sixteenth century, figures in at least ten plays, including a batch that retell the story of his assassination of his heir at the urging of Roxolana, one of his harem wives (but not the heir's mother) who sought the advancement of her own sons.

At a time when the Ottoman empire was more important to England than the New World and many definitions of identity, including what it meant to be English, were unusually fluid and contradictory, terms such as *Turk, Moor, blackamoor,* and *negro* were widely applied as catch-all labels regardless of culture, faith, or geographical origin, combining and confusing peoples from Asia, Africa, and the Americas. Although geography was as much a matter of imagination as science and drama was not intended to be ethnographically authoritative, theatrical creations, nevertheless, were a means to handle actual engagements with a rapidly changing and intensely contested, multicultural world. As travellers and translators made often highly dubious information about the Other increasingly available, notions of the racialized Other inherited from the Crusades were reassembled through, and in turn were transmitted back into, trade, war, politics, and cultural exchange. The messages from the Crusades, however, were not straightforward, and nor were the new perceptions: Islam, for example, was seen as the enemy but also as a site of extraordinary knowledge, from astronomy and finance to mathematics and poetry.

Though the Other was a threat, it could also be magical and wonderful, and lack of discrimination between Others did not mean they were treated the same all the time; Persians could be presented as different to the Turks, and both could be seen as enemies of Spain, whereas in *The Jew of Malta* (1592), in which Marlowe questions religion itself, Jews, Muslims, and Christians are all shown as corrupt. In plays that deal with conversion – political and religious apostasy was common and often enforced – the superiority of the Christian world is asserted even when Islam is allowed positive features. Yet, though conversion may offer a narrative resolution of the contest with the Other, it does not always represent a secure victory, as can be seen in the case of Shylock.[10]

Before the Restoration, religion remains paramount in defining the Other, and clothing, rank, and manners are more important external indices than physical attributes. Yet, though the use of colour was not always a sign of the Other or of racism, there was an accumulation of negative notions ascribed to the colour black that increasingly yoked an array of anxieties to it. Amid the plethora of stage images of the infidel Turk and the merciless Moor that link lust and irreligion to darker skins can be found deep unease concerning a range of meanings: honour, virtue, morality, sex and its progeny, religion, status, class, conquest, national identity, gender, and governance and its legitimacy.[11]

Though skin colour on stage may have been more a metaphor for difference rather than a description or explanation, pejorative language and imagery are, nevertheless, pervasive; Queen Isabella, for instance, is called an 'Aethiope, Gypsie, thick lipt Blackamoor' in *The Death of Robert, Earl of Huntingdon* and, in *Love's Labour's Lost*, the King and Berowne discuss love in terms of colour – 'black is the badge of hell'. In *Much Ado About Nothing*, a repentant Claudio says he will marry Hero 'were she an Ethiope'.[12] The very title of John Webster's *The White Devil* underlines the point that devils are assumed to be black and, when the devil appears as a dog in *The Witch of Edmonton*, it is black.

The stock black character was the vengeful male, the earliest significant representation of which seems to be Muly Mahamet, a defeated and malevolent usurper in George Peele's *The Battle of Alcazar* (c. 1588), a part played by Edward Alleyn, one of the most celebrated actors of his day. The play draws on an account published in 1587 of a recent famous battle when Morocco defeated Portugal. Although a topical play about real people, it is presented within the conventions of the day, which can be traced back to the morality figure of Vice and the depiction of a black Satan in medieval drama. Mahamet has been seen as standing at the head of a tradition of black stage villains that can be traced through characters such as Aaron the Moor in *Titus Andronicus*, Eleazar in *Lust's Dominion*, Mulymumen in *All's Lost by Lust* and, after the Restoration, to Eleazor in *Abdelazer*, Zanga in *The Revenge*, Hassan in *The Castle Spectre*, and beyond into later centuries.[13] Shakespeare gives Aaron, the one black villain to survive in the theatre from the Elizabethan period, a frankness that is lacking in both the Goths and the Romans. As a colonial victim, he is also given a plausible justification for his actions.[14] In a barbarous world where the reaction to the Queen of the Goths having a black baby is overtly racist, Aaron refuses to kill his child when commanded. Prefiguring Shylock, he defends his skin colour and that of his son:

> Is black so base a hue? –
> Sweet blouse, you are a beauteous blossom, sure.[15]

When the child is further threatened, Aaron protects the boy, shouting at his would-be assassins:

> Ye white-limed walls! Ye alehouse-painted signs!
> Coal-black is better than another hue.

Degrees of colour were used to express different levels of disquiet about the Other: in *A Midsummer Night's Dream*, Hermia is called 'an Ethiop' and a 'tawny Tartar'.[16] Such calibration becomes more important in subsequent periods, for example, when aristocratic men could be acceptable as tawny rather than black. How such verbal indices were reflected in the physical appearance of actors is not always known (both black and white required makeup), and this makes interpreting the colour codes more problematic. There was little evidence that the home community regarded itself as white until the early seventeenth century. Gary Taylor points out that white, the colour of beauty for women, was the colour of cowardice for men, or signified a ghost, a corpse, or a eunuch (black being the colour of sex). He claims the first reference to a collective English whiteness comes in Middleton's *The Triumphs of Truth* (1613), a pageant celebrating the return of four East India Company ships bearing profitable pepper in which a black King of the Moors addresses the audience as 'these white people'. The King is shown positively, the antithesis of the stock black figure, and the black Queen also speaks, in what Eldred Jones considers the first sympathetic portrayal of a black and monogamous marriage (because like a Christian one). Indeed, the pageant has the monarchs and all the Moors convert; hence their acceptability and effective disappearance as non-white people.[17]

Black was not just the colour of sex; it was the colour of the physical, sensual, and wanton aspects of sex. Black was a code word on the Renaissance stage for female genitalia, and the fact that female roles were played by white boys added another layer of meaning to possible interpretations. Though virtue and beauty were often defined in contrast to blackness, which was deemed ugly and licentious, the stage conjured titillation in blackness, in the prospect of uninhibited sex. Black could be voyeuristic, compounding a cocktail of popular views about Islamic polygamy, the nakedness seen in Africa, black skin denoting an inability to blush and show shame, and the black male threat to white women symbolized by the alleged huge size of the black penis. Similarly, black women, though ugly by white standards (unless they are aristocracy), are often endowed with large external markers of their sexual threat to white men, such as large lips, breasts, and backside. Such stereotyping contains an implicit critique of white men, whose appetite for such excess is seen as a weakness.

Theatrically, black women are generally under-represented and seen mostly as servants and/or prostitutes. In morality plays such as *The Trial of Treasure* and *The Tide Tarrieth No Man*, they are seen as lecherous and, in *The Merchant of Venice*, the clown Launcelot Gobbo talks about an off-stage black lover as a whore. A black woman, Celanta, appears in Peele's *The Old Wives' Tale* to represent inner virtue. She is a 'foul wench' and very ugly, but says, 'Though I am blacke, I am not the divell'.[18] The only way she can marry is to find a blind husband who will respond to her goodness rather than her skin colour. John Marston in *Wonder of Women, or The Tragedy of Sophonisba* offers a deceitful and lascivious maid, Zanthia, as do John Marston et al. in *The Knight of Malta* and Webster with Zanche in *The White Devil*. A new take on the bed trick, a standard convention in which one woman, the anticipated partner, is swapped for another, was to use a black woman, as Beaumont and Fletcher do with the loyal maid Kate in *Monsieur Thomas*, presumably to make the shock all the greater and funnier. Disguise as a Moor, another stage convention, was also used to explore morality: Richard Brome's *The English Moore, or, the Mock Marriage* has a husband insist his wife disguise herself as black when she wants to prove her virtue because this will be the best deterrent, and William Hemings's *The Fatal Contract* shows the sexually abused Chrotilda wreaking revenge as a black Moorish eunuch.

The paradoxes of sexuality and the black woman are reworked in the case of black nobility such as Cleopatra, Dido, or Sophonisba, who were popular subjects at a time when European courts were full of foreign queens. Black queens are presented with less emphasis on their pigmentation but with an added sexual allure: the threat is greater because they are more like whites. Dispute continues as to whether Cleopatra was or was not black, being from Macedonia, not Egypt, but, regardless of skin colour, she clearly represents the colonized Other and the colonized female and is a major influence on the myth of Rome. Her story, which is told in at least four plays, represents a significant encounter between cultures. Shakespeare shows her black from exposure to the sun, connoting sensuality but not ugliness and, as a political ruler, standing for a culture distinct and separate from Rome's. His version places female identity within a patriarchal structure, which she challenges, even though her demise reinforces the sense of a disappeared world.[19]

Shakespeare was also responsible for *Othello*, the most canonical Western play concerning race.[20] Whatever the playwright's intentions, *Othello* holds a central place as the most important portrait of the racialized Other until the twentieth century and, even in the twenty-first century, the play cannot be read without race being critical. Whether Othello is black or brown, whether he represents a particular ethnicity or is an imagined amalgam, he is the Other, and he is commonly both darker than the other protagonists and the only character of his skin colour on stage.[21] *Othello* was probably distinctive at first because it broke with the stock black role of villain and offered the star of Shakespeare's company, Richard Burbage, a rich part in which he could display his mimetic skills. The story exploits two other conventions – of the flawed military hero and cross-cultural love, known mainly through the legend of a Sultan infatuated with a Christian prisoner. Like Cleopatra, Othello has political clout, is a leader, and represents a distinct and separate culture but, unlike her, he is caught at a moment when the state needs to accommodate the Other, and he responds to assimilation. The play depicts the consequences; the worst fears of Desdemona's father are the same as Othello's, that he will be what the stage Moor is supposed to be, and this comes to pass through a white rather than a black villain. Othello is Shakespeare's second Moor in Venice after the benign but unsuccessful Prince of Morocco in *The Merchant of Venice*, whose colour is commented on by Portia. In *Othello*, Shakespeare tests the black stereotype and the expectations associated with it but, finally, the Moor has to conform to type.

Othello shows both the limits of acceptance of the Other and the limits of self-assertion by the Other. What Othello represents and how he is seen, along with his race, have changed over subsequent centuries. Until the second half of the twentieth century, Othello was generally taken as an example of the stereotype Shakespeare was trying to avoid. Slavery exacerbated the situation by narrowing perceptions of blackness, so that it was hard for a black Othello to be seen as tragic. To resolve the tension between his nobility and his blackness, white actors tended to make him brown or emphasize his distinctive, particular individuality. Sometimes, he might even be almost English. Othello became one of the leading roles for a white actor to play, in some degree because its blackface demands presented an extra mimetic challenge. For black actors, the role was presented as a pinnacle, too – though this centrality brought its own problems and has been disputed – yet it was only toward the end of the twentieth century that it became unacceptable for white actors to play the part.[22]

Shakespeare also wrote what became one of the key texts in post-colonial readings. *The Tempest*, as with *Othello*, also tests limits, in this case notions of civilization and society. Caliban, like his parallel slave spirit Ariel an openly theatrical creation, is a dispossessed monster at the mercy of white, European, male power but is capable of both tenderness and terrible, sexual revenge and can articulate the possibility of a hopeful new world and its converse. Caliban can be taken as an anti-colonial symbol at the same time as being trapped in the colonizer's culture.

> You taught me language; and my profit on't
> Is, I know how to curse: the red plague rid you,
> For learning me your language.[23]

Behind his linguistic complexity, Caliban possesses a good conscience and a bad conscience in the manner of a Morality play. While drunk, he is a caricature of the evil stage Moor, which Shakespeare challenged in *Othello*, and he also makes overt what was latent in *Othello* as the embodiment of a nightmare stereotype, the black rapist. Yet there is even more ambiguity about Caliban's colour and race than Othello's. For years, he was played as a monster and, although after Darwin he was seen as a colonized inferior native, scholars suggest he was not portrayed on the British stage as black until 1934.[24] Anti-imperialists such as Aimé Césaire, George Lamming, and Fernández Retamar have been drawn to *The Tempest* more than *Othello* because Caliban is seen in overt opposition to the dominant culture; after Frantz Fanon, he became a symbol of the effect of colonialism on the colonized psyche.

Whatever the subtleties of Shakespeare and his contemporaries, nuance was generally outweighed by – and may, indeed, have accentuated – the broad strokes of the stereotype that fed and required popular support to survive. The facts that drama of the period relies on stereotype – the fawning Englishman, the doltish peasant, the honourable noble, the nagging wife – and that the perfidious Spanish are treated more unsympathetically than the villainous blackamoors do little to mitigate the impact of the negative images. Furthermore, the move away from the type toward greater individuation clearly favours the dominant group, which was white. This bias cannot be attributed wholly to ignorance, even taking into account the justifications that were advanced for the negativity represented by blackness. The skin colour of Africans, for example, was linked to the curse on Noah's sinning son Ham, which is visited upon his descendants who were turned black and condemned to slavery. This Biblical account sat alongside other explanations that were later also found suspect, including the view that weather shapes character (in the case of black Africans, the sun is to blame for skin pigment and the related sin of promiscuity).

The body of plays of this period, hailed as unsurpassed by many, reflected, reinforced, and shaped popular views and anxieties, which were projected onto and back from characters on stage. Fascination and fear of foreigners were mixed together. Drama, like some of its audience, was heterodox and capable of showing gradations, distinctions, ambivalence, and contradiction as well as utter prejudice. This was a volatile period in the use of stage conventions and in society, and it is difficult to judge to what extent the shifts reflected opinion outside the theatre or were driven from within. It is also difficult to judge to what extent the stage reinforced or nurtured the growing racism that was crucial to the expansion of slavery and colonial power as the seventeenth century progressed. The evidence suggests the stage played an important part in confirming white subjectivity and securing the ideological apparatus that was required to build and sustain colonialism and imperialism, but this process was not rapid, automatic, or uncontested.

Commonwealth and after

After 1642 and the closure of the theatres, the first performance to be allowed (in private) was William Davenant's opera *The Siege of Rhodes* (1656), which used the Other, in this case the Islamic Ottoman empire, to debate religious tolerance and apostasy. Remarkably, the play that signalled in 1660 the new theatrical and political era of the Restoration was *Othello*, a choice that offers multiple interpretations, touching on the manifold political and cultural connections of race, gender, and sexuality, particularly given the sexual axis of the play and the historic introduction of actresses to the public stage. The iconic moment became the bedroom scene, which was pictured in many illustrations. *Othello* remains a key text for the Restoration, the only major Shakespeare tragedy to be performed throughout the period without substantial revision.

Development of the theatre was intimately linked with the Court, which maintained its fascination with foreign attire, a predilection that reflected personal taste and the makeup of the Court – the King's mother was French, his grandmother Danish, and his wife Portuguese. Charles was known as 'Black Boy', according to one view because his mother was ashamed of his dark complexion, and this may have added another layer of meaning to the use of the word black (as well as possibly influencing the naming of a number of pubs). Charles subjected the restored stage to tight control, limiting the spoken word to licensed or patent companies (though this rule was flouted). Representation of the Other was still governed by the needs of narrative and remained a means by which national identity and other pressing issues could be examined.

The Other was still mainly to be found in what was loosely thought of as the Orient, an inherently theatrical notion because it was both exotic and enigmatic. Bridget Orr says there were at least forty plays with Asian or Oriental settings seen in London between 1660 and 1714.[25] At their heart was the Ottoman empire, in plays such as Roger Boyle's *Mustapha*, Elkanah Settle's *The Empress of Morocco*, or Joseph Trapp's *Abra-Mule*, but the obsession with stability and governance, especially the topics of succession and legitimacy, took playwrights around the globe and across history. They turned to earlier imperial adventures, of Persia, Egypt, Rome, or to those nearer in time and place such as Spain and Portugal. In *The Indian Queen* and *The Indian Emperor*, John Dryden looked to the Peru and Mexico of Montezuma the previous century and to contemporary Mughal India in *Aureng-Zebe*, considered the first major dramatic representation of India.[26] Thomas Killigrew, Nahum Tate, Thomas d'Urfey, and Peter Motteux followed the common practice of reworking pre-1660 material and, in versions of John Fletcher's *The Island Princess*, relocated the Stuart Court to southeast Asia.[27]

Playwrights also began to include characters and plots reflecting the new economic situation in and strategic importance of India, such John Crowne's *Sir Courtly Nice; or, It Cannot Be* (1685) featuring a nabob (a Briton who makes fortunes in India). Terminology regarding the Other remained loose, and depictions of colonial subjects, regardless of any underlying curiosity, generally reproduced the disdain or indifference that underpinned such imprecision or contained a critique of those (as had happened in India) who had 'gone native'. East India Company employee James Cobb, for instance, in *Love in the East* (1788), confuses those of East Indian and African origin. Travel writer and playwright Mariana Starke, who grew up in Madras (later Chennai) and who uses Indian settings, echoes in her comedy of manners *The Sword of Peace* (1788) the common unconcern toward distinctions between indigenous African, North American, and South Asian peoples. At the same time, she reproduces a hierarchy of colour that maps white angst against degrees of blackness while exploring the abiding topic of 'mixed' marriages and their issue.

Paradoxically, there was a simultaneous appetite for authenticity (regardless of accuracy). Starke's *The Widow of Malabar* (1790), for example, was commended for its recreation of a sati (or suttee), a funeral practice among some Hindu communities in which a recently widowed woman immolates herself on her husband's funeral pyre. A production of *Love in the East*, which is set in Calcutta (later Kolkata), was applauded for the designs based on drawings of the city and, similarly, praise was given for the scenery of Cobb's *Ramah Droog* (1798) and James Messink's *The Choice of Harlequin* (1781), which were inspired by watercolours, drawings, and engravings of India. Such gestures of the authentic, like the need for each age to find realistic speech on stage, oddly enough enhance rather than undermine the currency of the exotic and the fantastic, in which the theatre habitually trades when dealing with the Other. Spurred by advances in seafaring and a new taste for science, the English stage of the late eighteenth century spread its net for locations and themes as wide as the empire it was servicing. *Omai, or A Trip Round the World* (1785, by William Shield, John O'Keefe, and Philip de Loutherbourg) not only capitalized on the continuing celebrity of the Tahitian Omai, who sailed with Cook and was feted in London as a 'noble savage' exotic exhibit, but was noted for its spectacular scenic effects, which were directly influenced by John Webster, chief illustrator on Cook's final voyage to the central and south Pacific. Reviews even talked of the educational worth of the pantomime, despite the songs' being racially offensive and the cod Tahitian speech an invented farrago.[28]

Theatre was frequently promoted as a conduit for information, often dramatizing topical events. A series of shows presented at Philip Astley's theatre from 1791 to 1800 acted like a tabloid Living Newspaper in following (albeit some months afterward) British campaigns in the southwest of India against a favourite 'hate figure' Tipu Sultan: *Tippoo Saib, or British Valour in India*; *Tippoo Sultan, or the Siege of Bangalore*; *Tippoo Saib, or, East India Campaigning*; *Tippoo Saib's Two Sons*; and the last, *The Siege and Storming of Seringapatam*, which saw the final defeat of Tipu. Others were less direct. Elizabeth Inchbald, playwright, actress, and novelist, used South Asian settings to compare the values of Europe and the East while dealing with dilemmas at home rather than those of Mughal India. Her farcical afterpiece, *The Mogul Tale*, satirizes in an allegory of a runaway balloon that descends into a harem the recent defeat of Prime Minister Fox's India Bill; her *Such Things Are*, which finds the English in Sumatra, prefigures *The Sword of Peace* in its criticism of the extravagances of East India Company leaders such as Robert Clive and Warren Hastings, who had been impeached for corruption two years earlier.[29]

Aspects of colonialism, such as the mercantilist mentality of the slavers, the decadence of the nabobs, and the repression of the East India Company, were challenged on the British stage, even if the underlying ideological thrust of British superiority that promoted and sustained colonialism and imperialism was seldom questioned head-on. An embrace and even enjoyment of the Other seems possible but only at the expense of historical specificity; the theatrical effect comes to mask the oppression it might be criticising, thereby mitigating any discomfort the audience might feel at complicity with that oppression.

Validation (where it existed) of the indigenous culture of the colonized peoples was mostly confined to the study. Sir William Jones in 1789, for example, translated the Sanskrit classic drama *Sakuntala* into Latin and then into English, but the play was not performed in Britain for more than a century afterward. Taken from the *Mahabharata* by Kalidasa, the story of a king in love with a young woman raised by birds was the first Sanskrit drama to be made available to the European reader. It was reprinted at least five times in England in the next two decades and translated and published many times across Europe. Such enthusiasm has subsequently been attacked by writers such as Edward Said as part of an Orientalist discourse that venerated Sanskrit because it validated the European enlightenment project.[30]

Colour

As the colonial enterprise expanded, particularly through the African slave trade, there was an increasing concern to differentiate ruler and ruled by colour. Although colour was never the sole or an unambiguous indicator of difference, it came to replace categories such as religion, which had previously held sway in the hierarchy of racialization, and developed its own refinements (however uncertain) of pigment grading. Pure (racially speaking) white came on top and black at the bottom with ludicrous gradations between, from mulatto (one black, one white parent) to quadroon (one-fourth African) to octoroon (one-eighth African) and so forth. Just as masculinity had reached a stage of being the gender norm whereby it was unconsciously accepted and therefore did not need to be constantly present or acknowledged as such, whiteness and its cultural correlatives, whether explicitly stated or not, became regarded by the British as the universal benchmark against which other virtues were to be judged. This uneven process was under way in the Restoration period but did not reach maturity until the nineteenth century.[31]

An ambiguity in colour signification, as seen in the prevalence of plays featuring American Indians, is reflected in the practicalities of theatrical representation, itself an expression of social custom. In Georgian times, for example, whitening agents were common, yet were sold not as English but as Jewish, Polish, Cyprian, or Turkish. Before gas or electricity was introduced to the stage, a neutral or white role was often played with red makeup. Blackface, which could involve excessive use of lard, topped off by burnt cork soaked in beer, reduced the visibility of the actor's face, especially when deeper colours were required in larger auditoria, and it was uncomfortable to wear. There are accounts of black coming off during performance, and its stage use is satirized in several plays.[32]

Fluidity in the meaning of colour is also reinforced by the presence of strong female characters of colour. They appear in plays both by men (for example, Dryden's *The Indian Queen* and *The Indian Emperor*; Nathaniel Lee's *Sophonisba*; or Congreve's *The Mourning Bride*) and women (for example, Mary Delariviere Manley's *The Royal Mischief* and *Almyna*). The colour of these characters, however, is ambivalent and signals sexual associations of the female Other rather than anything specific to the colonized female Other. After the so-called Glorious Revolution of 1688, the impact of women changed: Queen Mary was installed as an equal to King William, and their successor, Queen Anne, became in 1707 the first sovereign of Great Britain. This public rise of women was reflected in drama – as actors (often with considerable power to affect the repertoire and styles of performance), as playwrights, and as a distinct section of the audience. The new theatrical place of women led to a different exploration of the power exerted by and over women, using foreign and racialized settings. Mary Pix, for instance, mines connections between gender, race, and liberty in *The Conquest of Spain* (1705), in which the violated woman disguises herself as a Moor, and white female subservience to men is defined in terms of black slavery.

As shown by the choice of *Othello* to usher in the post-Commonwealth dramatic era, the role of women and the issue of interracial sex were central to depictions of the Other. They figure in a raft of plays, from *The Indian Emperor* and *The Mourning Bride* to Aphra Behn's *Abdelazer* and *The Widdow Ranter*. Dryden in *An Evening's Love* suggests the volatility of racial definition and its colour coding when he has Jacinta court Wildblood first as the Lady Fatyma and then as a mulatta. One strand in this attraction to interracial sex was fear of the consequences. Shakespeare had avoided the issue of progeny in *Othello* because Desdemona is killed but, in *The Tempest*, he raised the prospect of rape and, by implication, a child of mixed parentage crossing class and racial boundaries in what would have been a reversal of the experience of the female Other at the hands of white pirates and colonialists. Laws were passed in the colonies banning interracial marriage and sex whereas the rape of black women for pleasure and to increase the slave population continued unchecked. As Ania Loomba argues, patriarchy was a motor, not an addition, to colonialism.[33] This can be seen in the mythologizing of the American Indian Pocahontas, who came to England in 1616 as Rebecca, wife of tobacco planter John Rolfe. Rolfe said he had married her not for sexual reasons but to convert her. She met James I and became a celebrity, an iconic figure for the representation of the non-white female Other. Her story, and by extension that of the native woman in general in relation to the white male, acted as a symbol for the capture of colonial lands in the New World. In her case, violent seizure was justified because she had been saved and had agreed to be saved.[34]

Oroonoko

Interracial love lies at the heart of *Oroonoko*, one of the key texts of the period when Stuart rule at the end of the seventeenth century gave way to the Georgian era, which dominated the following century. *Oroonoko* was adapted for the stage from a 1688 novella by Aphra Behn about an enslaved African prince who leads an unsuccessful slave revolt to save his enslaved lover and unborn baby. He kills her to free them from slavery and is captured and horribly put to death before he can kill himself. The first stage adaptation, by Thomas Southerne at Drury Lane in 1695, probably made the story more popular than Behn's book did. A High Tory such as Behn, Southerne was more interested in aristocratic notions of virtue and liberty than in slavery or race. As anti-slave feeling grew, the story was taken up in other versions, by John Hawkesworth in 1759, Francis Gentleman in 1760, in an anonymous version, and an adaptation by Dr. John Ferriar entitled *The Prince of Angola* in 1788 (probably unperformed). They each offer variations on Behn, but the main departure, begun by Southerne, is to turn Oroonoko's lover Imoinda white, a change to which all the versions adhere.[35]

Various explanations have been offered. Some are practical, such as the erroneous view that actresses were forbidden to wear black makeup or the suggestion that the absence of black actresses made the convincing portrayal of a black female tragic figure too difficult.[36] Some explanations are explicitly racial, from acknowledgement of the open suppression of a black character to consideration of perceptions of female beauty and the temperature of contemporary sensibilities (an audience could cope with reading about a black-to-black romantic tragedy in the confines of their own home but not in a public playhouse). Imoinda becomes another Desdemona, white but also morally black (because she loves a black man), and is redeemed through her own death, which, as with Desdemona, avoids the progeny problem. The colour change removes a major black voice from the story (and adds, therefore, to persistent under-representation) while allowing the relative privilege of a white woman in a man's world to resonate erotically. Imoinda becomes the embodiment of feminine empathy for the enslaved but also separate from and superior to them as white. As Felicity Nussbaum points out, English masculinities and femininities rest on establishing black femaleness as different, and making Imoinda white keeps black women at a further remove.[37] Her whiteness also serves to render Oroonoko tragic because, despite his skin colour, his moral sensibilities allied to her love show he is really white at heart. This transposition is aided by the fluidity of Oroonoko's colour and origins, which, as with Othello, shift from production to production: sometimes Oroonoko sports a beard, or is half-naked, or wears a furry loin cloth like a kilt, or is even dressed like an English gentleman. Furthermore, the tragedy is made individual rather than social or racial by the sentimentalizing of Oroonoko and his separation from the other slaves, whom he leads in revolt not to free them but to free Imoinda and his future child.[38] Underpinning the useful ambiguities of *Oroonoko* is the likelihood that until the African-American actor Ira Aldridge played the part in the 1820s, the eponymous role was performed by white actors.

In its various versions, *Oroonoko* is considered by many the most influential racial text of the eighteenth century after *Othello* and, having spread to many non-patent theatres across the country, the second most performed (after Nicholas Rowe's *The Tragedy of Jane Shore*). The play has a tragic hero who is not white – the first major portrayal of an African slave, albeit of royal descent – and marks a shift toward the association of the slave and Africa. The title role was played by the leading actors of their day, such as Pope, Cooke, Kemble, Garrick, Kean, and Booth, and was translated into French and German. Srinivas Aravamudan links the popularity of *Oroonoko* to the vogue for pets, including black servants.[39] William III, king at the time of the first stage adaptation, had a favourite black slave who was displayed at Hampton Court, complete with padlocked collar like a dog. An important factor in the public profile of the play was the visit to a performance in 1749 of William Ansah Sessarakoo, a prince from modern-day Ghana. His father was a slave trader who interceded with the British government when his son was sold into slavery. In London, he became a celebrity, memorialized in paint and poetry, and was likened to Oroonoko. Apparently at the end of the performance, he wept to the applause of the rest of the audience.

The history of *Oroonoko* on stage is linked to rising anti–slave trade sentiment. Although an anonymous farce, *The Sexes Mis-match'd*, which surfaced in the early 1700s as a blend of Southerne's subplot and John Fletcher's *Monsieur Thomas*, is hostile to Africans, later, more direct adaptations portray the unpleasant aspects of slavery and suggest the need for better treatment of slaves, if not an outright end to the trade.[40] The most popular of these latter texts is by Hawkesworth, who also wrote of Captain Cook's expeditions. His version of *Oroonoko* is an adaptation of Southerne commissioned by David Garrick, who played Oroonoko with Mrs. Cibber as Imoinda. Hawkesworth gives voice to the slave Aboan, who urges the revolt. In common with the other anti-slavery adaptations, which tend to embrace enlightenment notions of essentialism and human rights rather than equality, Hawkesworth's attack on slavery is humanitarian and says little about race. The anti-slave versions, as Joyce Green MacDonald argues, also use Imoinda as a white woman to naturalize the collusion of patriarchy and slavery, her whiteness being the price of admission for white women to a racial authority.[41] Ferriar, unlike Southerne and Hawkesworth, drops Oroonoko's apology for slavery, replacing his plea for tolerance by opposition to the trade. This version was produced in Manchester by the local Abolition Society but banned in Liverpool because of a line about the city's links to slavery and the play's anti-slavery attitude.

Also from the abolitionist camp comes Thomas Bellamy's variation of the story in a sentimental afterpiece, *The Benevolent Planters* (performed as *The Friends* in 1789, the summer after Wilberforce introduced the abolition Bill).[42] Bellamy reverses the Oroonoko situation by having his couple enjoy a happy reunion, having been freed thanks to their respective masters. The hero (called Oran) opens the play as an African sailor pleading abolition and saying Europe is destroying African life, but slavery, nevertheless, is presented as preferable to life in Africa because slaves get to become Christians. This contradiction, as Jeffrey Cox points out, is replicated in the difference between the Acts of 1807 (ending the slave trade) and 1838 (ending slavery).[43] Appearing between the two Acts is Thomas Morton's popular *The Ethiopian* (a.k.a. *The Slave*), which reworks the Oroonoko story, with the central figure of Gambia a 'super-patriotic, colonial slave' who, in true noble savage style, is isolated from his people, eulogizes England, the land of liberty, and tells the audience the good black slave can and should be freed because he will go on serving the white man afterward.[44] With emancipation, the Oroonoko story loses its purchase. More than 150 years later, in 1999, 'Biyi Bandele, a Nigerian-born playwright living and working in Britain, adapted the Behn novella for the Royal Shakespeare Company and probably for the first time on the British stage presented Imoinda as a black African.

This trajectory of *Oroonoko* from the end of the seventeenth century to the beginning of the nineteenth shows the strength both of its hold and of the idea of the noble savage that lies at its core. The idea can be traced back to *Othello*, the begetter of *Oroonoko* and, with variations, to other predecessors, such as Dryden's honourable Indians, Montezuma and the two half-brothers, Morat and Aureng-Zebe. After *Oroonoko*, the noble savage can be seen in a range of eighteenth-century roles, including Ulamor in *Liberty Asserted*; Juba in Jospeh Addison's *Cato*, the most popular political tragedy of the period; Cawwawkee in John Gay's *Polly*; Julio in James Miller's *Art and Nature*; Cannassatego in John Shebbeare's *Lydia*; and Itanoko in *The Untutored Savage*, attributed to Thomas Sheridan and reworked by his more celebrated son, Richard Brinsley, in a rare comic treatment of the motif. The noble savage is not always associated with skin colour or ethnicity (for example, the Dacian prince in Behn's *The Young King*) but, with *Oroonoko*, this connection becomes crucial.

The noble savage – an oxymoron evoking a fantasy, pre-lapsarian state, coined to accommodate unpalatable consequences of conquest – chimed with the conventions of stoicism and sentimentality. Noble-savage plays remained primarily moral rather than political, which allowed contradictory political interpretations – *Cato*, for instance, was championed by both Tories and Whigs, and became a symbol of the American Revolution as well. The plays did not break with the general view that saw blacks as inferior and the threatening Other, despite the occasional existence of singular individuals (of royal or noble birth) who may be treated as white or even almost English. The fact that the English could accept such people (albeit at arm's length, safely on stage) allowed them to justify the feelings of superiority that shaped colonialism in the first place. Such acceptance could not be extended to ordinary slaves or black people as a whole, any more than the working class could be treated as equals of the upper class or women the equal of men. The theatre was complicit in a system that underpinned colonialism, yet it also engendered support for actions that put an end to certain outrages. This progressive aspect – attacking mercantilist excesses in the plantations, for example – flattered audiences while ignoring or attacking one of the major motors that brought the eventual end of slavery, the collective effort of the slaves themselves. Black-for-black solidarity is absent, as is black-for-black love.

In the wake of the many slave rebellions, the black African was further denigrated, and a brown (if aristocratic) noble savage became the acceptable face of the Other. Both the place of the noble savage and its fluid colour coding were underpinned by the roles of the leading actor Edmund Kean who made a speciality of playing racialized parts and gave an apparently electric revival of *Oroonoko* in 1817.[45] The lighter-skinned Other allows new possibilities for male emotion (even a feminized eroticism in the Other's Oriental guise), for a fuller relationship with a white (or lighter skinned) woman, and for the black male to be consigned to the stereotypes of lust and revenge. As a consequence, the noble savage supplants the figure of the avenging, promiscuous black man, though does not eliminate him.

If the male noble savage lives in the shadow of fictional Othello, the female variety is overshadowed by the mythologized though real Pocahontas. The female noble savage is used as a contrast to flawed white characters, as in Pix's *The False Friend*, in which, unlike her white mistress, the intensely loyal and royal slave Zelide belies her 'swarthy veins' by showing true Christian virtue.[46] The most important of the female noble savage figures is Yarico in George Colman Junior's *Inkle and Yarico*, first seen in 1787 at the Haymarket Theatre. It was an extraordinarily popular comic opera, with music by Samuel Arnold, in which the moral failings of an Englishman are highlighted by the virtue of an idealized American Indian, who grew up 'natural', untouched by capitalist society.

The piece reverses the colour balance of *Oroonoko*: Inkle, an English trader, survives a shipwreck in the Caribbean with the help of Yarico and they fall in love, but he plans to sell her as a slave to recoup his losses and marry a white woman to ensure his status. He is finally made to see the error of his ways and marries the devoted Yarico. In telling this story, Colman does not seem to be concerned with racism itself or slavery but with the morality of mercantile trade, which involves both. Criticism of plantation culture (while leaving the notion of Christian and English superiority that supported colonialism unscathed) was common and can be found from the end of the seventeenth century in dramas such as Nahum Tate's *Cuckold's Haven*, Charles Sedley's *Bellamira*, and Behn's *The Widdow Ranter*.

The Yarico story, which predates *Oroonoko*, was already well known when Colman's version appeared. The story was taken up in Germany and, to a lesser extent, France and can be found in poems, epistles, ballets, operas, and novels and in plays and pantomime. Yarico had become a generic name for an American Indian, like Mustapha for a Turk.[47] A version attributed to a Mrs. Weddell was banned mid-eighteenth century, perhaps because the central relationship was between a white Englishman and a woman of colour but, by Colman's time, this was clearly not a problem – three years earlier, Robert Jephson's play *The Campaign; or, Love in the East Indies* had sympathetically shown a young Indian officer courting a white woman.[48] Perhaps Phillis Wheatley was an influence: taken as a child from Africa to America, she was a slave in Boston who came to London in 1773 to issue a volume of poems, possibly the first published work of any black writer in England, and she returned to Boston a celebrity.

Colman adds a 'happy' ending to the Yarico story, with no overt reference to the usually contentious question of offspring. Some commentators regard the sentimental resolution as implausible, whereas others argue that it is set up by the narrative of the play or is in keeping with the fable-like quality of the comic opera (a version of beauty and the beast in which a base human is redeemed by the love of a righteous woman). Another interpretation is to see the ending as more like that of *Measure for Measure*, where the future for the couple is ambiguous and the ending is, therefore, not conventionally 'happy'.[49] Colman also introduces a comic counterpoint to the main story by providing Inkle with a white servant, Trudge, and Yarico with a black maid, Wowski. This allows Colman to play across a wider register of colour, class, and gender differences.

Yarico and Wowski are discovered in a cave decorated with skins of wild beasts' feathers. Inkle immediately calls Yarico 'my charming heathen' whereas Trudge notes that Wowski is darker.[50] Yarico is serious, remains pure, and speaks perfect English, whereas Wowski, a burlesque of the noble savage, is comic, becomes tainted instead of improved by contact with English civilization, and speaks 'pidgin' English, which she learned from the same shipwrecked sailor who taught Yarico. The social distance between the two parallels that between Oroonoko and the other slaves and reinforces the emphasis on the individual nobility of the exceptional main character, who is not to be seen as representative in the way the slaves or Wowski might be. (This distance is reinforced by the fact that the part of Yarico attracted leading actors such as Elizabeth Kemble.)[51] Yarico, though nominally an American Indian, has no fixed ethnicity but is clearly not white. Her colour changes in different versions and productions, from copper to black, although an 1827 actors' manual says by then the part was played uncoloured. Wowski, though also an American Indian, remains black. Colman has Trudge say of Wowski's colour that it does not rub off, yet elsewhere shows it does by wiping her makeup onto his face.[52] Stage anecdote suggests the actors used profuse amounts of makeup to reflect the moral message that racial difference is only skin deep; all is caricature.

Such a message, however, did not plead or demand equality for people with different skin colour or ethnicity and, as with *Oroonoko*, stage versions were generally less subtle than their more-nuanced literary counterparts. Nevertheless, despite its racist representations, *Inkle and Yarico* was perceived to carry liberal sentiments and was used to galvanize people in the abolitionist cause. As happened to *Oroonoko*, the text was changed to suit location and the political climate. David Worrall estimates that in the decade after its first performance, the audience for *Inkle and Yarico* probably approached around 1 million and, for many, was their primary point of contact with artistic expression of anti-slavery.[53] Like *Oroonoko*, however, *Inkle and Yarico* lost currency after the abolition of slavery in the 1830s while remaining popular in America and the Caribbean.

Comic line

If the tragic noble savage represents a tacit marker of white discomfort about aspects of its own society, figures such as Wowski show comedy exposing those anxieties more openly and directly. The role of comedy is very complex and is related to its connections with everyday perceptions and experience; comedy can accommodate and suppress, it can be trivializing and demeaning, but it can also be challenging and allow the voice of the Other a space denied elsewhere. This double-edged nature of comedy may help explain why it became the major vehicle for the development of the black, as opposed to the brown, Asian, or Oriental stage character, a development bound up with the role of African slavery in the development of Britain and its psyche.

Wowski forms part of a line of comic association with the colour black that can be found in the Elizabethan stage (for example, Launcelot Gobbo's references in *The Merchant of Venice* to the black Moor whom he has made pregnant). More directly, there is the Restoration example of Davenant's and Dryden's popular reworking of Shakespeare in *The Tempest, Or the Enchanted Isle*. A precursor of *Inkle and Yarico*, it has Sycorax, Caliban's sister, as 'a racial and sexual monstrosity' who later in Colman becomes Wowski.[54] Unsurprisingly, the association of such black characters is with servitude, and the black comic servant soon became a stock figure. James Townley's *High Life Below Stairs* (1759), which has two comic black servants, Kingston and

Cloe, working for a white 'West Indian of Fortune', was still being performed nearly a hundred years later in 1850, but the key role in this strand of representation is that of Mungo in Isaac Bickerstaff's short comic opera, *The Padlock* (1768). It is loosely drawn from a Cervantes story, which contains a humorous black servant but centres on an old miser and his young fiancée. The padlock refers to her imprisonment by Mungo's jealous master but, as a symbol of slavery and an allusion to the locked collar commonly worn by black servants in Britain, it brings wider associations to bear. These are reinforced by the words and actions of Mungo, the classic stage servant of the period, dutiful when sober but defiant when drunk. In traditional vein, Bickerstaff uses comedy to criticize the master's cruelty. Mungo, a cross between the earlier Caliban and later Figaro, pointedly complains:

> Dear heart, what a terrible life am I led!
> A dog has a better, that's shelter'd and fed;
> Night and day, 'tis de same,
> My pain is dere game.[55]

The Padlock first appeared at Drury Lane after *Hamlet*, and was often paired with *Othello* and *Oroonoko*, the comic contrasting with the tragic, thereby more explicitly locating these plays in a racial context. It seems *The Padlock* was written at the suggestion of the actor John Moody, who played Kingston in *High Life Below Stairs* and who had been to Barbados where he took an interest in the lives of its inhabitants. Moody apparently dropped out when the singing part proved too difficult and was replaced by Charles Dibdin, who wrote the music and was the main reason for *The Padlock*'s original success.[56] It ran for fifty-three nights (a long run in those days) and was successful in America, too, where it probably contributed to the development of blackface minstrelsy. Though noble savages such as Oroonoko remained a dramatic fantasy, the characterization of Mungo attempted to be more realistic, or more recognizable, within the limitations of contemporary attitudes. Dibdin's music was not Caribbean or African, though the songs offer opportunity to present Mungo directly to the audience outside the confines of the plot, but Mungo does essay ordinary speech, an approximation of dialect, as seen in the example cited earlier (possibly the first time in any significant way this had occurred for a black character).

Bickerstaff, who came to London in 1755 as an outsider himself (being Irish and gay) had already written a female black servant, Quasheba, in his comic opera *Love in the City*. She does not speak and appears only twice but is used to criticize her mistress's poor treatment of the 'Neger' in an attack on plantation manners (nevertheless, the mistress, who stands for everything the middle classes hate, is the heroine of the piece).[57] After the success of *The Padlock*, Bickerstaff kept Quasheba in *The Romp*, his comic opera reworking of *Love in the City*, this time with dialect, a trend that both acknowledges difference but exposes it to ridicule.

Dibdin published an anthology, *The Padlock Open'd, or Mungo's Medley* (1771), and made a one-man show out of Mungo, who became so popular that he appeared in cartoons, prints, magazine articles, poems, masquerades, burlesques, and even on tea caddies. His name became shorthand for a presumptuous black person – indeed, in a demeaning sense, for any black person – and appeared in dictionaries as a typical name for a black slave. During the milestone Somersett case in 1772, when slavery was judged to be unlawful in England, Mungo's name was evoked in the wider debate. Though *The Padlock's* popularity in slave-holding colonies implies that the comic portrayal of the enslaved Mungo reassured British West Indians about their treatment of African slaves and it was used in private houses by English gentry to deride black people, *The Padlock* also offered a critique of the audience's prejudices and played a role in the struggle to end slavery. An epilogue by an anonymous clergyman, written soon after the first performance, makes the case for Mungo and his plight to be taken seriously:

> Comes freedom then from colour? Blush with shame,
> And let strong nature's crimson mark your blame.

And the epilogue finishes with the line, 'For, though no Briton, Mungo is a man!'[58] It is unclear whether the epilogue was or was not performed, but its matter was still of sufficient interest to be reprinted in 1787 in *The Gentleman's Magazine*, the biggest-selling publication of the time. Mungo and *The Padlock*, however, declined alongside *Oroonoko* after emancipation.[59]

Mungo showed that black representation could be profitable at the box office and, at a time of increase in the British black population, it is not surprising that the role had a discernable effect on that representation, as the following examples from the three decades after *The Padlock* show.[60] The Rev. Henry Bate's comic opera, *The Black-a-moor Wash'd White*, has a disguised lover as a 'negro' who, after Mungo, uses words such as 'massa' to signify authenticity. The piece, which includes a white servant singing 'times are turn'd topsey-turvey, that white Englishmen should give place to foreign Blacks!', gained notoriety because of riots during its run, which forced cancellation of the show.[61] Dibdin's *The Mirror, Or Harlequin Every-where*, echoes Mungo directly when a black character says 'me work dam hard; and yet, Massa, Heaven forgive him, strip and whip, and cut, poor Negro man all to piece', and the title of *Harlequin Mungo, or, A Peep into the Tower*, by William Bates with music by William Reeve, overtly acknowledges its source.[62]

Black comic servants tend to follow either in imitation of Mungo or in contrast: William Macready's farce, *The Irishman in London; or, the Happy African*, includes the servant Cubba who, like Mungo is a link between white men and women rather than having her own sexual desire, although, unlike Mungo, she is loyal and quietly spoken and, by refusing to take her freedom, is seen to gain in moral authority. William Dimond in *The Lady and the Devil* gives the main female role, a widow, a trustworthy servant called Negombo, described by the widow's uncle as 'my tiny bit of tropical darkness'.[63] Negombo speaks in stage black dialect, sings a ballad, and is used as a veiled and be-gloved stand-in for her mistress to dupe a man. On being revealed, she is taken to be 'that black gentleman in petticoats', the devil.[64] In Frederick Reynolds's abolition drama, *Laugh When You Can*, there is a moralizing black comic servant Sambo, who is very clever but does not speak in dialect, and *Obi* has a female black servant Tuckey.[65]

A significant strand in the Mungo heritage seems to be the denial of the sexuality of black characters aside from association, usually through comic exaggeration, with promiscuity, as is the case with Wowski's desire for Trudge. In *The Padlock*, which concerns older male sexual anxiety, Mungo may represent the threat of black sexual prowess, but he is the only character who has no erotic pursuits of his own, an erasure heightened by his pairing with the female servant, Ursula, whose farcical nature resides in her lascivious behaviour. Similarly, the black servant Cymbalo in John Cartwright Cross's *The Surrender of Trinidad* or Hassan in *The Castle Spectre* are denied an erotic existence while assisting the sexual adventures of their masters. This denial of the erotic, says Julie Carlson, can also be seen in the portrayal of sentimental or tragi-comic black males, such as the black slave Caesar in *The Sword of Peace*;, the escaped slave Jack in *Obi*; or the patriotic Gambia in *The Slave*, in love with another slave, the quadroon Zelinda, who proves his nobility by facilitating her union with a white captain.[66]

Black females, fewer than their male counterparts, are often used in a directly sexual manner but not as expressions of their own erotic impulses. *The Sexes Mismatch'd* repeats the comic bed trick with a white woman being swapped for a black Moor, a convention also revisited in Samuel Foote's *The Cozeners*. Black Marianne, who is brought from Boston (possibly an allusion to Phillis Wheatley) and speaks in dialect, like Mungo and Wowski, becomes part of a marriage scam where the joke is all about her colour. To fool the suitor, she has to keep the curtains drawn, not use a candle, and stay silent. When the dupe sees she has 'turned all of a sudden as black as a crow', he reckons it is judgement on him for discarding his true love.[67] Foote auditioned a black actress for the Little Theatre, Haymarket, which he opened in 1766, but there is no record of her joining his company, and Marianne was played by white actresses.

Harlequin

Treatment of interracial themes was not always this crude; the examples of the black slaves in pantomimes who turn into Harlequin offer a more intricate use of blackness on the white stage. Indeed, the figure of Harlequin himself, a comic servant from the commedia dell'arte who traditionally wore a black mask, makes the context for the development of the black comic servant more complex. Harlequin was a very popular figure in eighteenth-century British theatre where he had been related to the notion of blackness since the 1720s, most notably in *The Necromancer or Harlequin Dr Faustus*. Written by John Rich, the leading Harlequin of his day, it linked black-faced Harlequin to the 'black' or dark arts. Wittingly or not, it also chimed with black as the colour of resistance, an association reinforced by the 1723 Black Act, which prohibited the wearing of blackface in groups as a response to poaching and rural protest against land privatization. The first explicit reference in English pantomime to Harlequin being black ('that blackamoor man') is thought to come in 1759, in Garrick's *Harlequin Invasion* at Drury Lane.[68] This attribute of colour is highlighted, however, to define Harlequin as an unwanted Other. The show is virulently patriotic, produced in the middle of the Seven Years War to celebrate a naval victory (and it features the debut of 'Heart of Oak', the Royal Navy anthem by Thomas Arne, who composed for other racialized shows). Harlequin, the audience is reminded, is French as well. He is banished from the stage by a statue of Shakespeare, the supreme symbol of national identity.

Harlequin, or the little devil, is an iconic symbol of the Other, associated with blackness through his mask, his sexuality, and his animalism. He is believed by some to wear a black mask because of his roots in ancient Roman slavery. The mask commonly had a mark where a horn would have been, referencing his association with cuckoldry, and he also wore a phallus, another connection to blackness in the English imaginary. He was also likened to certain animals, particularly the cat, another association with 'black' magic and related to his role in stage transformation scenes where he could touch one of his black patches to become invisible (a trope central to the black trickster tradition, as Henry Gates points out).[69]

The complex sets of signs linking colour to class, sexuality, and protest that coalesce around Harlequin are reinforced in shows explicitly containing racial references, such as *Harlequin Mungo* (1787) and its direct descendant, *Furibond, or Harlequin Negro* (1807). In both, a despairing black slave who is about to commit suicide is transformed into Harlequin by magic and marries the white planter master's daughter (who is or becomes Columbine). They live 'happily ever after' in what could be taken as an endorsement of interracial union. In *Furibond*, it is the slave's choice to reject the option of becoming a noble savage or a tyrant and to become instead the liberal Harlequin; the white actor in blackface would embody this choice by donning the black mask, a significant gesture open to rich readings in relation to the meaning of blackness. Ignoring the historical role of slave revolt and the fact that Britain is the perpetrator of the slavery the play apparently abhors, *Furibond* praises British liberty not only for giving the slave his personal freedom but for emancipating the other slaves. *Furibond*, nevertheless, was an abolitionist pantomime created in response to the Act abolishing the slave trade, which had been passed earlier in the year. Both pantomimes premiered when the anti-slave movement was in full swing but also at a crucial time when the development of racism in Britain saw the distinction between the British and the Other increasingly defined by skin colour and become embedded in science and religion.

By the time of *Harlequin Jim Crow and the Magic Mustard Pot* in 1836, the elements of the earlier shows that prefigure minstrelsy had now subsumed Harlequin, who loses his distinctive, iconoclastic personality. This historical journey of Harlequin's neutralization is part of the development of the pantomime into a British phenomenon.[70] It marks a passage that closely involves the iconography of encounters with the colonized Other in, for example, versions of the Robinson Crusoe story with stereotypical Man Fridays or exultant Captain Cook spectacles. A continuum can be traced from eighteenth-century shows such as *Aladdin, or the Wonderful Lamp* through *Sinbad the Sailor* and other nineteenth-century popular theatre to the wider popular culture of the subsequent centuries, whether in pantomimes, TV shows such as *It Ain't 'Alf Hot Mum*, or cinema, in, for instance, the *Carry On* series. It should, therefore, come as no surprise that young British soldiers fighting in Iraq in the twenty-first century are reported as calling local men 'Ali Baba'.[71]

The earlier, iconoclastic strand seen in *Harlequin Mungo* and *Furibond* was symptomatic of theatre's espousal of countervailing views. Much of this oppositional sentiment was to be found in non-patent or 'illegitimate' theatres, which expanded in number and spread at the end of the eighteenth and first decades of the nineteenth century, reacting to, resisting, and challenging the limitations of the patent system introduced by Charles II at the Restoration. This growth accompanied the industrial revolution, fuelled by the profits of slavery and colonialism, and with it the beginnings of a working-class and modern urban culture. In the theatre, there was on occasion an overlap between middle- and working-class aspirations, which tied in politically with the great reform movements of the day for social and parliamentary change and against slavery.

The theatrical struggle against authority increased the complexity and diversity of theatrical entertainment, especially in forms regarded as hybrid, such as pantomime, and resulted in performance – for example, the black slaves becoming black-masked harlequin – that reflected meta-theatrical questions about the character and function of theatre itself.[72] These so-called hybrid forms, which became very popular, were shared by patent and non-patent theatres alike and became vehicles for anti-slavery ideas, which formed a distinct presence in British theatre. Slavery had been a common topic on the stage before the African-Caribbean connection became central, and it was usually metaphorical (for example, standing for enslavement to love or one world view suppressed by another).[73] Drama of Oriental or Spanish slavers looked at both the subjugation of women, particularly through the harem, and the subjugation of indigenous peoples, whereby Spanish cruelty to American Indians or the Moors was often emphasized. In a blurring of slavery and colonialism, the reality of British expansion was masked by dealing with the viciousness of others (for instance, in Davenant's *The Cruelty of the Spanish in Peru*, 1658). Some plays celebrated colonial encounters and aspirations, such as John Dennis's *Liberty Asserted* (1704), in which the hero, Ulumar, an Iroquois general, fights with the English in Canada against the French.

As the anti-slavery movement gained great momentum at the end of the eighteenth century – a moment of transition from sentimentalism to Romanticism – not only were plays such as *Oroonoko* and *Inkle and Yarico* commandeered to the cause but likewise were the likes of Jean-François Arnould-Mussot's *The Death of Captain Cook*; *The Negro Slaves* (dedicated to Wilberforce, translated from a play by the German August von Kotzebue); *Pizarro* (also from Kotzebue, and said by Julie Carlson to be the period's most popular play of colonial resistance); and Archibald M'Laren's *Negro Slaves; or, The Blackman and Blackbird*.[74] The rise of the anti-slavery movement affected the representation of the Other by giving greater voice to slaves and occasionally to their resistance and future aspirations, however marginalized, distorted and framed within a racist perspective. Yet the liberal view was severely limited. Besides being noble, heroes or heroines were usually light-skinned rather than unambiguously black. In *Harlequin Mungo* and *Furibond*, when the black slaves become Harlequin, they still remained to the audience white actors.

Though the Other may be seen as human (a view that has been linked to the prevalence of women in the anti-slavery debate), the true test is to become English, and the Other can become English only on ceasing to be the Other. Starke, for example, whom Amal Chatterjee identifies as belonging to a Christian faction that condemned Indian practices and the East India Company for tolerating them, sums up such contradictions: in *The Widow of Malabar*, a tragedy set in southern India, she questions human trafficking while simultaneously trumpeting Britain, the dynamo of the abhorrent practice, as the cradle of liberty (the trope of *Furibond*).[75] She adapted her play from the French and has an Englishman rescue the widow from the pyre, but, unlike in the original, offers no romantic connection between the widow and the rescuer, thereby avoiding a racial challenge.[76] In *The Sword of Peace*, Starke has a black slave who is bought to be freed but only if he regards himself as English. In Thomas John Dibdin's *The Two Farmers*, a black farm labourer, a former African slave called Caesar, tells his landowning employer that British justice will protect him if he is maltreated. As Julia Swindells argues, the liberal representation of black people, because it was popular and bogus, promoted anti-slavery sentiment by diverting attention from the cruel and violent reality of slavery and the racism that supported it.[77]

Among the anti-slavery plays, however, were a few that attempted to portray black resistance, for example, John Cartwright Cross's *King Caesar; or, the Negro Slave* (1801), which tells of the 1752 rebellion of Haitian Maroon leader François Mackandal, and the more influential account of another Maroon figure-head, *Obi, or Three-Finger'd Jack* (1800), whose story had already been popularized in print. This pantomime was based on the life of Jack Mansong, an escaped Jamaican slave who had run away from his master in 1780 and organized a group of escaped slaves (maroons) into a gang feared by the colonizers. The name obi refers to *obeah*, a folk magic in which Jack was said to be expert. Mansong, who lost two of his fingers in a clash with the authorities – hence the subtitle – was murdered soon after a monetary reward for his capture was made along with the promise of freedom to any slave who killed him. As befits other Gothic black anti-heroes such as Hassan in *The Castle Spectre*, Jack is both evil and estimable, as is the culture he embraces and embodies. A flavour of this is spelled out in the text: the first Act ends with a spectacular Negro Ball led by Master of Ceremonies Jonkanoo, and the pantomime closes with an elaborate procession fit for a king. In performance, these scenes and the powerful presentation of *obeah* ritual would have conveyed Jack's valiant aspects. Yet, although he is given moral justification because of slavery, emancipation is conditional on his murder by his peers: freedom means betraying one's own people and joining the side of the oppressor.

Obi was written by John Fawcett, who had played Trudge in *Inkle and Yarico*, and it featured music by Samuel Arnold, who had composed the music for Colman's play. *Obi* enjoyed the longest run in one season of any production at the Haymarket Theatre between 1789 and 1811, and one of its songs, 'A Lady of Fair Seville

City', became a popular success.[78] As was common, the pantomime was altered in subsequent productions, and other versions appeared. *Obi* continued to play at both patent and non-patent theatres throughout England at least until the 1830s and in America. The addition of text in a melodrama version made the show more racist and had Jack guilty of crimes the historical record says he did not commit. However, it did give him a voice, which he uses to denounce the injustices of slavery and the hypocrisy of Christian morality – a virtue not extended to 'our dusky children'. Touching a profound fear of the colonizer that echoes through time, he also voices his desire for revenge:'The times have changed, and the white man must now labour for the black'.[79] Mansong became a mythic figure like Spring Heeled Jack or Captain Swing and, especially after the 1791 revolution in Haiti, came to embody white fear of the colonized Other that lodged in the British national consciousness in diverse forms, including that of *Frankenstein*.

The 1807 Act abolishing the slave trade marked a change of emphasis. George Colman in *The Africans* (1808) affirms the decision and deals more directly with slavery than in *Inkle and Yarico*. Inspired by the explorer Mungo Park's descriptions of Africa, Colman writes an ethnographic piece that chimes with the nineteenth century's passion for apparently authentic display. He departs from usual dramatic practice and attempts to portray realistically the world of the Foulahs, a Muslim slave-raiding people, including the devastation suffered by a village after a European attack. The play, which sentimentalizes by having Africans speak in blank verse, contains a black hero and heroine who remain noble and self-sacrificial to the happy end.

Though theatre could feature criticism of the system that sustained both it and the social milieu of its audiences, this was compatible with a national pride that increasingly combined conscience and xenophobia. Drama played its significant part in sustaining the ideological apparatus that oppressed throughout the empire along lines of class, nationality, gender, and colour or ethnicity. The theatre (its structures, financing, and social position) was itself closely connected to the profits of the slave trade, and the values forged on stage in Britain were exported to and in the colonies. The proscenium arch auditorium was introduced in the eighteenth century to India by the British, and East India Company officials, both military and civilian, acted in English plays, for example Sheridan's *The School for Scandal*, which was sent to Calcutta, along with personnel, by David Garrick, London's leading theatrical figure, at the behest of the Company. Plays such as *The Padlock* proved popular in slave-owning colonies, and British touring companies were probably the first to bring theatrical images of black people to America in the shape of Othello, Mungo, and Oroonoko – a banjo tune was added to a production in 1799 to liven it up. This export of British culture connected the heart of empire with its outer limbs and, in the case of America, even its former colony. In this way, British culture added to the distortion, omission, or expurgation of indigenous culture, whether through suppression or the sustenance of imperial culture among the colonizers ruling in the colonies. As Edward Said wrote, European culture did not cause imperialism and racism, but it validated its own preferences and advocated them in conjunction with imperial rule.[80]

Image and reality

White society confirmed to itself its own sense of adaptability and dominance by its ability to play the non-white Other who, as far as is known, did not form a significant part of either the audience or the performing theatre community. After the Restoration, non-white performers, however, continued to appear in pageants and at Court, particularly as musicians: the great horn and trumpet player, Cato, for instance, was given as a present to the Prince and Princess of Wales in 1738, and the violinist and composer George Bridgetower, to whom Beethoven dedicated the 'Kreutzer' sonata, came under royal protection in the 1790s. This tradition spilled over to the employment of non-white musicians in military bands. By the middle of the eighteenth century, amateur musicians (free and slaves) were also being employed outside royal circles as servants who played instruments and composed. Besides providing entertainment for their masters, they did so for themselves, organising all-black music and dancing events, which were autonomous spaces for their artistic creativity.

Contemporary literature, drawings, prints, and plays record African and Asian people trying to make a living in the world of travelling fairs and street entertainment as dancers, jugglers, acrobats, card-tricksters, 'freaks', contortionists, fire-eaters, puppeteers, boxers, musicians, and magicians. Ned Ward's play, *The London Spy* (c. 1698), has a black female rope dancer, 'half acrobate, half posture girl' at Bartholomew Fair.[81] Numbers were swelled at the end of the following century by stranded lascars (South Asian seamen) and freed slaves, African Americans who had fought for Britain in the American War of Independence. Several buskers-cum-beggars became well known, such as a Caribbean tenor called J. Alexander, who carried around Liverpool in the early 1790s a black bag in one hand and a music book in the other; or Billy Waters (a.k.a. the Ethiopian Grimaldi), an African-American crossing sweep in London who lost a leg serving in the British navy and who was commemorated in porcelain and ballads. He wore a feathered bicorn hat and played fiddle while spinning on his wooden leg. He performed outside theatres such as Drury Lane and the Adelphi Theatre, Strand, where he is thought by some to have appeared as himself and at the Caledonian Theatre, Edinburgh.[82] Waters was allegedly elected King of the Beggars not long before he died in the workhouse in 1823. Also captured in a print was Joseph Johnson (a.k.a. the New King of the Beggars and Black Joe), an ex-merchant sailor without a pension who sang sea songs to earn his living and wore the model of a ship on his head, which he moved to make it seem as if the ship were on the high seas. Having animal skills was also a means to survive. In 1795, a horse rider known as 'The Famous African' appeared at the New Circus, Strand, and trainers were brought to Britain in the same period to keep tigers, elephants, and other exotic beasts for the rich. It is likely that those with animal skills would have been employed in other circuses and theatres that presented such shows.

There is scant record of the appearances of non-white actors. In an English journal of 1889, an item titled 'The First Real Negro On Stage' said the honour

FIGURE 1.2 Crossing-sweep entertainer Billy Waters and street entertainer Joseph Johnson (Courtesy of Victoria and Albert Museum, London)

of that crown should go to 'a negress' more than a century before.[83] This was the black actress who auditioned for Samuel Foote and who had already played Juliet and Polly in *The Beggar's Opera* in Lancashire. If she were performing such leading roles, she must have acted in more parts, but these have not been unearthed, and her name remains lost.[84] The journal item, while claiming that British theatre had hosted a black actor before America, also referred to an anonymous black actor who had played Mungo in *The Padlock* in Dublin in 1770, but the date is wrong. A 'real Moor' appeared in three performances of the play in 1773 at the Crow Street theatre, but he remains unnamed, and other appearances have not yet been traced.[85]

It is possible that non-white actors would have performed in the British non-patent or 'illegitimate' urban theatres, which are likely to have had more diverse audiences than the patent theatres. Such spaces ranged from penny gaffs, song-and-supper clubs, dukeries, and spouting clubs in taverns to saloon theatres, music halls, and open-air venues. Many had short existences, changed management and function rapidly, and left little archival record. There is evidence, however, that Julius Soubise, brought from St. Kitts to England as a slave with the name Othello, performed in spouting clubs extracts from Shakespeare, especially Richard III, Othello, and Romeo's garden scene. These clubs were formed mostly by young, lower-middle-class or artisanal men to try out roles and were part of the Georgian vogue for private theatricals. A relatively privileged servant and friend of the noted African writer and composer Ignatius Sancho, Soubise was supposed to have been taught elocution by the elder Sheridan, was said to be a favourite of Garrick's, and earned a reputation as a flirtatious dandy. The subject of mocking engravings, he fled to India, having been accused of rape, where he taught riding and fencing, and may have appeared as Othello and Mungo.[86]

Sancho, who disapproved of Soubise's lifestyle, was possibly the author of two plays, but none has survived, and they seem not to have been performed or given a reading, though they may have been, if only in private. Sancho was said to have been employed briefly in the theatre company of his acquaintance Garrick, who apparently asked him to act at Drury Lane in the 1770s, but perhaps either declined or was dissuaded because of a speech impediment. Evidence for this relationship with Garrick, however, is dubious.[87] Britain had to wait until the second decade of the next century, with the arrival from America of Ira Aldridge, for any non-white actor to challenge the white hold on the representation of the non-white Other.

2

ALDRIDGE AND THE AGE OF MINSTRELSY

Ira Aldridge is the first black actor of note in Britain whom historians have unearthed, and the more that is uncovered, the more astonishing his achievements and resilience appear. It is difficult to get a true picture of his stature because he was doubly removed from history: as an itinerant actor and as a black actor. Yet one specialist, Bernth Lindfors, judges he was the most famous black man in Europe, and the actor who, of his era, had 'travelled farther, was seen by more people in more nations, and won a greater number of prestigious honours, decorations, and awards than any other'.[1] Though there is a danger of idealizing him, he is, nonetheless, a key piece in the jigsaw not only of British theatre history but of the influence and innovation of the African diaspora.

Born in New York on 24 July, 1807, Aldridge attended one of the African Free Schools in the city established by abolitionists and became fascinated with the theatre (as far as can be surmised) against the wishes of his father, a lay preacher. It appears likely that Aldridge managed to see from the balcony of a 'white' theatre Shakespeare performed by visiting English actors and watched from the wings of another while helping out backstage. It is possible he saw other plays from the British repertoire, such has *Inkle and Yarico*, *The Africans*, *The Irishman in London*, and *The Padlock*. Aldridge also attended the first black theatre in America, the African Theatre, which William Brown opened in 1821, and may have seen there *Obi* and *Tom and Jerry* (in a version by Brown) and the company's leading actor James Hewlett as Richard III and Othello.[2] Aldridge is said to have made his stage debut at this theatre as the Peruvian rebel Rolla in Sheridan's adaptation of Kotzebue's *Pizarro* and subsequently played Romeo, although definitive evidence has yet to be found.[3]

Aldridge became acquainted with James and Henry Wallack, two English actors working in New York, who may have encouraged him to try his luck in Britain. Aldridge probably came because he knew opportunity in America would be scarce. He had even been assaulted by a circus performer in 1822 in an attack that was probably linked to a campaign by a local white theatre manager to shut down the African Theatre, which had been harassed since its opening and was forced to close in 1824. That year, armed with a letter of introduction from Henry Wallack (who had hired him as a costume carrier), Aldridge worked his passage to Liverpool.

Remarkably, Aldridge made his debut aged only seventeen, on 11 May, 1825, at the Royalty Theatre in London's East End. It was an area with a multi-ethnic population, and the theatre had a reputation for presenting Shakespeare and having a relatively benevolent view of the Other. Presumably hired as a novelty, Aldridge was billed as 'a Gentleman of Colour, from the New York Theatre,' and he performed Othello. He was well reviewed in the only publication to cover his appearance but had problems with his lines and repeated the role a few days later in truncated form, 'being the second time the character was ever represented in this Country by a Person so formed by Nature for the part'.[4] He played the role a third time and, on each occasion, was accompanied by an afterpiece in which he did not appear. He then played Gambia in *The Slave*, Thomas Morton's reworking of the Oroonoko legend, in which role Aldridge was said to be better than as Othello. Aldridge stayed at the Royalty sporadically until the autumn, reprising Gambia at least nine times and playing in at least two melodramas: as Hassan in *The Castle Spectre* (not a leading part but crucial for mood as the most defiant and eloquent of four black slaves with angry speeches railing against his subjugation) and as another Hassan, again a slave, in a naval melodrama, *The Divan of Blood!, or, the Demon of Algiers*. As Lindfors says, it was a 'truly impressive' debut season, even if he had been a veteran.[5]

FIGURE 2.1 Ira Aldridge as Othello (Courtesy of Victoria and Albert Museum, London)

In September, he married Margaret Gill, a white woman from Yorkshire and, in October, he appeared at the recently opened and larger Royal Coburg Theatre (later to become the Old Vic), just south of the Thames, most likely because of his success at the Royalty.[6] He appeared for seven weeks in a run of plays, starting with *The Revolt of Surinam, or A Slave's Revenge* (another adaptation of *Oroonoko*); followed by *The Ethiopian, or the Quadroon of the Mango Grove* (better known as Morton's *The Slave*); *The Libertine Defeated, or African Ingratitude* (possibly an adaptation of Frederick Reynolds's comedy *Laugh When You Can, or Sambo's Courtship*, in which he later appeared as the eponymous quick-witted servant); *The Negro Curse, or the Foulah Son* (said to have been written for him by H. M. Milner, a writer associated with the Coburg); and J. H. Amherst's *The Death of Christophe, King of Hayti*. Reviews generally acknowledged he was well received, but the critics offered divided opinions; some were favourable, but others were openly racist, abhorring the very idea of a black actor appearing in the English theatre. The *Times* critic wrote that Aldridge was not able to pronounce English 'in such a manner as to satisfy even the unfastidious ears of the gallery' owing to 'the shape of his lips'. By December, he was playing Othello at Brighton's Theatre Royal, with a local reviewer commending his 'real and undoubted talent'.[7]

It was outside London in the thriving regional network of theatres that he learned and honed his craft and was celebrated for his expertise in a wide range of contrasting roles and for playing the guitar, dancing, and singing. It looks as though he did not return to London until 1833 and then only briefly. He toured extensively, visiting in his early years places as far apart as Sheffield, Edinburgh, Manchester, Dublin, Belfast, Bath, Brighton, Norwich, Liverpool, Bury, Sunderland, Newcastle, Lancaster, and Halifax. His itinerary shows a high work rate, and he was able to get material written for him, such as the revised version of *Obi*, a pantomime Aldridge may have seen in New York. Theatre manager William Murray, who had already presented Aldridge on stage, supplied him in *Obi* with rousing denunciations of hypocritical Christian slave owners and inspiring justifications for the revenge he visited upon them by recalling the carnage English slave traders had wrought when they raided Jack's village in Africa. Aldridge also used Jack's African name, Karfa, possibly as a further validation of his own heritage.

Touring made it hard to establish a reputation, as Aldridge never stayed long in any one place. Yet, despite difficulties – in 1826, his second year performing, he faced severe money problems – he clearly managed to establish himself very quickly; that year, he had his portrait painted by Royal Academician James Northcote. The selling point was obvious, though managements tapped into an empathetic sentiment as well as his exotic appeal. A 'Gentleman of Colour' was seen as an oxymoron and, therefore, heightened interest. He was exaggerated as 'the celebrated American Tragedian', but American was soon dropped and he became 'Tragedian of Colour' and 'the African Tragedian' (another apparent and tantalizing oxymoron). After he was derisively dubbed 'the African Roscius' by *The Times*, a reference to the leading Roman actor Quintus Roscius Gallus and commonly associated with precocious theatrical talent, Aldridge, as he was to do so often, turned the insult to his advantage and adopted the title himself. Aldridge's name was given at first as Mr. Keene, possibly his mother's maiden name and part of the name he was given at birth or baptism (he signed his first marriage certificate Frederick William K. Aldridge). Or, it may have been used to evoke either an Irish actor called Arthur Keene or, more likely, the leading English actor Edmund Kean, both of whom Aldridge may have seen in New York. (Kean even wrote a letter recommending Aldridge to the manager of the Theatre Royal, Bath, an important venue.) By 1833, however, when Aldridge had gained a reputation and Kean collapsed on stage, Aldridge had dropped Keene completely in favour of his father's last name, and he was using the first name, Ira.[8]

Identity was a critical issue. Aldridge exploited his uniqueness – the first plays he performed are set in the Caribbean and Africa – but, in keeping with his desire to be taken seriously, he presented himself as the son of a Foulah prince from Senegal (perhaps prompted by the play, *The Negro Curse, or the Foulah Son*, and/or because the British glorify aristocracy, as was seen when the visiting Taihitian Omai was transposed into nobility). Aldridge pretended his wife was the daughter of an MP, presumably to confer status on them both at a time when interracial marriages were frowned upon in many quarters.

In addition to titles already mentioned, Aldridge's repertoire of plays with black characters included *The African's Vengeance*, *The Galley Slaves*, *The Cannibal King*, *Savage of the Desert* (the latter two apparently written for him), *The Revenge*, *Dred* (adapted from Harriet Beecher Stowe's novel), and *The Padlock*, in which he famously played Mungo. He also played an 'Esquimaux' Chief in *Captain Ross* (a topical play about an Arctic voyage), all the parts including that of a runaway slave

FIGURE 2.2 Ira Aldridge as Mungo in *The Padlock* (Courtesy of Victoria and Albert Museum, London)

in the anti-slavery musical drama *Paul and Virginia*, and a black head waiter called Ginger Blue in *The Virginian Mummy* (one of his most popular comic creations). This latter show included the song 'Opossum Up a Gum Tree', which was associated with black folk culture and which Charles Mathews the Elder, after a visit to America, made popular in Britain in a sketch about a black would-be Shakespearean actor, often mistakenly believed to have been Aldridge. [9]

In the sketch, a black actor murders the roles of Richard III and Hamlet, whose soliloquy 'To be or not to be' becomes a cue for 'Opossum'. Mathews was probably mocking the snobbishness associated with Shakespeare as well as the black actor's aspiration, presumption, and delivery. The idea for the sketch most probably derived from Mathews's experience of James Hewlett but it attached itself to Aldridge, who was subjected to many requests to sing the song 'in character', which he did. Possibly recalling Hewlett's own satire on Mathews, Aldridge turned the song into a lampoon of the English comedian – a black actor parodying a white actor parodying a black actor trying to play a white role – and used it to endorse countervailing values of emancipation and equality. Aldridge repeated this satire in the role of Massa Jeronymo Othello Thespis, a stage-struck servant in the farce *Stage Mad*, and also added to his repertoire burlesques of himself that had appeared in minstrel productions, similarly making them his own.

'Opossum' featured in Aldridge's solo shows (often called *Classic Entertainment*), which he performed from the late 1830s to the mid-1840s. They offered a compilation of his roles and sometimes included a lecture in defence of drama, which he aimed at puritans who were attacking the theatre. He even performed 'Jump Jim Crow', the minstrel signature tune, which he added presumably because of its popularity. Aldridge's biographers Herbert Marshall and Mildred Stock believe he performed his own version and, as with 'Opossum', 'brought out aspects of these songs which the others [e.g., white actors such as Mathews] could never comprehend'. [10] In this, he prefigured later attempts by black performers such as Bert Williams to exploit for their own ends the white entertainment forms within which they had to work.

In looking for new black roles, Aldridge, it seems, commissioned plays, adapted existing plays for his own purposes, or collaborated with others to do so. In 1847, he appeared in a version of *The Black Doctor* (billed as being written by Frederick Lemaitre), which was later published under his own name. [11] There were at least two English versions in existence of this French melodrama about the love of a Creole doctor, Fabian, for a white aristocratic woman, which has been seen as the first contemporary melodrama to take interracial marriage seriously (a subject close to Aldridge). [12] Aldridge moved the text away from stereotype as a retort to the grotesqueries of black representation in minstrelsy and Mathews-style attacks on black aspiration. Making reference to *Othello* and *Oroonoko*, two plays with which Aldridge was already associated, *The Black Doctor* deals with a dangerous subject and was acceptable probably because Fabian was of mixed heritage and he dies. In a parallel to Aldridge's own life, Fabian proves the equal of whites in his profession and in his romance.

Aldridge's revival of *Titus Andronicus* in 1849 goes further in its departure from the original. Said to be the first production for more than 100 years (and a rare British outing in the nineteenth century), it was rewritten as a melodrama for Aldridge by playwright C. A. Somerset, who borrowed from other plays as well. The Somerset-Aldridge version makes the play Aldridge's own not so much by omitting the play's horrors, which Victorian taste probably required, but most notably by turning Aaron the Moor from villain into hero. Edward Ravenscroft's reworking of the play in the 1670s had made Aaron more prominent to make the villain more fascinating, whereas Aldridge wanted to stress his colour and place him, as Jonathan Bate points out, as much in the line of Othello as Iago.[13] Critics complained of Aldridge's altering the texts of plays, but he remained unrepentant about taking liberties, as a letter regarding *Titus* makes clear. He defends such changes because 'Being from my Colour [I am] limited in my Repertoire'.[14]

Though certain plays or spectacles were discarded quickly, presumably because they found no favour with his audiences, Aldridge embarked on a brave course to present a sufficient number of roles that touring demanded: he tackled non-black roles as well. The first, which came in 1827 in Lancaster, was the Peruvian anti-colonial leader Rolla in *Pizarro* (believed to be his first role in New York). Three years later in Kendal, he played a white European role, the firebrand Captain Hatteraick in the swashbuckling tale of smuggling, *Guy Mannering*. He also played Massaroni in *The Brigand* and William Tell, the count-turned-pirate hero in *Bertram*. In what was considered the greatest test for an actor, he also played white Shakespearean roles: Shylock, Richard III, Macbeth and, later, Hamlet and King Lear.[15] Aldridge played his white roles in whiteface, possibly the first black actor in Britain to do so. He used white makeup and sometimes a wig and/or beard to transform his head completely.[16] It seems that his whiteface was criticized only in London. His chief media antagonist, *Figaro in London*, for example, attacked him for subverting the tenets of racial essentialism.

His chance to conquer the London elite came in 1833. As it happened, it was also the year of a racialized Mathews burlesque, *Othello, the Moor of Fleet Street*, and of Parliament's passing an Act to abolish slavery in many (but not all) of the British colonies. Aldridge's appearance at Covent Garden, the equivalent of a National Theatre, followed the collapse of Edmund Kean, regarded as the leading actor of his day, who was playing Othello there. A fortnight later, Aldridge, at the age of 26, took the same role with virtually the same cast at the same theatre. The announcement of his appearance gave rise to virulent press assaults against him and, two nights before his debut, the City Theatre, Cripplegate found a black ship's steward to play a character called Tom Tug in *The Waterman* to counter Covent Garden's claim to be presenting the only man of colour on the stage. This type of spoiling ploy was common, but so harsh were the racist attacks on Aldridge that supporters in the Garrick Club, a redoubt of the theatrical establishment, felt compelled to respond in his favour. Subsequent commentators have reasonably assumed the pro-slavery lobby to be behind the slurs, and there is evidence that the lobby funded papers that were critical of Aldridge. They may have been goaded by his robust portrayal of black characters, his marriage to a white woman (not to mention his reputation as a womanizer), and his palpable demonstration that a black man can be as good as a white. He aroused in his opponents a toxic combination of racial, sexual, and class prejudice: Aldridge had come to represent far more than an actor, whichever camp one was in.

Criticism of his performance at Covent Garden was mixed. In general, the press found Aldridge a little lacklustre and, not surprisingly, compared him unfavourably to Kean, a stricken national hero, though they mostly acknowledged the applause he received from the audience. *The Times* said, 'Such an exhibition is well enough at Sadler's Wells, or at the Bartholomew Fair, but it certainly is not very creditable to a great national institution'. The *Morning Post*, while admitting Aldridge possessed a 'fine, full, melodious voice', complained that his 'enunciation is far from correct or pleasing; it is frequently broad and strikingly un-English'. The performance 'was doubtless sufficiently good to be considered very curious, but it was not an Othello for Covent Garden, where we do not, or rather should not, go to witness mere curiosities'. The *Theatrical Observer* cracked a punning joke about Aldridge not 'being obliged to dye himself!' whereas the *Athenaeum* gave vent to a racist outburst that also combined patriarchal and class prejudice. In its indignation at the impertinence of Aldridge tackling a 'masterwork' in 'an English national theatre', it believed it was impossible for Aldridge to 'fully comprehend the meaning and force or even the words he utters'. The critic protested at the ignominy of the 'decent girl' playing Desdemona being 'pawed about' by Aldridge, described as 'Mr Henry Wallack's black servant', and concluded that 'if this exhibition is to be continued' acting should cease being 'dignified by the name of art'. The *Spectator* asserted that 'English audiences have a prejudice in favour of European features, which more than counterbalance the recommendations of a flat nose and thick lips'. It found Aldridge's declamation 'ineffective' and 'very faulty; it is marked by numerous instances of false emphasis, incorrect readings and interpolations of the text even'. Nevertheless, the critic confessed that the 'beauties' of Aldridge's performance 'surprised us more than its faults'. The *Globe* agreed that 'those who go to see the mere novelty of an African Othello will find more than mere curiosity gratified', whereas the *Standard* was unequivocal: 'We at once gladly express our unqualified delight with his delineation of this masterpiece of the divine Shakespeare'.[17]

Aldridge was invited back for a second performance of *Othello* 'in consequence', said the playbill, 'of his enthusiastic reception'.[18] This performance was to replace planned appearances as Zanga in *The Revenge* and Mungo, which were rearranged for a third appearance, but this third appearance was cancelled. Whether this was due to 'the indisposition of several of the principal performers', as *The Times* announced, or to covert intervention by the anti-Aldridge, pro-slavery lobby is not clear.[19] There was an outbreak of influenza in London (which may have affected Aldridge's first, under-energized performance), and Aldridge had not attracted large numbers of audience. Perhaps both were factors, yet neither explains why he was virtually barred from the capital's main stages thereafter, an enforced absence described by certain papers at the time as the result of a boycott. Apart from visits to London theatres outside the privileged inner ring, his only return to the mainstream was as Othello. The first reprise came in 1858 at the Lyceum, not on a par with Covent Garden but a significant West End venue nonetheless, and then in 1865 at the Haymarket, under the management of J.V. Buckstone, a friend who had appeared with him in his first season at the Coburg (Buckstone, the year before Aldridge's Haymarket debut, had proposed Aldridge's health when he was guest of honour at an Actors' Supper in London on the tercentenary of Shakespeare's birth, with 400 present). The two latter London performances won praise, however cool, even from the *Athenaeum*.

Looking at reviews of his many Othello performances, it seems that Aldridge played the part with discretion to demonstrate that, in the words of the French novelist Théophile Gautier who saw him in Russia, he was 'no less cultured than the white man'.[20] Rather than accentuate the wild and fierce Moor, as Kean had done, Aldridge acted majestically with wisdom and poise to show Othello as someone who had lived a long time among Christians and was rightly valued by them. His performance was a form of emotionally realistic acting ahead of its time. Kean had moved Othello away from blackness by playing him tawny; Aldridge (who according to some sources was not very dark), nevertheless – and more importantly – rooted the role in his own culture and, through his performance, proposed an alternative to the blackface tradition. One critic said that, having seen Aldridge, he could not imagine any white actor, even Garrick, playing Othello.[21] In Britain, it was another 150 years, however, before white actors were ousted from their monopoly of this role.

Aldridge left Britain for continental Europe in 1852 and spent much of the remainder of his life touring there, where he was lionized. He became a British citizen in 1863, though his adopted country, in contrast to its neighbours, never decorated him. Apparently he was set to return to the United States – which would have been a landmark – but he died on 7 August, 1867, aged 60, on tour in Poland where he was given a state funeral. After his death, he disappears from the records, though some kept his name alive; a troupe in Philadelphia named themselves after him in the 1860s and, at the end of the century, some amateur African-American groups followed suit. In 1920, Oklahoma City opened a theatre bearing his name. When the Stratford upon Avon Shakespeare theatre burned down in 1925 and nearly half the money to build the new theatre came from the United States, African-American poet James Weldon Johnson presented a gift from the 'Negroes of the United States', and a bronze plate inscribed with Aldridge's name was attached to one of the seats. Paul Robeson, who took elocution lessons with Ira's daughter Amanda as he prepared for his first Othello, wanted to make film about Aldridge, and work had begun on a script, but the loss of Robeson's passport in postwar, McCarthyite America prevented this. A 1958 biography of Aldridge led to new interest in him: Howard University, Washington DC opened its Ira Aldridge Theatre in 1960; novels, plays, a rock-and-roll musical, documentaries, and more biographies were written or made about him; and in 2004, the Old Vic, responding to campaigners, agreed to display a picture of him as Aaron in *Titus Andronicus*.[22] In 2007, on the bicentennial of his birth, English Heritage agreed to raise a commemorative blue plaque on a house where he had lived in south

London, an honour at last for one of the major actors of the nineteenth century from the country where he developed and practised his craft.

Living proof that people of African heritage were not intellectually or emotionally inferior, Aldridge used his performances not only to demonstrate but to promote this view, resisting, complicating, and challenging prejudice that confined and demeaned him. Fittingly, he received his first state honour from Haiti, the first black republic, which was created by slaves who defeated their masters. In his own sphere, Aldridge sought to conduct a similar struggle, using his own presence and skills and reworking material to suit his culture and perspective. He responded to anti-slavery feelings both in sympathetic abolitionist roles such as Gambia, Oroonoko, and Christophe in *The Death of Christophe, King of Hayti* and in less-sympathetic roles such as Zanga or Hassan.[23] He gave voice to Dred, who calls for fellow slaves to revolt; was regularly seen as defiant Karfa in *Obi*, the leader of a band of escaped slaves; and emphasized the pride and blackness of Aaron in *Titus Andronicus*.

Aldridge sent large sums of money to America to help fight slavery and was particularly popular in Hull, the home town of the anti-slavery campaigner William Wilberforce, which town he visited frequently and where he launched several new roles. Aldridge also sympathized with national liberation movements, and sometimes in continental Europe, he performed in the country's home language as well as in English. He also had the custom of addressing his audiences directly at the end of particular engagements on 'the plight of the slave and his hope of freedom', making explicit what remained implicit in the plays he performed. After one appearance (as Zanga at the Surrey), he is reported as saying that he 'hoped the prejudice was fast dying away, when one man should be deprived of a hearing on the stage, because his face was another colour'.[24] He was also known to end performances with a plea for the rights of all, regardless of colour.

This attitude was in keeping with his portrayal of the Other, for example as Shylock, the white Shakespearean role he performed most often and over the longest span of time, second only in his Shakespearean repertoire to Othello. He ended *The Merchant of Venice* with Shylock a despised and exploited Jew, derisive of his judges and utterly repulsed by his forced conversion to Christianity. It was an attitude also to be found in the two main parts of his career, Othello and Mungo, which he coupled not just to display his versatility but to challenge audience preconceptions. In the vein of Mathews's caricature of the black actor mauling the Bard, audiences might expect Aldridge to flounder in Shakespeare, which, Lindfors suggests, he may even have encouraged by calling himself initially Mr. Keene, as if to invite unfavourable comparison with Edmund, a joke at his own expense.[25] However, by performing Othello skilfully and with dignity and by bringing a black body and sensibility to this key Western representation of the Other, he contradicted the audiences' expectation.

By following Othello with Mungo, he returned to the image of the original prejudice (the black man as simple and inept) and subverted that, too. Thanks to his poignant playing of Othello, Aldridge showed an audience that with Mungo he was also acting a part rather than 'manifesting his own innate racial peculiarities'.[26]

Through the juxtaposition, Aldridge showed both roles to be a kind of mask and, as Lindfors argues, 'enabled one disguise to comment on the other'.[27] Though Aldridge would not have been able to avoid the racist aspects of the plays he performed, he tried to exploit the space he was allowed on stage to his own advantage: thus Mungo became a 'rebel against slavery' in what Kean described as one of the finest pieces of acting he had seen on the British stage.[28] As Lindfors says, Aldridge's Mungo was a 'signifyin(g) flunkey whose hilarious antics indirectly subverted and revised nineteenth-century racial stereotypes'.[29] Aldridge tried the same strategy in other pairings of comic and tragic roles, and, as happened to Robeson in the following century, he was often praised while the plays he appeared in were attacked. He evidently brought something to his performance that made it stand outside the limitations of the plays and allowed him to embody and animate ideas about his character and even his people not promoted by, and even at odds with, the plays themselves.

His performance strategy looked forward to the multiple aesthetics of self-realising diasporic performance in the twentieth century that were developed as a response to, and as a way of challenging, the issues of identity formation for the non-white Other. Literal and figurative acts of self-affirmation can transform debasing discourses, as Daphne Brooks observes, and connect marginalization and estrangement to innovation.[30] His daring use of whiteface challenged notions of white supremacy (as if – through blackface – whites could become the Other but not vice versa). In tragedy, he used what was considered a realist mode to convey humanity and the value of black subjectivity against the dominant expectation, whereas in comedy, he used overt expressiveness and the hypervisibility associated with minstrelsy to highlight the social constructions of blackness and offer alternative definitions of his own.

White control of the Other

Many of the preconceptions Aldridge was challenging had been and were produced or reinforced by white theatre's control of representation of the non-white Other. In the wake of Britain's loss of America but expansion to the east, importantly in India and Africa, theatre in the nineteenth century reflected a new notion of being British, which intersected with changing and often contradictory views of gender, class, and national/regional identity. In helping construct this identity, theatre continued to order and interpret the body and culture of the Other at a time when urban migration, greater wealth and literacy, and an emerging concept of leisure led to increased public engagement in entertainment. Theatre was linked ideologically to the panoply of other nineteenth-century performance, whether opera, ballet, panoramas, dioramas, waxworks, exhibitions, and lectures or local and amateur mumming plays (which enjoyed a renaissance), pantomime, melodrama, saloon theatre, circus, and street and pier shows.

The visual and textual vocabulary of imperial attitudes, the foundation of much popular British ideology in the twentieth and twenty-first centuries, was mapped out through such entertainments and through fashion, interior and architectural design, and the new intellectual disciplines, such as ethnology, anthropology, biblical archaeology, and geography, that fed them and were fed by them. Promotion of rampant empire building pervaded all aspects of British life. It fuelled the racial theorizing that gave an apparently scientific rationale to an assumed yet refashioned sense of national and ethnic superiority, which deemed the governed as immature and incapable of self-rule, belonging to a pre-capitalist, pre-urban world, less advanced but also more innocent, coming under the protection of Christian virtue. Even the mere possibility of equality of the Other (albeit on white, male Christian terms) was denied by supremacist Victorian racism.

Commercial competition in the theatre mixed with and exploited genuine interest in other species and their habitats, stimulated by debates around Darwinism and the 'missing link' of human evolution. The need to create the human subject, as Edward Ziter argues, organized the nineteenth-century theatre as much as it did the nineteenth-century prison and clinic.[31] Central to this need was the idea of exhibition that, as Lindfors shows, fostered a tradition dating back at least to the early sixteenth century when, in 1501, Eskimos were put on display in Bristol.[32] Such display was a practice that increased as navigational techniques and travel improved: toward the end of the eighteenth century, Amelia Newsham, the 'white negro woman', was exhibited at Bartholomew Fair, and Primrose (John Bobey), the 'celebrated piebald boy', was shown at the Haymarket as 'the Spotted Indian', even though he was from African slave stock in Jamaica; another West Indian with piebaldism, George Alexander Gratton from St. Vincent, was taken aged 15 months to Britain to be exhibited as the 'Beautiful Spotted Negro Boy'.

British occupation of the Cape Colony in 1806 led to a Khoikhoi, Saartjie 'Sarah' Baartman, being toured around Britain as the 'Hottentot Venus', a supposed freak with huge buttocks and elongated labia. She was followed by a wave of Southern Africans: in the 1830s, for instance, another 'Hottentot Venus', Vikaitus Vessula, San or bushmen at Croydon Fair in the 1840s,and, in the 1850s, thirteen Zulus exhibited as Native Zulu Kafirs, acting out incidents 'typical' of Zulu life with song and dance (about whom Charles Dickens wrote racistly) and Ubangi women, who, with other troupes, performed for Queen Victoria. The British Museum opened an ethnographical gallery in 1845, and the Crystal Palace Great Exhibition of 1851 boasted all manner of foreign exotica, including Africans on display and an Arabian Nights apartment relocated in India. William Leonard Hunt (a.k.a. the renowned funambulist, the Great Farini, who crossed Niagara Falls by tightrope) was responsible for importing many Southern Africans, such as the short Kalaharians and Lala, the Black Venus, who hung upside down from a trapeze with a cannon ball in her mouth that was ignited and fired. This kind of display continued in theatres and exhibitions on a regular basis through to the following century and proved immensely popular. The Ituri pygmies, for example, displayed at the Hippodrome from 1905 to 1907 were seen by an estimated 1 million people.

The British empire made commodities of other people's cultures; knowledge and artefacts were consumed, as wider travel, more readily available accounts of travellers and reports of foreign affairs, and improved and cheaper reproduction of images made the colonized both more familiar and less historically specific. This was the symbiotic relationship of fantasy and reality, which, as has been seen, are not necessarily in contradiction. The symbolic authenticity of selected realism allows the 'natural' order to be organized and reinforced through representation. Conventions of display mediate the 'real' in conformity with a discourse, as Jackie Bratton says, and in this case the discourse is imperial.[33]

Audiences were thrilled by fabulous depictions of naval skirmishes, Redcoat victories, far-away storms, and harem titillation, aided by the introduction of gas and lime light in the early nineteenth century and the general development of stage technology in increasingly large auditoria. Drury Lane in 1823 showed William Thomas Moncrieff's melodrama *The Cataract of the Ganges! Or, the Rajah's Daughter* with real horses and cascading water, as if to emphasize the theatrical nature of Britain's subjugation of both nature and India. Later, under Augustus Harris, the same theatre specialized in imperial spectacle whereas venues such as Astley's continued to impress with grandiose display (George Sanger's *The Fall of Khartoum and the Death of General Gordon* in 1885 featured camels and Arabian horses alongside a cast of several hundreds). Imre Kiralfy's *India*, a ninety-minute spectacle at the 1895 Empire of India Exhibition, which had the Empress Theatre, Earl's Court decorated like a Mughal temple, employed a cast of 1,000 (not Indian) to portray nearly 2,000 years of Indian history in justification of the British Raj by, among other things, ignoring discordant episodes such as the 1857 Uprising.[34]

Theatre mapped out all manner of British foreign policy interests, whether against Napoleon and his conquest of Egypt, which threatened important trade routes, or in favour of keeping intact and fighting on the side of the Ottoman empire against the Russians in Crimea, although this was at odds with support for Greek independence. A crop of Crusader plays underpinned the significance of the Holy Land (Jerusalem was sacred for many Christians and for linking the British to the Roman and Ottoman empires), while numerous plays also maintained the view of Islam as the enemy of Christianity. Apprehension of the Other was often expressed in metaphor, for example, in plays that featured symbolic underground or enclosed spaces such as *The Captive Vathek, Azael the Prodigal* or the many versions of the Bluebeard story set in a labyrinthine castle.[35] There were few figures of resistance such as Obi, and the convention of the disgruntled black avenger was ridiculed in C. P. Thompson's 1829 nautical melodrama *Jack Robinson and his Monkey*, when a mutinous African called Muley is outwitted by the eponymous animal.[36] Plays and other spectacles produced in the aftermath of events such as the 1857 Uprising generally reinforced notions of British liberty. Dion Boucicault's *Jessie Brown, or the Relief of Lucknow* (1858) – in which the author played the villainous Sepoy Nana Sahib apparently because the other actors were fearful of the audience response – was sufficiently pro-British, despite Sahib putting the anti-colonial case with conviction, that it was toured to India.[37]

The few counter-narratives that can be found, however heavily circumscribed, tend to come in educational/lecture performances (dioramas, for instance) or in shows at so-called illegitimate theatres (or their successors after the 1843 Theatres Act that passed into law the reality of the failure of the patent system). David Worrall offers the case of the Royal Coburg, which gave space to Islamic Indian pride and protest at the British invasion of India in plays such as William Barrymore's *El Hyder* or H. M. Milner's *Tippoo Saib*.[38] Many such theatres, especially in London, sprang up in river areas with a multi-ethnic population linked to East and West trade; the opening in the early 1800s of the West India and East India docks, for example, completely altered the local demographic. An adjacent area with a high proportion of Indian lascars (seamen) and Chinese sailors who had arrived with the East India Company became known by the 1830s as the Oriental quarter, or the black hole of the East End, echoing a derogatory (and historically inaccurate) phrase that had entered popular usage from the campaign to subjugate India. Unsurprisingly, the quarter gained a reputation for danger and exoticism, the staples of Asian representation in British drama.[39]

By their nature and location in lower- or working-class areas, these theatres enjoyed a close correlation between audience and repertoire, and shows may have included diasporic performers in their casts. The makeup of the audience would have affected styles of performance and the meanings audiences took from them, perhaps countering aspects of the dominant imperial view. Nevertheless, it is important not to romanticize or impose an agenda – let alone a unified one – on such venues. Though audiences might boo the villainous plantation owner in stage versions of *Uncle Tom's Cabin* and cheer an escaping slave, they might also applaud violent racist misogyny or British military might conquering in Africa.

Though most of the focus on the African or Asian Other was aimed abroad, a noteworthy shift occurred with stories set in Britain, a development associated with the non-patent theatres and a reflection of the multi-ethnic presence in British cities. Symptomatic of this change were the many stage adaptations, primarily as *Tom and Jerry*, of a picaresque novel of 1821 by Pierce Egan called *Life in London*, which recounts the metropolitan adventures of two gentlemen who mingle with the 'lower orders'.[40] This allowed stage versions to bring on a throng of black beggars and musicians and named roles such as African Sal and Billy Waters, both inspired by real street entertainers who, some commentators believe, appeared as themselves. Heidi Holder argues that in such shows, the thrill of seeing the classes mix and the sense of strangeness intensified by the presence of the Other reinforced the existing social hierarchy: black people were inferior and to be laughed at, whereas the superior whites can become anyone they choose.[41]

Characters from the African and Asian diasporas were generally marginal and restricted to negligible and subservient roles, such as Caliban (or Calaban), a malicious black attendant attached to the Old Bailey in various versions of *Jack Sheppard*; Sally Slack, a 'pauper negress' (played by a man) in Gilbert Abbott à Beckett's *The Revolt of the Workhouse*; Ah Luck, a Chinese comic servant in Paul Merritt and George F. Rowe's *New Babylon*; or Rampunkah, a 'hindoo' servant in Joseph Derrick's *Twins*.

In the rare plays where diasporic figures do take centre stage, their depiction remains stereotypical. Edward Fitzball's *The Negro of Wapping* (1838) features a sailor called Sam who robs and commits murder but offers as justification what had become a common explanation: the evil of slavery. Despite his attack on the rich and powerful, a regular motif in popular theatre, he remains the familiar figure of the diabolic black avenger. In *The Street Arab* (1871, author unknown), Clement, King of the street Arabs and pinnacle of rootless criminality, turns out to be the long lost heir to a fortune, marries a rich upper-class woman, and calls on the poor to be virtuous.[42]

Holder, however, identifies two plays in which central diasporic characters present more complex images of ethnicity in the modern city. In J. B. Johnstone's *How We Live, or, London Labour and London Poor* (1856), the figure who acts as guide through the urban jungle no longer comes from the privileged class but is not only a coster (someone who sells fruit and vegetables) but also a 'Hindoo' called Araxa.[43] In James Willing and Frank Stainforth's *Glad Tidings* (1883), the plot's pivotal figure is a female Indian beggar, Juanna (who is later discovered to be related to the main character). Both Juanna and Araxa criticize the cruel treatment of the poor by the ruling class and, instead of passively carrying notions of race, class, and gender, are the active agents of social restoration and humane values, even if they renovate the existing social order by eventually being sacrificed. Both achieve their dynamic role in deathbed confessions and then are required no more, a device also seen typically in noble-savage plays. As Holder says, the two characters are not 'fully incorporated' into society; they are used symbolically as well as realistically, and may have been cast as Indians rather than been given darker skins to allow a blurring fluidity of colour.[44] This profile also fits the fact that they are women; the Other used as critique is often feminized, even in the Oriental confections that transpose British desire to a make-believe land.

Feminization and blurring are parts of the ontological and psychological ambiguity regarding the Other, which reflects anxiety at, and a recognition of, the instability of skin colour coding. Such concerns were sharpened in the wake of the abolition of slavery and the accompanying sense of urgent need to secure racial categorization. They are specifically captured in plays that treat the stock character of the tragic mulatto or mixed heritage figure, of which there were many in the mid-nineteenth century: for example, *The Quadroon Slave, The Creole, Lugarto the Mulatto, Sarah Blangi, American Slavery or the Creole of St. Louis*, and *The Slave Hunter or the Half Caste*. Dion Boucicault's *The Octoroon* (New York, 1859; London, 1861) manages to appeal to both pro- and anti-abolitionists using melodrama, minstrelsy, and spectacle but does offer what seems to be the most significant debate in the British theatre since *Inkle and Yarico* on issues related to mixed relationships. Racism is removed from immediate focus, as the eponymous heroine Zoe is ostensibly white (and was played by the author's white wife). The initial assumption that she is white is used by Boucicault to make more poignant the revelation that her black blood, even if it is only 'one eighth' (hence octoroon), prevents her under the law from marrying her white lover, a fate she resolves by committing suicide. In response to pleas from his British audience, Boucicault replaced Zoe's death with a 'love triumphs over adversity' ending, allowing the lovers a future – in England – that was not possible in America. Coming after the Indian Uprising, the show successfully pandered to British nationalist superiority and challenged the US racial system while simultaneously using blackface minstrel stereotypes that perpetuate white control of the black body and accommodate the violence associated with that power.

Minstrelsy

Blackface minstrelsy became central to the performance of Otherness in Britain, rising with the abolition of slavery and the renewed attempts at racial fastening. Enormously popular for more than a century, it offered the least compromising view of the non-white body, yet, paradoxically, could be highly complex as well. Unravelling the roots and the manifold meanings of blackface minstrelsy is a difficult and often highly speculative task. Outside urban theatre, blacking up was associated both with illegal activity – whether poaching or politics – and with seasonal mumming or other rural festivities such as Morris dancing, the history of which is itself confused, particularly because folk traditions were reinvented during the industrial revolution as the country/city balance altered. Mummers might use blackface to present satirical or challenging material anonymously without fear of retribution or as part of the fun in making a local audience guess who from the neighbourhood was performing for them. Black could also signify a non-naturalistic aesthetic, as might be found with cross-dressing or other devices of parody or exaggeration.[45] According to Worrall, rural mummers dealt conservatively with topical issues such as piracy linked to the North African Islamic states and the campaign against Tipoo Saib.[46] With the onset of minstrelsy, the mumming/Morris customs came to embrace 'nigger' musicians, and one annual event, in Padstow, Cornwall even took the name 'Darkie Day'. (This day continues to be celebrated. Despite some participants wearing 'Afro' wigs in the late twentieth century, organizers denied any racist connotation, though the name was changed to Mummers' Day in 2005 in response to campaigning, a tacit recognition of the possible contradiction between intention and effect.)

Though there is continuing debate about the origins of blackface minstrelsy, it seems likely that English theatre played a key role in its development via such actors as Charles Dibdin and Charles Mathews. On the back of his Mungo success, Dibdin in the late 1780s and 1790s began presenting solo musical entertainments called *Readings and Music*, or later *Table Entertainments*, several of which involved impersonating a black character and more representatives of the Other: the Irish, the Italians, and the Jews. His satirical comedies were so popular that he built his own theatre in 1796 to perform them and took them to America. These shows launched some of his best-known songs, especially 'Kickaraboo', which describes the death of a black man as ludicrous but says black and white are the same in the grave.[47] Dibdin, playing all the parts in the shows himself, would use a keyboard with a set of bells, side drum, tambourine, and gong, an echo of the minstrelsy to come.

Mathews, the chief British comic actor of his day and also noted for his solo shows (called *At Home*), lampooned the absurdities and affectations of the middle and working classes and included caricatures of black people in his satire. Indeed, he may have been the first white to impersonate an American black person. After visiting New York and the African Theatre, he created several black characters, including a preacher whose sermons foreshadow the minstrel 'stump' speech. In *Mr. Mathews' Trip to America* (1824), he performed the black roles of a stage coach driver, a fiddle player, and a black Shakespearean actor. In his 1833 burlesque, *Othello, the Moor of Fleet Street*, which transplants the story to contemporary working-class London, Othello is a street sweeper (a stock drunken, violent husband) and Desdemona a brass worker. At the end, she survives and highlights the pretensions of blackness ('he's far more fair than black'), playing, as English theatre had done before, with the fact that the audience knows the actor performing Othello is white.[48]

In his ridicule of black speech and vocabulary and the ambition of his black characters, Mathews employs a racism that resurfaces in minstrelsy. It is likely he reproduced and exaggerated aspects of black performance he had seen at the African Theatre, which may themselves have been embellishments of the style of English actors who had played New York. The African Theatre's main actor, James Hewlett, who was said to have replicated Kean's rolling eyes and flashing teeth, performed a riposte to Mathews at the African Theatre in 1823 called *Imitations of Mathews' At Home* and may have repeated a similar show in Liverpool in 1825. A letter from Hewlett to Mathews, published in *The Times* the previous year, criticizes American racism, defends British tolerance, and says that 'Shakespeare is *our* bard as well as yours'. Furthermore, adds Hewlett, 'when you next ridicule the "tincture of the skin", do not forget the texture of the mind'.[49] Mathews, who prepared the ground for blackface minstrelsy as well as more directly influencing the representation of black people in British music hall, ignored this injunction and continued his mocking for the rest of his career.

The white American T. D. Rice first visited Britain in 1836 with his 'Jump Jim Crow' song and dance that heralded the arrival of blackface minstrelsy. The routine was said to have been copied from a black stableman who had a damaged leg, and it is possible that Rice, or his followers, may also have been imitating black slave caricatures of the white master. He started a fashion in America with his frenetic black minstrel act, and he set in train a hugely popular trend in Britain, too. His celebration of excess clearly had tremendous theatrical vitality, and his preposterous exaggerations, which were first seen in London at a theatre that featured acts depicting Otherness (a Bedouin Arab, a Parisian giant), were welcomed as authentic representation. American minstrel troupes followed Rice to Britain, where a local version soon took root, fed by indigenous blackface traditions and a curious post-abolition sense of superiority over America, which still had slavery. Minstrelsy in turn fed back into those traditions, producing regional variants, and gained respectability quickly: Queen Victoria attended a performance in 1846, and blackface minstrels were invited to the command performance at Balmoral in 1868. Fanny Kemble reportedly brought the house down as Lady Teazle in an 1847 production of *The School for Scandal* when she entered humming a minstrel tune.

Use of blackface minstrelsy in stage versions of Harriet Beecher Stowe's *Uncle Tom's Cabin* not only helped make the story reach a mass audience in Britain but gave new impetus to minstrelsy itself. When the book appeared in 1852, the Fugitive Slave had become a hero figure in the wake of visits by former slaves. Within months of publication, *Uncle Tom's Cabin* was on stage and, by the end of the year, there were at least eleven different dramatizations on offer.[50] Tom appeared in pantomimes, burlesques, equestrian spectacles, circuses, sketches, children's adaptations, songs, new fiction, illustrations, paintings, and poems; as a puppet and a toy; and was used to sell other merchandise, such as china and coffee. 'Tom mania' (as the vogue became known) spread across Europe but was mainly felt in Britain, where stage versions remained popular until World War 1. Adaptations mostly used white performers but, at the end of the trend, a few black performers were included, for example, Lizzie Allen, Carlton Bryan, Ada Cuffy, and J. G. Johnston.

The anti-slavery message of, and portrayal of black people in, *Uncle Tom's Cabin* helped secure the acceptability of blackface minstrelsy. Different versions of the story were used to express different views, and there were shows that criticized 'Tom mania' from an openly racist standpoint.[51] The legacy of *Uncle Tom's Cabin* turned out not to be its abolitionist aim but, with the aid of minstrelsy, a clutch of demeaning stereotypes that dominated representation of black people for decades to come: the mammy, the lazy slave, the tragic mulatto, the comic zany youngster, the Jezebel and, above all, the supine Uncle Tom, whose negative characteristics were not intended by Stowe but were emphasized in the stage versions.

Stowe's lesser known novel, *Dred* (1856), possibly inspired by the slave rebellion of 1831 led by Nat Turner, also appeared in many stage adaptations, often using minstrelsy. With the eponymous escaped slave who espouses violence at its centre, *Dred* reinforced the stage tradition of the vengeful black man, even though it was portraying black empowerment. Judie Newman argues that the stage versions, peopled as they were with plantation stereotypes, nevertheless showed that the British public had accepted black violence as the likely outcome of the controversy over slavery, an outcome that Stowe herself evades.[52]

The British strain of minstrelized blackface spread to an astonishing range of pursuits, both amateur and professional: fetes, festivals, fairs, race meetings, markets, street and seaside entertainments, wakes, religious assemblies, Punch and Judy, local concerts, circuses, and itinerant shows. There were white minstrels and blackface minstrels and black performers who donned blackface because it provided job and travel opportunities. It was a major influence on the music hall, with its many 'coon' songs and turns that became increasingly absurd and further removed from lived black experience. British blackface minstrelsy was exported to India and Australia and even visited the United States. One of the earliest films to be seen in Britain, *The Wandering Negro Minstrels* (1896), featured blackface minstrels. Augmented by the popularity of the golliwog phenomenon it had fostered, the genre continued into the twentieth century as 'family entertainment', a declining force in music hall but still active in vaudeville, ragtime, popular dance, film, radio, and television. Having spawned a West End version that ran for twelve years, *The Black and White Minstrel Show* remained on television for two decades before coming to an end only in 1978. Blackface outside of minstrelsy began to fade in Britain in the 1950s, though it survived in major productions of *Othello* until 1980 and was notably seen in the supposedly more realistic media of film when Alec Guinness 'browned' up in the 1984 film of *A Passage to India*.

Theatrically, blackface minstrelsy was indomitably non-literary and stood against the tenets of the Romantics ('the willing suspension of disbelief'). Its extravagant style has been linked not only to slave performance and circus but to the garish uniforms black bandsmen wore, the livery of eighteenth-century footmen and pages, and the excitement of the servants' all-black entertainments. It brought audiences into the domain of the clown, who can turn the world upside down in safety. Like melodrama and pantomime, this was a world of recognizable types, seen through a racial prism that suited the Victorian love of an exhibit.

Differentiated reception and interpretations, especially by class and gender, reveal much that is contradictory in a form that relied on strong audience rapprochement. In its working-class manifestations, there was satire of the middle and upper classes and also a prevalent male presence (with some exceptions, it was 'an aggressively segregated form', without room for female or black performers).[53] It offered temporary escape from the grind of factory work or the vacuity of unemployment through the association of wage and slave labour and identification with the unashamedly 'lazy' attitudes on display. At the same time, there is validation of the male body via racist caricature. Despite the traditional connotation of black as bad and ugly, nineteenth-century artists admired the black male body in a way that echoed ancient Greek and Roman classicism. In blackface minstrelsy, the ugly is acknowledged with brio and (for men) turned into its opposite. Male sexuality, the rhythm and 'naturalness' of the body, are celebrated, even as black men – and more so, black women – are belittled for the consequences of these very qualities. Misogyny offers another kind of bonding. Black minstrel women, often seen in outrageous drag (an extension of the exaggerated image of sexual promiscuity promoted by the Elizabethan theatre), reinforce stage pictures that can be found elsewhere, such as the grotesque Cuffa in George Dibdin Pitt's *Toussaint L'Ouverture* or other brutal caricatures in shows such as Edward Stirling's *The Cabin Boy* and *The Buffalo Girls*; A. L.V. Campbell's *More Ethiopians!! Or, Jenny Lind in New York*; or *Somebody's in the House with Dinah, or Invitation to the Nigger Ball*.[54]

For the middle classes, blackface minstrelsy allowed a self-satisfied feeling of anti-slavery, 'pro-black' sentiment untroubled by the realities of black life. The exotic was thrilling and allowed the British to be very un-British without disturbing their sense of self and Britishness. Jingoism crossed class and gender boundaries in spite of its different meanings. Fun was poked at the British both at home and in their imperial adventures abroad while celebrating their power and superiority, not just over the non-white Other but also over slave-holding America, the democratic revolution of which was seen as a threat to the British parliamentary-monarchy system. *More Ethiopians!!*, for instance, ends triumphantly with 'Rule Britannia' sung in minstrel style.

As Britain's post-abolition exploration and exploitation of Africa increased and Africa itself became a more distinct and particular creation, the black body became central to white theories of existence, operating as a reverse image, or negative, of the white. In theatre, just as the Mungo type had supplanted the noble savage, so blackface minstrelsy superseded Mungo, channelling the comic servant stereotype into a more pervasive humiliation of black people that was both more sophisticated and more unpleasant. Whatever positive readings can be found – common cause of the disenfranchised, a celebration of Otherness, the possibility of multiple identity – its dominant feature is representation of inferiority through infantilization. Any possible connections that might be made or desired are both invited (through engaging theatricality) and dismissed (by the overt separation that informs the caricature). Minstrelsy's clownish disruption is distanced by disdain, and the 'natural order' is reinforced. The white body has the power to mimic the black body, to wear the black mask and, by possessing and controlling, to confirm black disempowerment. If white can become black without losing its whiteness, white can conquer anything. In such a world, where white is the universal standard, colour can even be considered ephemeral like makeup when white chooses. As such, colour can be disregarded as a marker for collective violence while that violence continues unchecked. For all the complexity surrounding interpretation of blackface minstrelsy, the practice was vital to contemporary and later concepts of race and to the position and identity of white and black within them.[55]

Blackface may have become taboo in the twenty-first century – and even its ironic or critical use remained contentious – but what it has bequeathed has not entirely disappeared; opportunities for black actors remain constrained by the legacy of stereotypes inherited from minstrelsy, which, at root, rely on and promote racist essentialism.[56] Frederick Douglass, the outstanding African-American emancipationist who first came to Britain in 1845, blamed minstrel shows for the intolerance he met. Aldridge had to act in the context of minstrelized perceptions, and subsequent African-American performers in Britain found they had to black up to be accepted: for instance, audiences in Liverpool in 1866 did not like a minstrel troupe of ex-slaves until they returned with burnt cork applied. Blackface minstrelsy was both one of the major currents of white control and, because of its pervasiveness, one of the major outlets for black performance. That black performers were able to find space within the convention or against its dominant backdrop to express their own and counter messages is hugely to their lasting credit.

3

AFTER ALDRIDGE

Diasporic artists of colour who came to Britain after the arrival of Ira Aldridge do not form a coherent group, and they range across genre and performance style. One such artist, Henry 'Box' Brown, made spectacular theatrical interventions in the 1850s that used theatricality in a way opposite to minstrelsy. Replicating his method of escape, Box posted himself from Bradford to Leeds in (it was said) the box in which he had escaped, a symbol of the confinement to which he and other slaves were subjected and the means by which he resisted and overcame that constraint. He emerged on a music hall stage, gave a lecture, and then finished with an abolitionist panorama. He wrote slave narratives, too, and his exploits were celebrated in song, broadsheet, and illustration. Daphne Brooks points out that his box show, a metaphor of rebirth, references Victorian love of magic, escapology, and spiritualism and prefigures the allure of Houdini by stressing the potency, and expanding the possibilities, of the black body as agent, made all the more real because the magic of his escape was not an illusion.[1] Box's kinetic panorama *Mirror of Slavery* used the latest technology to support his narration of the evils of slavery and sometimes included songs such as the 'Hymn of Thanksgiving', which he was said to have sung on removal from the original box. As Brooks says, he used his body – that which made him a slave – as a tool of defiance; he made his body vanish from the slave masters and thereby demonstrated he was the true master. He also added non-slave-related material, including pro-British references to the 1857 Indian Uprising, showing that both slavery and insurrection could be turned into entertainment, and he remained on the circuit as a hypnotist and conjuror. He was praised by some white critics for his veracity but attacked by others both for his 'unfair' and 'false view' of America and for his use of English (a recurring theme in patronizing the Other), though he won a celebrated court case against a newspaper editor whose paper had attacked his 'palpable exaggeration'.[2]

Following Aldridge's precedent, another African-American, Samuel Morgan Smith, travelled to England in 1866, a year after the abolition of slavery in the United States, to be an actor. Born in Philadelphia in 1832, he was well educated, worked as a barber and hairdresser, and had published *A Critical Review of the Late Speech of Charles O'Conor: 'Negro slavery not unjust'*.[3] Morgan Smith had moved to Boston and New York to pursue a stage career, found professionals to coach him in acting, and gave public readings and recitals but was denied backstage access 'on account of his color'.[4] Within days of arriving in Britain with his wife and small child – never having appeared on stage in public in a full-length play – he had leased the Theatre Royal in Gravesend, Kent where among the roles he played for twenty-one nights were Othello, Hamlet, Richard III, Macbeth, Lear, and Shylock.[5] He then went on tour, to further mixed reviews and little financial success. He also played in Edward Bulwer-Lytton's *The Lady of Lyons* and *Richelieu*; Thomas Morton's *The Slave*; Thomas Southerne's *Oroonoko*; and Walter Scott's *Rob Roy* before, later that year, appearing in a short season at the Royal Olympic Theatre, London.

FIGURE 3.1   Samuel Morgan Smith, actor (Courtesy of Westminster Library archive)

He maintained a gruelling schedule. During his first year, he performed in at least twenty-nine locations across Britain and Ireland and, by the following year, he had established a respectable reputation, billed variously as 'the Coloured American Tragedian' and 'the great African tragedian'.[6] His other parts included the eponymous role in Kotzebue's comedy *The Stranger*; Iago, Romeo, Zanga, Dred, Uncas (a Mohican chieftain in *All But Love*); an Ethiopian monarch in *The Fall of Magdala, or the Death of King Theodore*; a freed South American slave in *War*; and Fabian in *The Black Doctor*. This latter part he also reprised in a new spectacular version called *The Rising of the Tide*. Three new plays were reportedly written for him, but none has yet been traced to verify this. They include a romantic drama, *Child of the Sun; or, The Bondsmen Brothers*, in which he played the role of the celebrated musician, swordsman, and equestrian Chevalier de Saint-Georges, known as the Black Mozart.[7] A short season Morgan Smith undertook at the Elephant and Castle Theatre, London in 1877 opened with this play and ended with T. W. Robertson's *Birds of Prey*.

After the death of his first wife, Morgan Smith married a white actress, Harriet, who appeared opposite him in several roles. He did not play major theatres but maintained a strong presence in the regions and so-called minor London venues for more than a dozen years, performing some thirty-five roles. Not surprisingly, one account of him recalls his 'habit of leaving the theatre in a four-wheeled cab, on the top of which he always had piled sundry garish garments of his wardrobe and all his swords and daggers for his different characters'.[8] According to Errol Hill, he did not play Mungo or any other comic black character, instead taking on only those characters 'who were unfairly victimized or who suffered for a noble cause'.[9] He appeared only once in *Uncle Tom's Cabin*, not as Tom but as George Harris, the proud black man who detests slavery. In 1868, he gave a benefit for the performer Nellie McEwen, who herself may have been of African descent.[10] He died in Sheffield of pneumonia in 1882 aged 49.

Besides receiving a slew of bad reviews, Morgan Smith was also favourably described as an 'intellectual and dignified' actor of 'decided talent', a 'careful and agreeable elocutionist…painstaking…earnest and spirited'.[11] A review in 1873 summarized his prowess as 'good reading, unexaggerated action, a clear, powerful voice, a correct memory, and an intelligent apprehension of dramatic requirements'. Standing in contrast to minstrelized performance, he was noted for 'natural delivery and accompanying deportment'.[12] Hill says Morgan Smith was not of Aldridge's rank, having less range, power, and originality, yet he was (quoting one critic) a 'superior performer', talented and painstaking, and a worthy successor to Aldridge.[13]

A third example of an African-American actor coming to Britain in the nineteenth century for the opportunity to act in Shakespeare is Paul Molyneaux Hewlett. Born in 1856 in Cambridge, Massachusetts, he trained to be an actor and received positive reviews for his portrayal of Othello in Boston in 1880 when he assembled his own company of supporting players. Seeking more training he knew would be difficult to obtain in the United States, he worked his passage to England where he played London and the regions as Paul Molyneaux. Billed as by 'the great American tragedian and black Roscius', an 1883 performance as Richard III was poorly reviewed (though in a letter to the same paper, Molyneaux pleaded he was new to England and had to rely on amateurs to make up his cast).[14] There are few details of his appearances, though the *New York Globe* in 1883 quoted two reviews of his performance as Othello without giving their source or identifying the theatre or date. One review said, 'His impersonation was at all times careful and conscientious; it was occasionally very impressive' whereas the other was even more effusive: 'Mr Paul Molyneaux gave one of the best, if not the best, impersonations of the Moor we ever saw…the whole heart and soul of the actor were thrown into the character and the result was perfection'.[15] The *Globe* also revealed that Molyneaux had written an account of the troubles he had faced finding work and recognition, entitled *The Curse of Prejudice; or, A Struggle for Fame*. In addition to the racism he encountered, the novelty of another black actor was apparently wearing thin. In 1886, he wrote to Frederick Douglass, the great emancipationist, that he still had not made his fortune.[16] With emancipation no longer a rallying issue, Molyneaux clearly 'found life very difficult indeed'.[17] In 1889, he returned to America and died two years later of brain trouble.

Tantalizing but incomplete references exist to another black performer, Joseph Jenkins, who performed outside the theatre circuit. He was known for his speeches from *Othello*, notably at the Eagle Saloon in London (of 'Pop Goes the Weasel' fame). Described as a genius by William Wells Brown, a prominent African-American abolitionist who visited London in the 1850s, Jenkins did an assortment of jobs, including psalm singer and crossing sweeper.[18] Diasporic performers remained a common sight on the streets, to the extent that white buskers were known to pretend to be black, and they were also popular at fairgrounds and circuses and in horse and animal entertainments. Along with several black boxers, such as Bill Richmond, who appeared on theatre bills, could be found circus performers such as William Beaumont ('the African Lion King'), George Christopher (tightrope dancer), Carlos Tower (tightrope walker) and, probably the most celebrated, William Darby, a Norwich-born black Briton known professionally as Pablo Fanque. Proprietor of many circuses, he was a horse rider and acrobat, immortalized in the Lennon and McCartney song 'Being For the Benefit of Mr. Kite'. In the associated world of juggling and conjuring, there were strong links with India going back to the end of the eighteenth century and, through a subtle process of Orientalization, connections later with China, too.[19]

Music and dance still provided the main arena for non-white diasporic performance. In 1838, African-American violinist, bugler, horn-player, conductor, and composer Frank Johnson toured Britain with his woodwind and percussion band and was honoured with a command performance. Spanish singer Dona Maria Loreto Martinez, dubbed The Black Malibran after the leading opera diva of her day, appeared in London in 1850, and soprano Elizabeth Taylor Greenfield, a former slave from Mississippi known as the Black Swan, came to Britain for additional training and sang for Queen Victoria in 1854 during a tour. 'Blind Tom' (Thomas Bethune from Georgia) drew large crowds in 1866 to hear him sing and play the piano. One of the few black performers to thrive in minstrelsy was the renowned dancer William Henry Lane, known by many names including Master Juba (the name of his

characteristic dance and also the name of the major black character in the play *Cato*).
He appeared in 1848 in Liverpool and London, where he settled after touring with a
white minstrel troupe until his death in the early 1850s. Acknowledged as a pioneer
of tap dancing, he influenced British music hall acts and clowning, performed with
an English dance company, and opened his own dance school.[20]

Choirs singing spirituals came to Britain because of the opening created by
minstrelsy, but they traded on their difference from minstrelized performers. The
Fisk Jubilee Singers first toured Britain in 1873 to raise funds and spread the gospel.
They were welcomed as authentic, in contrast to the blackface minstrels who, in
retaliation, impersonated them. The choir returned in 1875 and toured Europe
and Britain until 1877. They are credited with introducing Britain to spirituals and
inspiring the founding of white gospel choirs. Similar African–American choirs
were formed and visited Britain, some exploiting the name Fisk. Songs from the
repertoire – 'Deep River', 'Steal Away', and 'Nobody Knows the Trouble I See', for
example – aided by recording in the early twentieth century, became absorbed into
British culture, and one song, 'Swing Low, Sweet Chariot', was even adopted later
as England's Rugby Union anthem. Notions of authenticity remained contentious,
however. Though the choirs eschewed the exaggeration of minstrelsy, the singing
was not representative of the slave experience from which the songs came and was
delivered in a style that would appeal to the religious sensibilities of a white audience,
who, as a result, were hearing the slaves' message anew.[21]

By the end of the nineteenth century, there were many African-American
entertainers performing in Britain as comedians, dancers, musicians, and singers; in
minstrel troupes, jubilee choirs, and quartets; and as solo artists. They appeared in
different types of entertainment and in a variety of venues and locations, from pier
shows to music halls. Fashionable society took up black dances such as the 'Cakewalk',
which lampooned the stiff pomposity of slave owners and white aristocracy, who
themselves may have been mimicking black slaves, as T. D. Rice had done. Such
dances paved the way for the warm reception given in 1903 to *In Dahomey*, hailed
as the first all-black musical comedy to arrive in Britain. Suitably altered for British
taste (adding the 'Cakewalk', the expected badge of the public black body), the show
ran for 251 performances in the West End and successfully toured the country. The
large cast, led by the vaudevillians Bert Williams and George Walker, were invited
to meet the King. It even became chic to throw parties for cast members, an echo
of the aristocratic patronage of exotic servants as fashion accessories from an earlier
age. Created, produced, and performed by African Americans, contributions were
not always easily compartmentalized, but the principal creators were composer-
conductor Will Marion Cook, who led the team; scriptwriter-stage manager Jesse
Shipp; composer-lyricist Alex Rogers; and the performers Williams and Walker. It
contained work by other composers, including white ones. The celebrated writer,
Paul Laurence Dunbar, wrote lyrics with Cook in the early stages and featured
prominently in the publicity but apparently had little to do with the production
itself. *In Dahomey* combined elements of different entertainments, such as operetta,
variety and, above all, minstrelsy. White vaudeville promoters put up the money for

the show, which began life in the United States in 1902 and continued in different versions until 1905.[22]

The plot features a hoax land scheme in Dahomey, a kingdom in west Africa – the first time an African theme (albeit not treated respectfully) had been dealt with in a major musical. Two confidence tricksters (played by Williams and Walker) try to trace an heirloom to make money from it. Loosely structured to allow the presentation of a series of turns as might be found in pantomime, the action sees the two embark on a journey during which they meet many aspirant black characters and satirize racial stereotyping (when marketing skin and hair products, for instance). The show, which Audrey Fisch describes as a Pan-African extravaganza, revelled in chaos and hybridity, undercutting any attempt at coherent racial interpretation while reflecting a desire for social mobility among the American post–Civil War black population.[23] According to Fisch, the extraordinary image of Africa, duly exotic but unlike anything the British had seen before, was an African-American vision of a fantasy land from which African-Americans came. *In Dahomey* traded in imperial imagery but exploded it through majestic excess, refusing to accept an essentialist vision that promoted Africa as both an unspoiled kindergarten and a threatening, unknowable continent of darkness. There was genuine counter-cultural and ethnographic intent that attempted, within the confines of an overwhelmingly minstrelized and racist entertainment system, to offer a vision of the black body and the black person as joyful and human rather than dangerous and monstrous.

In Dahomey made its mark in Britain in several ways: Dahomey became a byword for things African and for black entertainment (for example, the Dahomey Quartet was a black song-and-dance troupe that toured Britain in 1904); the show became the first black musical to have its score published (and this happened in England rather than America); and the show created a new interest in, and impetus for, black entertainment in Britain, helping, for example, raise improvisation to new levels and popularize syncopated ragtime music.[24] Exploiting the success of *In Dahomey*, African-American impresario Will Garland staged a 1906 British version of another important American black musical, *A Trip to Coontown*, by Robert 'Bob' Cole and William 'Billy' Johnson. Popularity brought problems, however. With the influx into Britain of African-American entertainers, white journalists picked on the bad behaviour of a few, some London pubs introduced a 'race' bar, and white variety artists complained about unfair competition. Nevertheless, a number of African-American artists found Britain relatively benign compared to America and remained or returned to settle, appearing in variety, revue and film as well as in the 'straight' theatre and on disc.[25] Norris Smith, for example, went on to understudy Paul Robeson in *Show Boat*, appeared from 1928 on as part of a top-billing piano and vocal duo Marino and Norris (later a trio) and, in the 1940s, had a number of roles on stage, including in Lillian Hellman's *Watch on the Rhine*, which ran for almost two years at the Aldwych Theatre.

Henry Francis Downing

Just as Britain had been central to the earlier anti-slavery movement, at the end of the nineteenth and beginning of the twentieth centuries, it was becoming a focal point for Indian independence, Pan-Africanism, and anti-colonial struggle in general. Taken broadly, these movements valued culture highly (often within a European definition), both as a self-improvement aspiration and a benchmark of universal equality, regardless of race. Among those active in such movements who had prominent cultural connections were Frederick J. Loudin, who led a spirituals choir to Britain in the 1890s and then settled there; the African-English composer Samuel Coleridge-Taylor, one of the first black composers of international standing; the Egyptian actor, writer, and theatrical promoter Dusé Mohamed Ali, who founded and ran the anti-colonial *African Times and Orient Review*; and the African-American playwright Henry Francis Downing, probably the first person of African descent to have a play of his or her own written and published in Britain.[26]

Downing was born in New York in 1851 to a family of free African Americans who ran an oyster business and cafeteria. Downing's uncle was a renowned civil rights activist, a cousin became President of Liberia (where Downing lived for a while and about which he wrote two books and a novel), and Downing himself became a well-known Democrat and a leader of the National Colored People's Protective Association. After taking a variety of jobs – messenger, clerk, waiter, sailor (serving twice in the US navy), and editor of a Brooklyn paper – he was made US consul to Angola. In 1895, he and his Bostonian wife, Margarita, who was of Irish descent, moved to London and lived there until 1917, when German bombing drove them back to New York.[27]

During his time in London, Downing addressed the first Pan-African Conference in 1900, was a member of the executive committee of the short-lived Pan-African Association formed at the Conference, and attended the 1911 First Universal Races Congress.[28] He managed Paul Laurence Dunbar's first recital with Samuel Coleridge-Taylor, contributed in serial form part of a novella for the *African Times and Orient Review*, and wrote at least one novel, *The American Cavalryman*. Downing also wrote the lyrics for 'Where the paw-paw grows' by Amanda Aldridge, daughter of Ira Aldridge. In 1913 and 1914, Downing had published at least eight plays. Two of these were self-published, and one was written with Margarita.[29]

His precise theatrical activities are unclear but, in the early 1910s, he seems to have presided over the Players and Playwrights Association, which aimed to help dramatists have their work produced.[30] Such bodies held competitions and organized performances of plays by their members. It is possible, especially given Downing's position, that some of his plays were seen in this kind of outlet, a speculation given substance by the action of a short comedy, *Placing Paul's Play*, which he wrote with Margarita about such an event. Downing evidently sought access to the powerful; several of his plays are dedicated to grand figures such as US President Woodrow Wilson, Lady Randolph Churchill, the catering magnate Sir Joseph Lyons, and May Sheldon, an expatriate American explorer and author. Downing even gained endorsements from a number of leading theatrical people and apparently used these to help arrange production of some of his plays at the Royal Court, but the theatre closed with the outbreak of war. His moment was lost, along with the 'considerable amount of money which he had already expended' on souvenir medallions for his plays, a loss that led to 'arrears with his rent' and subsequent legal problems.[31]

Downing believed in the importance of the author and therefore of being published, a position probably reflecting his temperament and the reality of cultural production in a white society where the few black actors that might be available would have to perform in relation to the expectations of minstrelsy. The plays, which follow the prevailing conventions of the day, are literary and allusive: *Human Nature; Or, The Traduced Wife* refashions *Othello*, and *Incentives* alludes to *Hamlet* in its use of a play within a play. Downing's plays are also dramaturgically and morally conservative. In *Placing Paul's Play*, there is a dig at the contemporary taste that favours Ibsenite drama – if the thwarted hero's play had been called *Crooked Way* or *Soiled Dove* and had dealt with neurotics and immoralities, it would have been acceptable. He complains: 'purity, cleanliness and simple fun appeal no longer'.[32] Downing's own taste for sentimentality and melodrama nevertheless accommodates issues of empire, displacement, and the diaspora. Espousing a philanthropic capitalism, he tends to focus on inequality rather than racism, but race and the discriminations associated with it are dealt with in several of the plays, a couple of which contain important black characters.

Despite Downing's generalist stance, which can be seen as a strategy to avoid the limitations of parochialism, the plays can be read as addressing the international interests of Downing's circle: *The Arabian Lovers; Or, The Sacred Jar* retells an *Arabian Nights* story of the Bagdad Caliph in an approach consistent with *The African Times and Orient Review*'s Pan-African/Pan-Asian perspective; in *Lord Eldred's Other Daughter*, a staid comedy of intrigue and double identity, it is suggested that the heroine may have been of part-African descent; *The Shuttlecock, or Israel in Russia*, set in St. Petersburg in 1900, has only one black character of thirty or so (an African-American woman still under the control of a man who seems to have ignored the demise of slavery), but it deals with the culture of exile; and *Voodoo*, a historical drama written on an epic scale, venerates Britain's Glorious Revolution by linking characters exiled to Barbados for involvement in rebellion against James II with the suppression of a slave revolt. *Voodoo* includes black roles but the topic of racism is incidental; *Incentives* deals with a British capitalist who wants to extend a war loan to a predatory nation called 'Nightmaria' (probably meant to evoke the Netherlands), but an unsavoury incident in his past when he was a gold prospector in America comes back to haunt him; and a comedy, *A New Coon in Town*, questions representations of Africa. Downing also wrote with Margarita *A Terrible Dilemma* (possibly a.k.a. *Which Should She Have Saved*), about which nothing is known.

In *A New Coon in Town: A Farcical Comedy Made in England*, Downing openly confronts racism and lampoons colonial attitudes in a multilayered, comic deconstruction of gender, class, and national stereotypes. A poor African American Terminus Quoddy, who is in London on his way to Liberia to claim an inheritance, gets involved in two confidence tricks aimed at an English family rich from the African jewel trade. The spur for both scams is class-based: the first results from a snub to an Irishman for being common by the aristocratic wife of the diamond merchant, the second from the desire of the merchant's daughter to marry the 'unsuitable' man she loves (a sculptor). Furthermore, it is an aristocrat who turns out to be a thief, not Quoddy. In the first con, Quoddy impersonates an African prince and, in the second, a statue of an African 'savage' in leopard skins. Quoddy works within and against minstrel stereotypes, and Downing is careful to instruct the actor playing him to 'act with restraint, and thus avoid debasing the character to the level of the music-hall, minstrel type of Negro'.[33]

Downing is challenging stereotypes and playing with the representation of Africa and those of African descent at a number of levels. While working against the minstrel type, Downing gives Quoddy minstrel language and, echoing *In Dahomey*, a project to find fortune in an inheritance in Liberia ('de country whar cullud folks de equal o' anybody else'). Downing debunks the use of offensive words such as *nigger*, which the Irishman calls Quoddy as a term of affection, and *coon*, which is used in the title as if in keeping with common practice. Downing also exploits the assumption that white people would believe other whites before Quoddy. Downing exposes the reactions of the rich white family to Quoddy, both as an African prince and as a statute that the sculptor has to 'touch up' because Quoddy is 'not exactly the correct thing'.[34]

As Brian Russell Roberts points out, by using the idea of, and white obsession with, the 'primitive' African to explore the gaps between image and reality, Downing pokes fun at both the habit of exhibiting exotic imperial conquests and contemporary aesthetic ideas that remove the image from its real-life referent. With his use of the Liberian project, he also challenges African–American ideas of, and their relationship to, Africa and their claims to be authentically representative. He is also addressing the view of Africa portrayed in *In Dahomey*. Downing's preoccupation with the nature of diasporic representation is signalled by the play's title echoing a hit American song of the 1880s and the 1890s musical *A Trip to Coontown*. Downing's subtitle, *A Farcical Comedy Made in England*, also emphasizes the diasporic focus and the concern with legacies of slavery and colonialism. Though Downing clearly attacks colonial exploitation of Africa (and makes a barely disguised reference to a then well-known imperialist Sir Harry Johnston), he explores at the same time, as Roberts says, 'the power motives and legitimacy of African American involvement in speaking on behalf of diasporic populations generally and African populations specifically'.[35]

When Downing returned to New York in 1917, he settled in Harlem and became vice-president of an African-American little theatre group, the National Ethiopian Art Theater, which had James Weldon Johnson as treasurer. Downing arranged for the Quality Amusement Company (affiliated with the Harlem-based Lafayette Players) to produce one of his plays, *A Racial Tangle*, but the production was either cancelled or its details have been lost. The play was an adaptation of his novella that had been incompletely serialized in *The African Times and Orient Review*. According to Bernard L. Peterson, it tells the story of a 'mulatto' brought up white whose black lover refuses to marry him on racial grounds until his real identity is revealed. Oscar Micheaux, the first major African–American film director, used *A Racial Tangle* as the basis for his 1928 silent film, *Thirty Years Later*, and, for his 1930 film, *A Daughter of the Congo*, Downing's novel *The American Cavalryman*, which he had written in London but had published in the United States.

In his lifetime, Downing's writing was mentioned alongside the work of leading African Americans such as W. E. B. Du Bois and James Weldon Johnson but, after Downing's death in 1928, it has been forgotten. In 1925, an article in the *Messenger: The World's Greatest Negro Monthly* observed that Downing was 'undoubtedly our foremost Negro dramatist—yet we hear little of him'.[36] The neglect of a person whom Francis Griffiths, the London publisher of his plays, described as a dramatist 'of unusual originality and power' can be ascribed to several factors: the probable loss of his papers as he hurriedly left London under German bombardment; his plays' being published in Britain; their not being staged (at least commercially); and their apparent lack of an 'ethnic' profile, offering utopian, universalist appeal for justice and equality in general rather than racial equality or a racialized message in particular.[37] However, as Roberts says, Downing was a 'a consummate denizen of the black Atlantic world' and his work 'ought to be accessed via a tradition of anti-colonial literary utopianism, a tradition less concerned with nationally specific racial formations and more inclined toward comparative or transnational approaches to questions of racialized oppression'.[38]

Dusé Mohamed Ali

Another member of the London Pan-African circle was Dusé Mohamed Ali, who founded and edited *The African Times and Orient Review*, which serialized Downing's fiction and reviewed his plays. Ali, who was probably born in Alexandria in 1866 to an Egyptian father and Sudanese mother, was an actor and a writer of journalism, fiction, autobiography, history, and plays.[39] It is not clear when he came from Egypt to Britain but, by his own account, he was educated in Britain from the age of ten. He returned to Egypt in 1882 on the death of his father at the battle of Tel-el-Kebir fighting the British (among others) as a compatriot of Ahmed Urabi, an Egyptian national leader. Back in Britain, Ali studied medicine at King's College, London and stayed from the early 1880s to the early 1920s. He pursued two main lines of work, acting and journalism, both, for different reasons, linked to race.

Apparently a friend who saw him play the Prince of Morocco in *The Merchant of Venice* at school – racial casting early on – suggested he become an actor. Though details of his theatrical life are not complete or fully verifiable, what is known of his attempts at survival as a non-white actor at this time is instructive. He found non-speaking work in 1883 aged seventeen, probably as a black slave being prepared for sale in the Roman drama *Claudian*, which was presented for a year by the leading actor-manager Wilson Barrett. Ali went with this production to the United States in 1886 and, while there, toured for famous lecture agent Major Pond as 'The Young Egyptian Wonder Reciter of Shakespeare'. On his return to Britain, Ali joined Sarah

FIGURE 3.2 Dusé Mohamed Ali, actor, playwright, producer and journalist

Thorne's company performing along the south coast in towns such as Brighton, Margate, and Ramsgate and, in 1890, appeared in Lilly Langtry's production of *Antony and Cleopatra* at the Royal Princess's Theatre, Oxford Street, which ran through to 1891. In 1893, he was typecast as a Nubian slave in *Hypatia* at the Theatre Royal, Haymarket, with Beerbohm Tree playing the lead role of a vengeful Jew. In Liverpool, Ali was a walk-on in the Shakespeare Theatre and a lead at an unnamed venue where audiences would pelt actors with food, possibly playing Tom in *Uncle Tom's Cabin* and the villainous Nana Sahib in Boucicault's *Jessie Brown*.

Ali's autobiography has him waiting at theatres trying to get work from impresarios such as D'Oyly Carte and Augustus Harris (with whom he did work in pantomime at Drury Lane). It also tells of encounters with the famous: of chancing upon Oscar Wilde in the green room at the Haymarket where *A Woman of No Importance* was rehearsing before it took over from *Hypatia*; of exchanging words with Edward, Prince of Wales, about Egypt and his pride in his father; and of meeting in the House of Commons Dadabhai Naoroji MP, an India Home Rule campaigner, whom he interviewed.[40] Ali also met him at the 1892 West End première of *The Round Tower*, a play about the 1857 Uprising, for which play Ali had missed out on playing the major role of the wicked rebel.

In 1900, Ali landed such a part, playing Osman Digma, a stereotypical nasty, disloyal, and lustful Arab in a tour of *On Active Service*, an imperialist melodrama by Herbert Leonard. Ali was also assistant stage manager, calling rehearsals on the second tour, which began in Lowestoft. The publicity billed him as the son of an Arab chief, presumably in keeping with the Sudanese subject matter of the play, then much in the news and figuring prominently in the popular imagination. He was well reviewed, and afterward was cast in a touring production of Maurice Goldberg's

Secrets –, or the Cross and the Crescent as a cruel and hypocritical Arab slave dealer Ibrahim al Murad who abducts beautiful white women. Often titled for titillation as simply *Secrets* – and set in a fantasy Eastern city of Balsora, this was standard Oriental nonsense, demeaning Muslims as sexually and morally corrupt and thereby validating civilized imperialism: the heroine is rescued by a noble English naval officer whose men clear the stage of 'black swabs' with fixed bayonets to rousing cheers.

Ali was well reviewed again, as he was in his next touring role, in 1903, as Nemo, the 'man vulture' freak in the melodrama *Because I Love You*, where his 'dusky countenance' was seen as enhancing the effect of his weird and 'creepy' impersonation.[41] As Ian Duffield points out, the attributes of the part – violent, lustful, drunk, ugly – would sum up the popular image of the black man fostered over several centuries. Despite his success, Ali was dropped when another actor, who wanted to play Nemo, bought the rights to the play and the remaining bookings. Nevertheless, actor-manager Walter Melville was so impressed by Ali's portrayal that he apparently told him were he not a 'negro' he would be in the first flight of West End actors.

Though Ali had little option but to appear in such cliché roles, his unhappiness is apparent; the author of *Because I Love You* and the show's manager had to induce him to play the role of Nemo by offering to stage two of his short plays. This seems to have happened in Newcastle but without success; no titles or details survive, though the plays may have been among others he was known to have written and which may constitute the first original plays by a person of the non-white diaspora to have been professionally performed in Britain. In the late 1890s, he wrote a short play or tragedietta, *The Jew's Revenge*, borrowed from *Hypatia* and also set in ancient Egypt with a stereotypical 'cunning Jew' at its centre, a part he played several times in the early 1900s. His short dramatic melange, *All the Fun of the Fair*, was performed in Gloucester in September 1907, and his play, *A Cleopatra Night*, was probably produced, but it is not clear when, possibly Dundee in 1907. A Hull journal, *The Hull Lady*, to which he contributed, described him as a playwright and author of the blank verse plays *Eunice the Greek* and *Matho the Libyan*, both dealing with classical subjects and one specifically African. The same paper published Ali's 'Hull Coronation Ode', written to mark the coronation of Edward VII, whom he had met, in which he tells the history of Hull and praises Hull's William Wilberforce as a slave emancipator. Ali spent time in Hull doing various dock-related and other jobs, including work as an elocution teacher, and organising concerts and 'at homes'. He founded a Hull Shakespeare Society with Sir Henry Irving as Patron, which, recalling his American lecture tour, presented costumed Shakespeare recitals. It is claimed he performed Othello and the Prince of Morocco in Hull in 1902, following in the footsteps of Aldridge, but these appearances may have been recitals rather than full stage performances (Shakespeare presumably offered him an escape from his usual formulaic roles).

Pursuing his ambition to produce, Ali took a show ('stale musical airs, dancing chorus girls, and ludicrous plot') to the Liège International Exhibition in 1905 in which he played an Oriental Sultan.[42] He was retained in the Extreme Orient section as a guide to celebrities visiting the exhibition. He later joined Melville as a publicity agent dreaming up stunts to sell shows outside London. To establish himself as a touring actor-manager, Ali formed the Vaudeville Company, which appeared at least for one night in Carmarthen in November 1906. The following year, Ali revived *The Jew's Revenge*, hoping to secure a place on the Moss-Stoll Empire circuit. He won a trial contract, one week in Manchester and one in Glasgow (where it is possible he had appeared in *A Daughter of Judah* at the Empire Palace the year before). Favourable reviews in Manchester promised much, but an accident on stage in Glasgow forced him to cancel the engagement and convalesce. After further occasional engagements in Scotland, he formed a variety company with another actor to tour small towns in the Glasgow area but failed to find a patron. His partner quit after three unprofitable performances, and Ali followed suit after one last try in Inverness. He earned his fare back to London by giving recitals in Glasgow. In London, he performed *The Jew's Revenge* again. He found work as an electrician in 1908 building the Franco-British exhibition in Shepherd's Bush, where he subsequently appeared as 'The Great Egyptian Actor-Author' dressed in Egyptian costume to give lectures on Moses in a piece called *Pharaoh's Daughter*. He was replaced with six weeks to go because another actor agreed to accept lower pay.

Ali decided to change tack and became a literary and theatrical agent with an office off Shaftesbury Avenue, ghosting, doctoring, and giving advice on plays. He rewrote or co-wrote the libretto of the musical comedy *The Lily of Bermuda* by Bermuda-born black actor Ernest A. Trimmingham, which Ali's company, now called Vaudeville Enterprises Syndicate, produced. In June 1908, Ali announced the show would be seen in London by the end of the year, but this did not happen. Trimmingham was to play a principal role in the show but was not at that time listed as its author.[43] The following year, on the strength of only verbal guarantees for the future of the production, which boasted a cast of nearly seventy (though now minus Trimmingham), Ali booked the Theatre Royal, Manchester in November as the start of a pre-London tour to Middlesbrough, Sheffield, Liverpool, Bradford, Oldham, and Sunderland. The review in the *Stage* was not promising ('the piece…did not go too well' and the familiar story of a rich American with an eligible daughter was 'slender'). Several actors, however, were picked out for praise, including Charlie White, the black actor playing a waiter.[44] The leading lady left before the transfer to Middlesbrough, where Ali cancelled further bookings and pawned the scenery and costumes to pay off the cast. *The Lily of Bermuda* was a huge financial and artistic flop.

Subsequently Ali devoted more time to journalism and became more active in politics, particularly in the Pan-African movement. He spoke at the 1911 First Universal Races Congress in London, an international gathering bringing together a wide range of people concerned to promote interracial and East-West harmony. The chair of one session was Sir Harry Johnston (a likely target of Downing's satire in *A New Coon in Town*), who spoke on the world position of the 'Negro' along with W. E. B. Du Bois. Duffield says Ali organized the entertainment at the Congress, including a performance of the third act of *Othello*, a role Ali might

GRAND NEW PRODUCTION,
MONDAY, NOV. 8th,
Theatre Royal, Manchester,
" THE LILY OF
BERMUDA, "
A Colonial Comedy, with Music, in Two Acts.
By DUSE MOHAMED and ERNEST TRIMMINGHAM.

FIGURE 3.3   Announcement of the 1909 production of *The Lily of Bermuda* by Dusé Mohamed and Ernest Trimmingham (Courtesy of *Stage*)

have played himself. As a result of the Congress, Ali the following year founded the influential *African Times and Orient Review*, where he gave Marcus Garvey a job and which reviewed plays by Downing and published serial fiction by him.[45] Ali's history of Egypt, *In the Land of the Pharaohs*, published in 1911 and said to be the first history of Egypt by an Egyptian, made an international impact, but much of the book turned out to have been plagiarized. Ali, a cofounder of the African Progress Union, was also said to have been influential in early British Islam; he was linked to the All-India Muslim League and founded the Anglo-Ottoman Society in London and, in 1915, the Indian Moslem Soldiers', Widows' and Orphans' War Fund. He went to the United States in the 1920s, where he worked briefly for Garvey's Universal Negro Improvement Association and helped set up the Universal Islamic Society in Detroit before moving to Nigeria in 1931, where he became an editor and journalist again. He produced a play, *A Daughter of Pharaoh*, in Lagos in 1932 and died there in 1945.

Taking their cue from Duffield, several commentators have speculated that the demeaning and cliché stage roles on offer to diasporic actors such as Ali, combined with his failure to be accepted by white society, influenced his Pan-Africanism and desire for Asian-African unity.[46] Mustafa Abdelwahid sees him as a Muslim pioneer of black resistance in the twentieth century whose ideas are echoed in the work of Garvey and other black nationalist leaders.[47]

Ali's collaborator, Ernest Trimmingham, author of *The Lily of Bermuda*, appeared on the British stage for three decades from the early 1910s, mostly in variety, revue, and light comedy, sometimes performing burlesques of other actors. He was seen in a revival of Joyce Carey's *Sweet Aloes* (1936) and *No Sleep for the Wicked* (Streatham Hill, 1937). From 1912 to 1921, he also appeared in several films and has been described by Stephen Bourne as Britain's 'first black film actor until others of African descent are identified'.[48] In 1928, he appeared for a Sunday performance at the Strand Theatre in *Jordan*, by Mary Kennedy, a new play about interracial relationships in the American South, but his 1922 role in a Ben Travers farce, *The Dippers*, as 'leader of the Coon Band' is more typical of the fare on offer to actors such as he. As the *Stage* announcement of his death put it: 'He was a clever character actor, especially in butler and similar parts'.[49]

The Lily of Bermuda, possibly Trimmingham's first play, deals in stock characters, such as a crass American millionaire with his marriageable offspring, an amorous Frenchman, a foppish Lord, and comic black servants alongside a Suffragist and a Socialist. Its main roles are white but, in the final scene, under the influence of the hallucinatory scent of a mysterious flower, the characters change roles: the ingratiating black servant becomes the object of attention and favours, he is served champagne by his master, and the duchess, who calls him Lord Niger, makes love to him. When the effect of the scent wears off, however, she still wants to marry him, thus snubbing her suitor, the American capitalist. Through fantasy, the poor black man is exalted at the expense of the wealthy whites.

With Leslie Russell, Trimmingham wrote an entertainment called 'A Revue of Their Own' (1915) and originated a musical play *Eldorado* (Daly's, 1930, book by Gerald Robinson and Gus Dale, directed by Oscar Asche). This story of young lovers battling against their fate set in South America and on board a steamship was poorly received by the *Stage* ('not at all satisfactorily dealt with, and the general action needs drastic cutting').[50] James Mason, who for a time in 1933 lived in the same house as Trimmingham, described him as 'cheerful and good natured' and said he was known 'the length and breadth of Charing Cross Road'. 'Unusually tall,' wrote Mason, 'often affecting a swallowtail coat, he was a character'.[51] Trimmingham died in Clapham, south London in 1942, the year after probably his last stage appearance (in an undistinguished West End play, *Room V*).

India

The situation for Indian performance was different from that of the African diaspora. Not only was there a different cultural history and relationship to the 'mother' country but, besides the lascars and nannies (ayahs), there were also students and professionals (teachers, doctors, lawyers) in Britain, although they did not form a unified community and, apart from a concentration in London, were spread out and relatively few in number. The activities of the middle-class Indian community and student body in Britain sought to distance them from the stereotypical view that still located their culture somewhere within the broad and ill-defined mysterious Orient.

In the last decades of the Victorian period and up to World War 1, Orientalism echoed through drama and the other arts, particularly music, and in various branches of social design (the auditoria of late Victorian and Edwardian theatres such as the Hackney Empire display a dazzling array of 'Eastern' reference). In the field of musical comedy and light operetta, which reinforced the stock characteristics found in pantomime, fantasy collations of China and the Middle East and South Asia proved extremely popular. As in pantomime, they often featured actors in 'yellowface', signalling with different degrees of exaggeration physical qualities assumed to belong to 'Oriental' people.[52] Aside from *The Mikado*, which survives in the repertoire, successful shows included *The Geisha* (1896, which ran for 760 performances); *A Chinese Honeymoon* (1901, 1,075 performances); the musical play

The Cingalee (1904, 365 performances, set in what was called Ceylon); and *Chu-Chin-Chow* (1916, 2,238 performances during the war, then a record for the longest stage run). The presumed box office appeal of specifically South Asian titles also appears to have grown, as the breadth of a selection of titles suggests: *The Nautch Girl*; *My Friend from India*; *Indian Prince*; *The Prince of India*; *The Great Mogul*; *The Nabob's Fortune*; *The Saucy Nabob*; *Carylon Sahib*; *Carnac Sahib*; *The Mahatma*; and *The Star of India*.[53]

A constant theme was interracial relationships, in which women (often in a generalized 'Eastern' sense) tended either to be chaste innocents or titillating yet dangerous sirens. They might be part of a harem, an Oriental chorus, or a procession symbolizing the East (as in *Aladdin* at Drury Lane in 1885 or *The Crown of India* at the Coliseum, 1912, which had major cities of the subcontinent personified by women who were virtuous but in need of protection). Alternatively, the women might appear as individuals with particular metaphorical weight: Cleopatra, Scheherazade, the Queen of Sheba, or Salome, for example. In 1913, however, the India Office banned an Earl's Court spectacle, *The Romance of India*, not because of the eroticism of the 'nautch girls' (dancers) but because the piece portrayed human sacrifice in lurid terms, and this was deemed to cause offence to religious feeling.[54]

Indian performers themselves could be found among street, circus, and fairground entertainers and as magicians. As part of a European tour, a South Indian dancing troupe, Les Bayaderes, were brought as a novelty to London's Adelphi Theatre in 1838 after success in Paris. Unlike in France, they were not able to present their own repertoire but had their dances framed by other material, regarded by the London management as commercially attractive. For instance, they appeared in a short burletta, *The Law of Brahma or the Hindoo Widow*, based on *The Widow of Malabar*, in which the widow is rescued from the funeral pyre by British troops. The troupe also performed in *Arajoon, or the Conquest of Mysore*, one of the shows that celebrated the British victory over Tipu Sultan. The management must have felt vindicated – Les Bayaderes or Dancing Priestesses of Pondicherry, as they were billed, gave 55 performances and appeared daily at the Egyptian Hall, Piccadilly. Apparently they started a vogue among actresses at the Adelphi of dying their hair black and eating olives in the belief it would darken their skin.[55]

In 1868, a troupe of strolling players was brought to England from Bombay and appeared as an exhibition at Crystal Palace and elsewhere in London, in Manchester, Liverpool, and Norwich before the tour ended in acrimony and the English promoters were arrested for debt.[56] Novelty was still the driver when, in 1885, the Parsee Victoria Dramatic Company from Bombay appeared at the Gaiety and Opera Comique theatres in London. The company performed four items: *Solomon's Sword*, the story of the capture of a nobleman's wife by a ne'er-do-well in league with the devil and of her release by a youth with an enchanted sword was played in Hindustani with songs of English or American provenance; a sketch of American origin prepared for performance by 'nigger troupes'. Britain sent minstrel troupes to India, in keeping with its 'divide and rule' strategy of making the colonized Asian feel superior to the colonized black, and here the Parsee company was returning the favour. It was announced that this sketch (about black servants being duped to let uninvited guests into the master's ball) would be performed in English, but *The Times* said the 'chief character struggled, the remainder proved unequal to the task and the result was a confusion of languages'; then came scenes from Kalidasa's *Sakuntala* and a Hindustani version of Bulwer-Lytton's popular play *The Lady of Lyons*. According to *The Times*, the latter simply evoked derision instead of sympathy because the audience could not understand it, an attitude that apparently summed up the entire programme and revealed condescension, especially toward the use of English and its pronunciation, that was to persist.[57]

Also toward the end of the nineteenth century, in the face of burgeoning urban bustle and Victorian materialism, a different kind of Orientalism looked East for aestheticism, asceticism, and a spirituality that often embraced mysticism and the occult. The subcontinent, like the rest of the East, was seen as unchanging and therefore a possible source of transcendental balm, in contradiction to the political situation in South Asia and among the diaspora where political radicalism was on the rise. The pioneering actor and director William Poel, who believed in universalism, turned to *Sakuntala* for inspiration and produced an open-air performance in the Conservatory of London's Royal Botanical Gardens in 1899 for the Elizabethan Stage Society, which he had founded to explore continuous and ensemble methods of staging and acting.

Open-air performance was integral to Indian theatrical practice and, in search of further authenticity, Poel enlisted the help of R. C. Dutt, an Indian National Congress leader, on the translation. Giyani Singh Giyani, a law student at Gray's Inn, coached the cast in posture and gesture. He and a Captain Nath lent costumes, there were Indian performers, although not in leading roles, an Indian singer was used, and music was played on Elizabethan instruments by Indian musicians.[58] Poel says that 'Oriental notabilities' were present in the audience at what appears to be the first British production of the play. His inclusion of a stuffed tiger and antelope provoked hilarity, however, and The *Times* reviewer, who found the performance 'very inadequate', decided that the 'imperfect English' of the Indians 'hardly added to the dignity of the production'.[59] Poel prepared a revival of *Sakuntala* in 1912 for a body called the Council of the Oriental Guide. A public production was held in Cambridge indoors (because of bad weather), with the white English actor Clarence Derwent as the king and Indian students playing non-speaking parts. Poel was aided by Mrs. P. K. Ray and Mrs. P. L. Roy, who attended rehearsals and showed the women how to wear saris and the men how to fold turbans.[60]

By this time, the first stirrings of autonomous South Asian theatrical activity were evident, possibly inspired by the visit to India of King George V in 1911.[61] That year, according to Poel, Indian students mounted a series of 'very beautiful' tableaux illustrating the incidents in *Sakuntala* (he gives no details, and none has so far come to light). The following year, Poel directed performances at the Royal Court of *Buddha*, an adaptation by S. C. Bose of Edwin Arnold's narrative poem *The Light of Asia*, presented 'under Indian management' (which was, in fact, Kedar Nath Das Gupta). The production featured six episodes from the life of the spiritual leader, who was played by Clarence Derwent alongside a 'company of Indian actors, mainly composed of students of law and medicine'.[62] Bose, said *The Times*, made 'an interesting and beautiful series of spectacles' from a not very dramatic work.[63] The run was extended from three to seven performances and, as a result of *Buddha*, says Poel, a group of Indian students formed the Hindusthan Dramatic Society and presented *Ayesha* in 1912 at the Whitney Theatre, Aldwych. This play was a dramatization by Nirajan Pal and Harendra Nath Maitra of the romantic nineteenth-century Indian novel *Durgeshnandini* by B. C. Chatterjee, which they named after the story's Bengali heroine.[64] Poel said the production did not reach the level of *Buddha* and was without merit or distinction. *The Times* reported it as a new Indian play and said proceeds were to go to St. Bartholomew's Hospital and Indian charities.[65]

According to Poel, 'perhaps the most valuable object-lesson as regards Indian dramatic art that the English public and English actors have ever received' was seen at the Royal Court in March 1912 for two performances; it was the story of Kalidasa's poem, *Kumarsambhava*, presented as *The Birth of the War-God* in eighteen tableaux vivants. Proceeds went to the Indian Women's Education Association, to train women to be teachers in India, another charitable motivation in keeping with Indian performance tradition. Mrs. Roy arranged the tableaux, costumes were copied from antique Indian prints lent by the librarian of the India Office, and it was acted anonymously by some thirty Indian women and children. *The Times* said the cast showed some faults common to the amateur, the chants were weird to Western ears but 'full of atmosphere', and there was a 'curious exotic fascination' about the entire production. This last comment encapsulates a continuing imperial attitude to the Other despite 300 years of Anglo-Indian encounters and the presence in Britain of well-established though small and disparate South Asian communities.[66]

Indian Art and Dramatic Society

Clearly there was a momentum in South Asian theatre, and driving it was the indefatigable Kedar Nath Das Gupta, an activist against British Rule and the partition of Bengal, who arrived in England from India in 1907 to avoid the possibility of imprisonment.[67] He was born in 1878 in Chittagong, East Bengal in what later became Bangladesh. He moved to Calcutta and became involved in nationalist campaigns, including the promotion of indigenous goods in place of British ones. He was appointed manager of a shop selling home-grown produce set up by a relative of the Bengali writer Rabindranath Tagore. Das Gupta asked Tagore to edit a patriotic Bengali monthly magazine, *Bhandar*, which he wanted to publish, and Tagore (reluctantly) agreed. Subsequently, Das Gupta published some of Tagore's books. Das Gupta's anti-partition activities brought him to the attention of the police, and his brother sent him to England to study law.

In England, Das Gupta, who was a follower of Swami Vivekananda (an interfaith proselytizer and major figure in nineteenth-century Hinduism), wanted to increase understanding between the two cultures and formed the Union of the East and West. It was supported by several leading figures, including H. G. Wells, and organized a number of often prestigious events. These could range, for instance, from a talk on Indian painting by Laurence Binyon, writer and assistant keeper of Oriental Prints at the British Museum, to lectures on the political situation in India, past and present, by speakers such as Surendra Nath Banerjea, founder of the Indian National Association and a leader of the Indian National Congress, and Bhupendra Nath Basu, who had become president of the Indian National Congress. The majority of the Union's activities, however, were theatrical, spurred, according to a Das Gupta family source, by the motto 'a nation is known by its stage'.[68] These activities were presented in association with the Union by the Indian Art and Dramatic Society (a.k.a. the Indian Art, Dramatic and Friendly Society). The aims of the Society were 'to bring before the Western public the Art, Drama and Literature of India, with a view to promoting a closer understanding between India and Great Britain'.[69] The Society staged a remarkable collection of Indian plays, mostly in the afternoons or when theatres were not being used for commercial productions, and involved white British performers (the majority), some of whom were among the most famous names sat the time.

Buddha appears to have been the catalyst for the formation of the Society in May 1912 at 21 Cromwell Road, west London, which was owned by India House, a nationalist body, as a hostel and cultural centre for students from abroad. The Society's first venture came in July 1912 at the Royal Albert Hall when it presented

FIGURE 3.4 Kedar Nath Das Gupta in the Indian Art and Dramatic Society production of *The Maharani of Arakan* (Image by Walter Benington)

an evening dedicated to Tagore. The programme comprised an address by the painter William Rothenstein on Tagore's ideas, a recitation of Tagore poems by the eminent feminist actress Florence Farr, and a short play, *The Maharani of Arakan*, in which Das Gupta appeared, adapted by British playwright George Calderon from a story by Tagore. A review in *The Times* called the play 'attractive' and praised the Indian music under Inayat Ali Khan, a distinguished exponent of Indian classical music and a leading Sufi. The review, however, was critical of a note in the programme concerning politics:

> We cannot tell who was responsible for the statement that 'below the surface' of the comedy lay a political lesson on the relations of England and India. Whether Mr Tagore's story were a political allegory or not, such references [probably penned by Das Gupta] are better omitted from the programmes of artistic entertainments.[70]

Some months later, *The Maharani of Arakan* was revived at the Albert Hall along with an adaptation of *Sakuntala* by Das Gupta, a play that was also presented the following year at the Cosmopolis Theatre, again using Indian performers, though not in the lead roles.[71] In 1913, the Society held a meeting in Cromwell Road presided over by the illustrious actor-manager Sir Herbert Beerbohm Tree, whose daughter, Viola, appeared in Society productions. At this meeting, Tagore, who was that year to become the first Indian – and the first non-European – to win the Nobel Prize for Literature, read an English adaptation of his play *Chitra*.[72] In 1913, the Society also presented at the Cosmopolis Theatre another Sanskrit historical play, the romantic comedy *Ratnavali*, or *the Necklace*, translated by Das Gupta.

During the world war, Das Gupta enrolled in the Indian Field Ambulance Corps in London and organized performances to raise money for wounded Indian troops, who were admitted free to these events: in 1914, there were two such performances at the Grafton Galleries, London of *Savitri, or, Love Conquers Death*, an adaptation from *The Mahabharata* by Das Gupta. William Poel directed, and Das Gupta played the manager in the Prologue and Epilogue, which seemed to have been written for the occasion. Part of the manager's opening speech was described in a review as a 'patriotic outburst celebrating the unique spectacle of the present Union of the East and the West', presumably a reference to the contribution being made by India to the war effort.[73] In 1915, at Chiswick Town Hall, west London four pieces were presented in a *Grand Performance in Aid of the Wounded Indian Troops*: *Caliph for a Day*, a comedy adapted from the *Arabian Nights* by Das Gupta; a revival of *Savitri*; Tagore's poetic duologue *The Gardener*; and *The Maharani of Arakan* again.[74] There was also music from the West and the East, including Indian songs performed by Ali Khan (presumably Inayat). The Society published *Caliph for a Day* accompanied by illustrations and remarks on Indian music by Tagore.

A costume recital was also given in 1915 – the year Tagore was knighted – of his play *Malini*, at which the celebrated actor John Martin Harvey presided and spoke. *Malini* was revived along with *Savitri* in open-air performances in 1916 in the gardens of Sir George Reid and Sir William Lever (later Lord Leverhulme) under the direction of alfresco production expert Patrick Kirwan. Das Gupta played the lover of the princess Malini who converts to Buddhism. Also in 1916, the Union presented a dramatic reading of Shudraka's *The Little Clay Cart*, another Sanskrit classic, with the leading actor-manager Arthur Bourchier presiding. Das Gupta's adaptation of Kalidasa's *Vikramorvasie*, under the title *The Hero and the Nymph*, was performed later that year at the Grafton Galleries, with Sybil Thorndike as the nymph. It was Kalidasa's last play, and Das Gupta said it had never been performed anywhere before.[75]

In May 1917, at the King George's Hall, YMCA, Tottenham Court Road, the Union gave the première of Das Gupta's musical play *Bharata* (India), an educational and philosophical conversation explaining aspects of India to Europeans. It was accompanied by a lantern slide show of Hindu and Buddhist temples. Written in conjunction with Margaret G. Mitchell, who appeared in several of the Union and Society's productions, *Bharata* was intended as the first but independent act of a four-act play that would follow the four stages in the ideal life of the Hindu Aryan. The other three acts do not appear to have been written. Das Gupta played Ram Lal, who offers the explanations to, among others, a teacher played by Mitchell, and to young scholars played by pupils from a school in Stoke Newington, north London. The Union published the play text and Adela Maddison's music to the song with which the play ends, a free adaptation by Das Gupta of a song by Tagore. The children sang the chorus and Inayat Khan the solo. The *Stage* said he also played a 'quaint stringed instrument' and, like Das Gupta, was 'picturesquely attired'.[76] Das Gupta's version of the song became known separately as the 'National Hymn for India'.

Also in 1917, the Union revived *Chitra* at the St. James's Theatre and organized in Lord Leverhulme's Hampstead garden (the Hill) a celebration of Holika, a festival dedicated to a female Hindu demon of that name, at which the prominent Shakespearean actor and director Ben Greet staged Bhavabhuti's love story *Malati and Madhava*, dating from 800 CE. In Glastonbury, Das Gupta directed *The Maharani of Arakan* as part of a three-day miniature festival and, at a second festival the following year, Tagore's *Sacrifice* was performed, with music by Rutland Boughton, the originator of the Glastonbury Festivals. The Society revived *Sacrifice* in London in early 1918; H. K. Ayliff, who became celebrated as a Shakespearean director, played one of the lead roles (the King).

After the war, the Union and the Society continued their activities with even greater intensity: in 1919, they presented at the Comedy Theatre in a programme with *Savitri* (featuring Sybil Thorndike and the noted actor-manager Henry Ainley as the Prologue) the British première of Tagore's *The King and Queen*. The 'National Hymn for India' was sung at the interval. This event was followed, at the Hill, Hampstead and then at the Prince of Wales's Theatre in the West End, by *The Ordeal* (a.k.a. *King Harischandra*) by Das Gupta and K. C. Chunder, directed by the actor-dramatist Miles Malleson. The play is based on a legend taken from the Puranas, an ancient Indian genre of literature, and celebrates faith, love, and endurance. *The Ordeal* offers 'an extreme instance of priestly domination', said *The Times*, 'permeated with spirituality' that was probably impossible for 'an Occidental' to understand: 'Much of it was extremely moving and it was all simply and effectively told. It was well acted, too, in an unpretentious way.'[77]

At the end of 1919 came a major event, a production (two matinee performances) of *Sakuntala* at the Winter Garden, Drury Lane. A twenty-two-strong committee of mainly Indian and a few white British notables was formed to oversee it.[78] Using an English version by Laurence Binyon based on a text prepared by Das Gupta for an English audience and with a prologue specially written for the production, it was directed by Lewis Casson and featured Sybil Thorndike playing Sakuntala.[79] *The Times* declared it was the first 'worthy' production of the Indian 'masterpiece', a 'panegyric to love'. Although a fragment, the version 'has been so well done (and part of the credit is probably due to Mr. K. N. Das Gupta…) that it is complete and single.'[80] Despite the main roles still being performed by white actors, the production had cultural importance as an index of acceptance and was attended by a bevy of British aristocracy as well as the Aga Khan and Maharaja of Baroda. The Union revived the play in 1920 in two open-air performances at Lord Leverhulme's garden. Such connections with the elite, both artistically and socially, were in keeping with the general intention of validating Indian culture as worthy of respect and the assimilationist strategy associated with this project.

In 1920 at the Wigmore Hall, the Union presented two more Tagore plays: *The Autumn Festival*, a short play with music, and the allegorical *The Post Office*, accompanied by a programme of Tagore songs. This production was followed at the same venue four months later (with help from Tagore in rehearsal) by five short Tagore dramatic lyrics, the first time, it was said, they had been performed in English.[81] At the same time, the Union had organized Tagore to lecture at Caxton Hall, accompanied by dramatic presentations, including Tagore songs and Sybil Thorndike reciting Tagore poetry. The year 1920 also saw open-air revivals of *The Hero and the Nymph* and a return to the Prince of Wales's Theatre with a double bill of *Chitra* and *Sacrifice*, which was toured to Oxford, Cambridge, Manchester, and Croydon. In late 1920, Das Gupta accompanied Tagore to the United States and decided to remain for a while. He staged productions there, including *The Post Office*, *Sacrifice*, and *Buddha*, and founded an American branch of the Union of the East and West. By 1921, there were branches in Washington and Boston and New York. Das Gupta became more involved in attempts to bring religions together and, in 1924, founded the World Fellowship of Faiths, of which he was general secretary. From this point, he divided his time between New York, where he became based, and London, serving the cause of global unity.

The London Union of the East and West in the meantime did not cease its activities: in 1921, at Lord Leverhulme's garden again, it presented three Indian plays – Tagore's *The Farewell Curse*, *Kunala* by D. G. Mukherji, and *Savitri* – and at the Prince of Wales's Theatre a play called *Affinities* by Zula Maud Woodhull about mysticism. Also in 1921, at Wigmore Hall, there was a revival of *Malati and*

Madhava along with a première of Tagore's *Trial by Luck* and performances of five plays from the Union's repertoire in Cambridge's Guildhall under the patronage of the university's vice chancellor and the town's mayor. A review of *Trial by Luck* described it as 'simple' and 'delicate', but another said,

> It is a matter of serious doubt whether the performances of Indian plays…are really worth the pains and the money expended on them. Experience of these productions shows increasingly that we do not get…anything of the quality which make them to be acclaimed …literary masterpieces in their original tongue.[82]

Das Gupta returned to Britain in 1924, and that year there were more performances of Tagore in Lord Leverhulme's garden along with *Sakuntala*. At the Devonshire Park Pavilion, Eastbourne, Das Gupta produced a programme of three revivals: *The Farewell* (presumably a version of *The Farewell Curse*), *Savitri*, and *The Maharani of Arakan*, in the latter two of which he appeared. In September 1924 at the Wigmore Hall, the Union staged *Divine Vision*, an adaptation by Das Gupta of G. C. Ghose's Bengali drama *Vilwamangal*, which had enjoyed a long run in Calcutta. The production was described as a 'Hindu morality play' with 'brilliant costumes, and native music and dancing'.[83]

The activities of the Union and the Society fade from the mid-1920s as Das Gupta's energy increasingly focuses on his promotion of world peace and interfaith unity, though *Savitri* was given an open-air revival independently in 1936 in the grounds of Mrs. Gloria Gasque's house. She was a well-known American proponent of vegetarianism who spoke the following year alongside Das Gupta on 'Non-violence is the Key to World Peace' at a London celebration of Gandhi's birthday organized by the World Fellowship of Faiths and chaired by the writer and socialist pacifist Laurence Housman. By 1939, Das Gupta was being described as the general executive of the World Fellowship of Faiths (British Centre) when he arranged a celebration of the great Hindu festival of Dashana at the Dorchester Hotel with a programme of speeches, dancing, music, and film.[84]

Besides staging and writing plays, Das Gupta wrote *Consolation*, published by the Union of the East and West in 1916, comprising four stories from ancient Indian culture, and *Essence of Religions*, a book published in the United States in 1941 that describes the world's living faiths grouped according to their place of origin. It seems he received a doctorate from a New York University before he died in Manhattan in 1942.

Indian players

It did look, briefly, as if a former medical student Niranjan Pal, who had appeared in *Buddha* and co-wrote the adaptation *Ayesha*, might carry on Das Gupta's pioneering work, bringing a South Asian presence to British audiences and asserting cultural pride for Indians in Britain. Son of leading nationalist Bipin Chandra Pal, Niranjan began writing while a student in London, where he was involved in the Indian independence movement. In 1922, he formed the Indian Players to present his play *The Goddess* for 'two special matinees' at the Duke of York's Theatre.[85] The play, which the Indian Players published, deals with the life of a Brahmin priest who propounds rationalism to challenge deceit and pronounces a beggar woman with whom he is in love to be the incarnation of the goddess Kali. Despite being unhappy with the deception, she agrees to appear as Kali to please him, but she then commits suicide to atone for her sacrilege. This act brings much needed food and rain to the village, an ending one reviewer called a 'compromise between faith and religious "reform"'.[86]

Importantly, the production (by American writer and director Guy F. Bragdon) had an all-Indian cast and Indian stage management and used Indian music.[87] Though the *Era*, which thought the principal recommendation of the production was its 'picturesqueness', found the pronunciation of English 'a little precarious' and *The Sunday Times* said the production was acted in the 'quaintest of English', *The Times* praised the 'remarkably good' diction of the cast, and the *Stage* found the production was 'acted admirably'.[88] *The Goddess* (shorn of its prologue and epilogue but with enhanced musical and dance contributions) also played at the Ambassadors'

FIGURE 3.5 Cover of a programme for *The Goddess* (Courtesy of Mukul Dey Archives, India and Victoria and Albert Museum, London)

Theatre (evenings and matinees) and proved sufficiently successful to be transferred under the direction of B. N. Dey to the Aldwych Theatre for a run of sixty-six performances, a remarkable accomplishment. At the end of the run, rehearsals were due to begin for the next production by the Indian Players for an Indian Repertory season, but nothing seems to have come of this.[89]

Pal next wrote a farce with an English setting called *The Magic Crystal*, which was performed in 1924 on tour for two months, beginning in Swansea, and then at the Scala Theatre, London. In the play, a visionary Indian with the gift of a box appears to a bankrupt Englishman Reggie when he has nothing left. As Reggie takes the box, his personality is transported into the body of his butler, and the comedy unfolds but, in the end, it turns out that Reggie has only been dreaming.[90] The opportunity to satirize the English through humour could be taken only, it seems, in the context of the unmistakably unreal. Pal also wrote *Shiraz*, which was due to appear in the West End in 1926, but there is no record of a production. Instead, it became a film, with members of the Indian Players in the cast, including Himansunath Rai, who had come to London to train as a lawyer and had played the lead in *The Goddess*. Pal used his experience in *Buddha* to write the successful film version of Arnold's poem *The Light of Asia* (*Prem Sanyas*), in which Rai, a pioneer of Indian film, acted and directed. They collaborated on this film with the German director Franz Osten, with whom they also made *A Throw of Dice*, *Untouchable Maiden*, and *Shiraz*. *The Goddess* was staged in Calcutta after Pal and Rai had moved back to India to work in films, but the Indian Players by that time were no more.

One link did endure between this period of the 1910s and 1920s and the subsequent years of British South Asian theatre practice, and that was the work of Tagore, India's major literary figure. A supporter of Indian independence who renounced his knighthood after the British massacre at Jalianwalabagh, Amritsar in 1919, Tagore remained a towering influence. His first play to be seen in England (as opposed to a stage adaptation from his writing) was *The Post Office* in a production by the Abbey Theatre that transferred from Dublin to the Court Theatre in 1913. Its reception encapsulated key issues surrounding his place in British culture of the time: Tagore was seen as dreamy, symbolic, and spiritual, a novelty that soon wore off, and there was awkwardness both in the translation and in the fact of non-Indian actors' (in this case, Irish) playing Indians.[91] *The Post Office* was followed by the Union of the East and West productions and a performance in 1916 by Lena Ashwell's company of *The Maharani of Arakan*.

Tagore's reputation, however, was fashioned more by reviews of the published texts of his plays than by their production, the peak, according to Ananda Lal, being *The Post Office*, which appeared in 1914, and the nadir *Red Oleanders* (1925). Lal says he was adulated in Germany but welcomed 'less whole-heartedly' in England where his political significance was misunderstood.[92] He frequently read from his plays while in Europe but, following the demise of the Union of the East and West, his plays were produced in Britain only intermittently from the 1920s to the 1970s: *The King of the Dark Chamber* was seen at the Clifton Boarding School for Girls, Bristol in 1920; in 1928, *Sacrifice* appeared at the Little Theatre, London with an all-Indian cast; *Suttee* in an open-air production in north London in 1936; *Sacrifice* in Shoreham, Sussex, and the Working Men's College, London in 1937; three of his plays were performed at the small Irving Theatre in the 1950s; in 1963, Bristol University Drama Department invited Ram Gopal to dance in and choreograph *The King of the Dark Chamber*; and Tara Arts's choice for its inaugural production in 1977 was Tagore's *Sacrifice*, adapted by its founder Jatinder Verma from Tagore's *Balidaan*, which he had written in support of World War 1 pacifists and translated into English in 1917.

It is likely there is more autonomous South Asian theatrical activity to be uncovered from the late nineteenth and early twentieth centuries. Indian students, who played an important role in the beginnings of British South Asian theatre, were well organized and ran their own cultural events in their hostels, but this phenomenon, along with the amateur work of groups such as the India Office Drama Society, has not been adequately researched yet. For example, little is known about the Indian Students' Union Play-Reading Circle. There may also be more to discover about Cornelia Sorabji, a Christianized Parsi from western India who came to England to study at Oxford in 1889 and was asked to provide the leading English actress Mrs. Patrick Campbell with a play. Sorabji turned to an ancient Sanskrit drama, but Mrs. Campbell, whose role turned out not to be the lead, wanted changes that Sorabji refused to make. Her text was sent to Bernard Shaw, who made what Sorabji took to be a disparaging comment, and she abandoned the play.[93] It is possible that Sorabji was active in one of the many amateur dramatic societies that flourished at the turn of the century or was involved with student cultural activity. Her play *Gold Mohur Time: 'To Remember'* was published in Britain in 1930, but there is no record of its having been performed.

Though English directors such as William Poel may have sought South Asian involvement to encounter a world new to them and to refine production values, when South Asians began to organize themselves theatrically, their desire was to reclaim authenticity, celebrate their own culture, and change perceptions of the host audiences. Against the larger political background of the growing demand for Indian independence, the strategy adopted in the theatre insisted on parity, that the 'real' India had a culture that could be judged in Western terms as being as rich as (and older than) the West's.

The early activists such as Das Gupta and Pal worked within conventional, liberal British-Indian discourse. The challenge they offered British audiences was not so much what they were presenting, which the British seemed to like as exotica, but their aesthetic, the ways in which they performed and the fact that they performed at all. However slight it may seem decades later, to gain a measure of acceptance in the Britain of the early twentieth century and to demonstrate a capacity for self-organization and artistic expertise in a generally unreceptive environment was a notable achievement.

4

BETWEEN THE WARS

Asian theatre

In the period between the two global wars, despite the massive, though at the time under-recorded, influence of the East on Western theatre (for instance, on Artaud, Brecht, Copeau, Craig, Stanislasvky, and Yeats), the Asian contribution to British theatre was generally much less than that of the African American and the Caribbean.[1] Nor was there a drama equivalent of the influential dancers Uday Shankar and Ram Gopal, who changed the traditional British-Indian discourse. Up to the early 1920s, it looked as if the activities of the Indian Art and Dramatic Society and the Indian Players might tell a different story, but the impetus was lost with the departure of their leading figures.

Asia in mainstream culture still tended to be collapsed into the fantasy exotic East that had been highly popular and lucrative in the years leading up to and during World War 1. Although cinema was taking over this niche, Oriental settings (still loosely defined) remained in vogue in the theatre of the 1920s and 1930s, for instance, in 'sheikh' shows such as *Prince Fazil* or the musical *The Desert Song*. Asia also featured occasionally in the repertoire of 'serious' theatre: Shudraka's Sanskrit play *The Toy Cart* (a.k.a. *The Little Clay Cart*) was performed in 1916 and 1930; Lena Ashwell's company appeared in *The Maharani of Arakan* in 1916 alongside Arthur Bourchier's company in J. B. Fagan's *The Fourth of August*, which dramatized German plans to induce the Maharaja of Mulpur to revolt against the British Raj at the outbreak of World War 1; and *Sakuntala*, as well as being broadcast on BBC radio in 1929, was revived by the Norwich Players under Nugent Monck in 1931, accompanied by a series of tableaux drawn from the poetry of Omar Khayyam. The 'Indian' extravaganza *The Golden Toy* (complete with elephants) and *Clive of India* appeared in the West End in 1934, while in the political sphere, the Workers' Theatre Movement in the early 1930s produced *Meerut*, an agitational piece about an Indian railway workers' strike and imprisoned union leaders in which class was more important than nationality or race.

Scarborough, Blackpool, and Battersea's Festival Gardens had their exotic Indian Theatres, which featured novelty acts and various types of variety performance that accorded to the popular imagination. The latter two theatres were run by Amir Bux, Royal Indian magician who came to Britain in 1924, the year of the British Empire Exhibition at Wembley. The Exhibition boasted an Indian Pavilion with a full set of clichés: snake charmers, jugglers, and a Madras Chow Chow, described by the *Stage* as a sort of Indian variety show with novelty 'girl' dancers.[2] Sometimes performers in such shows were of South Asian origin and sometimes from elsewhere, assuming the role as a passport to entertainment acceptance, just as black performers often assumed African identities to further a professional career.[3]

The end of the Indian Art and Dramatic Society and the Indian Players led to the demise of collective South Asian activity. South Asian immigration was already less than that from the Caribbean, the movement for independence was growing stronger in India, and entry restrictions into Britain were placed first on political grounds (in the 1920s) and then (in the 1930s) on financial grounds. In 1922, the Little Theatre, however, staged a week of Indian productions under the title *The Glorious East in the West*, presented by Pandit Shyam Shankar (Uday's father). It comprised Indian magic (familiar in Britain), music, dances (including Uday), a romantic drama by the Pandit called *The Queen of Chittore*, and *The Dreamer Awakened*, a comedy adapted from *The Arabian Nights*, which, according to a report, mirrors the Induction to *The Taming of the Shrew*, with Shankar Senior playing Abu Hussain, the Christopher Sly role.[4] Tagore's *Sacrifice* was seen with an all-Indian cast during an international theatre season at the Little Theatre, London in 1928. A few South Asian individuals, such as the Punjabi Princess Indira of Kapurthala (a.k.a. Maharajkumari Indira Devi) and Devika Rani, often referred to as India's first film star, studied at the Royal Academy of Dramatic Art (RADA) but made no wider impact in the absence of either an outstanding individual profile or a collective South Asian presence. Princess Indira apparently aroused much gossip in India when she spurned her parents' wishes, saved her allowance in secret, and escaped to enroll at RADA. She appeared in films in the 1920s, made her stage debut in 1938 as a Turkish slave in *The Heart Was Not Burned*, a forgotten play about Keats, Byron, and Shelley, and also appeared in a children's revue, *Let's Pretend*. She gave up acting but became a theatrical backer, a St. John's Ambulance driver during the war, and a long-serving BBC news reader.[5] Two plays by S. N. Ghose were published in 1924 under the title *The Colours of a Great City*, and five mystical plays by the poet Harindranath Chattopadhyaya were published in 1929 but, apart from a single performance of *Tukaram*, one of the latter's plays, at the Little Theatre, there appear to have been no productions.[6]

Two artists who were briefly involved in theatre in Britain and did secure productions were the Indian-Irish writer Aubrey Menon (a.k.a. Menen), who is dealt with later in the chapter, and the Indian painter Samuel Fyzee Rahamin, whose play, *Daughter of Ind*, had three performances at the Arts Theatre in 1937. The story of a young Indian 'untouchable' woman whose love for a white English tutor brings down political and religious wrath, it began and ended with votive tableaux and acknowledged none of the European conventional rules. Fyzee Rahamin demanded the audience 'discard their notions of what a play ought to be and exchange development of action for an unvarying situation only gradually revealed'.[7] The cast, it seems, was mixed white and non-white, as it was for Fyzee Rahamin's play *Invented Gods* (Embassy, 1938), which presents a philosophy of mystical acceptance through the life of its lead Indian character, played by ex-RADA student from India Vera Dantra.[8] Also in the cast was Mayura, whose solo performance of the Indian Temple Dance had been a highlight at the Mask Theatre Club the year before.[9]

Chinese-American actress Anna May Wong had already made an impact as an exoticized silent movie star by the time she made her British stage debut in 1929, two months before she was seen in the British film *Piccadilly*, in which she plays a dishwasher whose dancing expertise rescues a failing night club. Her stage debut was as the heroine Hai-Tang in a West End production of *The Circle of Chalk*, adapted from a fourteenth-century Chinese play from the Yuan dynasty about jealousy and treachery in which she played the honourable second wife of a powerful nobleman maligned by the spiteful first wife in a struggle over inheritance. Although still trapped in Orientalism, its attempt at engagement with Chinese culture marked a break from the *Chu-Chin-Chow* type of fantastical parody.

As in her film roles, Wong was being used to authenticate Orientalism while she was using it to find work in a cultural context that denied her expression in other modes. British critics attacked Wong's accent for being American, a reaction perhaps encouraged by the fact that she was well known as a face but not a voice in films, yet the production had a successful run (and she took elocution lessons). She was not able to appear in the 1931 revival and was replaced by a white actress. Wong quickly came to prominence again when she was caught up in a press-fuelled scandal in 1930 because of her kissing white actor John Longden in the film *The Road to Dishonour*; the American censors removed the kiss, but it continued to be shown in Britain.[10] Inter-racial sex, however, was still a sensitive issue in Britain. At the same time, Paul Robeson, who was playing *Othello* in London, became embroiled in a similar row over a black-white stage kiss with Peggy Ashcroft as Desdemona, and Wong offered Robeson her support. Wong performed cabaret and songs at London's Embassy Club and Holborn Empire in 1933 and, later that year in London, the Midlands, Leeds, Scotland, and Dublin sang in a variety revue, *Tuneful Songs and Intriguing Costumes*. As the title implies, she was dressed in lavish Chinese outfits, which she swapped for other national dress as she moved on to the next song amid the other singers, acrobats, novelty dancers, and comedians.

Opposite Wong in *The Circle of Chalk* playing the treacherous wife was Rose Quong, an actress from Melbourne and of English, Australian, and Chinese heritage, who remained with the play for the 1931 revival. (In a 1945 production, white actresses played both her and Wong's roles.) Quong's story is instructive because it shows not only the limited opportunities available to an actress who appeared to be Asian but the legacy of empire in the importance an Australian actress attached to the London stage, even if she saw her roots, or came to see them, as being Chinese.[11] She won an elocution prize in a competition run by the Australian Natives' Association in 1903 and became active in amateur dramatics, helping to found, and then performing in a range of plays presented by, the Mermaid Play Society (a.k.a. Melbourne Repertory Players). In 1924, Quong, who had ambitions to be a Shakespearean actress, won a scholarship to study under Rosina Filippi in London and acquired an 'English' accent. In 1925, she appeared in a regional production by Edith Craig and, in London, in *The Maid's Tragedy*, *The White Devil*, and an *Old English Nativity Play*; in 1926, she appeared in *Martinique* in the West End.

According to Angela Woollacott, Quong went to gatherings of Australian artists in London where she would perform scenes from *Macbeth*, but when it became evident she was not going to succeed as an actress, let alone in Shakespeare, her friends apparently encouraged her to exploit the one trait she had that was distinctive in England. Overcoming an initial ambivalence, she promoted herself as Oriental, performing her own version of Chineseness and thereby showing, as Woollacott says, the plasticity and transportability of ethnic categories. Quong adopted Chinese dress and hair style and made a career reciting and lecturing on Chinese poetry and culture, at private receptions, on tour, and on BBC radio and television. She toured the United States in 1934 and, from the late 1930s, made the United States her home. The price she paid was separation from home, trapped within an essentialist stereotype that prevented her pursuing her desired career in Shakespeare.[12]

The Orientalism of the early 1930s found another outlet in *Lady Precious Stream*, a play by Hsiung Shih-I, adapted from a traditional Chinese story of the Tang dynasty, several hundred years earlier than the setting of *The Circle of Chalk*. Hsiung, a lecturer in Peking (later Beijing), was a translator into English of Chinese literature and into Chinese of Barrie, Galsworthy, Hardy, and Shaw. Hsiung had literary friends in England and was prompted by them to write a play about his homeland. After eleven rejections, he found a management willing to accept the romantic story of a Premier's daughter who elopes with a gardener. Nancy Price, a celebrated actress, author, and founder in 1930 of the People's National Theatre, agreed to produce the play at her 350-seat Little Theatre off the Strand. She had suffered a couple of flops and said if this production failed, it would bankrupt her. *Lady Precious Stream* opened in November 1934, co-directed by Hsiung and Price using a Caucasian cast and with costumes – uncredited – designed by the celebrated Beijing Opera master Mei Lanfang, who was staying with Hsiung. It was probably the first play by a Chinese writer to be seen in London, and it ran over the next two years, being revived in 1935 and 1936. It was critically well received, being compared favourably to *Twelfth Night*, *A Winter's Tale*, Dickens, and Hans Christian Andersen. The Chinese Ambassador spoke at some performances, hailing the production as a link between East and West. The Japanese invasion of China in 1937 aroused much sympathy, and the play was revived at the Kingsway Theatre in December 1939 after the outbreak of war (Hsiung appeared as the Honourable Reader, a role which did not exist in the other productions). *Lady Precious Stream* was revived again in 1943 and 1944 at the Regent's Park Open Air Theatre and once more, at the Arts, in 1950. Overall, the play must have achieved around 1,000 performances. A leader in *The Times* even cited wartime attendance at the 1944 production as an example of bulldog Londoners not cowering underground but getting on with life by enjoying plays.[13]

After the war, attitudes toward East Asia changed in the wake of the 1949 Chinese Revolution and China's involvement in Korea in the early 1950s, but the stereotypes – demurely exotic, inscrutable, sinister – remained robust.

Black theatre

Music was still the chief vehicle for the black presence in British theatre. Though occasional visits to Britain by internationally renowned African-American artists, such as the tenor Roland Hayes, who had studied in London and made his concert debut there in 1920, and the contralto Marian Anderson, who toured Europe in the 1930s, showed the concert world that black performers could be the equal of their white peers, the wider theatrical context remained dominated by revues and light entertainment. Here, the immense and transforming African-American contribution was helped by the growth of the recording industry and the introduction of radio and television. Black performers were also present in fairground and summer entertainment as boxers, magicians, spielers, medicine sellers (such as Ernest Marke or Prof. E. B. Knight, the great Abyssinian herbalist from British Guiana), and racing tipsters (such as Prince Monolulu). Such entertainments often confirmed racial stereotypes but, within the constraints, some performers promoted an alternative identity, particularly through a strategy of extravagance, as certain predecessors had done.

Objections to foreign incursions were voiced but usually swept aside in the interests of good box office; white audiences used to blackface minstrels still found non-white performers a novelty and were prepared to pay for it.[14] Early jazz orchestras, gospel singers, and quartets such as the Four Harmony Kings remained popular. The singer John Payne, who came to Britain in 1919 with the Southern Syncopated Orchestra, stayed on in London, was taken up by the white social elite, and became an important focal point for visiting fellow black artists while continuing a successful career in variety and offering voice training.[15] Payne and Alberta Hunter, who played Queenie in the musical *Show Boat* opposite Paul Robeson, appeared in *Robinson Crusoe* at the Hippodrome, Lewisham in 1934, billed as 'England's first all-coloured pantomime'.[16] Vaudeville stars Turner Layton and Clarence 'Tandy' Johnstone came to London in 1923 to work in nightclubs and made their stage debut as a duo in 1924 at the Queen's Theatre in *Elsie Janis at Home*. By 1935, their popularity on stage and radio had led to sales of 35 million records, including quintessential 1920s songs such as 'Bye Bye Blackbird', 'Happy Feet', and 'You're the Cream of My Coffee'. From the mid-1920s to the late 1930s, Will Garland toured black revues with names such as *Coloured Lights*, *The Black Bottom Revue*, *Brownbirds*, *Swanee River*, *Black Berries*, and *Down South*. American bandleader Lew Hardcastle formed a popular dance group in the 1930s called the Eight Black Streaks, who appeared in variety shows in theatres such as the Holborn Empire and London Palladium.

Grenadian singer/pianist Leslie 'Hutch' Hutchinson was the toast of cabaret, and the Guyanese bandleader Ken 'Snakehips' Johnson, who was front man for the Emperors of Jazz band, took over the band when it folded in 1936, brought in musicians from the Caribbean, and restyled it under different names: Ken Johnson and his Rhythm Swingers, the West Indian Orchestra and the West Indian Band. British and British-based black performers were to be found especially in the nightclubs and revue chorus lines, and one version of the Garland revue *Brownbirds* had an all-British black cast in the early 1930s, including Cockney Charlie Woods, a Black Streaks member.[17] Though there were many black musicians in show bands and orchestras in the West End, trumpeter and band leader Leslie Thompson recalled in his autobiography that big shows with large black casts were not that successful: promoters would hire a top name such as Elisabeth Welch and employ the rest just because of their colour. Only the likes of Welch, says Thompson, survived the stigma resulting from poor quality all-black shows.[18]

The world of musical revue, however limited, was not only a site of black expression but a platform for black women such as Florence Mills, Adelaide Hall, and Elisabeth Welch to gain exposure and leverage. Mills, a versatile comedienne, dancer, and singer who was a key figure in the Harlem Renaissance, came to Britain by way of Charles B. Cochran, the leading English producer of revue. In the face of racist opposition, Cochran presented in London's West End as part of their European tours two successful African-American revues, *Dover Street to Dixie* (1923) and *Blackbirds* (1926), both with Mills at their centre. She was featured in magazines such as *Vogue* and *Vanity Fair* and, with the second show, which ran for nearly a year and was seen by the Prince of Wales several times, initiated a brief, negrophiliac 'Blackbird' mania such as had greeted *In Dahomey* nearly two decades before. Mills was vocal on race and endorsed the National Association for the Advancement of Coloured People in America. Her signature song, 'I'm a Little Blackbird Looking for a Bluebird', was taken as a challenge to racial discrimination. She was touring in Britain in 1927 when doctors advised the exhausted performer to return for treatment to the United States, where she died of infection after an operation aged 31. The *Blackbirds* revue format was revived in 1934, 1935, and 1936 with other US performers, such as Valaida Snow, Jules Bledsoe (the original Joe in *Show Boat*), and the tap dancing Nicholas Brothers; the 1936 show had Nigerian composer and musician Fela Sowande on piano.

Elisabeth Welch and Adelaide Hall came to Britain as stars in the wake of Mills's success, and both became British residents. Welch, whose mother's family came from Scotland, made her West End debut in 1933 in the revue *Dark Doings* while waiting for rehearsals to begin for the show that had brought her to England, another Cochran transfer, Cole Porter's *Nymph Errant*. In *Dark Doings*, she introduced what would become her theme song, 'Stormy Weather', and began an entertainment career that lasted into the 1990s and spanned records, radio, TV, and film as well as the stage. Jazz singer Adelaide Hall moved from New York to London when she made her stage debut there in 1938 at Drury Lane in a musical version of Edgar Wallace's jingoistic *The Sun Never Sets*. She enjoyed a similar durability to Welch in her adopted country. She entertained civilians and troops throughout the war and remained very popular on stage, radio, TV, film, and disc, making more than seventy records for Decca.

Cochran brought many of the top African-American entertainers to Britain. He produced the musical play *Porgy* in London, forerunner of the better-known *Porgy and Bess*. At Fred Astaire's instigation, Jessie Matthews persuaded Cochran to bring the African-American choreographer Robert 'Buddy' Bradley to the West End in 1930 to stage the dances for the Matthews show, *Ever Green*. He worked with Matthews again the following year in *Hold My Hand* and on a string of her films and the postwar revue *Sauce Tartare*. He appeared in *Cochran's 1931 Revue* and choreographed several other West End shows, including Jerome Kern's *The Cat and the Fiddle*, Cole Porter's *Anything Goes*, *Blackbirds of 1936*, and the British musical entertainment, *It's Time to Dance*, in which he also performed. Dubbed Britain's Busby Berkeley, Bradley collaborated with and influenced the ballet choreographers George Balanchine and Frederick Ashton, and opened his own dance school in London, which continued until the late 1960s, when he returned to the United States.

The urban edge of African-American light entertainment was counter-balanced by a more 'folksy' image symbolized in the late 1920s by London productions of *Show Boat* and *Porgy*. Both productions, originated by white artists, demonstrated the growing African-American influence on mainstream white culture, although it was still common to see blackface productions of *Uncle Tom's Cabin* with their 'Pickaninny' choruses, and, in non-lyric theatre, people of colour were still mostly played by blacked-up whites. For example, the 1926 British première of Eugene O'Neill's *All God's Chillun Got Wings*, a play that deals with the coruscating effects of racism in a mixed marriage, had an all-white cast, demonstrating the lack of indigenous black actors and the means by which to develop them. The Gate revived the play in 1928 with an all-white cast again but, in 1929, it included some black actors, notably, as the main character Jim Harris, the African-American Frank H. Wilson, who had just appeared in the title role in *Porgy*. Also in the O'Neill cast were the African-Americans Anyce Frances as Jim's sister and Emma Williams as his mother. Henry Brown (the future band leader Ray Ellington, who was London-born) played Jim as a child. Williams had already been seen in London in minor roles, in *On With the Dance* (1925), *Still Dancing* (1925), and *And So To Bed* (1926, and its later 1931 revival). She had also appeared in Shaw's *Back to Methuselah Part III* (1928) as the Minister of Health, known in the script only as The Negress, a sexual fantasy of a future president of the British Isles.

Paul Robeson

Such appearances did not signal the stirrings of autonomous diasporic cultural activity, as conditions for that were not yet present. Nor did the achievements of stars such as Paul Robeson, although his political and cultural struggles came to epitomize the challenge of the era, moving as he did from the dominant performance terrain, which he conquered, to the alternative landscape to express more fully his developing political awareness. Robeson spent much of the 1930s in Britain, though he was not part of the British empire's diaspora, a fact that sometimes led to resentment in the job market when British-based Caribbean and African actors were overlooked in favour of him or told they had to emulate him. However, his commanding role as a hugely successful non-white actor, his stature as catalyst and inspiration, his interest in his African heritage, and his involvement in British projects that validated diasporic values and aspirations have secured him a significant place in the history of British diasporic theatre.

His British debut came in 1922 as the male lead – an itinerant minstrel – in *Voodoo*, a melodrama by white socialite Mary Hoyt Wiborg set in an antebellum southern plantation. The play chimed with the vogue for 'primitive' exotica, this time by including an African scene in which the minstrel returns to his roots in a dream singing 'Go Down Moses' and is transformed into a voodoo chief who brings rain to end the drought that was threatening the plantation crop. A tour was planned to include Blackpool, Edinburgh, Glasgow, Liverpool, and finally London. However, during the pre-London run, Mrs. Patrick Campbell, who played the lead and had received neither good reviews nor any pay, quit, and the production folded. Robeson wrote to his wife, Eslande, that the prospects for black performers in Britain were not promising and that the theatre seemed in as bad a state as in New York, if not worse. 'Vaudeville pays here better than the legitimate,' he wrote, and the idea of 'Negroes making money here is bosh'.[19]

Nevertheless, Robeson returned in 1925 as Brutus Jones in O'Neill's *The Emperor Jones,* this time in the West End, the first occasion a black actor had played a central role in a serious drama on the British stage in sixty years.[20] To add to this novelty, the play itself was innovatory, with its stream-of-consciousness regression through flashback. Despite the play and production being heavily criticized, Robeson was praised. There seemed to be little awareness in Britain, however, of the racial issues the play raised – and these were controversial, particularly among African-American critics who were divided over both O'Neill's psychological stereotyping in his portrayal of a Pullman porter who becomes a dictator and Robeson's involvement. Dockworkers and other non-professional performers were recruited to play non-speaking roles – convicts, spectators, inhabitants of the fictional Caribbean island – in a move that would be repeated and extended in the immediate future as a way of increasing the pool of diasporic actors.[21]

Robeson was already a star when he made his British breakthrough in 1929 as Joe in *Show Boat* singing 'Ol' Man River' to acclaim in the London production. Black experience frames the show and provides the dominant motifs, but Joe is still the 'lazy nigger' of white cliché. Black critics were again divided, as they had been over Robeson and O'Neill, in ways that echo through the years; many found *Show Boat* offensive, and there was criticism of Robeson for aiding its success, whereas others believed progress was necessarily compromised and individual accomplishment was a crucial element in any prospective advance. Robeson understood the critics but answered that if he waited only for parts in which he believed, he would not work, and there would be even fewer black performers in employment.[22] It was an acute dilemma Robeson shared with past and future generations of non-white performers.

He followed *Show Boat* with a milestone British production, as Othello in 1930, only to be greeted in certain quarters with a furore over black-white stage kissing reminiscent of the treatment meted out to Ira Aldridge by some of London's journalists nearly a century before. Amid innuendo of her own affair with Robeson, Peggy Ashcroft, who was playing Desdemona, had to answer media questions about whether she minded the kiss. Newspapers also reported that Robeson was being paid the highest rate for a play (though less than the amount paid to musical entertainers), but this did not prevent his being refused service at the Savoy Grill because of his skin colour, puncturing the notion that London was free from such prejudice. A shocked friend of Robeson's gave the story to the papers, and subsequently a protest meeting was called by Africans and West Indians living in London, which was attended by a Labour MP, who raised the matter with the Prime Minister.

The production of *Othello* was made possible because the American Maurice Browne, who had recently accumulated great wealth from producing *Journey's End*, had persuaded Robeson over a period of eighteen months to overcome his anxieties regarding his ability to play the part. Records suggested few black actors, perhaps only two, had been allowed to play the Moor in Britain since Aldridge in the 1860s, and none was known to have done so in the current century. Browne promised Robeson an excellent Iago and director, but neither promise materialized. Though without experience, he cast himself as Iago and offered the directorial post to his wife, Ellen Van Volkenburg, who also lacked experience and had never directed Shakespeare. By way of preparation, Robeson studied phonetics, Elizabethan speech, English pronunciation, and the history of the role on stage. He took voice and diction classes with Amanda Ira Aldridge, whom he had met in London in the 1920s and who had given Robeson the earrings her father had worn for the part. Unfortunately, the short rehearsal period was fraught. Robeson even had to resist Browne's insistence that he arrive in Cyprus singing. At one point, Robeson asked in vain for the director to be replaced; she was issuing orders through a megaphone from the back of the stalls and treating Ashcroft very badly. He was helped by friends and other, older, cast members and, despite a wobbly start, received twenty curtain calls on the first night at the Savoy Theatre. Robeson judged the end result clumsy and his own performance not that good.[23]

Journalist Hannen Swaffer said one London editor walked out 'because there were negroes around him in the stalls'.[24] The doyen of English critics James Agate called the production 'nigger Shakespeare' and thought Desdemona's decision to 'choose a darkie' showed she had a 'fragile intellect'.[25] Some critical comment centred on whether Othello should be Arab or Negro, a debate Robeson entered equivocally, though later was to say that by Moor Shakespeare meant Negro.[26] Several critics praised Robeson as outstanding, others damned him as pedestrian, and a few complained he was too civilized, as if the presence at last of a black actor in the role required him to fulfil their preconceptions of racial behaviour. Robeson did feel awkward, however, not only because of his awareness of his own limitations as an actor but because of the press harassment about his kissing a white actress.

In playing Othello, Robeson nonetheless had broken a barrier. Unsurprisingly, the role remained a symbol of his own life, a connection underscored by the fact that he played it in three different productions stretching across almost three decades and that in his regular concert repertoire he included Othello's last speech before he stabs himself: 'I have done the state some service and they know't./ No more of that. I pray you, in your letters,/ When you shall these unlucky deeds relate,/ Speak of me as I am. Nothing extenuate,/ Nor set down aught in malice'.

His *Othello* in the United States in 1943 offered a more racially accented reading, not of uncontrollable jealousy and personal tragedy but 'the problem of my people. It is a tragedy of racial conflict, a tragedy of honour, rather than jealousy'.[27] The production broke New York records and was a landmark in African-American culture. Robeson contemplated Macbeth and Hamlet ('if I thought anyone would accept a black Hamlet'), but his postwar struggle with the American administration made any such experiment even less likely.[28] It was to be Othello instead, for the final time, at Stratford upon Avon in 1959, triumphing in Shakespeare's birthplace as a fitting accolade at the end of his career; it was his last stage appearance. He had been asked to play Gower in *Pericles* at Stratford the year before, but a number of reasons, including his battle with the US authorities to regain his passport and his poor health, made this impossible. He was able to play Othello in Britain because he had won his passport battle (without capitulation), and his success at Stratford seemed a vindication of his stand. Appropriately, Sam Wanamaker, a fellow victim of US anti-Communist persecution, played Iago. Directed by Tony Richardson with Mary Ure as Desdemona, this third interpretation of the role by Robeson reprised his romantic reading of the noble Moor as an outsider destroyed by a hostile host culture. Richardson's production, however, had a contemporary tone at odds with this reading, and Robeson lacked the energy and technique he once possessed. The critics on the whole sided with Robeson, and the public unambiguously did; the entire seven-month run was immediately sold out.

Robeson's fondness for Britain and his work opportunities made him a regular visitor in the 1930s, during which time he developed a Marxist view of history and politics, placing his own stand for the rights of black people and his deep interest in black and African culture into a global and class context. In Britain, he became friends with many people of the left and, in particular, with leaders of the anti-colonial struggle such as Nnamdi Azikiwe, Jomo Kenyatta, Kwame Nkrumah, and Pandit Nehru. Robeson met diasporic communities in London, Liverpool, Cardiff, and elsewhere and became a leader for them. At the same time, he played a critical role as an educator of the white people, not just through his own artistic achievements but through his discussions on racism and a black perspective on life.

His film career took off in Britain, where the diasporic population was able to find a certain amount of work as extras, especially from the end of the 1920s onward when sound was introduced. Extras work provided a meeting place for the black population as well as money, and often politics were discussed.[29] From 1935 to 1940, Robeson made six feature films that turned him into one of the British screen's most popular stars. Yet his film career troubled him because of the racial stereotyping involved and his lack of control over the finished product. His experience in film made him realise the limitations of the individual in challenging the dominant cultural system and the impossibility of overcoming it from within. The theatre, especially in the non-commercial, independent sector, offered him more direct leverage if less popular influence, but the problem remained of finding suitable material while also earning a living. If he were to find a play that matched his ideological persuasion, he knew it had little chance of finding a mainstream outlet.

In 1931, he appeared in the West End as the stoker Yank in O'Neill's *The Hairy Ape*, a part not written specifically as a black character. Ill-health cut the run short (it lasted only five performances) and, after that, Robeson began to turn his back on the West End and devote his energy to the non-commercial theatre. He appeared twice at the Embassy Theatre in north London, run by Ronald Adam and André van Gyseghem. It was one of the country's 'little' theatres, which presented a fortnightly repertoire that dealt with pressing social issues using club membership to circumvent censorship. Despite (and because of) Robeson's star status, he agreed in 1933 to revive his portrayal of Jim Harris in *All God's Chillun Got Wings*, a role he had created in New York, for the standard rate of the theatre. Both mother and sister were played by white actresses. The production, directed by van Gyseghem, transferred to the West End, where a short run at the Piccadilly was extended to three weeks, all sold out; Robeson remained on the same Embassy rate, and seat prices were kept below the West End norm.

Stevedore by Paul Peters and George Sklar, the second production at the Embassy (in May 1935) and also directed by van Gyseghem, was a play Robeson had read about and said he wanted to perform. Adam, according to a friend of Robeson's, accepted because it formed part of a plan Robeson had to establish a black theatre, along the same lines as the Jewish Habimah theatre and possibly like one being formed in Harlem.[30] The play tells of black and white dock workers uniting to defend a black worker, Lonnie Thompson, who had complained about being cheated by his boss and was then wrongly accused of raping a white woman. Lonnie's call to act is challenged by a fellow black worker:

> Lonnie says stand up and fight. How you gwine fight? What you gwine fight with? White man own dis country. White man rule it. You can't fight against him.

To which Lonnie replies:

> We can't wait for de judgement day. We can't wait till we dead and gone. We got to fight fo' de right to live. Now – now – right now.[31]

The workers rally but face a braying white mob, and Lonnie is shot dead. Just before Lonnie is killed, his rallying cry is:

> Dar black folks all over de country looking at us right now: dey counting on us, crying to us: 'Stand yo' ground. You fighting fo' us. You fighting fo' all of us.[32]

Another black worker takes his place to carry on the struggle: the end is only the beginning. *Stevedore* carries a clear, if optimistic and idealized, political message of unity and resistance, which appealed to Robeson.

From the point of view of British diasporic theatre, although *Stevedore* was written by white Americans, its significance lies in the fact that it had a majority of black characters (three times as many as the white) who were played by black actors rather than white actors blacking up, as was still the custom, and that the black characters were seen as agents of their own lives, not just victims. Unlike O'Neill's plays, *Stevedore* connected its black characters in both class and racial terms to a broader collective experience.

The production was also important because it became a focal point for cultural expression among the diasporic population. Help in casting the play came from a Miss Maukaus, an African anti-imperialist whose house was a hub for Africans in London, and from the Jamaican Pan-Africanist Amy Ashwood Garvey, the first wife of – now separated from – Marcus Garvey, who ran the Florence Mills Social Club with Trinidadian actor and musician Sam Manning. George Padmore, the Trinidadian revolutionary, introduced his friend Robert Adams and recruited seamen and African and Caribbean students. Robeson's African-American entertainment friends also helped out: the singer John Payne was the music director, and his choir sang in the production: it seems likely he helped recruit, too, given the number of variety artists involved. Lawrence Brown, Robeson's pianist and collaborator, acted one of the roles. The lack of a readily available pool of diasporic actors to call on was due partly to the relatively small number of the diasporic population resident in Britain and partly to the debasing roles usually on offer, which did nothing to encourage anyone who might be interested in acting. Productions such as *Stevedore* helped change this situation and began to create a group of actors who found work as extras in film and looked to the stage for less-well-remunerated but more productive roles.

Robeson intended to tour *Stevedore* in repertoire with Peter Garland's *Basalik*, in which he had appeared the previous month at the small Arts Theatre. However, this wooden depiction of an African chief resisting British interference did not last beyond its three-performance trial, and the idea of a tour was dropped.[33] Finding the right material, politically and artistically, was difficult and made more urgent when film roles such as Bosambo in *Sanders of the River* turned out to be pro-imperialism. Plays such as *Stevedore* were unlike any British plays being written at the time, both in terms of political content and muscularity of language, but they came from the militant American theatre of dynamic social realism, which suited Robeson, whereas the emerging diasporic community in Britain sought plays more closely related to its own agenda. When offered the part of the Haitian revolutionary Toussaint Louverture, leader of the first black Republic, in C. L. R. James's play of the same name, Robeson found that his needs and those of the British diasporic community coincided.[34] The result was a production that has been celebrated as a milestone in both Caribbean and British theatre, not only because it marked the first time black professional actors had performed a play by a black playwright on a British stage but because of its historical significance in recovering 'the collective memory of the historic experience uniting people of the African diaspora: the experience of slavery and the resistance to it'.[35]

James, activist, essayist, historian, had come to Britain in 1932 and was cricket columnist for the *Manchester Guardian* from 1933. He was part of a Caribbean diaspora that he said formed a distinct group among other colonial subjects in London who were described by the Africans they knew as the 'Black Englishmen' or as the 'black white men'.[36] He stayed in the United States from 1938 until he was expelled and returned to Britain in 1953. After this, he travelled between Trinidad and Britain until he settled in Britain in the late 1960s. He died in Brixton, south London in 1989, acknowledged as one of the leading black revolutionaries of his day. In writing about the origin of *Toussaint Louverture*, he said a 'play was required' and, to write it, he drew on material he was collecting for a book called *The Black Jacobins* and the more general *A History of Negro Revolt*, both of which appeared in 1938.[37] James says he conceived the idea of the play in 1932, the year he left Trinidad for Britain, and finished the script by the autumn of 1934, a period during which both he and Robeson became more radical in a process that deepened during the next few years.[38] Though theatre in Trinidad never had particularly strong or popular roots, the young James seems to have taken an interest in what little there was and involved himself in amateur dramatics. He also studied Shakespeare and the Greeks and was a cultural activist in 1920s. In writing *Toussaint Louverture: The story of the only successful slave revolt in history*, he was spurred by a dual desire. One was to counter imperial versions of history, as could be found, for instance, in the programme of British events commemorating the centenary of the 1833 Emancipation Act. The other was to validate black achievement, an example followed by other playwrights in the reclamation of the past.[39] James's play is both an historical re-imagining and a call to arms in the anti-colonial struggle as well as an exploration of the difficulties that this struggle throws up.

Toussaint Louverture is an ambitious and exhilarating epic work in three acts running from 1791 to 1804, in which Toussaint establishes a free society in the name of the French Republic. On behalf of the white planters, Napoleon sends a force to Haiti and tricks Toussaint, who dies in prison. In the face of attempts to reestablish slavery, a permanent Republic is created under the leadership of another black leader, Dessalines. The play ranges in location from the forests of Haiti to the French Convention and in music from Mozart's *Don Giovanni* and African drumming to spirituals and the revolutionary songs of France. (There was even a song added for Robeson.) The play's direct engagement with the birth of the modern European world at the time of the French Revolution challenges the history of the Enlightenment by focusing on the centrality of slavery to it. Yet the play is also conceived within an Enlightenment frame: Toussaint is a tragic hero in classical mould, though his 'fatal flaw' is not psychological but political.

He declares: 'White men see Negroes as slaves. If the Negro is to be free, he must free himself. We have courage, we have endurance, we have numbers…'[40] However, he believes in the values of the Enlightenment and trusts revolutionary France, which lets him down. When Dessalines argues for total independence, Toussaint replies:

Freedom – yes – but freedom is not everything. Dessalines, look at the state of the people. We who live here shall never see Africa again – some of us born here have never seen it. Language we have none – French is now our language. We have no education – the little that some of us know we have learnt from France. Those few of us who are Christians follow the French religion. We must stay with France as long as she does not seek to restore slavery.[41]

As Christian Hogsbjerg points out in an introduction to the play, it is only after the betrayal of Toussaint, in his last lines – 'Oh, Dessalines! Dessalines! You were right after all!' – that James shows the great leader 'acknowledging his tragic failing not to have placed more trust in the black masses'.[42]

When Robeson was handed James's play, the actor had already read several scripts on the Haitian revolution as part of a discussion with the Soviet film-maker Sergei Eisenstein about a film project on the subject, but it is unclear whether or to what extent James knew about this. A mutual friend of James's and Robeson's had given the play to the Stage Society, a leading non-commercial play-producing company, though now past its heyday. James recalled that the Society agreed to present the play if he could persuade Robeson to play the lead, and it took some time for him to track Robeson down. When he did, Robeson accepted on the spot. *Toussaint Louverture* received two performances on 15 and 16 March, 1936, at the Westminster Theatre, then boasting a modern profile through its association with the experimental Group Theatre. The play's director was Peter Godfrey (white) who, with his wife, Molly Veness, had founded and run the pioneering Gate Theatre, where he had directed the first British production of *All God's Chillun Got Wings* in 1926 and his own burlesque version of *Uncle Tom's Cabin* in 1933 (both with white actors). Production of James's play was an important event for the diasporic community, and the audience is likely to have included major anti-colonial figures such as Jomo Kenyatta, George Padmore, and Eric Williams.

Among the diasporic members of the cast were a number who had appeared in *Stevedore*: Robert Adams, John Ahuma, Lawrence Brown, Rufus E. Fennell, Charles Johnson, and Orlando Martins. Fennell and Johnson had been in *Basalik*, as had Frank Kennedy. Casting a large number of black parts was becoming easier, even if the skills levels remained drastically inconsistent.[43] James later wrote of Godfrey's absences and having to rehearse the cast himself. He came under pressure to make cuts, not least from Robeson, but remembers a good collaboration with him. James later freely admitted that he lacked 'the instinct of the playwright' – 'I am not a dramatist by nature or inclination' – and several critics agreed.[44] The *Times* critic, who found the play 'informative rather than suggestive', complained of its 'woodenness'. The *Sunday Times* described the play as a 'somewhat tedious recital of the historical facts', and the *Observer* wished the play had been less a prose-record of Toussaint's tremendous struggle and more poetic, but said it was 'continuously interesting'. The critic added that 'the coloured actors contributed far more of value than the white.' Another critic wrote that *Toussaint Louverture* exposed audiences to a great black hero who 'emerges as a man of greater capacity and honour than the white men who contrived his downfall'. Or, as the *New Leader* noted,

The whole play cogently puts the problem of empire with its exploitation and slavery of the coloured people. The 'civilising' missions of the Capitalist Governments, their promises solemnly made and lightly scrapped, their trickery, makes a pretty picture for an audience whose rulers have the largest empire in the world under their domination. The production with its minimum of scenery, is excellently done by Peter Godfrey, and the large cast, many of them Negroes, succeeds in convincing the audience that an Empire is nothing of which any white civilisation can be proud.[45]

Robeson, as was often the case, fared better than the play, which had no further immediate life, despite its generally warm reception. The *New York Times* reported: 'although unevenly written and produced, [the drama] nevertheless held an appreciative audience's attention throughout, receiving an ovation at the final curtain'.[46]

The production came against the backdrop of the Italian invasion of Ethiopia in October 1935, an event that became a rallying cause for the Pan-Africanists in Britain and possibly led to tension between James and Robeson over the role and direction of the Soviet Union under Stalin. James, by now a Trotskyist, was openly critical of Soviet lack of support and of its selling oil to fascist Italy, news of which caused a major break with Stalinism for many black activists. Robeson, whatever his private thoughts, was steadfastly pro-Soviet in public. It is not clear what or how many attempts were made to transfer the production, remount the play, or have it published but, although James does not record any disagreement with Robeson over Ethiopia, this political difference may have contributed to the play's demise.[47]

Padmore recommended the play's publication and performance in the United States but without success, and the Eisenstein project collapsed, as did another involving the team responsible for the 1936 *Show Boat* film featuring Robeson, who were pursuing a similar idea using the James script. The original playtext itself appeared to be lost, and most subsequent critical comment focused on James's book, *The Black Jacobins*, especially as James did not continue his playwriting. In the 1960s, with help from fellow Trinidadian Dexter Lyndersay, James reworked the play under the new title of *The Black Jacobins*. It had its première under Lyndersay's direction at the University of Ibadan in 1967 and was published in 1976. Fifty years after the first production, this new version was chosen by Yvonne Brewster to launch the London-based black company Talawa.

In 2005, however, Christian Hogsbjerg, a doctoral student, discovered the original text during his research on James.[48] In his introduction to this text, he says the later play, *The Black Jacobins*, follows the same chronological structure as *Toussaint Louverture* and contains many scenes built around incidents depicted in the earlier play. There is the same humour, the lively music and drumming ebbing and flowing into the action on stage, and there are still moments of rare dramatic power. Yet, Hogsbjerg believes, 'the richness of character that defines *Toussaint Louverture* is absent from the later play'.[49] Hogsberg says James made three major modifications. While still a Greek chorus, the ordinary slaves are given greater emphasis, and James seems more conscious of the role and experience of women during the Revolution. The most striking difference, however, lies in the role of the individual in history. The later play ends not with Dessalines the heroic leader of the Haitian people but with Dessalines the corrupt despot who betrayed Toussaint to the French. By the time of the rewriting, James had felt both the thrill and the frustration of colonial liberation. 'If *Toussaint Louverture* was about the vindication of national liberation struggles written in the age of colonialism', says Hogsbjerg, 'in *The Black Jacobins*, James and Lyndersay were trying to explore what lessons the Haitian Revolution might hold for national liberation struggles in the age of decolonisation'.[50]

After *Toussaint Louverture*, the only play in which Robeson appeared that was written by a writer of African heritage, he returned to the American left-wing repertoire for his next British stage appearance. This came in 1938 when, at the height of his British fame, he rejected lucrative offers to appear in the West End, preferring instead to perform at the Communist-affiliated, amateur Unity Theatre. He appeared in Ben Bengal's *Plant in the Sun*, a play about a sit-down strike in a New York sweet factory called to defend a colleague who has been sacked for 'talking union'.[51] (Robeson played a 'white' part in demonstration of Unity's rejection of surface naturalism.) Robeson sang at the official opening of Unity's own theatre and was a tutor at Unity's theatre school and a member of its general council. For Robeson, Unity offered a political context, which had been lacking with the James play. Robeson's career in the United States, where he returned when war broke out, meant he did not return to Unity as an actor, although the links remained firm until his death.

Available outlets

Robeson's presence in a number of productions that mixed professionals and amateurs or part-timer actors raised the profile of diasporic theatre and helped develop a growing body of diasporic actors. This expansion was supported by social and cultural organizations, in particular student centres, which were a good recruiting ground for actors, and remained so through to the 1950s. Such centres acted as a hub for a range of activities, a process in which the racism experienced in Britain played its part because university facilities were often barred to non-white students. The cultural activities, which featured more music than drama, ranged from concerts, dances, and plays to debates, lectures, and welcome gatherings for visiting dignitaries. Important among the various institutions were the Indian Students Hostel (1920), the West African Students' Union (1925), which had a magazine and branches in the colonies and, later, the West Indian Students' Union (1946).[52]

These institutions formed part of the embryonic support network that was created by diasporic people residing in Britain, such as the Negro Welfare Association and the League of Coloured Peoples (LCP). They were reinforced by informal but crucial centres that ranged from the homes of key individuals, such as John Payne, to venues such as the Florence Mills Social Club, a jazz club and restaurant that became a hub for black artists and activists and also presented musicals and revues at other venues.[53] The LCP, founded in 1931 as an integrationist, gradualist Pan-African body, open to all races but overwhelmingly with a black membership and under black leadership, had twelve centres in Britain at its height. It published a journal, *The Keys*, which backed campaigns; reported social activities, including dances, concerts, garden parties, and cricket matches; and addressed issues of representation of black people in cultural forms (it carried poems, book reviews, and occasional theatre and film items, for example on *Toussaint Louverture, Blackbirds of 1936*, and Robeson's activities). In 1933, the LCP took the brave and unusual step of producing a play. Even more uncommon, the play was written by a woman.

At What a Price, a formally conventional comedy written by Jamaican Una Marson when she was twenty-six, deals with women's experience in a male culture; spirited but naive young Ruth, daughter to a weak mother and patriarchal father, leaves her middle-class, countryside home to work as a stenographer in Kingston, falls for the charms of her white boss, and returns to her parents and a former admirer pregnant, deceived, rueful. Though her attempt at independence fails, the play applauds her feistiness and rejection of women's domestic marital subjugation. Mounting *At What a Price* was a huge undertaking, which Marson led. It is a four-act play, which calls for some twenty actors to play Jamaicans. Marson took the main role and was directed by Clifford Norman, who had to draw on people with little or no acting experience from different cultural backgrounds. Their original home was listed next to their name in the programme: Bermuda, British Guiana, England, Gold Coast, India, Italy, Jamaica, St. Lucia, and West Africa, an indication of the spread of the diaspora and LCP membership. The two white roles were taken by black actors. Of the cast, several went on to illustrious careers, including the future British Communist and noted Ghanaian anti-colonial fighter Desmond Buckle; Eric Campbell, who became a member of the Jamaican House of Representatives for the People's National Party; Fred Degazon, Dominica's first president after independence; Keith Gordon, a barrister who became a senior judge in the Caribbean and was knighted; founding LCP executive member and LCP librarian barrister Stella Thomas, a Nigerian of Sierra Leonean descent, Pan-African activist, the first African woman to qualify as a barrister, and the first woman to be appointed a magistrate in Nigeria (in 1943); and her brother, Stephen Thomas, LCP secretary who became a judge in Nigeria. Also in the cast were Amy Barbour-Jones, daughter of the colonial official and author John Alexander Barbour-Jones, and Edith, his wife, who were active in British black organizations; LCP foundation member Dennis Degazon, Fred's brother, who became a leading medical officer in the Caribbean; S. P. Khambatta, who became a QC in 1946; Sylvia Lowe, who became a prominent Christian activist in Jamaica, where she enjoyed a distinguished medical career; LCP founder Harold Moody's daughters Joan and Christine and son Harold; and LCP executive member Viola Thompson.

The production had one performance on 23 November, 1933, at the central London YWCA and was deemed sufficiently successful to transfer for a three-night run on 15 January, 1934, to the 1,130-seat Scala Theatre nearby. The *Daily Herald* ran a news story under the headline 'All-Coloured Play of Many Accents', reporting that among the actors, who were mostly students, 'Some spoke with the heavy, rich language of the

African coast, others in the staccato sing-song tones of Jamaica, and a few natives of London with a genuine Cockney accent'.[54] *At What a Price* was favourably reviewed in the *Manchester Guardian* and *West Africa*, which called this 'capital rendering of middle class life', 'a delightful Jamaican comedy'.[55] The key feature for the *Guardian* critic was 'the sheer beauty' of Stella Thomas walking across the stage in an orange dress, 'moving like a slim queen of night' – an entrance that brought a round of applause. Although the production failed in its original aim – to raise money for the LCP – it did succeed in another aspiration, as a political statement that demonstrated cultural autonomy. As *The Keys* said, the 'all-coloured' production aimed to:

> bring home to the British public the fact that we can manage our own affairs effectively and therefore need not to be for ever under tutelage. It will also bring our own people together and help us have more confidence in ourselves, dissipate from among us any inferiority complex in ourselves, and assist us to find a basis for fuller co-operation among ourselves. Its effect must also spread overseas and be a source of inspiration to our race.[56]

Marson, described by her biographer as the first major female poet of the Caribbean and the first black feminist in Britain to speak out against racism and sexism, had come to England in 1932 and became secretary of the LCP and editor of *The Keys*.[57] Her trip was financed by the small profit she had made from the first production of *At What a Price* earlier that year at Kingston's Ward Theatre, where she was credited as co-deviser with a friend, Horace Vaz (her biographer says it was mostly her work).[58] She later wrote two more plays, *London Calling* and *Pocomania*, neither of which was

FIGURE 4.1 The League of Coloured Peoples's magazine *The Keys* reports on Una Marson's play *At What a Price* (Courtesy of British Library)

seen in Britain. *London Calling* was another comedy and published in 1937 after she had returned to Jamaica, where she established the Kingston Dramatic Club and was an advocate of Jamaican national theatre. The play tells of an African prince from an imaginary colony who, as a student in Britain, has farcical encounters with the English upper classes but, in the process, nevertheless manages to counter the myth of black inferiority. *Pocomania* (1938), regarded as her most impressive and original play, was inspired by marginalized black culture, in language, folk song, and dance.[59] Her plays, however, have been overshadowed by her poetry.

Although *At What a Price* represents a minor element in her output, in its assertion of female independence and black pride, it echoes the central themes of better-known work, such as *Tropic Reveries* (1930), her first collection of poems, which are also set in Jamaica and explore a women's desire for self-expression and freedom. *At What a Price* also looks forward to later collections, such as *Moth and the Star* (1937), which validates black definitions of value and aspiration, and *Towards the Stars* (1945), which celebrates the autonomous female. Marson became known not only as a poet but as an activist who set up the Jamaican Save the Children Fund, worked in the Women's International League for Peace and the British Commonwealth League, served as secretary to Haile Selassie, and became an important figure in British black culture: she was freelance at the BBC before gaining a full-time job as programme assistant coordinating broadcasts under the title *Calling the West Indies*, later renamed *Caribbean Voices*, which was aimed at British-based Caribbean service personnel to help maintain contact with home.[60] Marson, the first black female programme maker at the BBC, gave *Caribbean Voices* a cultural agenda, especially in her use of short stories, and it remained an important influence until it closed in the late 1950s. She returned to the Caribbean at the end of the war and continued her involvement in the anti-colonial struggle. Her contribution was a herald of the significant role to be played by Caribbean women such as Pearl Connor and Yvonne Brewster in the post-war development of black British theatre.

In contrast to *At What a Price*, which was produced by a diasporic organization, the other distinctive manifestations of black theatrical activity in the 1930s were associated with white-led companies, as was the case with *Toussaint Louverture*. Most of this activity was also associated with the left. A group called Left Theatre, for example, which was founded in 1934 by progressive theatre professionals, staged that year an American play, *They Shall Not Die*, by John Wexley (a white writer) only three months after it had finished its run in New York. The play tells the story of a notorious case in which nine young black teenagers – some as young as thirteen – were falsely convicted of raping two white women, sentenced to death, and held in prison while their fate was debated through the courts. The Scottsboro Boys case, as it was known, became a rallying point for the international left in demonstrations, petitions, and pamphlets as well as in plays. In Britain, colonial students, especially in the West African Students' Union, were very active in the Scottsboro Defence Committee, which was chaired by Paul Robeson and Jomo Kenyatta.

They Shall Not Die, a three-act play that moves between the court room, the death cell, and the defence lawyer's office, fictionalizes the case but leaves no doubt as to its subject: the action follows the case closely, and quotations from transcripts are used in the trial scenes. An avowedly partisan play, which ends with the jury having to make up its mind, *They Shall Not Die* attacks the repressive and racist state apparatus of the American South, criticizes the response to the case of moderate black opinion, and supports the Communist-led attempts to free the accused. Left Theatre presented *They Shall Not Die* on a Sunday evening at the Holborn Empire, a huge variety venue with a capacity of almost 2,000.[61] Though London theatre managements were reported as refusing to host a benefit concert for the Scottsboro aid fund, Left Theatre invited a spokeswoman of the Defence Committee to address the audience during the interval to raise money and garner support.[62] With the Committee's cooperation, the play was performed again the following two Sundays, first at Greenwich Borough Hall and then East Ham Town Hall, at the end of which performance a resolution was moved by the local mayor and carried unanimously protesting at the trial and demanding the release of the 'boys' with compensation for their imprisonment.

The production was directed by a professional Left Theatre member, André van Gyseghem, a key figure in left-wing theatre of the time who had directed Robeson at the Embassy and who later joined the Communist Party. The black actors in the large cast included radio and stage actor Harry Quashie; Ernest McKenzie, a Socialist who attended the 1945 Pan-African Congress and established the Caribbean Bureau after the war; and three members from the cast of *At What a Price*: Amy Barbour-James, Una Marson, and Viola Thompson. The main defendant was played by Orlando Martins, who became the leading Nigerian actor in Britain. Martins's life was symptomatic: he had settled in London in 1919 and earned his living as best he could in a variety of jobs, working as a Billingsgate porter, wrestler, circus snake charmer, night-watchman, kitchen porter, road sweeper, merchant seaman, silent film walk-on and, for Diaghilev, a ballet extra as a Nubian slave.

Another link between Left Theatre and the anti-racist struggle was the Indian-Irish actor and writer Aubrey Menon, who had set up a theatre group at University College, London with students of several nationalities 'in order to expose the character of the world they were living in, fraught with fascism and war'.[63] With van Gyseghem and others from Left Theatre, Menon founded the Experimental Theatre, which performed at the West End's Fortune Theatre on a Sunday evening in 1934 Menon's anti-fascist and anti-racist play, *Genesis II*. It is an ambitious and sprawling reworking of the first books of the Bible that deals with the oppression of one race by another and journeys from Eden and the British Museum Reading Room to a swastika-clad German police station and an Indian tea plantation. The group subsequently found its own premises in north London, where they converted a house into a 120-seat venue with a 'floating' stage, which appeared not to be fixed to the ground (it comprised two platforms at different levels and a cantilever support underneath entirely covered in black so that the audience could not see it). The project promised much. The group, which incorporated dance and music in its programme, responded to current events in Living Newspaper form as well as presenting its repertoire of plays.

The initial, twenty-week season opened with an evening that comprised three dance-drama 'News Reel' items ('Bread Queue', 'Eviction', and 'Factory'), and

Menon's play *Pacific*, set on a Polynesian island and featuring Polynesian songs and dances; it was described by one critic as dealing in a semi-realistic way with 'the coloured problem' in an 'odd' production that had 'moments of interest and even power'.[64] Other offerings in the season included a classical Chinese play, *Apu Ollantay* (an Aztec drama of revolt against the Inca), classics from Tibet and Java, and Kaladisa's *The Hero and Nymph* from India (which the Indian Art and Dramatic Society had produced). The small auditorium, however, was not financially viable, and the venture soon collapsed. It is not clear how much of the programme was achieved, although one item, *The Mysterious Universe*, Menon's adaptation of the astronomer James Jeans's book, appeared at the Arts Theatre in 1935. Menon, who prefigured the mixed-heritage, hybrid perspective that became a striking feature of later diasporic culture, toured Britain with the India League campaigning for Indian independence before going to live in India, where he wrote at least one play for radio, and then Italy.[65]

Van Gyseghem and other Left Theatre colleagues also helped out at Unity Theatre where Robeson appeared. Unity offered opportunities to diasporic actors after Robeson left. In 1939, it hoped to present Robeson again in *Colony* but, despite his absence, went ahead with the production in conjunction with *After the Tempest* as part of a double bill on imperialism. Both plays, by Geoffrey Trease (a white Englishman), are set on fictional islands but, in *Colony*, the island is clearly recognizable as Jamaica, where sugar workers are striking for fair wages, better conditions, and the right to organize in a trade union. There were several black actors in the cast, including Orlando Martins and Robert Adams, who alternated the part written for Robeson of the strike leader, an impressive figure reminiscent of Alexander Bustamante, who, in 1943, went on to found the Jamaican Labour Party.

After a run of successful shows and under strong encouragement from the American Group Theatre, Unity decided to form a professional company and planned to revive *Colony* in the West End as its inaugural production, hopefully with Robeson, but the declaration of war interrupted the scheme. Unity kept operating throughout the war and included in its 1943 repertoire *India Speaks* (a.k.a. *Map of India*), a Living Newspaper in poem-form dealing with the famine in eastern India written by Mulk Raj Anand. He remembers there being a cast of some three dozen, including several Indians. At one performance to raise money for Bengali relief, an astonishing £2,500 was donated after a speech by Krishna Menon, a local Labour councillor, secretary of the India League, and future Foreign Secretary of India. Accompanied by Menon, Unity took the play to London's East End for a special showing to Indian seamen and to Birmingham, Leeds, and Cardiff as part of the India League's campaign on the famine and the need for Indian independence. Anand went on to write a similar Living Newspaper, *Famine*, for the Army Bureau of Current Affairs Play Unit, which was heavily influenced by people associated with Unity.[66]

When Unity finally launched a professional company in 1946, its artistic director, Ted Willis, invited Robert Adams to lead the opening show, *All God's Chillun Got Wings*, with Cheshire-born Ida Shepley playing his sister. (As the company did not employ any more black actors, white actors blacked up alongside them, although

Robeson had not whited up in his earlier role at Unity. One review, however, thought Shepley could be made darker so that the audience would believe more readily she was related to the character played by Adams.)[67] Unity continued to present plays on anti-colonial and race issues in the postwar years and be a home for diasporic actors in plays such as *Dragnet* (1947) by Joe MacColum; *Longitude 49* (1950) by Herb Tank; *Oh! Freedom* (1963), a show about the slave trade; *The Feather Pluckers* (1967, by John Peter Jones, which depicts the troubled lives of three British youths, two white and one black); and *South Africa '70*, a documentary play co-presented with the Stop the 70 tour and the Anti-Apartheid Movement to coincide with the campaign against the Springbok rugby tour; its cast included five black African performers, including actor/writer Yemi Ajibade playing Nelson Mandela. In 1970, Unity presented the work of a black writer, Obi Egbuna's *The Agony*, which tells of his time in Brixton gaol as editor of *Black Power Speaks* and the script of which play had to be smuggled out of the prison. Several of the actors who appeared at Unity were seminal to the development of black theatre in Britain, such as Ajibade, Mark Heath, Errol Hill, Errol John, Carmen Munroe, Anton Phillips, Frank Singuineau, and Rudolph Walker. Although Unity had always opposed racism, particularly anti-Semitism, and during the war had refused membership on the grounds of racial attitude, it nevertheless remained overwhelmingly white, like most of the left, yet continued to be staunchly anti-imperialist.

In *All God's Chillun Got Wings*, Adams and Shepley were reprising the roles they had played in a Negro Repertory Theatre production two years before under Adams's direction, which probably represented the first attempt to establish a black theatre company in Britain. Robeson had explored the idea, as had the League of Coloured Peoples at Adams's suggestion (he was a founder member), but nothing came of it until Adams revived the notion during the war. Born in British Guiana, Adams trained as a teacher and acted in and directed amateur drama before coming to Britain in the late 1920s to become a professional actor. He suffered from Robeson's pre-eminence and, like Orlando Martins, had to take a series of poorly paid jobs and was persuaded to take up wrestling, in which pursuit he earned minor celebrity as 'The Black Eagle', winning the heavyweight championship of the British Empire. Yet, besides appearing in *Stevedore*, *Toussaint Louverture*, and *Colony*, Adams made West End appearances, too, and in 1938 played the title part in O'Neill's *The Emperor Jones* at the Arts Theatre, Cambridge, the same year the BBC broadcast him in this role, the first black actor to appear as a leading character on British television. In 1942, however, he missed the chance to play Othello at the Old Vic. He had been approached for the part, he said a few years later, until a 'continental' was offered it instead. Adams does not name him, though it is almost certainly the eminent Czech actor Frederick Valk, who performed the role for the Old Vic in 1942. Adams said the actor's 'lack of knowledge of English was obviously a drawback, his power was alright but his inflections were ludicrous. Yet what was the explanation for rejecting me? I was told that I had not sufficient Shakespearian technique'.[68] Adams was to miss out again on the role more than a decade later when a BBC TV production gave the part to the American Gordon Heath.

FIGURE 4.2 Robert Adams in *Colony*, Unity Theatre, 1939 (Image by Herbert Paul. Courtesy of Victoria and Albert Museum, London)

In 1943, with help from a Unity activist, Peter Noble, Adams began planning a black-led company that would stage ballet and dance and plays by black playwrights. The idea was also to tour the United States and countries within the British Empire, in association with the British Council. The Negro Repertory Theatre was due to open in December 1943 at the Arts Theatre in a production of *All God's Chillun Got Wings* featuring Adams and directed by André van Gyseghem, but there is no record of this occurring.[69] Noble later recalled only one production by the company, in late 1944 of the same play but at Colchester Repertory Theatre.[70] Adams, who had become president of the Society for the Prevention of Racial Discrimination in Britain, directed and played the lead alongside black actors George Browne, Earl Cameron, Martins, and Shepley. Cameron remembers that Adams did not direct very well and that Robert Digby, Colchester's director, had to take over.[71] Apparently Adams left in shame but was coaxed back, yet it represented a blow to the future prospects of the group, which did not survive.

Adams, however, did not give up the idea of the group immediately. In 1946, Noble reports his announcing his intention, 'as soon as conditions permitted', of forming a Negro Theatre as part of the struggle for the 'artistic and social recognition for the negro race'.[72] One obstacle had been the lack of actors, says Noble, but this was no longer the case. Another barrier had been lack of plays, yet Noble lists a planned repertoire: *The Emperor Jones*, *All God's Chillun Got Wings*, and a new play by Adams on a slave revolt in the Caribbean (he is said to have written plays and a book, but none survives). Other productions, it was hoped, would include James's *Toussaint Louverture*, Richard Wright's *Native Son*, and *Porgy and Bess*. Noble sums up the case for the company:

> A theatre, such as Mr Adams is determined to form, giving regular performances in London and the provinces of intelligent plays acted by Negro *and* white actors, would be of unlimited value towards the creation of a wider understanding of the Negro problem. Such a theatre would indeed be a power for dispelling colour prejudice and there are indeed immense possibilities in a progressive Negro Theatre which would be an important liberal weapon for the uprooting of basic inhibitions and the sowing of seeds of tolerance.[73]

Unfortunately, these plans did not materialize, although Adams did play Bigger Thomas in *Native Son* in 1948 in an adaptation by Paul Green and Wright himself at Bolton's, a small club theatre in London. The *Stage* review said of his performance as the black chauffeur who accidentally kills his boss's daughter that Adams was a 'towering personality capable of expressing instantly every changing emotion'.[74] Although his company did not reach the Caribbean, he went there in 1949 to lecture for the British Council on theatre and cinema in Britain and, while in Jamaica, appeared as Inspector Goole in *An Inspector Calls*. In British Guiana, he directed *The Emperor Jones*. Back in Britain where, through his appearances on TV, film, radio, and stage, Adams had become the country's leading black actor, he felt tired and disillusioned, and took up the law. After a few acting appearances in the late 1950s, he returned to British Guiana where he became a head teacher prior to his death in 1965.[75]

In a letter to a friend explaining what had made him turn to the law – he qualified as a barrister in 1948 – Adams writes,

> The Stage as it exists for the Negro is a most precarious type of existence. If one manages to succeed on the Music Halls like HUTCH [pianist Leslie 'Hutch' Hutchinson] then one may if one lives carefully look forward to a somewhat secure old age. But the position is different for the Dramatic Artiste, and that is my Field. The parts are few and far between and when one reaches Stardom the position becomes more difficult still. Apart from this the main objection is the Negro stereotype which seems to be the standard for the Coloured Artiste. When one raises objections one immediately hears that one's head is getting too big.[76]

Before he left acting, he also wrote an article for the Unity magazine *New Theatre* on the struggle black actors faced in Britain and attacked the theatre industry bias in favour of Americans, a subject he spoke about at an Equity meeting at the time. Adams writes (in 1947) that when he arrived in Britain, he found the conception that 'only the American Negro artist had any talent. The African or West Indian was called second-rate'.[77] The problem was most pressing in 'the serious theatre' where the 'British Negro artist' is told either 'he [sic] has not the talent or that he will not be "box office"'. As a result, the 'Negro artist is still considered not an artist in his own right but as something contributory to the support of the white artists… However good he or she may be, the association must be with white artists and in a supplementary rather than a complementary role'. In the face of this, 'We British Negro artists claim respect for our individuality, and for the assessment of our contribution on its merit value'. Adams calls for government and Equity action and for 'British Negroes' to use trade unionism to overcome the difficulties he outlines. He ends with a wider challenge to the British public and its institutions, a challenge that offers a prophetic statement of the value of the future theatre he did not live to see but helped to create:

> Recognise us artistically as equals, give us the opportunity to contribute as equals. Ours will be a dynamic contribution.

Under the heading 'The Negro Actor – a Summing Up', the American Jamaican-born actor Frank Silvera responded in *New Theatre* to Adams's 'unwarranted and disparaging' remarks on black American artists.[78] Silvera acknowledges that plays such as *All God's Chillun* are compromised but argues they were great advances and notes the five years of 'unprecedented progress' achieved by the Federal Theatre Project in the United States in the 1930s in the advancement of black artists through training across the various theatrical skills and exposure to a range of classics and new plays – a period of state support that black artists in Britain never enjoyed.

Echoing arguments within black theatre that resonate through the years, Silvera quotes from an article in the *Stage* entitled 'Negro', which says *Anna Lucasta* and *Deep are the Roots* (both white-written and then playing in London with American casts) 'prove that Negro players can hold their own with actors of any colour or creed'. He sees the way forward as integration into the theatre, and cites the example of Canada Lee 'greased up' as a white Bosola in an American production of *The Duchess of Malfi*. 'By all means let us have a Negro production of *Hamlet*. Then let us have productions of *King Lear*, *Romeo and Juliet*, *Ghosts*, or a *St. Joan* done at the highest artistic level with several Negro actors in major roles… The process of development is slow and exacting, but this should not be discouraging.'

The same edition carried a letter from Orlando Martins, a great supporter of the idea of a black theatre company, backing Adams: 'We are tired of such plays as *Emperor Jones*, *All God's Chillun*, *Little Foxes*, etc. What we really need is some new material written by British authors'.[79] This was the challenge for the postwar period.

5

POSTWAR STRUGGLES: 1940s–1960s

Britain's postwar decline as an imperial power was accompanied by an invited but unprecedented influx of peoples from the colonized countries who found the 'Mother Country' less than welcoming and far from the image that had featured in their upbringing and expectation. Their own cultures continued to be simplified, homogenized, and demeaned as inferior, and the struggle in British theatre to create a space for, and to voice in their own way, their own aspirations and views of the world was symptomatic of the wider struggle for independence and to survive with dignity.

After the end of the war, both the Subject People's Conference in London and the fifth Pan-African Congress in Manchester called for common cause among the African, Caribbean, and Asian diaspora. Yet their cultural trajectories in Britain were quite different, though all suffered racism and discrimination, and responded by coming together for protection and to establish self-help and support organizations as well as participating in the British trade union and anti-colonial, anti-racist movements. Despite the pan-African umbrella, the links between the African/ Caribbean and Asian diaspora – themselves highly differentiated and internally fraught – were not strong, and the situation in their respective homelands did not bring them closer. For those of South Asian heritage, independence, with all its difficulties, came not long after the war. For those with African and Caribbean heritage, the wait was longer. A major shift then occurred in the 1960s as a result of the Vietnam War and the rise of black consciousness, which affected all non-white diasporic peoples living in Britain.

Asian theatre

Britain's immediate postwar reconstruction needed labour, which, very broadly speaking, resulted for immigrating Caribbeans in entry to public service, especially

transport and health, and for Asians work in factories or the small business sector.[1]
When India won independence and Pakistan was born, they attracted the intelligentsia
of the respective countries, and South Asian immigration to Britain was less than
that from the Caribbean. South Asian diasporic theatre remained much as it had
been before the war, the domain of the student population and middle-class migrant
community. In the 1960s, new levels of South Asian immigration introduced people
who were more religiously and culturally distanced from British society than the
Caribbean communities, most notably through their want of English. This tended
to keep large numbers outside the public sector and its consequent socialization and
instead concentrated them in industrial sites away from the capital, a focus reinforced
by chain migration whereby first settlers brought over to the same location members
of the same family group or village. Unsurprisingly, most of the cultural activity was
inward-looking and took place within these communities. For historical reasons
related to cultural tradition, religion, gender perceptions, and language, little of this
activity was associated with what the European elite defined as drama but with music
and dance, drawn from a culture older than and largely unconnected to Europe's
Renaissance traditions.[2] Own-language theatre, in Urdu, Bengali, Gujarati, Hindi,
and Marathi, developed in the 1960s as a force for community cohesion and identity,
drawing on the repertoire of the home country yet using European genres, such as
melodrama, drawing-room comedy, and the thriller.[3] Such shows tended to validate
values and traditions of the home culture and were aimed at distinct home language
groups, not at other Asian-language communities let alone non-Asian audiences.

Rare appearances in the commercial theatre by Asian performers, or those with
Asian heritage, in productions such as *This Way to the Tomb* (1946) and *Murder in
the Cathedral* (1947), in which ethnicity is not an issue, underlined the fact that
the Asian presence remained marginal and sporadic. It was most noticeable when
type-casting required it, for example in *South Pacific* (1951), *The King and I* (1953),
Teahouse of the August Moon (1954), or *Flower Drum Song* (1960). This limitation
reflects both a narrowness of vision by writers and a bias against artists of colour
by producers. South or East Asian actors, if used, often portrayed characters from
different parts of the continent regardless of any actual connection, as audiences still
were overwhelmingly white and, it was assumed, had little notion of the distinctions
but did like to see what they regarded as acceptably 'real'.

In the non-commercial sector, the Asian presence was equally inconsistent and
peripheral, but it was more varied and more under the control of the diasporic artists
themselves. Intermittent alfresco events continued in the spirit of the Union of the
East and West – Lord Leverhulme's garden was again the site for a performance of
Sakuntala in 1947 by an all-Indian cast. In 1950, Govindas Vishnoodas Desani, a
Kenyan born actor, writer, and mystic living in Britain, had *Hali*, a poetic play about
a prophet, published (with puzzled forewords by E. M. Forster and T. S. Eliot). It was
staged at London's Watergate Theatre club but little noticed. Indian impresario D. P.
Chaudhuri managed the Irving Theatre and acted as an agent promoter for 'coloured
artists' through his company the Eastwest Entertainment Exchange. The Irving
operated in the 1950s and early 1960s as a club theatre behind the National Portrait

Gallery off Leicester Square, above what was then the city morgue. It presented late-night revues and more traditional fare, including some diasporic shows. Edric Connor's *Cabaret Caribbean* was seen at the Irving in 1952, followed in 1955 by his *A Caribbean Revue* along with Douglas Archibald's play *Junction Village*. In a 1952 festival of international plays, the Irving revived Tagore's *Sacrifice* and *The Post Office*; both were directed by Tarun Roy, who had trained with the British Drama League, and were presented by the East and West Drama Society, which appears to take its name from Das Gupta's defunct pre-war organization. The following year, the Irving presented Tagore's *Red Oleanders* under the auspices of the Royal India, Pakistan, and Ceylon Society, with several South Asian performers in the cast. Also in 1953, the Irving presented the International Players in *Black Napoleon*, a play about Toussaint Louverture (Mark Heath) written and directed by Peter Munk (white), and *Magic from the East* (a magician, fire-eater, and other variety acts), a Christmas-time offering that mined the conventional variety appeal of an illusory Orient. In the second half of the decade, the Irving under Chaudhuri became known for its sleazy non-stop 'glamour' revue.[4] In the late 1950s, he also briefly owned the Princes Theatre in Edinburgh, which staged revue during the annual summer Festival, and in 1964 – again, briefly – he acquired Margate's eighteenth-century Theatre Royal, one of Britain's oldest working theatres, to stage revues there as well.[5]

It was still a time of individual initiative. Actors and directors such as Ebrahim Alkazi, Saeed Jaffrey, Zia Mohyeddin, Alyque Padamsee, Alaknanda Samarth, and Habib Tanvir who studied at RADA in the 1950s and 1960s were isolated figures, as Rani and Princess Indira had been before the war, despite the distinguished careers they went on to enjoy and the contributions they made to Indian theatre or to establishing a South Asian profile in British theatre. Collective activity was local and constrained by conservative attitudes within the diaspora and British racism without. The Indian government prohibited Partap Sharma's *A Touch of Brightness* from being performed at the first Commonwealth Arts Festival in London in 1965; the play tells of a young Hindu being tricked into becoming a whore and having to choose between the brothel and life with the man she loves. Eventually, there was a production (without décor) at the Royal Court two years later with a cast of Indian performers, including Saeed Jaffrey, Zohra Segal, and Roshan Seth, but it did not lead to any further projects.[6]

A breakthrough (however partial) in terms of mainstream commercial theatre came in 1960, when the Meadow Players' production of E. M. Forster's *A Passage to India* was transferred from the Oxford Playhouse to the West End, with Zia Mohyeddin, Rashid Karaplet, and South Asian extras in the cast. The novel was adapted with Forster's approval by Santha Rama Rau, an Indian-born writer who was educated in England while her diplomat father was based there. Her adaptation was seen on BBC TV in 1965 and used by David Lean for his 1984 film of the novel, in which Alec Guinness notoriously played Godbole in brownface. Rau told a journalist that she had undertaken the project in response to a director who had asked her why there were no plays being written that interpreted India.[7] She chose not to write a play of her own or to adapt an Indian play but turned instead to an

English novelist and an English view of India. This kind of response would be turned on its head in the 1970s with the forced arrival in Britain of South Asian exiles from East Africa, who, with their exposure to theatre, responded in drama as well as in politics to the racism they encountered to create their own theatre of self-expression and self-representation.

Black theatre

In the immediate post-war years when Britain was trying to rebuild, African-American theatre arrived as part of an energizing transatlantic wave. In 1947, the American Negro Theatre production of Philip Yourdan's *Anna Lucasta* woke up the West End with its ensemble vigour (it ran for fourteen months and was revived in 1953). Later in 1947, another white-authored Broadway hit, *Deep are the Roots* by Arnaud d'Usseau and James Gow, began a six-month run in the West End. In a plea for tolerance, the play tells the story of a black officer who returns home to the Deep South after serving in World War 2 only to find that he is still treated unfairly. Its achievement won the American lead, Gordon Heath, the role of Othello in 1951 on a six-month Arts Council tour, directed by Kenneth Tynan, who cast Pauline Henriques as a black Emilia to make sense of Iago's suspicion that Othello has slept with her. Building on similar initiatives that had taken place during the war, the Council wanted to tour the play to towns without theatres or regular theatre-going audiences. *Othello* played in a range of venues from traditional auditoria to church, welfare and school halls, and visited the Midlands, north of England, Scotland, and Wales. Heath went on to play major roles in cinema and British television, including Othello in 1955 (probably the first time a black actor had performed a major Shakespearean part on British television). The success of Americans such as Heath irritated Commonwealth black actors living in Britain who were British subjects, a status underpinned by the 1948 British Nationality Act. Robert Adams, for example, was overlooked for the television role of Othello despite being auditioned, and challenged Heath's right as a foreigner to be given the part. The actors' union Equity allowed it because Heath was classified as an international star. Heath, however, complained that he was often passed over for black British actors and was typecast as Caribbean. He felt the black British actors were, on the whole, 'insufficiently trained and spoke English with their own accents and lacked discipline and organization'.[8]

Black British actors knew they needed to be organized to gain experience and become better trained. After the demise of Robert Adams's wartime Negro Repertory Theatre, several attempts were made over the next two decades to rectify the situation. The number of black British actors was still relatively small, but it had been – and was – growing. Many were not trained but had aspirations, some were students with drama experience, and some were semi-professional, whereas the few who were professional struggled to find work and decent parts. Though television and film offered money and exposure, opportunity was severely limited. Access to the stage was also restricted, though amateur or semi-professional club theatres such as Unity or Bolton's offered a few openings. Radio, however, provided a haven, exploiting the fact that the black body was hidden from view. With programmes such as *Caribbean Voices, Caribbean Carnival, African Theatre*, and *Caribbean Theatre*, BBC radio made an important contribution to the development of theatre in Britain and Commonwealth countries by broadcasting original plays and adaptations of novels, and raising the profile of the actors and playwrights concerned.[9]

Radio's contribution to black theatre in Britain came mainly through providing a meeting place, a testing ground, and employment for black playwrights and actors, who were able to acquire valuable experience. Performers could develop articulation and diction, the lack of which skills was regularly used as an excuse to bar them from playing non-racially specific roles on stage. Two important figures in the radio world were Una Marson, whose contribution is noted in the previous chapter, and Louise Bennett (known as Miss Lou), who won a British Council scholarship to RADA in 1945, the first black Caribbean student there. A poet who cherished Caribbean folklore and celebrated its vernacular, she worked for BBC radio and was resident artist on *Caribbean Carnival*. She also appeared in repertory theatre, with the Midland Theatre Company, and in intimate revue (for example, in Edric Connor's *Cabaret Caribbean*). In 1965, during the first Commonwealth Arts Festival, she appeared on stage at the Royal Court and performed her poetry.

The black British theatre community took its first post-war steps to organize during the run of *Anna Lucasta*, perhaps inspired by the achievements of the African-American theatre and the example of Les Ballets Nègres, founded in 1946 as Britain's and Europe's first black dance company. The existence of a large group of black British understudies for the show presented the opportunity for them to work together, and, after a call from Edric Connor, they formed the Negro Theatre Company (NTC) in 1948 to mount their own productions and try-outs. One of the participants, Neville Crabbe, recounted: 'One rainy afternoon in late January, several Negroes met together at the Dinley Studios [in Marylebone, London], and after introductions sat down to discuss an extremely important matter, namely the possibility of forming a Negro Theatre Company here in London.'[10] Since the days of the pioneer Ira Aldridge, wrote Crabbe, 'music, dancing and slapstick comedy have been the parts allocated to Negroes, apart from the stereotyped "Uncle Tom" characters in a great many plays'. The NTC aimed to change that situation. More meetings were held, an executive committee was formed, and a constitution was drawn up. The chair was Ulric Cross, Pauline Henriques was the secretary, Ida Shepley the treasurer, and the committee comprised Connor, Crabbe, and George Browne. Members included Orlando Martins and Harry Quashie. The artist and NTC supporter Sir Francis Rose persuaded his friend Dame Sybil Thorndike to become NTC's Patroness. Henriques later described the NTC as forming the 'nucleus of what we were beginning to think of as the British Black Theatre Movement'.[11]

Training was a priority, and it was decided to mount a show to raise both the NTC profile and funds for classes in stage technique. Henriques was chosen to direct because she had experience, but, along with the problem of no premises, no money, and a variety of accents to manage, ranging from West African to West Indian and

FIGURE 5.1   Negro Theatre Company rehearsing in 1948 (*Checkers* magazine. Courtesy of British Library)

Cockney, the biggest challenge was finding suitable material. Rudolph Evans (a.k.a. André Dakar, a mentor figure who had come to Britain before the war) invited the group to use the Caribbean Club in Denman Street behind Piccadilly Circus, and there they rehearsed what turned out to be a programme of variety and dramatic items called *Something Different*. Crabbe, the producer of the show, had been on the point of giving up in his search for a venue when Maccabi, an international Jewish sport and culture organization, offered the theatre its headquarters in Hampstead, north London. Frederick O'Neal, from the *Anna Lucasta* cast, who had attended the inaugural NTC meeting, spoke on the wealth of black existence that was crying out to be dramatized, and there were extracts from Clifford Odets's *Golden Boy*, *Othello* (performed by Evans), and *Love From a Stranger*. The show was to include Thornton Wilder's *The Happy Journey to Trenton and Camden* but a review of it did not mention this item.[12] An article, however, in the November issue of *Checkers*, which styled itself as 'Britain's Premier Negro Magazine', said Rita Stevens, a coochee dancer in the 1943 London production of *Show Boat* and understudy for Hilda Simms in *Anna Lucasta*, had made her straight theatre debut in *Happy Journey* at Maccabi House.[13] The magazine became the postal address for the NTC, which advertised for new members through its pages.

'There were many mistakes made,' reported Crabbe, 'but many lessons learned. Perhaps the most important of these was the fact the group learnt to appreciate the value of team-work, and it was in this co-operative spirit that they are going to work in the future.' Weekly meetings took place, one of which was addressed by the film director Thorold Dickinson on the making of *Men of Two Worlds*, in which

Robert Adams became the first non-American black actor to play a leading role in a British film.[14] The services were obtained of Richard Angerola, a former teacher at the Goodman Theatre, Chicago and husband of Hilda Simms, who was playing *Anna Lucasta*, to run the classes. Plans for a second NTC production were disrupted by several NTC members' going on tour with *Anna Lucasta*. The show they were rehearsing included songs from Edric Connor, Ida Shepley, and guest, the bass Joseph Pereira, and three short plays with roles not written for black actors: Sidney Box's play *Solomon's Folly*, Eugene O'Neill's *Before Breakfast*, and George Bernard Shaw's *Village Wooing*.[15] It is possible some of this material was presented, but details have not come to light. The NTC also planned to perform *An American Primitive*, but it is not clear whether this was seen either, nor how many shows NTC performed.

Some of the original *Anna Lucasta* cast helped the NTC and more generally promoted the need for a black arts movement in Britain: Simms spoke at several meetings (and later appeared in other shows, including *Desire Caught by the Tail*, Picasso's only play, presented by the Institute of Contemporary Arts at the Rudolf Steiner Hall, 1950); Frank Silvera attended the 1948 British Theatre Conference in London, which occurred during the *Anna Lucasta* run, and contributed to the debate on 'The Negro Actor' in Unity's *New Theatre* magazine; and Frederick O'Neal gave lectures, including one for the NTC on the development of the American Negro Theatre.[16] The *Stage* reported that O'Neal and Connor had been behind the NTC, but later said the British company had nothing to do with the American Negro Theatre (ANT), and that NTC policy was decided by its own committee.[17] A few years later, Connor responded to a leader in the *Stage* that praised the American show *Porgy and Bess* while complaining that 'negro artists' in Britain could not unite.[18] Connor referred to the experience of the NTC. He pointed out that it had done fairly well, had raised funds and had won help from the London County Council, with classrooms and teachers being placed at the group's disposal, but, being aware they were not quite ready to stage a drama, had invited some of the *Anna Lucasta* cast to appear in one of their Sunday concerts. This appearance and endorsement had been interpreted as the ANT's setting up the NTC. Although O'Neal issued a disclaimer, the damage had been done, according to Connor, and the group began to disintegrate. The problem, he said, was not disunity but 'finding a place at a reasonable rental, within easy reach of theatregoers, where we could put on shows on a professional basis'.

Opportunities to be seen as distinct from the Americans were welcomed by the likes of Connor, whose significance in the development of black British theatre is detailed below. For instance, he appeared in *Calypso* (1948), a British riposte to the American theatrical invasion and the first postwar musical to have a Caribbean angle. *Calypso* was devised and directed by white English actor, dancer, and designer Hedley Briggs, who was stationed in Trinidad during the war, but it was generally less well regarded than Katherine Dunham's *A Caribbean Rhapsody*, which played the following month. In *Calypso*, Caribbean dancing and singing, which were still a novelty for most British audiences, enlivened a tired musical comedy plot based on a woman mistaking a photograph of her lover's sister for a rival. This revivifying role was a major one diasporic theatre would continue to perform for the rest of the century.[19]

The acting career of Henriques, a central force behind the NTC, typifies the problems of the time that the NTC was trying to confront: she had come from Jamaica to Britain in 1919 with her family who read plays together at home. Supported by her parents, she went to the LAMDA drama school in 1932, aged 18, where she was the only black person, and played leading parts such as Lady Bracknell and Lady Macbeth. She worked in radio and in repertory theatre but says that, as she could not dance, she played maids, which she hated, especially given the roles she had played at LAMDA. 'I had an English accent,' she recalled, 'which was perfect for "classic" roles…but I had to play my parts in white face…I went along with it because I was very anxious to learn my craft, and to be taken seriously as a dramatic actress'.[20] On radio, she was able to perform a range of roles because she was not seen and was good at accents. After the war in 1946, she was seen on TV in *All God's Chillun Got Wings*, probably the first black actress on British television. She preferred the stage, however. 'I loved the excitement of working in the theatre but I felt I could do better', said Henriques. 'I had a voice but it wasn't until Kenneth Tynan cast me in *Othello* that I discovered what a wonderful thing it was to act in a Shakespeare play on the stage, and speak those marvellous lines…We encountered every type of audience, and it was a most exciting experience'. After that exhilaration, she could not return to playing maids and left the theatre for social work, later becoming the first black female British magistrate.

Despite the obstacles, Britain still represented opportunity to those living in the colonies, particularly those interested in theatre. Following Louise Bennett to RADA on a British Council scholarship, Errol Hill came to London in 1949 from Trinidad and Tobago, having written plays, acted and, with Errol John, helped start an amateur group, the Whitehall Players. Hill found himself the only black student at RADA and, like Henriques, had to don whiteface and a wig.[21] When one of the tutors responded to this humiliation by letting Hill perform the lead in *Deep Are the Roots*, a white student had to black up to play his mother. Hill graduated with distinction, having performed an extract from *Othello* (to the astonishment of the principal, it is said, who found his achievement in adopting an English accent all the more remarkable because he was Caribbean and not African). When invited to participate in a graduating showcase, however, Hill was cast not in a leading role but as the black servant in Kaufman and Ferber's *Theatre Royal*. Clearly, drama schools were as much part of the social apparatus as they were training establishments for artists.

Hill used his time in London to see as much theatre as possible, especially Shakespeare. Glad as he was to witness the likes of Laurence Olivier and the young Richard Burton, he noted the absence of black actors. It was evident he needed to set up his own productions if he was going to progress. Before leaving RADA in 1951, he directed Sophocles's *Antigone* in a West African setting complete with Ghanaian clothes borrowed from African students; Errol John, who was also now in England, played Haemon, and Hill, Creon. He collaborated with John again in 1952 when he staged at the Hans Crescent student centre and hostel in Knightsbridge the British première of Derek Walcott's *Henri Christophe*. John played the lead in a student cast in which (black) South Africa was represented as were several Caribbean countries (including from Trinidad the future Prime Minister, Arthur Robinson). Trinidadian Carlisle Chang, who became a noted painter and scenographer and who was then at the Slade School of Fine Art, collaborated on *Antigone* and *Henri Christophe*. Hill directed *Henri Christophe* on BBC radio for *Caribbean Voices*, with Edric Connor taking over the eponymous role. Earlier, in 1950, Hill had also directed for *Caribbean Voices* his short play, *The Ping Pong*, a pioneering story that used Creole in depicting the passion of steel band players for creating a new form of music, in which he played the lead. He continued to appear in radio plays and also worked as a radio broadcaster. He stage-managed a theatre company that performed in Wales and appeared at Unity Theatre. Back in the Caribbean in 1952, he became a leading writer and theatre historian. His best-known play, *Man Better Man* (1954), which represented Trinidad and Tobago at the 1965 Commonwealth Festival in Britain in his own production, uses rhymed calypso verse to explore carnival, a subject Hill wrote about in his influential book *The Trinidad Carnival* (1972).

Errol John

Hill's collaborator Errol John became a key figure in the development of black British theatre. Son of fast bowler George John, Errol acted in, wrote, directed, and designed plays, co-founded the Whitehall Players with Hill in Port of Spain, and briefly ran the Company of Five before coming to England in 1950. He had been invited by the British Council to pursue a technical course in theatre study but ended up an unpaid trainee stage manager at Bolton's club theatre in Kensington. Besides acting in the Hill productions, John appeared at Unity and won his debut professional role (one line) in the 1952 BBC radio production of *The Emperor Jones*. He read Lear on radio and appeared on stage in *Cabaret Caribbean* (1952); the 1953 American Negro Theatre touring revival of *Anna Lucasta*; four shows in 1954 – Felicia Komai's verse adaptation of *Cry, the Beloved Country* (and on TV), Joan Sandler's *Local Colour*, Sartre's *The Respectable Prostitute* as the Negro, and Wilde's *Salome* as a Nubian slave, and in 1955 Paul Green's *South*.[22]

John found good roles scarce and considered he was not offered sufficient stage work. His response was to write a play of his own, *Moon on a Rainbow Shawl*, which he entered for the *Observer* play competition, but he felt disillusioned enough with life in Britain to book a passage home. Two days before he was due to sail, he heard that he had won the competition. The following year, the play was staged at the Royal Court and won him a Guggenheim Foundation scholarship to study in America.

Moon on a Rainbow Shawl – the title evokes O'Neill – brings to vivid life the tribulations of the inhabitants of a yard of shacks in late 1940s Port of Spain, Trinidad, the most cosmopolitan of the Caribbean islands. It opens with steel drums playing, a guitar strumming and a calypso singer taking on a new refrain. The story focuses on

FIGURE 5.2 (From left) Vinnette Carrol, Clifton Jones and Jaqueline Chan in Errol John's *Moon on a Rainbow Shawl*, Royal Court, 1958 (Courtesy of David Sim)

Ephraim, an impetuous young trolley bus driver, who escapes his tough, cramped, and crowded backyard life and his pregnant partner Rosa for the dream of a better life in Liverpool.

Ephraim tells Rosa:

> I got a life to live! A whole big future before me! But is a kind of future I can't make here.[23]

His way of dealing with his dilemma is contrasted to that of the older generation, the strong matriarch Sophia and the weak Charlie, who might have been a renowned Test cricketer had he managed to keep quiet about racism.

One of the play competition judges, Kenneth Tynan, likened *Moon on a Rainbow Shawl* to Italian neo-realist cinema and described it as a 'hauntingly, hot-climate, tragic-comedy about backyard life in Trinidad'.[24] It became known as the definitive 'yard' play, written within the framework of Western dramaturgy but with an individual poetic realism enriched by the use of vernacular speech. The British-dominated Caribbean education system demeaned the commonly spoken Creole, which is a language in its own right rather than a dialect, with its own vocabulary, syntax, and cultural heritage (indeed, later referred to as nation language). Writers such as Sam Selvon and George Lamming (whose TV play *A Man from the Sun* featured John as the lead), who were exploring the same moment of Caribbean migration, used realistic language that made the theatre look backward by comparison. However, John's play helped it catch up. His dialogue challenged the idea that standard English was the norm expected in theatre. Language and accent are always related to power, and John was part of a wider challenge, spearheaded by theatres such as the Royal Court, to question the class and national assumptions carried by the domination of Received Pronunciation.

In the preface to the published text, Tynan says there was never much doubt that John's play would win first prize in the competition (though some questioned this assessment). Tynan wrote: 'its lyricism, compassion and harmonious, all-of-a-pieceness made it the obvious choice'.[25] In the competition, which attracted almost 2,000 entries, *Moon on a Rainbow Shawl* beat N. F. Simpson's *A Resounding Tinkle* and Ann Jellicoe's *The Sport of My Mad Mother*. Yet, amid rumours that Tynan had pushed for John to win for political reasons, both these latter plays received productions at the Royal Court before John's, which was first performed in a radio version as *Small Island Moon* in May 1958. When the promised stage production did occur (which was supposed to be at the Arts, but this fell by the wayside), it proved to be a taxing trial for John.

Two cultures were at odds. Hugh Beaumont, the West End's leading producer, optioned the play when it won the competition but, when he read it, he thought it uncommercial and placed it with his not-for-profit section Tennent Productions (the eventual producers, with New Watergate Productions, originally set up to circumvent censorship). Tennent gave the play to Frith Banbury, a major West End director, who believed the script showed great potential but needed rewriting, a view he found confirmed by a public reading at the Criterion Theatre. Having consulted his play reader, Christopher Taylor, Banbury gave John eight pages of closely typed suggestions, which Banbury's biographer Charles Duff says focused mainly on lack of plot and need for sharper dramatic development.[26] Duff describes some of the objections as 'rather literal-minded', but John made the changes, except for altering the title. Banbury travelled to Trinidad armed with a camera to take photographs for the designer, Loudon Sainthill. Back in England, Banbury began casting and decided the black British actors he saw, including Cleo Laine, were not experienced enough. He brought in three Americans in the main roles, and replaced John, who had played the lead on radio, with Earle Hyman, who had acted with the American Shakespeare Festival Theatre, Connecticut for five seasons and had played Othello in New York. The British actors complained to Equity, to no avail.

Management showed no interest in the project either in rehearsal or on tour in Manchester, Brighton, and Leeds, a neglect that Banbury found disgraceful, particularly as the cast were black. There was more trouble, as the London destination had not been fixed, and the Americans believed they were heading for the West End. Beaumont had never intended this and instead approached George Devine, artistic director of the English Stage Company, which ran the Royal Court, who sent Anthony Page, an assistant director, to see the show in Manchester. On Page's verdict, the production came to the Royal Court, where it filled a slot in December 1958 that had become vacant owing to the illness of the lead in the planned show. *Moon on a Rainbow Shawl* opened at the end of a year that was critical in Britain's history of racism. It was a notorious year marred by violent summer race clashes in Nottingham, which sparked into action the 'nigger hunting' teddy boy mobs in Notting Hill and across London and elsewhere. The Royal Court audience would know, therefore, that Ephraim's optimistic vision of the 'Mother Country' was far removed from the lived experience, and John's play exploited this tension.

The play received mixed reviews. The *Sunday Times* critic consigned it 'to the romantic past', the *Evening Standard* found it 'conscientious and moving at times' but 'predictable', and the *Times* critic felt the drama was slow to emerge and 'The author's compassion rings true as his attempted lyricism rings false'. Yet Doris Lessing in the *Observer* likened its use of language to that of O'Casey and said, 'The actors have a quality lacking in most British acting; a warm and tender sensuality which gives the production a deep delicacy of emotion'. The *Stage* said John 'by detached, unsentimental and mostly economical writing, has brought his characters convincingly to life, and must be reckoned an important dramatic spokesman for a group of people who are steadily assuming world significance'.[27] *Moon on a Rainbow Shawl* played for thirty-five performances to thirty-seven per cent box office (the Simpson, in a double bill, played to forty-one per cent and the Jellicoe twenty-three per cent). When the play was broadcast on television in 1960, with John back in the lead, it was well received.

Not only had the play been produced by England's leading new play theatre, it had been published by the prestigious Faber and Faber. In fact, Faber published two versions in 1958. The original version is more elegiac and loquacious; the revised version blunter, more insistently dramatic. At the end, Sophia now slaps Ephraim, who is presented as harder, more selfish, more desperate to escape. 'TAKE ME OUT OF THIS BLASTED PLACE!' he cries.[28] In the first version, his exit is in silence. Tynan privately was furious that Banbury had made John rewrite, and John found the entire experience of the rewriting and the production depressing. He was angry at the 'unreal' and 'sentimental' tone of the production and would not let the play be revived in Britain until he was allowed to direct it himself, in 1986 at the Theatre Royal Stratford East.[29] Philip Hedley, who was running Stratford East, said meeting John represented 'a serious turning point' in his commitment to black theatre.[30] The play was performed to much praise off-Broadway in 1962 with James Earl Jones and has been seen in more than two dozen countries since. A 1988 revival, just before John died, at the Almeida, north London was directed by Maya Angelou, who made cuts, which John did not like. Already angry, according to Tyrone Huggins, because he believed he had been promised the production, John prevented Angelou and her producer Oprah Winfrey taking it to America and filming it.[31] Underlining its importance, *Moon on a Rainbow Shawl* was revived again in 2003 as the first production of the Eclipse initiative aimed at overcoming racism in the British theatre.

Despite film appearances and lead roles in radio and television and having three plays broadcast on television, John remained frustrated, whether in Britain, the United States, or the Caribbean. He had picked up his stage career at the Royal Court in *A Member of the Wedding* (1957) and eventually won the honour he had been seeking, to play Othello. Caspar Wrede, who directed the 1960 TV version of *Moon on a Rainbow Shawl*, invited John to the Old Vic (because the first-choice white actor had died, it was rumoured). Here he played the Prince of Morocco in *The Merchant of Venice* in 1962 and, in 1963, Othello and Barnadine in *Measure for Measure*. He lacked practice in his verse speaking, and the reviews for his Moor found him introspective and underpowered; it was not the triumph he had hoped for. Subsequently, he was absent from the stage as he refused to accept debasing parts (though he had to pull out of a Hedley production of Barrie Keeffe's *The King of England* in 1987 because he could not remember his lines). Known as a perfectionist, John was, as Hedley put it, 'a respected, highly professional artist and a very proud man, with many qualities which justified his pride'.[32] Pearl Connor believes he became increasingly frustrated at not achieving what he thought he would and could achieve and that, had he been white, he would have received a great deal more recognition. 'The talent was always there but the ability to project it wasn't', she said. 'He virtually dropped out altogether....Isolated, lonely, feeling forgotten and dejected, he died alone in his bed – he was found by his landlady. It was a tragic end to one of our most talented artistes'.[33]

It was not surprising that *Moon on a Rainbow Shawl* had found its way to the Royal Court. Under the new management of the English Stage Company, there had been several productions that included black actors, and it became an important venue for the black theatre community, offering validation from the heart of liberal white theatre. The Court's second show, *The Crucible* (1956), had Brooklyn-born former variety artiste Connie Smith playing Tituba, and she appeared again the following year in *The Member of the Wedding* by the (white) American writer Carson McCullers, along with Bertice Reading, Errol John, and Orlando Martins; it was not a success, however, and had to be replaced after a month. The Court employed black actors in the late 1950s/early 1960s in other productions by both black and white writers, such as Tennessee Williams's *Orpheus Descending*; Donald Howarth's *Lady on the Barometer* (a.k.a. *Sugar in the Morning*); Wole Soyinka's *The Invention* (Sunday night without décor, his first professionally performed play); Harold Pinter's *The Room* (from Hampstead); a Derek Walcott double bill, *Sea at Dauphin* and *The Six in the Rain*; Jean Genet's *The Blacks*; and Edward Albee's double bill *The Death of Bessie Smith* and *The American Dream*. This presence continued in subsequent decades, enhanced by Writers Workshops and the Royal Court Young People's Theatre, both of which helped non-white artists to develop.

In 1957, Wole Soyinka had joined the Court as a play reader, becoming a member of the theatre's (later much heralded) Writers' Group. The following year, in addition to *Moon on a Rainbow Shawl*, the Royal Court presented a programme of black poetry – 'Black and Unknown Bards' staged by Gordon Heath with Earle Hyman and Cleo Laine – and its first play by a black British subject, *Flesh to a Tiger* by Jamaican playwright Barry Reckord.[34] It came six months before John's play – and was also the first at the Court to have a substantial black cast, which was led by London-born Laine – but it failed to make the impact of *Moon on a Rainbow Shawl*.

Set in a poor area on the outskirts of Kingston, Jamaica, *Flesh to a Tiger* concerns a woman's survival in the face of both superstition and colonialism. It was a revised

FIGURE 5.3   Barry Reckord's *Flesh to a Tiger*, Royal Court, 1958 (Courtesy of David Sim)

version of a play called *Adella*, which Reckord wrote at Cambridge University and which was produced at the Theatre Centre, north London in 1954, directed by brother Lloyd.[35] A friend sent the play to the Court, who had the title changed. The Court's associate artistic director Tony Richardson liked the poetry of the play and its use of local language but felt the play lacked dramatic tension.[36] Indeed, Richardson's production at the Court managed only fifteen per cent box office (but incurred the highest production costs of the year). One critic called it a shanty town melodrama 'which hardly at any point carries conviction', whereas another thought the play 'too strong meat for English stomachs'.[37]

    Flesh to a Tiger was the first of five plays by Reckord to be produced at the Royal Court. It was followed by *You in Your Small Corner* (a Cheltenham Everyman production seen on a Sunday night without décor in 1960, transferred to the Arts in 1961, and broadcast on television in 1962); *Skyvers* (1963, at first without décor on a Sunday night, and then in the main auditorium; it was staged with white actors because the Royal Court said they could not find any black actors, and was revived, with white actors still, in 1971 at the Theatre Upstairs under the Young People's Theatre Scheme before transferring to the Roundhouse. *Skyvers* remains Reckord's best known play. He turned it into a musical called *Streetwise*, which toured in 1982); *Give the Gaffers Time To Love You* (1973, Theatre Upstairs); and *X* (1974, Theatre Upstairs, co-produced with Joint Stock, about the sexual education of children - a taboo subject - who had to be sensual with each other in the show, which included nudity. Tynan and *Time Out* liked it while others said it was pornography). Reckord, who also wrote for radio and television, deals convincingly with class (*Skyvers* offers a vigorous portrait of comprehensive school students being failed by society); the dilemma of black aspiration (*You in Your Small Corner* explores the anxiety of an ambitious black mother in Brixton when the son, who is going to Cambridge, falls in love with a white female neighbour she considers beneath him); and the contradictions of white liberalism and sexuality in relation to race (for example, in *Don't Gas the Blacks*, seen at the Open Space in 1969, and reworked as *A Liberated Woman*, Greenwich Theatre, 1971). His body of work, which includes one radio and two television plays, does not fall easily into the reportage or documentary category beloved of critics for whom witnessing the black experience is a revelation. Reckord's plays have not been given the recognition they deserve and have been unjustly overshadowed by others.

Soyinka became the best-known of the non-white diasporic writers associated with the Court. The first African to win the Nobel Prize for Literature, he was born in Abeokuta, Nigeria in 1934, came to the University of Leeds 1954-1957 to study for a BA in English, and was attached to the Royal Court 1957–1959 as play reader. He had directed his play *The Swamp Dwellers* for a student drama festival in London before the Court presented his production of *The Invention*. Written while he was attached to the theatre but not published, *The Invention* addresses apartheid – a rocket wipes out skin colour, so scientists invent ways of bringing back racism. It was accompanied by poems for a play in progress, *A Dance of the Forest*, later performed on his return to Nigeria to celebrate independence in 1960. Soyinka acted in and contributed to the writing of and music for another Sunday night production without décor, *Eleven Men Dead at Hola Camp* (1959), a dramatization of the beating and stamping to death of suspected Mau-Mau prisoners in Kenya. Such a production was unusual in those days before documentary drama had made its impact and, coming after the violence of the 'nigger hunting' whites that led to the Notting Hill and other riots, it represents an important opportunity to reclaim space for an alternative perspective on current events.[38] Soyinka had left Britain by the time British theatre took an interest in him in the mid-1960s, with the world première of *The Road* (1965) at the Theatre Royal Stratford East (on which he advised), *The Trials of Brother Jero* (1965/6) in Cambridge and Hampstead, and *The Lion and the Jewel* (1966) at the Royal Court.

His astonishing tragedy, *The Road*, is a complex story drawing on the formal conventions that underpin much of western European dramaturgy but in an African setting and context, both physically and spiritually. A professor, trapped in his obsession with finding the meaning of life and death, changes road signs to cause accidents to experiment with the victims, who occupy a state somewhere between life and death. The play is remarkable for its use of a range of linguistic and dramatic registers that, through the carnage, embody a Faustian sense of dynamic possibility. *The Road* was presented as part of the first Commonwealth Arts Festival by Stage Sixty, which had taken over Stratford East in 1964 for a three-year period, and the cast included Horace James as the professor, and Bari Jonson, Alton Kumalo, and Rudolph Walker.[39] The play was later revived by Talawa to open the company's residency at the Jeanetta Cochrane Theatre.

The Trials of Brother Jero, a picaresque romp exposing the greed and hypocrisy of a self-appointed evangelist-cum-prophet, was presented with Athol Fugard's *Blood*

Knot by the Ijinle Theatre Company, founded to stage plays by African writers and supported by the Arts Council.[40] Fugard, a white South African writer, had formed Ijinle (Yoruba for *deep*) with a group of African actors resident in London, notably Lionel Ngakane, along with Denis Duerden, a white Englishman who had been involved in Nigerian education in the 1950s and who promoted African arts on his return to London.[41] Ijinle also produced *The Lion and the Jewel*. It played at the Leicester University Commonwealth Arts Festival in 1967, where the company also performed John Pepper Clark's *The Raft* and Lindsay Barrett's *Jump Kookoo Makka*. Soyinka won the John Whiting Award in 1967, the year he surrendered himself to Nigerian authorities, went on a hunger strike, and was tried for treason. A group called Harmony Culture Theatre Group performed his play, *The Strong Breed*, at the Mercury, west London, in 1968 while he was in prison. Despite the National Theatre's presenting the world première of *The Bacchae of Euripides* in 1973 and productions such as *Before the Blackout* (Leeds, 1981) and *Death and the King's Horseman* (Manchester, 1990), Soyinka has never been given his due in the British theatre. Perhaps the National Theatre revival of *Death and the King's Horseman* (2009) suggests a different future for his extraordinary mix of Yoruba heritage and world drama that has created a vibrant African theatre of ritual, dance, and song enthused by a strong sense of universal morality.

During the late 1950s, another progressive white theatre company, Theatre Workshop at the Theatre Royal Stratford East, was also employing a few black actors. This was most prominent in Shelagh Delaney's 1958 play, *A Taste of Honey*, which caused controversy because of the sexual relationship between the white teenage Jo and Jimmie, a black sailor, who fathers her child. Prefiguring a later strong commitment to supporting black and Asian theatre, the Theatre Royal Stratford East hosted not only *The Road* but productions by the Ira Aldridge Players, the New Negro Theatre Company, and the New Negro Theatre Workshop, each one an attempt to form a black theatre group. In the mainstream commercial sector, black theatre was still dominated by African-American input, but even this was a rarity, such as the Langston Hughes's musical *Simply Heavenly* (Adelphi, 1958 with Bertice Reading); Lorraine Hansberry's *A Raisin in the Sun* (Adelphi, 1959); and Hughes's *Black Nativity* (Criterion, 1962). Though such shows occasionally offered roles to black British actors, British commercial theatre had nothing to compare with television and generally was not responding as sharply to the black presence in Britain, though television itself remained a white bastion as well.

The much-celebrated 'new wave' of British playwriting that took off in the mid-1950s may have dealt with the effects of empire in plays such as *Serjeant Musgrave's Dance* or *The Entertainer*, but it did not deal with the experience of imperial subjects. Despite the major issues thrown up by the end of empire, it was rare for white stage playwrights to deal with diasporic topics or characters. There were exceptions, such as *A Taste of Honey* and *Hot Summer Night* by the British writer and ex-Unity stalwart Ted Willis, both of which have working-class settings and depict interracial sexual relations. In *Hot Summer Night*, the values of a white working-class trade union leader are tested when his daughter falls in love with a Jamaican (played by Lloyd

FIGURE 5.4 Sylvia Earle and Neville Munroe in *Anna Christie,* performed by the West Indian Drama Group, 1959 (Tropic magazine. Courtesy of British Library)

Reckord), an angry young black man as opposed to the angry young white men of Royal Court fame. The play, which opened a month before *Moon on a Rainbow Shawl* in November 1958, was well received but also elicited hate mail and press stories claiming it was the first time a black man had kissed a white woman on the stage (ignoring a similar ruckus over Robeson and Ashcroft in *Othello* nearly thirty years earlier let alone Aldridge's brush with newspapers the previous century). One Saturday matinee during the kissing scene, remembers Reckord, a 'frail, rather timid and very gentle voice called out from the stalls – "I don't like to see white girls kissing niggers." There was dead silence in the theatre, and we went on with the play'.[42] Willis claimed in his autobiography that it was the first West End play to confront racism – *A Taste of Honey* transferred to the West End a couple of months later.[43]

Shows rarely featured black performers centrally in either the art or the commercial sector. Again, there were exceptions, such as *Mister Johnson*, an adaptation of Joyce Carey's novel at the Lyric, Hammersmith in 1960 that had Johnny Sekka in the lead; *Cindy-Ella, or I Gotta Shoe* (1962, Garrick), a black Christmas entertainment by white Caryl Brahms and Ned Sherrin with George Browne (a.k.a. the Young Tiger), Cleo Laine, Cy Grant, and Elizabeth Welch; or *Martin Luther King* by Ewan Hooper, with Bari Jonson as King, which opened the Greenwich Theatre in 1969. Attempts to counter this situation often looked to the white Western canon: the drama society at the Commonwealth Institute under Peter Munk staged multiracial productions, such as *Miss Julie*, and the opening production in 1965 of the multiracial Concord Drama Group at the Commercial Hall in London's East End was a double bill of Sartre's *The Respectable Prostitute* and Albee's *The Death of Bessie Smith*.[44] Concord also appeared at Unity, which generated two white-led initiatives to form black groups: the West Indian Drama Group based at the West Indian Students' Union and founded by Joan Clarke in 1956, and the Ira Aldridge Players set up by Herbert Mai_ 1961. Clarke, a collaborator of Lionel Bart's who was responsible for training _ Unity and who introduced acting classes for the West Indian Drama Group, directed for the British Council Karel Čapek's *The Insect Play* and Robert Ardrey's *Thunder Rock* with all-black casts. The group also presented William Saroyan's *The Time of Your Life*, Jules Romain's *Dr Knock*, and Shaw's *Androcles and the Lion*. Probably her most successful production for the group was the all-black Caribbean production it took to Unity in 1959 of O'Neill's *Anna Christie*, an idea possibly motivated by the success of *Anna Lucasta*, which was said to have been inspired by O'Neill's play.[45] Clarke's production featured Carmen Munroe, who was to become an important figure in the development of black theatre in Britain.[46]

Intended as a permanent black theatre company, the Ira Aldridge Players, despite its aims, produced only one show, probably because its founder went to the United States and settled there. Marshall had directed Paul Robeson at Unity and was the co-author (with Mildred Stock) of the pioneering biography of Ira Aldridge. The Players' show, *Do Somethin' Addy Man!*, was a reworking of the Alcestis story set in contemporary Camden Town, London: a young singer, the black Alcestis, takes work in a night club to save her family from eviction and to give her husband the chance to write. The book and lyrics were written by Jack Russell (white), the music was by George Browne, and the twenty-two-strong cast was all black.[47]

Black theatre groups

The need for groups under black leadership grew stronger. The various initiatives described earlier came and went while a significant pool of black actors emerged hungry for work they could believe in. The duration of the groups that emerged was often brief, and they had similar and changing names, frequently crossing between amateur and professional, as, for example, the Caribbean Students Performance Group based at the West Indian Students' Centre, which acted as a vital base for cultural activity in the absence of a dedicated space. Lloyd Reckord founded the New Day Theatre Company in 1960 to present plays by black writers. He directed the British premières of two short plays by Derek Walcott – *Sea at Dauphin* and *The Six in the Rain* – in a production without décor at the Royal Court that transferred to the Tower Theatre, north London for a fortnight, but then the company folded. Young Jamaican actor Clifton Jones launched the New Negro Theatre Company in April 1960. He had studied at the Italia Conti stage school and appeared while a teenager in *The Good Sailor* (based on *Billy Budd*) in 1956, *Moon on a Rainbow Shawl* and the West End transfer of *A Taste of Honey*. For his new company, Jones directed and appeared in a Sunday performance of two plays by white Americans at the Theatre Royal Stratford East: *Hello, Out There!* by William Saroyan (in which a young man is falsely charged with rape and shot by a husband who cannot bear the truth about his wife) and *No 'Count Boy* by Paul Green (in which a dreamer turns a young woman's head but proves to be a waster). Jones mounted further Sunday performances at Stratford East that year: Molière's *The Imaginary Invalid* in June and, in November, two plays by himself set in Jamaica, *La Mère* and the *The S Bend*, which examines why young working-class Caribbeans leave the region. The group was using the Theatre Royal until becoming established and had plans to mount Soyinka's *The Lion and the Jewel*, but the company disbanded before producing any more plays, probably because Jones became a regular feature of *Emergency Ward 10*, the first black actor to gain a continuing role in a television soap.[48]

Another attempt at establishing a black theatre came in 1961 with the launch of the Negro Theatre Workshop, and it made a much-more-lasting impact. It was organized by Edric and Pearl Connor, two people who were central to the postwar history of black theatre in Britain, providing guidance and inspiration over many years. Edric Connor, born in Mayaro, Trinidad and Tobago in 1913, was a man of many talents: actor, singer, writer, director, dancer, filmmaker, folklorist, and advocate for Caribbean arts, who dedicated his time in Britain to improving opportunities for British-based black performers.[49] He recorded several albums, such as *Songs from Jamaica* (1954), *Songs from Trinidad*, and *Calypso* (both 1955), and his books include *The Edric Connor Collection of West Indian Spirituals and Folk Songs* (1945), *Songs from Trinidad* (1958), and his posthumously published autobiography *Horizons* (2007), written in the early 1960s when he was recovering from a heart attack.[50] His leading role is symbolized by the invitation extended to him to appear at the dedication of the new Coventry Cathedral in 1962.

By the time he came to Britain in the early 1940s, Connor had won a railway scholarship to study engineering and had been a reporter and a singer who had promoted indigenous culture. He arrived by way of New York, where he sang, and he enrolled in an Essex technical college before joining the war effort in a factory making gun components in London's docklands. He brought with him letters of introduction to the BBC, where he immediately began what became a long and distinguished broadcasting career, including the popular television music show *Serenade in Sepia* (1945–1947) with contralto Evelyn Dove. He moved between theatre, radio, film, and TV, appearing in the West End and club theatres and making guest appearances in student productions at RADA and Rose Bruford, where he was awarded the drama school's first honorary diploma. Connor arranged for what is thought to be the first Trinidadian steel band to play in England, at the Festival of Britain in 1951, and his own musical prowess was used in revue and in shows such as *Calypso* (1948); *The Shrike* (1953); *The Jazz Train* (1955, promoted as 'The All-Negro Musical'); and *Summer Song* (1956). At the Irving, he devised *Cabaret Caribbean* (1952) and, in 1955, directed there a double bill, *Junction Village* (by Douglas Archibald) and his own *A Caribbean Revue*, which featured a black cast including Nadia Cattouse and the West African Rhythm Brothers.[51] In 1958, Connor became probably the first black actor to appear in Shakespeare at Stratford upon Avon when he played a balladeer Gower in *Pericles*. He appeared in a multiracial cast in *The First Nowell* at Drury Lane in 1958 but was never invited to perform at Covent Garden, which, in common with the British opera world in general, preferred American singers. Possible extended exposure in Nigel Dennis's *August for the People* (1961) starring Rex Harrison at the Royal Court was denied when Harrison left the show after two

FIGURE 5.5 Edric and Pearl Connor (Courtesy of The Main Library, The University of the West Indies St. Augustine, Trinidad)

weeks, and the production was withdrawn. Connor also trained at the BBC to be a producer and director, but he was offered no commissions by them, and breaking into that side of the screen profession proved as difficult as getting decent work as a singer or actor. Nevertheless, on the strength of the documentary films he did make, on subjects such as cricket and carnival, he could claim to be Britain's first black film director. Ill health in the 1960s made finding work even more problematic, though he continued to make a number of screen appearances and, after suffering a stroke, he died in 1968 aged 55.

Pearl Connor, who was born Pearl Nunez in 1924 in Diego Martin, Trinidad and Tobago, was an actress, theatrical and literary agent, publisher and, like Edric, a cultural activist, promoting African and Caribbean arts. The ninth of twelve children, she came from an educated, mixed-heritage background and was immersed in the arts and anti-colonial ideology before she came to Britain. She met Derek Walcott when she toured the Caribbean arguing for a West Indies Youth Federation, and he and his friends invited her to speak at their school. She met Edric at Trinidad's Little Carib Theatre, started by Beryl McBurnie, her greatest influence, who helped her get into broadcasting in Trinidad. Pearl and Edric married in June 1948, the year she returned with Edric to Britain to study law. As a student, she co-founded the West Indian Students' Centre in Earl's Court, where activities included presenting plays. She gave up her studies to manage Edric's career and promote African and Caribbean culture. The Connors formed part of a circle of Caribbean expatriates who became leaders of their diasporic community in politics and the arts, people such as Winifred Atwell, Learie Constantine, Rudolph Dunbar, Cy Grant, C. L. R. James, Claudia Jones, Sam Morris, George Padmore, and David Pitt. The Connors's house became a gathering place for aspiring artists and for cultural and political activists, and it provided a forum for initiatives such as the founding of London's Carnival, which Edric directed in 1959.

Pearl studied at Rose Bruford, a drama school that offered places to several artists who became catalytic figures in black British theatre. She was involved with productions at the Hans Crescent Student Hostel, the British Council premises that housed a small theatre, and she worked as a broadcaster, and occasionally as an actor, for BBC radio, making regular appearances on their Caribbean Service. There were sporadic appearances on stage, including in Barry Reckord's *You in Your Small Corner* at the Royal Court in 1960; in events such as *Beyond the Blues*, a performance of civil rights poetry at the Aldeburgh Festival in 1962; and in films such as *O Lucky Man!* (1973). She served on the Arts Council Drama Panel and on the committee organizing the London celebrations of Trinidad's independence, and was secretary of a group opposing the 1962 West Indies Bill, which would dissolve the West Indies Federation and return the remaining eight colonies that had not achieved independence to rule from London. She also worked with anti-racist organizations, the Caribbean Artists' Movement, and on the Notting Hill Carnival Committee. After Edric's death, Pearl married the leading South African singer, Joe Mogotsi, in 1971.[52] Pearl contributed to various radio and TV documentaries and, in 2003, introduced a screening at the National Film Theatre of Edric's 1960 film, *Carnival Fantastique*, which had been thought lost. The Trinidad and Tobago government honoured her in 1972, but no recognition came in Britain until she received the National Black Women's Achievement Award in 1992. She died in South Africa in 2005.

In the mid-1950s, the Connors returned to the Caribbean where Edric was filming, and local performers who were planning to come to Britain asked their advice. When the Connors came back to Britain, they were determined to help such performers and the growing pool of black actors who were still finding many obstacles in their way. These actors were rarely offered 'non-black' parts on the grounds that audiences were not ready for this, and many of the 'black' parts were debasing. There was also the issue of accent. Caribbean actors found they were not considered to speak 'proper' English but were given no opportunity to develop the required Received Pronunciation, had they wanted to. Conversely, American English was deemed acceptable (in certain roles), but Caribbean actors did not have that accent either. In response to this lack of opportunity, the Connors set up the Edric Connor Agency in 1956. It later went under other names, including the Afro-Asian Caribbean Agency, and lasted for twenty years, during which time Pearl estimated it represented nearly ninety per cent of the non-white actors in Britain.[53] It campaigned for the rights of black British actors, for example, on the numbers of African-American actors allowed to work in Britain, and on replacing them after six months. After several years of agitation, the agency helped persuade Equity, the actors' union, to establish a Coloured Artists' Sub-Committee (in 1965) and to promote 'integrated' or non-traditional, 'colour-blind' casting, which the union undertook in 1968, even though in practice it did little to enforce the policy.[54] Equality legislation allowed exemptions for the needs of 'authenticity', which meant discrimination could continue without legal redress.

Besides being involved in casting 'black' plays such as *A Raisin in the Sun*, the agency helped cast actors for West End shows such as *The World of Suzy Wong* (1959), *Flower Drum Song* (1960), and *The Black Mikado* (1975). The breakthrough for Pearl came when she saw the 1961 South African township show *King Kong*, which tells the story of a black boxing champion who could not get a fight with the white champion and commits suicide. The expertise of the cast opened up the possibility of non-Americans being cast in major roles, a realization underpinned by a range of black performances from different countries seen during the World Theatre Seasons at the Aldwych Theatre. These seasons, however, fed nothing other than inspiration into the British theatre scene, and the agency was pleased when producer Robert Stigwood, in productions such as *Hair* (1968) and *Jesus Christ Superstar* (1972), aimed for at least a third of each cast to be non-European or non-white. The agency helped launch artists such as Joan Armatrading, discovered through a Manchester audition, Floella Benjamin, and Patricia Ebigwei (Patti Boulaye). Of her time trying to promote black artists, Pearl said:

> …to get any kind of money, any recognition was very tough. We were trying to build reputations, get people recognised. The moment an artist received a press review, you blew them up. You do whatever you could with them and send them round to let everybody know. After all, they had to build a history, a black history, a black theatre here.[55]

The agency was also involved in theatre production (e.g., the 'All-Coloured Revue' *Blackbirds of 1964*), in producing films, such as *Carnival Fantastique* and the cricketing documentary *West Indies vs England* (1963), and in helping distribute films such as *The Harder They Come* (1972), *Pressure* (1975), and *Smile Orange* (1976).

Central to the Connors's struggle was the recognition of the importance of autonomy, that space had to be created by and for oneself. As Pearl said,

> Nobody will honour us or keep our image alive or remember our contribution. We have to do so ourselves and record our history through books, literature, music and the arts. We need our own icons, our own heroes.[56]

Both the Connors had been associated with postwar attempts to establish black theatre and had helped keep alive the notion of forming a black theatre company. Edric had led the formation of the NTC in the late 1940s and had experienced its demise. Pearl, who wrote to friends in the West Indies such as Errol Hill asking for Caribbean plays, had been involved with the Hans Crescent Theatre in the early 1950s and had formed the Caribbean Theatre Trust with Lloyd Reckord to try out plays by Barry Reckord at a house in Hampstead. Edric and Pearl had seen other attempts to found a black company fail and the trauma of apparently successful individuals such as Errol John having to operate in an alien culture. The general situation had deteriorated since *Moon on a Rainbow Shawl* had opened in the wake of the 1958 riots, a moment when racism gained a new public profile and made a collective impact on the non-white community as a whole. The Connors were involved in the cultural response to the riots and what they represented when the forerunner of the Notting Hill Carnival was launched with costumes, singing, dancing, and Caribbean food, an assertion of the values of the community under attack.

This retort renewed their belief in the need for a theatre company, but they were aware of the problems they faced: there was still a relatively small community to draw on; there were tensions between Africans and West Indians and between islanders, each with strong particular loyalties who understandably resented having a common identity forced on them by a racist British society; there was the predicament of ambition, balancing personal survival against collective advance; and there was scarcity of resources, training, and experience. Nevertheless, in 1961, the Connors decided it was worth trying again to form a company, and they called together at the Mercury Theatre, Notting Hill a large group of black actors and writers, mostly Caribbean, to found the Negro Theatre Workshop (NTW).[57] The aim was to put on 'regular productions, so as to give negro artists and writers experience and by so doing to help develop and improve standards in every branch of the theatre'.[58] The actors included Nina Baden-Semper, George Browne, Ena Cabayo, Leo Carrera, Tony Cyrus, Horace James, Bari Jonson, Carmen Munroe, and Bobby Naidoo. Many were involved in the sporadic cultural events that were organized by the Caribbean community – such as Jonson, who in 1963 devised *Ex-Africa*, a programme of African, American, and Caribbean texts that went to the Edinburgh Fringe Festival and the ICA – but they wanted to create a context that was both more reliable and more in their control, hence the NTW.

Run initially from the Connors's agency in Paddington Street, the NTW was to be moved to the Mercury, a small and vacant theatre that also attracted the attention of the Royal Shakespeare Company, but this ambitious plan came to nothing owing to lack of finance, and the NTW had to survive without a proper base. The NTW organized classes for actors and produced plays in churches, town halls, community centres and purpose-built theatres. It rehearsed in places such as the West Indian Students' Centre and the Africa Centre in Covent Garden, which had also opened in 1961. Recognising the reality of the situation and wary of being seen as exclusively black (apartheid in reverse, as Pearl Connor once put it), the NTW reached out to sympathetic whites for support and involvement.[59] Indeed, Pearl always said the NTW wanted to show British audiences that black people were just like them, human beings facing similar problems.

The first production with which it was associated was seen at the Lyric, Hammersmith in November 1961 and began with a preview in aid of, and to launch, the NTW and the West Indian Theatre Trust (co-founded by Pearl to support the NTW). The preview featured a steel band and Creole supper prepared under Pearl's supervision. The play was *A Wreath for Udomo*, adapted by an African-American playwright William Branch from a South African novel by black writer Peter Abrahams. The play had been produced by the African-American Karamu Theatre and optioned for Broadway and was presented in Britain by two American producers. The director was Philip Burton, Richard's father, and the cast included NTW members Harry Baird, Earl Cameron, Edric Connor, André Dakar, Evelyn Dove, Joan Hooley, Horace James, and Lloyd Reckord. Pearl and others put in a great effort to make the preview a success, inviting a broad range of notables from the worlds of entertainment, politics, and business. Letters sent to Pearl suggest the preview, at which she spoke about the

NTW, was a success.[60] Unfortunately, on the following evening – the official first night – Edric Connor collapsed during the opening night performance and the understudy was not ready to go on. That meant the end for the show, and Pearl subsequently had difficulty getting the money the NTW was owed from the show's producers. The chaos and trauma of the first night left the company in disarray.

People associated with the NTW maintained involvement in various collective activities, such as the event mounted at the Royal Festival Hall by the Movement for Colonial Freedom in 1963 called *No Man is an Island*, but it was not until 1964 that the NTW mounted its first own production. This was *Bethlehem Blues*, a musical retelling of the nativity from a Notting Hill perspective, in which tolerance replaces hostility, written by Trinidadian singer George Webb and directed by a white BBC producer, Christian Simpson, the director of *No Man is an Island*. A pioneer of dance on television, Simpson played an important role in keeping the NTW afloat.[61] The show toured churches in London with a cast that included Nina Baden-Semper, Tommy Eytle, Isabelle Lucas (narrator), Carmen Munroe, Corinne Skinner, Rudolph Walker (the voice of God), and Webb as Joseph. The success of *Bethlehem Blues* fed the desire to establish a permanent, professional company with its own theatre, which Pearl Connor believed might be in a converted church. As the next step, NTW staged in 1965 another tour of churches with *Dark Disciples*, a blues version of St. Luke's Passion, adapted musically by the Guyanese pianist Mike McKenzie and directed again by Simpson, who had become the company's artistic advisor. Simpson adapted *Dark Disciples* for BBC TV, and it was filmed at the blitzed St. Mary-le-Bow Church in London's East End.

With new-found confidence, the NTW approached the Commonwealth Office to participate in the first Commonwealth Arts Festival to be held in Britain in 1965. The reply was negative: the festival was designed to present art by overseas citizens, not resident immigrants. There was discussion about the NTW's being involved with the Errol Hill play *Man Better Man* but, in the end, this contribution to the Festival was an entirely Trinidadian affair.[62] The NTW's suggestion of a Festival fringe was also turned down, but the company was able to stage a related event that was advertised in Festival literature. This production was another biblical show, *The Prodigal Son*, by Lawrence Waddy and was seen at St. Martin-in-the-Fields with a supporting programme of spirituals and poems selected by Caribbean writer Andrew Salkey. Among the audience was Britain's first Arts Minister Jennie Lee.

To compensate for the NTW's absence from the official festival, the first World Festival of Negro Arts, held in Dakar, Senegal in 1966, invited the NTW to represent Britain with *The Dark Disciples*, which was performed twice in Dakar's Cathedral, on Easter Sunday and Monday. Confusion over expenses, with only fares being paid, led the NTW to launch an appeal to cover the costs of accommodation, subsistence, and payment to artists. Also invited was the Pan African Players, another group rejected by the Commonwealth Arts Festival. The company comprised Yemi Ajibade, Illario Bisi-Pedro, the leader Earl Cameron, Bari Jonson, and Alaba Peters. It was based at African Unity House and aimed to be a platform for black actors in Britain. The group's only show was *Wind versus Polygamy* by Obi Egbuna, adapted from his novel about an African country newly emerged from colonial rule and caught between its own customs and those of its former rulers. The production, which was broadcast on BBC Radio, won Best Director award in Dakar for Ajibade and was nominated for Best Production.[63] Together, the NTW and Pan African Players presented in the Dakar stadium *The Journey*, a show about slavery and the evolution of African art, and a variety programme.

The NTW, however, was also involved tangentially in the official Commonwealth Festival, which featured theatre from Trinidad and Nigeria.[64] Pearl Connor helped cast Soyinka's *The Road*, the producers gave a charity preview for the NTW, and the play's director, David Thompson, joined the NTW advisory board. The charity showing was designed to raise funds for the NTW's not-for-profit trust, which was in the process of being formed. Establishing the Trust in November 1965 was the result of Pearl Connor's hard work to turn the NTW into an organization that would function properly and professionally. It had a council of management, which was chaired by the noted Barbadian novelist George Lamming, and a working committee that oversaw the planning and running of the NTW's activities.

Bari Jonson devised a show to celebrate the founding of the Trust, which had gathered an impressive list of patrons from politics, religion, and the arts. The list included its president, the celebrated cricketer Sir Learie Constantine; Sir Jock Campbell; George Devine; Oscar Lewenstein; Joan Littlewood; Spike Milligan; Sir Laurence Olivier; Sidney Poitier; Dr. Rosey E. Pool; Archbishop Michael Ramsay, the Archbishop of Canterbury; and the Rev Austen Williams. The company was emphasizing inclusivity in its repertoire and its ethos. This was reflected in adding the country of origin to the cast list of *The Prodigal Son*, as the League of Coloured Peoples had done for *At What a Price*. Links between the NTW and the church remained strong – it was a source of support and anti-racist activity – and in December 1966 with an act called 'We Real Cool, Christmas in a Negro Community', the company opened *The 1966 Christmas Matinee* produced by St. Martin-in-the-Fields at the Drury Lane Theatre in aid of the Bhoodan Movement of India and War on Want.

After several attempts, the NTW received its first Arts Council grant in 1965–1966, a sum of £300 (which it received again in 1966–1967 but nothing thereafter).[65] The NTW had been turned down before on the grounds that it was amateur, and it had been shunted from the music panel, which thought its standards insufficiently high, to the drama panel, which eventually made the award. Although the sum was small, this was probably the first grant a black theatre company had received from the Arts Council, an organization that, despite its roots in popular wartime initiatives, had become locked into its role as patrician guardian of the cultural pyramid rather than enabler and promoter of broad cultural activity. The Council ignored many theatre constituencies – amateur theatre, for example, or theatre for the young, and theatre with a non-European heritage. Non-white diasporic theatre missed out on the funding gear change of the 1960s, when Jennie Lee significantly increased grants for culture, and it did not claim much funding attention until the 1970s.

In 1966, the NTW wanted to prove its professional credentials with an ambitious project and tried to break free of its folksy religious image by producing Henry A.

Zeiger's *Mr. Hubert*, an American play about a Harlem Everyman figure (played by Horace James) and based on a novel by actor and writer Julian Mayfield. With a cast of more than thirty, it was presented in association with the Tavistock Repertory Company, one of Britain's leading amateur companies, to open the Tavistock season at the Tower Theatre. The production made nothing for the NTW at the box office and meant its being more realistic but, nonetheless, the NTW continued to look for venues and shows beyond the church sector. For example, the company presented folk music and *Chekhov in the Caribbean* (adaptations of two short plays) as part of the Camden Committee for Community Relations' International Festival during UN Week in 1966 and visited the International Students' Club. The NTW also presented evenings of poetry and programmes of song, dance, and music, such as *Jump Up* (performed at King's Hall, Hackney in 1967), and toured to places such as Manchester (for a West Indian Arts Festival), Southampton (for an Amnesty International event), and Leicester. Here they presented *The Prodigal Son* in the Cathedral as part of Leicester University's 1967 Commonwealth Arts Festival along with two short plays: Errol Hill's *Dance Bongo* and Derek Walcott's *The Sea at Dauphin* staged in the festival's theatre space. The NTW also appeared at events organized by associations within the black community, such as the West Indian Standing Conference, and ran well-attended weekly training sessions. There were plans to mount a show called *Jonah* and to take a production to the Edinburgh Festival, but nothing came of them.

As part of its drive to broaden its appeal and secure a base, the NTW wanted to move into Wilton's Music Hall in London's East End, which had been saved from demolition. A lease was agreed with the Greater London Council on the understanding that the NTW received a regular grant to manage it, an arrangement that was under discussion between the GLC and the Arts Council. The idea was to run a club, restaurant, and workshops as well as a repertoire that ranged from Shakespeare to new African and black plays by writers such as George Lamming, Barry Reckord, and Sam Selvon. By the time of Edric Connor's death in 1968, however, the funding had not been given, and the company had ceased to be active. It had helped forge a presence for black theatre and offer opportunities for black creativity that were to be developed in the succeeding years. The problem for the NTW was want of suitable material, working in a vacuum without a supportive contex, and, above all, lack of resources. There was also a discernable political shift in attitudes within the diasporic communities that took black theatre in a new direction.

Carnival

This shift occurred against a background of years of discrimination in housing, education, employment, and law and of rising white-on-black violence. The 1958 attacks were followed the next year by the racist murder of Antiguan carpenter Kelso Cochrane without anyone being convicted. The introduction of racist immigration legislation in 1962 raised tension further and contributed to a spiral of increased levels of public racism being accompanied in turn by anti-racist reform, culminating that decade in the 1968 Race Relations Act and Enoch Powell's infamous 'Rivers of Blood' speech. The cultural response to the 1958 riots had been Carnival, a proud display in performance and cuisine of self-validation and resistance. At the centre of the initiative was Claudia Jones, the Trinidadian Communist expelled from the United States for her political activity and founder-editor in 1958 of the *West Indian Gazette*, a project she hoped would bring unity to the British Caribbean community. Hardened by political struggle in America, she used her experience to mobilize with others what was probably the first Carnival in Britain. Sponsored by the *Gazette*, it was held indoors at St. Pancras Town Hall, north London as a celebration of Caribbean culture, complete with palm trees from Kew, at a time when many on the beleaguered community were still trying to secure their place in British society by 'fitting in' and imitating British mores.[66] In the souvenir programme, Jones wrote that, 'A people's art is the genesis of their freedom'. The BBC broadcast almost an hour of the Carnival cabaret (though no archive remains), and some of the proceeds of the sale of the programme went towards paying the fines of black and white youths involved in the Notting Hill 'events'.[67]

The Carnival subsequently alternated between venues in central London, with elements going to Manchester in 1962 and 1963, and did not take to the streets until 1965, when local social worker and community activist Rhaune Laslett, who knew nothing of the previous carnivals, staged a community event in Notting Hill. This week-long event was not specifically Trinidadian – the Caribbean roots of Carnival – but open to other Caribbean cultures, especially Jamaican with its sound systems, and to all the diasporic groups in the area. It turned into a street carnival by accident. A steel pan combo led by Trinidadians Russell Henderson and Sterling Bettancourt was playing when, according to Henderson, who had played at the first Carnival in 1959, he decided to walk his musicians up the street and back to liven up the event.[68] People followed, and the procession grew. Over the years, the Carnival became increasingly associated with the black British communities and evoked the spirit of the Trinidad original in its spontaneous, mass popular form, traditionally a platform for cultural resistance that authority has sought to contain. In Notting Hill, it became not just an expression of self-pride but a focus for struggles with the police (there was rioting in 1976 when police overstaffed the Carnival). The divisions within the diasporic community that Jones had hoped to overcome reasserted themselves, and organizing the Carnival has been riven by dissension and splits. Nevertheless, it continued to grow into an enormous and diverse street theatre event, one of the most important popular cultural manifestations in Europe.

Carnival influenced conventional theatre forms, both in plays about carnival, steel bands, and calypso and in the dramaturgy and use of music, dance, and costume in stage plays. In Britain, plays that dealt with Carnival have included Hill's *Man Better Man* (seen in Britain in 1965) and his version of *The Master of Carnival* (seen 1986); Beryl McBurnie's pageant, *Cannes Brulees* (1971); Mustapha Matura's *Play Mas* (1974) and *Rum an' Coca Cola* (1976); Trinidad Tent Theatre's *J'Ouvert* (which came on tour in 1982); and Earl Lovelace's *The Dragon Can't Dance* (1984). Carnival was not confined to London – Leeds, for instance, had its first carnival in 1967 – and its open-air cultural presence was not confined to Caribbean heritage, which, in the case especially of Trinidad, had Asian and African roots. South Asian communities, for example, hold their own, often massive melas (gathering or fair), and the one in Brick Lane in the East End of London is claimed to be the biggest in Europe and the largest Bengali event outside the subcontinent.

The self-help movement that gave rise to such celebrations of cultural identity spawned a multiplicity of projects in which social demands were inevitably framed according to political conviction, and that conviction was being altered as much by global as by national and local influences. Against the background of the Vietnam War, the growth of black power ideology in the United States embraced differentiated strategies for advancement and change, symbolized by the two leading figures in African-American politics: Martin Luther King and Malcolm X. Both visited Britain in the mid-1960s and helped galvanize ideas and the formation of organizations that in some ways overlapped but in other ways were quite distinct. For example, the militant Radical Action Adjustment Society, which aimed to connect African-Asian-Caribbean people, emphasized the importance of culture and identity and was non-white, whereas the more reform-minded Campaign Against Racial Discrimination, which brought together associations that represented Caribbean, Indian, and Pakistani people in Britain, focused on discrimination and allowed white people to join. The tensions between the two approaches were replicated in culture. Complex concepts relating to phenomenology, philosophy, and aesthetics were debated as part of the struggle to propel and manage the process of change. The debate played out a dialectic between notions of black identity: was it intrinsically damaged by being conceived within an oppressive white framework? Were universal notions inevitably racialized, or could they survive and outlast the imperial historical period as benchmarks of worth for all? Drawing on ideas that reached back to the 1930s and the negritude movement, one version of blackness saw it as a necessary antidote to and opposite of white colonial racism that would wither with time, whereas others stressed its integrity as forming one set of values among several, all equally valid.

The Caribbean Artists' Movement (CAM) was founded in 1966 amid this debate to raise the profile of Caribbean art in Britain and to create an aesthetic shaped by the values and perceptions of the African-Caribbean diaspora rather than by European concepts. The CAM became an important catalyst for diasporic cultural activity and helped give that activity a recognizable identity. The CAM discussed the role of the performing arts (for instance, at its first conference, held in 1967 at the University of Kent). Its members were involved in several shows, ranging from consciousness and fund-raising events to productions – for example, two plays performed in October 1967 at a week-long festival in Notting Hill: Langston Hughes's *Shakespeare in Harlem* and Ram Jam Holder's *Eviction Blues*, which deals with the notorious local slum landlord Rachman and the reality of London ghetto life.[69] The visit to Britain of the charismatic Black Power advocate Stokely Carmichael in 1967 gave added impetus to the wider debate, which can be seen represented in a play such as *Dutchman*, produced at Hampstead Theatre that year.[70] Written in 1964 by LeRoi Jones and set on the New York subway, it uses a claustrophobic structure and vivid, muscular language to dramatize through a shocking encounter of an amiable black man and a predatory white woman the violence of a society in which the coexistence of black and white is constantly being negotiated and mythologized. Jones changed his name after the assassination of Malcolm X in 1965 to Amiri Baraka and brought the notion of a black aesthetic to the fore. Black opinion was divided, but the assassination of Martin Luther King in 1968 and international radicalization after 1968 further fuelled the anger and determination to 'seize the time' and make change happen on terms set by the black, not the white, community.

6

NEW BEGINNINGS IN THE 1970S

Regardless of differences in response to ideas of black power, for African-Caribbean theatre in Britain, the rise of black consciousness and the general radicalization of politics reinvigorated the struggle for self-assertion artistically and organizationally. In the context of an intensification of clashes between the black community and the state, and given the nature of arts funding in Britain, this meant primarily creating space on the margins.[1] Yet, fuelled by its status as the Other and engendered despite and because of lack of resource, franchise, and access, the dynamic of black theatre carried with it a new sense of pride and even swagger that defied its marginal status.

Seeds of change

At the end of the 1960s, the nascent alternative theatre in London was deeply influenced by African-American music and 'seize the time' politics, but it largely ignored the black experience. A white British student, Roland Rees, who had completed his doctoral studies in the United States, returned to this vibrant scene and brought with him enthusiasm for the notion of black empowerment as well as a number of plays, including *The Electronic Nigger* by the African-American playwright and Black Panther Ed Bullins.[2] Rees took it to a newly formed cultural cooperative, InterAction, set up by former American Rhodes Scholar Ed Berman, and was given the chance to direct the play in July 1968 at InterAction's Ambiance Lunch Hour theatre in west London. Berman's showman instinct brought Bullins to the United Kingdom, and this gained much useful publicity. Rees soon directed two more of Bullins's plays, *A Minor Scene* and *It Has No Choice*, and two more the following year, *The Gentleman Caller* and *How Do You Do*. Bullins's energetic mix of naturalism and formal experiment, drawing on jazz and blues, chimed with the challenging style and content of British political theatre groups such as CAST. Berman caught the mood and suggested a season of black American plays, but Rees argued that it should include new plays about the black British experience. The problem was to find them.

Rees asked his contacts, and the solution arrived through actor Stephan Kalipha, who had appeared in *The Electronic Nigger*, and filmmaker Horace Ove. Thanks to them, as Rees recalls, Ove's cousin, Mustapha Matura, turned up with 'some scraps of yellow paper containing a number of short plays'.[3] Matura says the plays were crude and naïve but very real and beautifully typed. He had written them without any idea of having them produced; he 'did not think anyone would be interested in black people and the way we talk'.[4] Born in Trinidad in 1939 as Noel Mathura to Indian parents – father a car salesman, mother ('near white', says Matura) a shop assistant – he had come to Britain in 1961 and taken a number of jobs including hospital porter and stockroom assistant.[5] After spending some time in Italy, he settled in the Surrey suburb of Surbiton with his wife. Encountering English racism – 'I had to come to England to become conscious of myself as black'– and influenced by the new black consciousness, he became interested in his identity as a black person, dropped his first name Noel for Mustapha, and began writing.

Rees chose a trio of plays: first was *Dialogue*, in which three men watch TV and argue; second was *Indian*, an observational comedy about flatmates; the third and main play was *Party*, which satirizes white middle-class fascination with black lifestyle and politics. Together they comprised *Black Pieces* and were staged in 1970 as the second offering in the Ambiance Lunch Hour 'Black and White Power' season at the Institute of Contemporary Arts, preceded by David Mercer's *White Poem*, a monologue by a white Rhodesian farmer who, with gun in hand, vows to prevent independence.

The other plays in the season – LeRoi Jones's *The Baptism*; Israel Horovitz's *Chiaroscuro*; Victor Corti's *Arrest*; and Ed Bullins's *It Bees Dat Way* – came from America and made little impact. The season was influential through the discovery of Matura's plays, which were written in the everyday language of characters living in contemporary British situations and came as a revelation to the British theatre. (Irving Wardle in his positive review in *The Times* confesses the first piece passed him by because he was 'getting attuned to its language'.[6]) D. Keith Peacock describes the plays as the 'authentic voice of the working-class, black West Indians who are attempting to settle in Britain'.[7] This milieu and its language separated Matura from previous writers such as Walcott, John, and Soyinka and helped black theatre in Britain find a new confidence and character. Oscar James said appearing in *Black Pieces* 'gave me back my dignity and my strength'.[8] Two other cast members, Alfred Fagon and T-Bone Wilson, were similarly inspired and became playwrights. Rees later co-founded the Foco Novo theatre company, which used integrated casting and was dedicated to new plays. The company presented work by, among others, Tunde Ikoli, Fagon, and Matura.

Ambiance repeated the idea of themed seasons, and this led to the formation of the Women's Theatre Group and Gay Sweatshop, heralding the establishment of identity or constituency theatre in the 1970s, of which black theatre was both a beneficiary and a prisoner. While black opportunity, presence, and profile were expanded, the tendency for black representation to be judged by socio-political indices determined by whites was accentuated. Black artists also feared that all-black shows under white direction, such as *The Black Macbeth* set in Africa and *An Othello*, a black power reading of Shakespeare (both 1972), were exploiting the new interest in black culture to revivify the white canon without helping to develop black theatre itself.

On the back of *Black Pieces*, Matura was commissioned by leading producer Michael White; *As Time Goes By* – a development of *Party* in its Jonsonian revelation of the world of a mystic fraud – was directed by Rees at the Traverse during the 1971 Edinburgh Festival, then transferred to the Royal Court Theatre Upstairs and won the John Whiting and George Devine playwriting awards. Two more British plays followed at the Almost Free: *Bakerloo Line* (1972) and *Nice* (1973). After a brief visit to Trinidad in 1972, his first return, Matura moved his plays from the British experience to the Caribbean while continuing to focus on language and character rather than plot or overt ideology as his dramaturgical mainsprings. *Play Mas* (1974), set either side of Trinidadian independence and using carnival as a barometer of change, became the first play by a Caribbean writer to appear in the West End when it transferred from the Royal Court; it won the Evening Standard Most Promising Playwright award. Matura's reputation was confirmed with subsequent work such as *Rum an' Coca Cola* (1976, Royal Court), in which the Disneyfication of culture and its affect on independence is explored through the story of two buskers on a Trinidad beach trying to complete a song for a calypso competition when one is discovered to have killed a female American tourist. Matura takes this theme further in *Independence* (1979, Foco Novo), in which colonization is shown to be a state of mind as much as a political reality.

Success, however, did not open the doors as might have been expected. His own independence did not sit easily in white-controlled theatre, and Matura struggled to place his plays, which were becoming more politically connected. As a result, he co-founded the Black Theatre Co-operative, which produced his play, *Welcome Home Jacko* (1979), a return for Matura to the British experience and to the dynamic margins. In the 1980s, besides writing for television (notably *No Problem* in 1978), Matura reworked two European classics, a strategy that, symptomatically, found its outlet away from the mainstream. In *Playboy of the West Indies* (1984, Oxford Playhouse tour), Matura moved Synge's play to a remote Trinidadian fishing village in 1950 and, in *Trinidad Sisters* (1988, later renamed *Three Sisters*, Tricycle), Chekhov's *Three Sisters* is transplanted to Port of Spain at the start of World War 2. Employing an approach that marked much diasporic theatre, Matura's reconfiguring of these plays, using and validating a different vernacular and set of cultural values, alters the place and standing of diasporic people in the Western imagination. *The Coup* (1991), inspired by an attempted coup against Trinidad's first Prime Minister Eric Williams, was a further exploration of the nature of subjugation and autonomy. Its production marked the first play by a British-based black writer to be performed at the National Theatre. Matura had managed to earn the respect of the established theatre and, in the reach and acclaim of his work, distinguished by irony, humour, and sharp language that give his sometimes deceptively light plays a deep emotional pull, he had become the leading black playwright of his period.

Important to Matura's acceptance in the theatre world was the Royal Court's championing of him under Oscar Lewenstein in the early 1970s. In this period, another major British-based Caribbean playwright, Michael Abbensetts, also found a temporary home at the Court, an unsurprising connection as he was motivated to become a stage writer by seeing *Look Back in Anger*, which originated there. Born in Guyana, Abbensetts came to Britain in 1963 by way of Canada to fulfill his ambition but found work at first as a security guard in the armoury department of the Tower of London and as an attendant at the Sir John Soane Museum. Abbensetts showed his work to the leading play agent Peggy Ramsay, who advised him to write about what it feels like to be black in London. He went on the dole to finish his first full-length play, *Sweet Talk* (1973), which was performed at the Royal Court Upstairs, directed by Stephen Frears. Full of humour but also dealing honestly with the travails of a Caribbean couple for whom married life in a one-room flat in Shepherd's Bush is miserable, *Sweet Talk* offers a slice-of-life portrait of unrealized dreams. The play won Abbensetts the George Devine award along with Matura and, like Matura, he became resident dramatist at the Court. Plays such as *Alterations* (1978), *Samba* (1980), *In the Mood* (1981), and *El Dorado* (1984) showed Abbensetts's eye for the individual, which was most amply demonstrated in his creation of *Empire Road*, the first black drama series on British TV.[9]

Dark and Light

Although the achievement of individuals such as Matura and Abbensetts was important for the profile of the black theatre community, the struggle for collective existence remained the bedrock. The year of the 'Black and White Power' season saw a press conference given by Jamaican actor Frank (Franklin) Cousins outlining a very different type of initiative. Deliberately avoiding the vocabulary of black power, Cousins, a former post office worker, announced the establishment of a new company called Dark and Light, dark for the auditorium, light for the stage. The name was not intended as a reference to race, although people, he acknowledged, took it in its multiracial sense, which fitted the aspiration of the company.[10] Dark and Light aimed to become 'the first professional Multi-Racial Theatre Company in Great Britain' and to 'promote understanding between people of different races through the media of the performing arts. By examining the nature of prejudice it is hoped to identify its sources and therefore decrease its manifestations'.[11] It became the first British theatre company with any continuous presence and its own base to be shaped and defined by black talent.

Cousins had arrived in Britain in 1960 with his friend, the future playwright Trevor Rhone. On the ship, they came across Rudolph Walker, and together they formed a group to present a show on board. Cousins had been involved in drama at college where he had been taught by Lloyd Reckord and knew Mona Hammond and Charles Hyatt (like Walker, to feature as important actors in black British theatre). Cousins also had the address of Edric Connor, so he was well placed to be introduced to Britain's black theatre community. He won a scholarship to study at the Guildhall

School of Music and Drama in 1963 and gained an acting prize on graduation. He appeared in the 1970 all-black Oxford Playhouse production of Genet's *The Blacks*, which toured Britain and represented the country on a European trip, yet generally experienced the fate common to black actors – playing a pantomime genie or one of the lone and minor black roles in plays such as *The Respectable Prostitute*, *The Hostage*, or *A Taste of Honey*. Cousins set up Dark and Light in 1969 to address this problem. It was not a new idea, but it was to be the first time such a company led artistically and administratively by black people obtained its own building.

To achieve this, Cousins studied theatre management (thanks to an Arts Council bursary) and sought help from a broad range of figures with expertise in different theatre-related skills. He mounted charity shows to raise funds and profile, such as *A Race for Time* and *The Magpie World* in 1970, and the most ambitious, at Fairfield Hall, Croydon in 1971, featuring Eartha Kitt. Supporters included Joss Ackland, George Baker (who was a patron), Cy Grant, Keith Michell, and Diana Rigg. Lambeth Council in south London, where a sizeable population of Caribbean heritage lived, showed him several buildings that might serve as a base. Eventually, after much frustration and disappointment, he landed Longfield Hall, a 150-year-old church community hall in Knatchbull Road between Brixton and Camberwell. The local council helped with bills and charged nominal rent, but there was no money to refurbish the hall properly and turn it into a well-equipped theatre, let alone the multiracial arts centre Cousins had envisaged. For this to happen, he needed Arts Council funding. He felt, however, the Council saw Dark and Light as an amateur community effort, not a professional theatre and, as a consequence, did not afford it proper support. This, allied to the fact that its location made it difficult to reach and it had to run as a club, posed severe problems in attracting the local community, who were not used to theatre going (the National Theatre may have been only a bus ride away, but culturally it might have been on the other side of the moon).

Dark and Light's ambitious plans – productions of *Moon on a Rainbow Shawl* and Büchner's *Woyzeck* – had to be scaled back; yet, helped by £1,000 from the Arts Council, Cousins opened in December 1971. The inaugural production was a revival of Fugard's *Blood Knot*, a play that captures Dark and Light's philosophy, in which two half-brothers, one black, one light in tone, struggle to hold on to what they have in common in a world that divides them by skin colour. Aided by the Gulbenkian Foundation, an important source of support for diasporic arts that paid for an administrator and publicity officer, the company organized a tour, though it proved costly and difficult. Cousins followed the Fugard in January 1972 with a revival of a long-running off-Broadway hit, *Evolution of the Blues* by African-American jazz singer and lyricist Jon Hendricks. In March came the British première of *Kataki* by Shimon Wincelberg, a two-hander by a German-born white American seen on Broadway in 1959 and inspired by Balzac in which a Japanese and a white American soldier are stranded together on an island in World War 2. In May came a double bill. First was *The Tenant* by white British playwright Richard Crane, seen the year before in Edinburgh, in which a black man is refused a flat to let but ends up reversing the situation between him and the landlord. This was followed by the

British première of LeRoi Jones's *The Slave*, in which Cousins played the lead, a fable seen by many critics as a portrait of the author as the inept revolutionary who destroys the white society of which he was once a part. All the foregoing shows were revivals and directed by white directors, and none was written by a black British, or British-based, author.[12]

With grants from the Arts Council and the Community Relations Commission, the Crane/Jones double bill toured Britain, and the next production, which celebrated the company's first anniversary, undertook an even wider tour. The play was an adaptation of Robert Lamb's *Raas* by the Jamaican actor Charles Hyatt, who also directed, featuring Anton Phillips. Naseem Khan says the generation-gap play, written by a white academic, presents a sentimental picture of a so-called typical Caribbean family and was booed off the stage in Birmingham.[13] Cousins made a surer choice next for the 1972 Christmas show when he asked Yvonne Brewster to direct a Caribbean pantomime, *Anansi and Brer Englishman* written by Manley Young (the company's administrator) and Gloria Cameron. It was probably the first time a Jamaican pantomime had been seen in Britain and the first British outing for Anansi, the part-spider-part-human, national folk hero of Jamaica. In the show, Anansi and family settle in Brixton next door to a bigoted Conservative councillor whose son falls in love with Anansi's daughter. The script has familiar panto features such as male drag and contemporary references, including barbs at Enoch Powell, the Prime Minister Edward Heath, the local town hall administration, and the Royal Family. Brewster, who had worked on pantomime in Jamaica, was well reviewed for her handling of the mixed cast of black and white actors, amateurs, and professionals, and the show proved very popular.[14]

In 1973, Dark and Light continued with an eclectic repertoire under the influence of Sierra Leonean Pat Amadu Maddy, a former Rose Bruford student and artistic director of Gbakanda Afrikan Tiata theatre company in Freetown.[15] There was a distinct African bent, as after *The Emperor Jones* with Thomas Baptiste came *Gbana Bendu*, concerning the dilemma of contemporary Africa, written and directed by Maddy; *Dalabani*, a dramatic poem of dance drum rituals by Sierra Leonean Mukhtarr Mustapha; and Soyinka's *The Trials of Brother Jero*, directed by Maddy. *Anansi and the Brer Englishman* was revived at Christmas, and Maddy returned to Sierra Leone in 1974.

Managing the theatre on the available resources was taking its toll on Cousins's health. Besides running a Dark and Light Young People's Theatre, encouraging local involvement (for instance, Angell Town Adventure Playground put on productions), and presenting folk evenings and fund-raising shows, he had to cope with poor audiences and on occasion more harmful local antipathy (when thieves stole all the takings). Plans such as reviving James's *The Black Jacobins* had to be scrapped, and programming remained problematic. Not surprisingly, 1974 proved to be thin: another Fugard play, *Boesman and Lena*, toured, and guest performances continued, especially on Sunday evenings when the West Indian Student Dance troupe and the Caribbean Folk Singers would appear. The Radical Alliance of Poets and Players (RAPP) brought *Twisted Knot* and *Two Pieces of Roots* by Jamal Ali, following in the footsteps of earlier visitors such as the Bird in the Hand Theatre from New York and Fasimbas from nearby Lewisham. *Ceremonies in Dark Old Men* by African-American Lonne Edler III was followed by another popular Christmas pantomime, *Anansi and the Strawberry Queen*. It was written by Manley Young, music was composed by Ilona Sekacz, and it was directed by Guyanese actor, writer, and musician Norman Beaton, with Eddy Grant, songwriter and singer for The Equals pop group, making his live theatre debut.

Cousins had gone to Jamaica to recuperate and, on his return, he found the financial situation had deteriorated. There was pressure on him and his administrator, Manley Young, to resign. The black presence elsewhere in the theatre – Matura's mainstream success, for example, and the founding of the touring Temba Theatre Company and the Keskidee Centre – had marginalized Dark and Light. It ceased operation in February 1975 and, in June, the company formally became the Black Theatre of Brixton. The new title reflected a shift toward a more radical stance and one with which the local community could more strongly identify. A new team of Beaton, Ali, and Rufus Collins was running the company but, within a short space of time, there was no more money, and they had lost the building.

It was a powerful team: Beaton had come to Britain in 1960 with ambitions to succeed as a song writer and did odd jobs until he found work in Liverpool as a teacher, his profession in Guyana, where he was also calypso champion. He sang in Merseyside clubs and joined a group that became The Scaffold, which dropped him for a white performer when they were to appear on television. He turned his bitterness into a musical, *Jack of Spades*, written in 1965 with Ken Hignett at the Liverpool Everyman. Along with acting, Beaton followed this in 1968 with a second musical, *Sit Down Banna*, at the Connaught Theatre, Worthing. He led a black cast that included Frank Cousins, who had appeared in *Jack of Spades*. At this time, Cousins and Beaton discussed the idea of forming a company, which became the Dark and Light.[16]

Beaton opened a restaurant in central London called the Green Banana and, when business fell off, invited Ed Berman to bring the Ambiance there. It became known as the Ambiance in Exile Lunchtime Theatre, an early pioneer of the genre, featuring playwrights such as Tom Stoppard. After business problems and scrapes with the law, Beaton concentrated on acting and was highly regarded in many roles, from Ariel in Jonathan Miller's *The Tempest* (1970) and work at the Royal Court and National Theatre to *The Black Mikado* (1975) in the West End. A political activist and central figure in black British theatre, he played Toussaint in Talawa's opening production and achieved wider fame as the leading black actor of his period through radio and television appearances, in shows such as *The Fosters*, *Empire Road* and, most notably, *Desmonds*.[17] Ali was the founder of the RAPP, a touring performance collective that bridged drama and poetry, and Harlem-born Collins had been a member of the (then) nomadic American cooperative Living Theater. He brought its innovative and challenging style to London black theatre in the mid-1970s, invigorating Keskidee and Drum, and moved from London to the Netherlands in 1983 when he became director and choreographer of the Royal Ballet of Flanders.

The new team at the Black Theatre of Brixton had a political-cultural agenda to root the theatre in the needs of those living on the 'front line'. They made great efforts to meet community representatives and visited popular meeting places and social venues, such as the Caribbean Showboat above a Tooting hairdressers. An ambitious first season was planned, with training programmes, street theatre, and tours of plays such as Matura's *Play Mas* and T-Bone Wilson's *Jumbie Street March*. This scheme had to be watered down, and initially the new company presented a pilot series of six Sunday programmes of plays, music, and poetry in the summer of 1975. They staged one programme in a local park and included Ali's angry poems and Beaton reading aloud from James Baldwin's *Going to Meet the Man* a passage about lynching and castration and the burning of a black man. According to Beaton, they upset the council, who tried to remove them from Longfield Hall.[18] Lambeth did not want to support a theatre company, let alone a black one with which it was dissatisfied, and the company complained about the council to the Race Relations Board but pulled back when the council agreed to let them stay. This reprieve, however, turned out to be brief, and soon they were homeless.

As the Black Theatre of Brixton in Exile, the under-resourced team booked the Roundhouse for a week-long festival of drama, mime, music, and poetry in November 1975. It was called *Black Explosion* and involved Wall Theatre Company, the Ebony Steel band, folk groups, and others. The Black Theatre of Brixton was now peripatetic, cut off from their immediate audience, and survived on a project-by-project basis in whichever venue they could find. Beaton's involvement had diminished, and Collins had joined Keskidee. By March 1978, when the Black Theatre of Brixton folded, its productions had included: Ali's *Jericho* (written for the company and billed as the world's first reggae opera) and his double bill, *Dark Days, Light Nights* and *The Treatment*; *Jumbie Street March*; *Seduced* by Jimi Rand; *Father Forgive Them* by Aubrey Legal Miller; Steve Wilmer's *The Jolly Green Soldier*, and *Separate Classes* staged at venues such as Soho Poly, the Young Vic, the ICA, Battersea Arts Centre and the Roundhouse.[19]

The problems Cousins faced had not been overcome. With few exceptions, mainly the pantomimes, Dark and Light audience figures were poor.[20] Cousins blamed the funding bodies for not giving adequate support that would have allowed him the time needed to build a local base, a difficulty exacerbated when grant conditions forced him to tour as the preferred way of reaching new audiences rather than consolidating artistically and administratively at Longfield Hall.[21] He felt bounced between the Arts Council's New Drama and Touring committees and not comfortable with either. Despite the founding mission of the Council to broaden the arts, it did not fund amateur companies, which is how 'ethnic' groups were often regarded because they lacked access to training and professional experience. The Council recognized this conundrum by defining 'ethnic' arts as community arts. Cousins, in effect, had been told to undertake community work and was expected to resolve the riddle of attracting working-class black audiences when white theatre had failed to achieve this goal with its own working-class audiences, let alone black ones. The problem of funders' perceiving diasporic theatre as a vehicle for audience development and welfare work would remain.[22]

The community relations network helped Cousins find suitable non-traditional venues and supported the publicity work. Non-traditional venues, however, were hard to play, and there was insufficient help or money to target new audiences effectively. The company could not afford a new leaflet or poster for each town they visited or to send people in advance to promote the shows. By the time word of mouth had spread, the company had moved on; the result was small and often mostly white audiences. Low-budget touring was also difficult to sustain artistically. Cousins felt the limited funding and potential box office income restricted the type and scale of play he could present. Attracting actors was also difficult. There was reluctance to endure the trying conditions of a cheap tour and to leave the capital for fear of missing more lucrative TV or film work, which would take precedence. The quandary for the Black Theatre of Brixton was the same: the company was not well enough funded to continue touring but, if they played only at Longfield Hall, they would lose their grant. The bold opening programme, budgeted at £40,000, did not receive official support, and the tension between artistic and social demands, which was always much stronger for a black theatre than a white, proved too great to sustain.

The audience problem was further complicated because visiting companies to Longfield Hall – with rare exceptions such as the RAPP and Fasimbas, who wrote their own material and had strong local links – failed to raise the reputation of the Dark and Light company. The project also suffered because the multiracial approach failed to satisfy any constituency, whereas the pantomimes – aimed specifically at the Caribbean-based population – were well received (though this brought its own problems, as health and safety issues were immediately raised). Nevertheless, despite its many shortcomings, Dark and Light and the Black Theatre of Brixton had highlighted the issue of black theatre and the need for public funding to sustain it and played an important part in inspiring the influential first report into 'minority' theatre, *The Arts Britain Ignores*. They showed that, however hard it might be to realise, an artistic and administratively black-led company was not a fantasy.

Keskidee

Across the capital in north London, the Keskidee Centre took over the role Dark and Light had hoped to play and became an important focus not only for black theatre but wider black involvement in a range of cultural activities. Coming out of the self-help movement, it formed part of a crucial network of outlets such as New Beacon Books and its shop that served and supported diasporic communities. Keskidee was founded by Oscar Abrams, a Guyanese architect in his early thirties, who had returned to Britain after working in Tanzania and wanted to help black youth, who lacked facilities and – he thought – direction, especially in relation to their Caribbean heritage. He gave up his career, bought a rundown Victorian mission school in Islington and, in 1970, opened there the Keskidee Centre, which became vital to the social life of the local black youths, especially the males.[23] The Centre was named after a common Caribbean bird native to Guyana, tiny but resilient, which was believed to sing 'qu'est ce qu'il dit?' (and which also gave its name to a specialist Caribbean language programme that helps young children). The Centre used the bird as its logo, a reminder and symbol of both Caribbean roots and migration. Helped by friends and local volunteers, Abrams adapted the building to become a black-led arts centre, possibly the first in Britain, and set it up as a trust. Abrams was a Socialist with a vision, which was to provide a space for the community and to let the community have ownership of it – although not everyone in the local white community appreciated this and, on one occasion, a stage set was vandalized. Keskidee's founding motto was 'a community discovering itself creates its own future'. At a time when black youngsters could not walk the streets without fear of police harassment, places such as Keskidee offered a vital refuge and place to meet, learn, develop skills, and express oneself.[24]

Keskidee developed from an educational and social centre to a major platform for African and Caribbean culture, whether in lectures, exhibitions, film, poetry, literature, or plays.[25] There were homework groups, school holiday clubs, nurseries, games and competitions, legal, housing and welfare advice, political forums, an artist-in-residence, a library, and classes for a range of activities, from cooking, woodwork, and yoga to typing, pottery, and photography. At the heart of Keskidee's work was the Theatre Workshop, which opened in 1971. The first theatrical events happened by chance. One of the original influences behind the idea of Keskidee was the grassroots movement for supplementary schools that developed in response to the mis-description by the education system of many young black people as 'educationally sub-normal'. Abrams encouraged the parents of students attending classes to come and tell stories from the Caribbean and Britain, and the students then began to perform these tales. Abrams saw an opportunity not only to organize a youth theatre but to present plays by black writers and provide black actors with roles that were not the clichéd ones commonly on offer.

The Workshop's first notable production was *Sighs of a Slave Dream* (1972) by eseoghene (the Jamaican writer Lindsay Barrett), directed by Maddy. It was followed in 1973 by Maddy's *Gbana Bendu* and *Voices from the Frontline*, a programme comprising: *Babylon Ghetto* by Dam-X (Steve Hall); *The Bus Rebel* by eseoghene; and *Voices of the Living and the Dead* by Linton Kwesi Johnson, who was the Keskidee's Library Resources and Education Officer and who developed his dub poetry there. These were the voices of and from the street that Dark and Light was unable to tap. Other early productions included Jamal Ali's musical *Black Feet in the Snow*; T-Bone Wilson's *Body and Soul* and *Jumbie Street March*; Jimi Rand's *Sherry and Wine*; and two plays by Soyinka: *The Trials of Brother Jero* and *The Swamp Dwellers*.[26] Keskidee Young Gifted and Black Theatre Workshop took a musical, *The Father and Child Reunion*, to the Roundhouse Downstairs in 1976.

Lack of substantial and continuous funding – it received its first Arts Council grant in 1974/5 – meant programming was difficult, standards were inconsistent, and the premises were never refurbished. When Rufus Collins from the Black

Theatre of Brixton joined as head of the Centre in 1976, he found new funding (including a grant from the Arts Council's Housing the Arts scheme), revamped the building (in 1977) with help from those in the community who used Keskidee, and presented more regular programmes of work from Africa, African America, and the Caribbean at a generally higher standard than before. The new building conformed more to Abrams's vision; it had a food and drink area; drama, music, and dance workshops; a 200-seat theatre; a larger library; and a basement disco. The Centre had six professional actors and Collins as resident director, and it began to run professional workshops in acting, directing, and playwriting alongside its theatre-producing programme. Critics began to review the productions, which gained a reputation at home and abroad.

Collins directed several British premières by Edgar Nkosi White, who settled in Britain in the 1980s: *The Black Women* (1977), *Lament for Rastafari* (1977), *Masada* (1978), which transferred to Royal Court Theatre Upstairs and, for the Black Theatre Co-operative, *The Nine Night* (1983). White, a writer born in Montserrat but raised in New York where he became resident dramatist at Joe Papp's Public Theatre, played a key role alongside others such as Matura and Abbensetts in helping establish a black repertoire in Britain with plays of exodus and exile such as *Man and Soul* (1982), *Ritual by Water* (1983), *Redemption Song* (1984), *The Boot Dance* (1984), *Ritual* (1985), and *The Moon Dance Night* (1987).[27]

Other plays that appeared at Keskidee under Collins were Jimi Rand's *Say Hallelujah* (1977), which first brought Keskidee to wider attention; *A Play* by the Ugandan writer Robert Serumaga (1977); the British premières of Steve Carter's *Eden* (1978) and Lennox Brown's *The Throne in an Autumn Room* (1979), which Keskidee took to the Black Theatre Festival in New York the following year; the first London revival (in 1979) of Walcott's *Malcochon* since it was seen (as *The Six in the Rain*) at the Royal Court; and the British première of Walcott's *Remembrance* (1980), directed by Anton Phillips. Collins directed the Keskidee Theatre Workshop in *Running Fast Thru' Paradise*, a two-hander by the African-American writer Kulua Dundee (a.k.a. Calua Dundy), which toured the Netherlands in 1978. Festivals were held that brought visiting companies to Keskidee, such as the RAPP (which came in 1978 with *Now*, a piece about the frustrations of black artists); the Theatre of Contemporary Arabic Drama (TOCAD, founded 1975 to present drama from the Arabic world to Britain); Wall Theatre; and the Picket Theatre from Barbados. Keskidee toured Maori townships in New Zealand in 1979 and helped establish a companion organization, Keskidee Aroha.

By 1980, Keskidee was badly in debt, a situation Abrams later attributed to the New Zealand trip. After an investigation by the local council, new procedures, particularly in relation to financial control, were put in place. In 1981, along with other companies such as Gay Sweatshop and Croydon Warehouse, Keskidee lost its Arts Council Annual Programme Grant when the Council abolished the scheme, which had offered something between the security of revenue funding and the insecurity of one-off project grants. The Centre was forced to apply for grants on a project-by-project basis but, aside from sporadic shows such as Jimi Rand's *Hands*

Off My Mind (1981) and the Asantewaa Company in Rauf Adu's *Musa, Rahmatu and the Seven-Eyed God* (1983), its occasional attempts at revival failed, and it closed as a theatre space. During the 1980s, Abrams developed Keskidee as a vocational training centre for theatre crafts and other media. Despite a re-launch in 1990, Abrams had to sell the building in 1992 to pay off debts. He died of cancer in 1996 aged 58.

Keskidee was open to numerous activities and was very accessible as part of its community mission, which was the source of its success and, some commentators believe, its downfall as well because it tried to do too many things for too many people. Its influence and repute, however, were wide and went beyond theatre – black politicians from abroad would drop in, poets such as James Berry appeared there, model Naomi Campbell visited, Nina Simone played there, and Bob Marley used it as a location for his *Is This Love* video. More than Dark and Light, Keskidee provided a focus for black people to learn together a range of theatrical and other skills and to share their expertise, giving them a confidence that was hard to develop elsewhere.

Temba

Following in the footsteps of Robert Adams, Edric Connor, and Frank Cousins, two other actors, Oscar James and Alton Kumalo, founded a company – Temba, in 1972 – to offer work to black actors marginalized by mainstream theatre, often on the self-fulfilling grounds of inexperience. They were familiar with this when they met playing a number of relatively minor roles at what was considered the peak of the profession, working for the Royal Shakespeare Company (RSC). Trinidadian James had come to Britain in 1957 when only a teenager and did a variety of jobs – taxi driving, washing dishes, being a gymnast – before landing small acting parts. He joined the RSC in 1967 and thought, wrongly, he had 'arrived'.[28] South African Kumalo had first appeared in Britain in the township musical *King Kong* (1961) and had stayed when the apartheid republic left the Commonwealth. He studied at Rose Bruford, worked in radio, TV, and theatre, appeared in the 1965 première of *The Road*, and joined the RSC in 1968.

Temba (Zulu for hope or trust) was the name of a semi-autobiographical play Kumalo wrote while on tour to Japan with the RSC; the play was seen with James in the cast at the Young Vic for two Sunday performances. The Arts Council gave a small sum for it to tour to the Oxford Playhouse, and the company bearing the name of the play was born. Whereas James went on to a distinguished career as an actor, Kumalo ran Temba as its first artistic director. For the next decade, Temba toured new plays, often written by and starring Kumalo: premières of David Halliwell's polyphonic *Prejudice* (1978); Barrie Keeffe's *Black Lear* (1980); Edgar White's *The Boot Dance* (1984); and revivals of plays by Lewis Nkosi, LeRoi Jones, Jimi Rand, Mustapha Matura, and Athol Fugard. A strong political commitment and anti-racist stance came through the repertoire. During this time, Temba became the first British black theatre company to receive an annual Arts Council subsidy, beginning in 1974–1975. Although within a couple of years it was receiving more than Dark and Light/Black Theatre of Brixton had, Temba faced similar audience and venue problems associated with low-budget touring.

A squeeze on arts funding that began in the late 1970s and contributed to the demise of overtly political theatre led to the 1984 Arts Council decentralization strategy, *The Glory of the Garden*. Though echoing government regeneration programmes in its commitment to black arts – a public necessity after three months' of riots in 1981 in London, Liverpool, Bristol, Manchester, and elsewhere – it jeopardized Temba's future, along with other companies that were being moved to regional rather than central jurisdiction. In the process, Kumalo was replaced by Alby James as artistic director. James enjoyed an expanded administration and proclaimed his aim to broaden Temba's repertoire in an attempt to increase audiences and re-position the company within the theatrical mainstream by looking beyond (without ignoring) what he saw as the limiting focus of much black theatre on racism and a uniquely black experience.

James was British-born, university-educated, and middle class, with as much affinity to Britain and its cultural legacy as to that of his Jamaican parents. His appointment represented a move in the control of diasporic theatre toward those who were British-born or raised and who had a different relationship to their heritage than those who had come as immigrants. He brought with him to Temba an unusual level of experience in mainstream theatre for a black director. After graduation from the University of East Anglia in 1977, where he was president of the student drama society, James joined the Royal Court as an Arts Council Trainee Assistant Director and, in 1982, became assistant director with the RSC. He put Temba on a new footing with a blend of its own shows and co-productions (for instance, with theatres in Birmingham, Derby, and Leicester, which had significant diasporic populations), and he embraced the mainstream theatre world of glossy programmes and sponsorship.

His search for a new type of theatre that would give Temba a distinctive artistic profile took him on his first visit to the Caribbean (in 1985), which inspired him to seek new spectacular theatrical forms drawing on Caribbean and African heritage. An immediate result was the British première of Barbara Gloudon's *The Pirate Princess* in the 1986 Black Theatre Forum season, a show that combined Jamaican pantomime and music with contemporary black British culture. He revived and encouraged new black writing, undertook important outreach work, and introduced a diasporic dimension to European classics through a policy of integrated casting. *Romeo and Juliet*, for example, was set in nineteenth-century Cuba just after the War of Independence with Spain and had black Montagues (David Harewood played Romeo) fighting white Capulets (Georgia Slowe, nominated for an Olivier Award, played Juliet).

Temba's repertoire was broad and lively, like that of a national theatre in microcosm: new plays such as Michael Ellis's *Chameleon*; Jacqueline Rudet's *Basin*; Nigel Moffat's *Mamma Decemba*, which won the Samuel Beckett Best New Play Award; Benjamin Zephaniah's first play *Streetwise*; *Black Sheep* by Derrick Cameron; *A Visitor to the Veldt* by Mfundi Vundla; and *Back Street Mammy* by Trish Cooke mixed with the

British première of *Mother Poem* by Edward Kamau Brathwaite; Felix Cross's musical *Glory!*; revivals such as *Woza Albert*; and reworkings of classics such as *Romeo and Juliet* and *Ghosts*. Arts reporter Jim Hiley wrote that Temba was 'the very model of a modern theatre company, both expansive and conscientious. It tramps the land in search of fresh audiences, while carefully nurturing tyro talents'.[29]

The company, nevertheless, came under threat in 1990 when the Arts Council rejected James's plan for Temba to become a larger-scale touring company. James announced his resignation rather than seeing the company denied the chance to expand. The following year, the Council's grant was withdrawn amid criticism of the company's artistic and management standards, exacerbated by poor reviews for the 'colour blind' production of *Ghosts*. Temba campaigned to survive, with high status support from people such as Peter Brook and Trevor Nunn. Nonetheless, what turned out to be its final show came in 1992: *A Killing Passion* based on Thomas Mann's version of an Indian legend, *The Transposed Heads*. A programme note summed up what the company had tried to achieve: to make black theatrical expression and appearance in Western classics normal and expected, to be a catalyst between black and white, to create integrated multicultural theatre, and to promote theatre inspired by black artists but drawing on other cultures.[30]

James was quoted as stating that:

> not enough of us had been given the opportunity to acquire the skills to improve the quality and variety of our work. I wanted Temba to gain national status. I didn't want to stand around in community halls. I didn't want to work on minimum finances. There had to be somewhere where black actors could go to earn a good salary.[31]

His own verdict on the audiences the company attracted was that initially they were 'white, liberal middle-class, predominantly university centred'. But, he said, 'As years went by black community centres became established on a regional touring circuit. Temba visited and the audiences who came were on the whole black, middle class, with some black students too'.[32]

The Arts Council, which said Temba had not met the required standards, defended its support for black theatre by pointing to the rise in grant to Talawa and backing for groups such as the Black Mime Theatre and Double Edge Theatre. James felt the Arts Council had not liked Temba's trespassing on the classics – ground that should be left free for white companies to occupy – and preferred Temba to focus instead on black communities and black audiences.[33] This interpretation of the state funding strategy, which echoed what Cousins had felt at the time of Dark and Light, was supported by other diasporic groups, and it encapsulated the predicament state funding presented: it gave diasporic theatre a lifeline but at the expense of its own independence and growth.[34] In the absence of realistic alternative sources of funding, black theatre practitioners had established their right to be funded by the state and then had tried to free themselves from the essentialist categorization that underpinned the minimal support that was offered. They wanted to be seen as artists, with their diverse cultural heritages an important but not necessarily or always the determining element in their artistic vision. They did not want to be seen as super community workers or a subdivision of the fringe and wanted the interplay between heritage and other factors to be in their hands, not those of the funders or the white theatre establishment.

Initiatives in the mid-1970s

Dark and Light, Keskidee, and Temba were initiatives launched in the early 1970s when identity-based groups started to flourish as fringe and alternative theatre expanded. Like much of the fringe, many diasporic groups came and went quickly in the 1970s, sometimes changing names for different projects or grant applications and sometimes fading as the personalities behind them moved on. One of the most promising and ambitious projects of the decade was the Drum Arts Centre, set up by Cy Grant and John Mapondera in 1974 with the aim of establishing a national centre for the arts of black people, in contrast to local centres such as Keskidee.

Grant (considered coloured, not black, in his homeland of Guyana) had been in Britain since 1941 when he joined the RAF and became a flight lieutenant. He was a Nazi prisoner-of-war for two years after being shot down over Holland and qualified as a barrister on returning to Britain. Like Robert Adams, he found a disturbing barrier of racism in the law and ended up earning his living in entertainment. He had been involved in amateur drama while studying law and made the transition to the profession when he won the lead in what he describes as a third-rate touring production of a forgotten play called *13 Death Street, Harlem*.[35] In 1951, he joined Laurence Olivier's Festival of Britain company at the St. James's Theatre and encountered the ugly face of racist Britain one night after a show when a white actress, Elspeth March, was beaten badly by two Teddy Boys for being on the street with two black men, Grant and another actor, Neville Crabbe. Grant went on to appear on radio, TV, and film and became a national figure as a calypso news singer on the BBC TV *Tonight* programme in the late 1950s. He appeared in *Freedom Road: Songs of Negro Protest* (1961), a musical TV documentary on civil rights, and, on stage, in a range of work from *Cindy-Ella, or I Gotta Shoe* and the lead in *Othello* at the Phoenix, Leicester in 1965 to *The Iceman Cometh* (RSC, 1976).[36]

Zimbabwean John Mapondera, who became executive secretary and projects officer of Drum, had, together with a group of African artists, formed the Contemporary African Arts Organization in 1969 to present integrated programmes of theatre, poetry, music, dance, and exhibition. He joined Grant in creating Drum to reach a black British audience that was also Caribbean and not just African in its heritage. Aware of the problems that had beset previous black ventures, Mapondera undertook a feasibility study of black arts provision to enhance the strength of the Drum organization and secure a permanent infrastructure focused on a new, purpose-built performance centre in Covent Garden. Grant meanwhile sought influential patrons. He wrote to Laurence Olivier, who declined, saying Drum was separatist – a rejection that Grant interpreted as 'be like us because you have no culture of your own'.[37]

Fund-raising began in early 1975 and, in June, in conjunction with the Notting Hill People's Carnival Committee, Drum organized *Mas in the Mall,* a two-week season at the Institute of Contemporary Arts of plays by Caribbean writers (for example, *Talkshop* by Thomas Baptiste), combined with performances by steel bands and an exhibition of carnival photographs and costumes. One of these plays, a revival of *Sweet Talk* by Michael Abbensetts, went on to appear at the King's Head Theatre, Islington. In 1975, Drum also presented two plays at the Commonwealth Institute in response to a request from Oxfam to contribute to a programme of educational activities surrounding an exhibition called *Involved in Mankind.* The two plays were *How Do You Clean a Sunflower?* and Wole Soyinka's *The Swamp Dwellers,* which had entered the examination syllabus. The former play, one of the winners of a Royal Court/*Observer* competition, tells a familiar story of the clash between Caribbean dreams of the 'Mother Land' and the reality. The play was written collectively and performed by the young people's West Indian Drama Group from Bristol. The latter, directed by Horace Ove, toured London schools and was seen at Keskidee.

Drum's most influential venture came with a summer workshop at Morley College, Lambeth that resulted in the production of *Bread* by Mustapha Matura at the Young Vic as part of the National Theatre 1976 summer season there. The workshop, which covered theatre production, writing, direction, and stage management, attracted more than 70 participants, was led by writer and director Steve Carter of the Negro Ensemble Theatre Company, New York, and was opened by the Jamaican High Commissioner. Out of this project, workshops were also held with black actors at the National Theatre for two successive years. In 1977 – the Queen's Silver Jubilee – Drum held a play competition of its own to find work that reflected multiracial Britain. The winner, *Sonny Wesley,* a play set in the pop music world and written by Clive Duncan, a white British Leyland Coventry shop floor worker, was presented at the Oval House. In 1978, Ola Rotimi from the University of Nigeria directed more workshops at Morley College, leading to the production of his play, *The Gods are Not to Blame,* a Yoruba reworking of *Oedipus Rex,* at the Jackson's Lane Community Centre, north London and the Greenwich Theatre with the Aklowa Dance Group. Drum also staged art exhibitions in various galleries in London, notably *Behind the Mask - Afro-Caribbean Poets and Playwrights in Words and Pictures* at the Commonwealth Institute and the National Theatre in 1979.[38]

In 1977, Drum announced it had been offered £30,000 by the Home Office Voluntary Services Unit and a possible further grant from the Arts Council Housing the Arts Scheme for the establishment in Covent Garden of a national centre that, it was hoped, would open in September the following year. Also in 1977, Grant's professional career reached a personal turning point with a solo show, *Return to My Native Land* by Aimé Césaire. Originally a platform performance at the National Theatre, the show transferred to the Royal Court Theatre Upstairs and subsequently had a two-year tour. Performing this poem exalting negritude deepened Grant's desire to value what he saw as his own culture rather than aspire to what other cultures had achieved. He and Mapondera found themselves moving in different directions. Grant went on to be director of the Concord multicultural festivals that appeared around England in the 1980s, including a four-month presence in Devon, while Mapondera returned to Zimbabwe after independence was won in 1980.

Drum's final project occurred under fresh – and white – leadership but added to the Drum legacy. Funding from the Ministry of Overseas Development was offered in 1979 to form a new Drum group but along theatre-in-education lines. The new artistic director, John Burgess, who had worked with Roger Planchon's Théâtre National Populaire in France and as an Arts Council associate at Riverside Studios, decided to use the money instead to commission plays on the theme of the relationship between Britain and the 'third world'. As a result, Riverside and Drum presented a season in 1980 comprising *Black Man's Burden* by Michael O'Neill and Jeremy Seabrook; *One Fine Day* by Nicholas Wright; *A Dying Business* by Mustapha Matura (in association with Black Theatre Co-operative); *The Mother Country* by Hanif Kureishi (who attended playwriting workshops at Riverside with, among others, Caryl Phillips); and *Scrape Off the Black* by Tunde Ikoli, a play that has come to be regarded as a major text in black British theatre. The Black Plays Umbrella season – three white writers, three non-white – was performed by a company of twenty actors, fifteen of whom were black or Asian and five white. The directors all were white.

When Drum was wound up because of its debts, the influence of its season at Riverside was felt elsewhere. The lead in *Black Man's Burden*, Decima Francis, joined the Black Theatre Co-operative on the strength of her Riverside performance but found BTC very male-chauvinist and, in response, formed her own company, SASS, recruited from a youth drama workshop in South London. SASS presented *The Flatshare* by Ray Shell in 1984 and revived *Black Man's Burden* in 1985.[39] Francis asked Burgess and Peter Gill, who had moved from Riverside and were now running the National Theatre Studio, whether they would hold Shakespeare workshops for her group. Gill was already experimenting with Shakespeare in dialect, and the two agreed. Soon, with some more black actors added, the Studio programme was cleared for a workshop production of *Macbeth* and a devised play, *Black Poppies*, about black soldiers in the British army. *Macbeth* extended to an entire play Gill's shorter Shakespearean experiments: for example, the *Julius Caesar* tent scene performed using Jamaican accents and rhythms of speech. With its black cast led by Treva Etienne and Decima Francis, *Macbeth* had one performance in the Cottesloe Theatre in 1987. It was followed by *Black Poppies*, co-directed by Burgess and Francis, making her the first female black director to work at the National. The show toured to Paris, was seen at the Theatre Royal Stratford East, and was filmed by BBC TV.[40] The cast later formed the core of The Posse, performing satirical sketch shows at Stratford East.

The Arts Britain Ignores

Funders were forced to respond to this phenomenon of a burgeoning diasporic culture, which was in danger of being diverted into social rather than artistic work, sometimes because the projects were deemed to be of vital social importance but not yet sufficient artistic quality, and also of falling through funders' fingers because applications did not fit existing categories for support. After a broad consultative process that began in September 1974 came the key document of the period in this field, *The Arts Britain Ignores*, written by journalist Naseem Khan.[41] Published in 1976, it was commissioned by the Arts Council, the Gulbenkian Foundation, and the Community Relations Commission and had a steering group consisting mainly of artists and cultural activists. In putting the report together, Khan uncovered a breadth of activity across the country in a range of performance genres that had hitherto been hidden from wider view. It surveyed the activities of diasporas from Africa, Asia, the Caribbean, central and east Europe, and Cyprus.[42] The report argued for support of ethnic minorities' arts to be a matter of right, for the establishment of a central advisory body, and for the provision of buildings and training. *The Arts Britain Ignores* became pivotal in bringing the debate on cultural policy to a new level and opening up the reassessment of that policy in tandem with the debate on what constitutes Britishness. It also, however, reinforced the association of 'ethnic' arts with community arts, thereby underpinning their marginal position in relation to what was perceived as mainstream professional activity.

The major immediate outcome of the report was the establishment of the Minorities' Arts Advisory Service (MAAS), an agency that continued as an arts access unit until its demise in 1994. With the majority of the advisory group to Khan's report forming the MAAS board under the chairmanship of Norman Beaton, the MAAS acted as a bridge and a broker, campaigning for arts and artists. For its first few months, the MAAS was run by Khan from her house with her assistant, Veronica Lovindeer, but it grew rapidly. It organized regional and national conferences, and similar operations opened in Nottingham, Manchester, Cardiff, and the West Midlands. Jatinder Verma was the MAAS's Northern Coordinator for a time, and Parminder Vir its Midlands Coordinator. A black dance group, the MAAS Movers, also came under its wing. The MAAS published a monthly bulletin, *Echo*, which became the quarterly *Artrage* from 1982. Among other publications were the first national register of black artists and groups, a free listings guide, *Black Arts* (which included comment, reviews and poems), and a guide to medium- and small-scale venues in London for use by black and non-European groups.[43]

Khan's recommendations on premises and training fared less well than the proposal to establish an advisory body. Premises and training had been long-standing issues in the diasporic theatre community. The buildings question was not properly addressed centrally by funders until the following decade and then without adequate resolution. On training, Khan had received evidence in particular from the Afro-Asian Artists' Committee of the actors' union Equity. The committee was the successor of the Coloured Artists' Committee, formed in the mid-1960s under pressure from the union's own black members such as Bobby Naidoo and Thomas Baptiste and the two specialist casting agencies (that of the Connors and the Oriental Casting Agency founded in the early 1960s by Peggy Sirr).[44] This committee faded but, in the early 1970s, renewed pressure from the short-lived Afro-Asian Artists' Association and the advocacy of black Equity members such as John Worthy and Louis Mahoney led to the committee's revival and name change, accompanied in 1975 by its own representative on the union's Council.[45]

The committee's evidence to Khan dealt with both training and under-employment.[46] Career advisers were telling the committee they were turning young black or Asian people away from drama schools because of the scarcity of parts on stage and screen, while at the same time drama schools, like some theatre managements, were saying there was an absence of non-white actors.[47] The committee, led by Mahoney, who was an Equity council member and vice president, produced a directory of all 'ethnic minority' performers to counter this latter problem. Following the committee's submission, Khan's report identified the problems of training at both drama school and theatre company level. In spring 1975, there were only ten British-born/-raised/-based black drama students in eight London drama schools of a total of 675 students. In the regional theatre, the industry's 'hands-on' training ground, opportunity for non-white actors was almost nonexistent: no black actor was a permanent member of a repertory company (it was not until 1973 that a black actor, Olu Jacobs, had appeared on the main stage of the Birmingham Repertory Theatre).[48] The Arts Council eventually agreed to advertise training schemes in publications aimed at ethnic audiences, but the basic problems were not addressed.

Equity's committee connected the severe under-employment of non-white actors in relation to the proportion of the non-white membership to the types of roles on offer.[49] Main roles tended to be limited to black shows; otherwise parts were generally minor and usually associated with a (tense) racial aspect rather than non-racialized everyday life. The 'vicious circle' remained: black actors blamed directors/agents for not casting them, whereas directors/agents said they did not cast black actors because they lacked experience. The campaign for 'integrated' or 'colour-blind' casting was designed to tackle this but also had negative effects when its use overlooked racism and justified the practice of blacking up, for example when white actors played Othello. Integrated casting on its own could lead to inclusion of black actors without any challenge to prevailing ideology or conventions and, indeed, could reinforce existing hierarchies of inequality. For this reason, the term 'colour blind casting' was opposed by many black actors, because it implied, and in practice could often mean, using a white benchmark and ignoring the importance of difference, which in turn could mean ignoring discrimination.

The debate frequently revolved around playing and speaking Shakespeare, as global icon and barometer of British theatre. Terry Hands, when RSC artistic director, was quoted as saying the 'iambic pentameter just doesn't sound right with a strong Asian or Caribbean accent', yet Peter Gill's work on *Macbeth* at the National Theatre Studio showed that a Caribbean accent did not diminish the text or make it sentimental.[50] Some within the black theatre community saw the problem differently, however. They did not think training for and entry into white theatre was the answer. At an Equity meeting in 1978 called to discuss the situation of black actors, Jamal Ali was reported as asking why black actors should want to play Hamlet and similar roles when they had not yet had the opportunity to play themselves.[51]

For artists such as Ali, acting like whites or in white theatre had nothing to do with black theatre. Conversely, directors such as Yvonne Brewster argued vehemently that black actors should have access to the classic repertoire; otherwise they would remain marginalized, and the classics would remain irrelevant.

This debate reflected wider differences on social and political strategy, such as an integrationist 'melting pot' multiculturalism set against a diversity approach that validated each cultural strand. For those struggling to establish an autonomous non-white theatre, self-determination was central, but did this mean ceding ground and power by abandoning the white culture within which non-white theatre had to operate, or accepting the compromises involved in accommodation with white theatre and risking a dilution or loss of identity? To avoid ghettoization on the one hand and incorporation on the other, funders and the white theatre establishment had to both support diasporic theatre without imposing their own agenda and recognize, and then overcome, the artistic and cultural obstacles that restricted or denied non-white participation.

Arrival

Driving this debate were the artists themselves. During the 1970s, the profile of immigration changed, particularly with the passing of the 1971 Immigration Act, which introduced new notions of the right of abode and restricted non-white primary immigration. As empire gave way to Commonwealth, the balance tipped away from the diasporic exile to the British-born or -raised citizen. The postwar settlement was breaking down, and monetarism was soon to bury it, as the decade was abruptly catapulted into the Thatcherite 1980s, and the new demographic became clear: British-born children of migrants in a 'post-industrial', expanded higher education context created a critical mass for the blossoming of the arts.

The seeds were evident in the mid- and late 1970s. Distinctions were porous between the professional and the non-professional, between pure and applied art, and between art forms themselves. Groups came and went and interchanged personnel freely. The political use of culture as a means of resistance reached new heights, especially in countering the rise of overt racism and far-right groups through initiatives such as Rock against Racism (white led) and the expansion of the Notting Hill Carnival. Diasporic theatre was asserting and exploring a new sense of identity in crisis-ridden, post-imperial Britain, moving beyond the immigrant Other to claim its stake and confront notions of what it meant to be British. As a Trinidadian worker says to his boss in Matura's *Play Mas*, 'of course I is English, I does talk English, so I is English, we is English, all a we is English, man'.[52]

In the maelstrom of social unrest and industrial militancy of the time, there was an extraordinary mushrooming of groups such as Acacia, African Dawn, Birmingham Youth Theatre, Black Expression in Birmingham, Black Grass, Black Theatre Workshop, Brixton Arts Theatre, Calabash, Carib Theatre, Early Start, Grasshopper, Group 3, Hewanorra, Images Theatre Company, Impact Theatre, Lambeth Ensemble Theatre, Legba, L'Ouverture, Omnibus, Pigment Theatre in Nottingham, Sahar Arts,

Sassafras, Staunch Poets and Players, Tara Arts, Theatre of Black Youth, TOCAD, the United Caribbean Association of Leeds, Wall Theatre, and the West Indian Drama Group in Bristol. As the 1970s spilled into the 1980s, the number and spread of diasporic groups, the emergence of a diverse, British-based repertoire that introduced a new energy beyond the confines of naturalism, the availability of a growing pool of skilled actors, and the existence of a network of university, community, and arts venues prepared to present diasporic work signalled that an irreversible if fraught and fragmented black and Asian presence had been established in British theatre.

7

ASIAN THEATRE: TARA ARTS AND BEYOND

A distinctive British Asian theatre that defined its own image and identity along with that of the African and Caribbean diaspora began to take shape in the mid-1970s and established itself in all its variety in the 1980s and 1990s. Mainstream theatre still largely ignored the Asian experience, which surfaced occasionally in fringe theatres. In 1968, Gopal Sharman's play *Full Circle* came to the short-lived International Theatre Club at the Mercury Theatre on a global tour from India. In 1970, there was a production without décor of Partap Sharma's *A Touch of Brightness* at the Royal Court (about life in a Bombay brothel) and a London fringe production by a group called Navakala, with Saeed Jaffrey in the cast, of Dilip Hiro's *To Anchor a Cloud* (about the emperor who built the Taj Mahal for his favourite wife). Incidents such as Roshan Seth being hired at the Royal Shakespeare Company in 1974 as assistant director on *Cymbeline* or the appearance at the National Theatre in 1975 of Alaknanda Samarth in *Phaedra Britannica*, which was set in British-ruled India, remained both supplementary and rare. The 1975 European première of *Tughlaq*, the story of an infamous fourteenth-century sultan by the Indian playwright Girish Karnad, directed by Rajiv Mehrota for the Oxford Experimental Theatre Club, continued the tradition of student theatrical activity.

Community theatre groups, mostly ad hoc, were usually working in home languages; in 1975, the Birmingham-based L and P Enterprises produced a Gujarati play, *Kona Bapu Diwari?* (Who Cares?) in Leicester and London. Based on Molière's *L'Avare*, it told of family life in India dominated by a miser who is faced with a defiant son and daughter. The self-styled Indian National Theatre (founded 1974) also produced a Gujarati play, *Kadam Milake Chalo* (Let's Pull Together – Nehru's slogan). Set in an opulent Bombay apartment and dealing with generational conflicts and the theme of freedom versus obedience, the play was seen in London, Leicester, and Luton. There was also the drama section of London's Bharatiya Vidya Bhavan (Institute for Indian Culture); Leicester Literary Arts and Lights; the Maharashtrian

Theatre Group, which presented an annual play; the Asian Artists Association, which performed in Hindi and Urdu; and various expressions of Bengali theatre in the East End of London.

Muslim communities often remained suspicious of theatre because of the link in Islam between human representation and idolatry, and for moral reasons the concern was even more acute in relation to women. According to Naseem Khan, Ros Lyle's East-West Community Theatre Group in Birmingham for Hindi-speaking youngsters and Southall's pioneering Indiyouth had difficulty involving girls.[1] Without community support (mosques and other religious institutions, high commissions and embassies, or local councils, for instance) and without backing from state funders, which did not as policy support amateur work, it was often a struggle to mount any kind of activity.

Forced migration from Kenya and Uganda in the late 1960s and early 1970s, however, added another dimension. The exiles knew they could not return (unlike migrants from the Caribbean), and this affected their response to living in Britain. They brought with them an East African tradition of amateur drama, especially among the Kenyans whose country was more embedded in English-language culture and infrastructure than, for example, India because it had won independence much later.

The catalyst for change in British-Asian theatre was the racist murder of seventeen-year-old Gurdip Singh Chaggar in Southall, west London in 1976. The killing led to the mobilization of South Asian youths in defence and welfare organizations and, as part of that response, to the formation of Tara Arts, an English-language company that was a voice of and for Asians in Britain.[2] None of the founders was from a theatre background, but 'our anger told us we needed to inhabit a public space', said artistic director Jatinder Verma.[3] At first, the group met in Tooting Bec, south London and, along with drama, included in its activities poetry, talks, and debate. Culturally outside the mainstream, they found themselves aligned with the alternative theatre movement of the time, which used non-traditional spaces to reach their audiences with the kind of socially aware work that would not normally be seen in regular theatres. This birth has left its mark on the company ever since, the longest-surviving diasporic theatre in Britain and the one that has made the most significant contribution to theorizing post-colonial difference and negotiating the relationship between the margin and the centre and between its homelands and Britain.

Verma was born in Dar-es-Salaam, Tanzania in 1954 to Indian parents, grew up in Nairobi, Kenya, came to Britain aged fourteen; and was in his last year at university (studying for an MA in South Asian Studies) when Chaggar was killed and Tara was co-founded. In Verma's words, those who comprised the group were 'twice born': once when their families had moved from British India to Africa and the second time when they came to Britain. Here, when they were forced to answer the question, 'Where are you from?', tracing one's roots to South Asia was easier, says Verma, than Africa.[4]

With an all-Asian cast, the first play Tara performed was *Sacrifice* (1977), which Verma adapted from a Tagore play set in sixteenth-century Bengal dealing with the clash between self and tradition, duty and truth. Verma saw the piece as offering a 'perspective on our lives here today'.[5] According to Kadija George, this production involved fifty young Asians from the local community wanting to develop a distinct theatrical vocabulary and to have a voice on stage as Asians.[6] Using English in a play about the oppressive nature of communalism positioned Tara in contrast to existing Asian theatre in Britain, which was mainly own-language, amateur, and, aesthetically and ideologically, conservative. Tara's generation, in Verma's words, had 'a deep ambivalence' to Asian languages at a time when to succeed, to be modern and to be treated as equal rather than part of the ethnic ghetto required fluent use of English.[7] Tara believed Asians had a need and a right to make their voice heard in the dominant tongue.

In Tara's first phase, which lasted until 1984, the group explored the historical anchor points of their lives – India, East Africa, and Britain – either through plays set in the present or through seeing the past in relation to the present: the difficulties faced in Britain by a newly arrived boy (*Fuse*, 1978); sexual relationships and family pressure (*Playing the Flame*, 1979); the creation of modern East Africa by colonial Indian labour (*Yes, Memsahib*, 1979); the Amritsar massacre related to riots in modern Britain (*Inkalaab 1919*, 1980); a warrior queen defying the British in India in the 1850s (*Jhansi*, 1980); the early presence of Asians in Britain confronting the problems of the present (*Vilayat or England Your England*, 1981); a young woman's journey from Africa to England (*Scenes in the Life Of...*, 1982); and inter-generational tension (*Ancestral Voices*, 1983).

The company brought in white directors, such as Gerald Chapman, Tony Clark, and David Sulkin, to learn the craft of theatre, and mounted three shows a year before, in 1982, turning fully professional. Funding had come from the Greater London Arts Association and the local council (later to be cut) and, in 1985, the first Arts Council support. As Tara survived this initial period of touring community-based political theatre, it began to forge a new identity through its investigation of theatrical vocabulary to express more fully the complexities of the British-Asian experience. A visit to London's Riverside of the Theatre Academy of Pune in 1980 with Vijay Tendulkar's *Ghashiram Kotwal* crystallized for Verma a way of approaching theatre, which he explored in the subsequent years.[8] Tara moved beyond use of English and the tendency toward naturalism that accompanied it toward a more Indian-influenced aesthetic, returning to the languages they had at first rejected. Now, Tara looked forward to a time when it would not be embarrassing – indeed, it would be enhancing – to speak an Asian language in public.

In 1984, this stage of Tara's development was represented by contrasting shows: its topical *A Cabaret for All Seasons; Chilli In Your Eyes,* a critique of Asian communities and of white society, which depicted the contemporary experiences of young Sikhs, Muslims, and Hindus in east London; and the Sanskrit classic *Miti Ki Gadi* (*The Little Clay Cart*), a fable about poverty, romance, and revolution, considered one of the greatest in Indian culture, in which role reversal and intrigue lead to a peasant becoming king. The play had surfaced briefly in the English repertoire at the beginning of the century and had been revived in 1964 at Hampstead but seen through white eyes.[9] Tara's revisiting of the classic marked a turning point for the company. It was first shown at the Institute of Indian Culture and included added material to highlight the parallels with contemporary racism, a move criticized by some reviewers but in keeping with Tara's mission.[10] The company performed the play again in 1986 and 1991.

Tara continued to link past and present in other productions from the Indian repertoire, such as *Shikari* and *Exile in the Forest* (1983 and 1987–1988, respectively, both of which took stories from the *Mahabharata*); *Anklets of Fire* (1985, based on a medieval Tamil epic); *Tejo Vanio* (1986, an adaptation of a sixteenth-century Bhavai farce); *Bicharo* (1987, adapted from a film based on a Bhavai farce about the plight of the untouchables); *Bhavni Bhavai* (1988, a fourteenth-century Gujarati folk play); *Hayavadana* (1988, Girish Karnad's post-independence play inspired by the eighth-century *Katha-Sarit-Sagar* by way of Thomas Mann's short story, *The Transposed Heads*); and *Heer Ranja* (1992, the British première of Waris Shah's celebrated eighteenth-century Punjabi play).

Verma was beginning to develop a distinctive methodology he termed Binglish, a name that captures the fractured, overlapping hybridity of modern Britain. Binglish is distinguished textually by transposition to an Indian setting often using storytelling devices and, in performance, through costume, set, and the actors' accent, inflection, tone, gesture, and stance. For Verma, Binglish denotes 'a distinct contemporary theatre praxis: featuring Asian or Black casts, produced by independent Asian or black theatre companies…to challenge or provoke the dominant conventions of the English stage'.[11] Crucial to this practice was not only the use within the same show of several languages – Gujarati, Hindi, Punjabi, and English, for instance – but the use of different theatrical modes, whether based on the *Natya Shastra* (the ancient Indian treatise on performing that predates European notions of total theatre); Brecht; Bunraku; Indian folk forms such as Bhavai or Bollywood film conventions; and *commedia dell'arte*. As with the refashioning of European classics by Matura and others, Binglish ideologically and physically decentres English and all the power that flows from this, presenting it not as the supreme authority but as another language among the vast family of languages.[12] Like John and Matura, Verma in his Binglish productions suggests that standard English (itself a moveable entity) is just a variant, however influential and rich, among the many Englishes that can be gathered under the umbrella of the English language.

The acquisition in 1983 – thanks to a Greater London Council grant – of a former snooker hall, in Earlsfield, south-west London, and its renovation in 1985 as a studio, rehearsal/performance space and offices, allowed the company to explore the notion of Binglish further. They collaborated with Theatr Taliesin of Wales on *Talishna* (1984) exploring Celtic and Indian myth, and with the Calicut University Little Theatre on *Kalari* (1987) and *Exile in the Forest* (1987–1988), both of which benefited from a visit by Sankara Pillai from Kerala, an expert in performance traditions in South-West India, including the martial art Kalari. Other specialists, such as Anuradha Kapur, director of New Delhi's major street theatre group Theatre Union and professor at the National School of Drama, were invited to teach Asian performance techniques, a rarity in Britain. Kapur directed *This Story's Not for Telling* (1985), which explored communalism in a devised piece using techniques of popular Indian theatre that proved influential in Tara's future work and consolidated the new direction the company had taken since *The Little Clay Cart*. Shobana Jayasingh was invited to choreograph a revised version of this play that Tara performed under its English title in 1986 at the Arts Theatre as the opening production of the third Black Theatre Season. Verma revised it again for the National's Cottesloe Theatre in 1991, completing a journey with this play from the periphery to the British theatre's mainstream. The performance at the National emphasized the stylized, physical expression of character and used song, dance, and music played live on Asian instruments throughout. The *Times* critic wrote: 'a few more shows like this and western linear theatre will start looking primitive'.[13]

Kapur returned in 1989 to adapt and direct Gogol's *The Government Inspector*, transplanted to post-independence India. It was a production that marked Tara's sustained investigation into the canon of European theatre seen through 'Asian eyes and ears'.[14] A long list of Binglish productions, which ranged from Sophocles and Shakespeare to Molière, Ibsen, and Brecht, included *Danton's Death* (1989); *Tartuffe* (1990); *Oedipus the King* (1991); *Marriage Of Convenience* (1991, a double bill of Brecht's *The Emperor and the Beggar* and Chekhov's *The Proposal*); *Le Bourgeois Gentilhomme* (1994); *Troilus and Cressida* (1993); *Cyrano* (1995); *A Midsummer Night's Dream* (1997); *The Merchant of Venice* (2005); *An Enemy of the People* (2006); and *The Tempest* (2007). This Binglishing re-imagined the classics in the context of the Other and adjusted the power structures contained within them, thereby challenging the established ladder of representation associated with those structures.

Appropriately, Binglishing found its way to the National Theatre, symbol of hierarchical Western cultural values. First came Verma's 1990 production of *Tartuffe*, in which the exposure of hypocrisy becomes focused on an Indian fakir. Verma set the story as a play-within-a-play that is presented to a French visitor at the court of the Mughal Emperor Aurangzeb (about whom Dryden wrote). In his production notebook, Verma explains the notion of translation behind the adaptation – or tradaptation, as it has been called – which lies at the heart of Binglishing:

> I am setting out to translate a seventeenth century French farce through an all-Asian company of performers. This entails a double translation: once from the French original to English; and secondly to an English spoken by Asian actors, who have their own history of the acquisition of English speech. In other words, who are themselves 'translated' men and women – in that they (or their not-too distant forebears) have been 'borne across' from one language and culture to another. In order then to lay bare the full dimension of 'translation', I must take account of the specificity of my performers (their history): by conveying Molière's original playtext into a form that allows the performers to make creative connections between their ancestral traditions and their English present.[15]

In the programme for the production, Verma wrote that to transform a text is 'to do no more than give a voice to what is being done by the act of living in Britain'. By performing the tradaption at the National Theatre – the first Asian play to be seen there performed by an Asian cast and directed by the first Asian director to work there – Tara was showing it was part of redefining what the term *national* means and asserting authority over representation.[16] *The Little Clay Cart* and *Cyrano* followed at the Cottesloe – the latter not being well received – and there the road to the mainstream ended for more than a decade.[17] Bruised, Tara returned to its roots but with a new set of skills and experience. Aided by a more secure financial footing and lottery money, Tara moved beyond the translation phase to telling stories of migration across a century from India to Africa and from Africa to Britain. The result was an epic diasporic trilogy, *Journey to the West*, a millennial example of global hybridity, several years in the making and first staged in its entirety in 2002. The titles of the constituent parts – *Genesis*, *Exodus*, and *Revelations* – are redolent of the Western tradition but, through inspiration derived from a range of cultures in addition to that represented by the Bible – drawing on, for example, the *Odyssey*, the *Ramayana*, the *Mahabharata*, and the *Hsi-yu Chi-Xi You Ji* (the Monkey King legend) – it was storytelling steeped in the ancient landscapes of Asia too.

Genesis (1999) offers an account of the Indian workers who were transported to Kenya at the end of the nineteenth century to work as indentured labour for the British, building the East Africa Railway but denied the land they had been promised on completion of their work. The play ends on an optimistic note with the discovery of a baby abandoned on the railway and adopted by Fateh, a Punjabi Sikh worker. *Exodus* (1998), set in Kenya in 1968, follows three teenagers, a Sikh, a Hindu, and a Muslim, descendants of the workers in Part One, who face increasing hostility from the Africanization policy set in train after independence. They leave for Britain

FIGURE 7.1 *Genesis,* 1999, the first part of the Tara Arts trilogy *Journey to the West* (Courtesy of Stephen Vaughan and Tara Arts)

ahead of the deadline limiting Kenyan Asian immigration, only to meet racism from the white society, which raises their political awareness. The play ends on a pessimistic note, with the stabbing to death of Ranjit, an echo of the murder that led to the founding of Tara. *Revelations* (2000), set in contemporary Britain in thrall to popular music and lifestyle culture, has the son of a Hindu mother and Muslim father, who appeared in the second part, travelling Britain to scatter his grandfather's ashes at Hadrian's Wall. Kamaal's journey is one of self-discovery, confronting the draw of both assimilation and separatism, neither of which he favours, as he questions his own identity. Arriving at his destination, which, as Dominic Hingorani points out, is a tangible reminder of England as a once colonized nation and a colonizing nation, Kamaal accepts and celebrates his hybrid identity and is determined to 'make this England, our England, full of all your long journeys West'.[18]

Journey to the West began and ended with the communities whose story the trilogy set out to tell. Invitations were sent in Hindi, Urdu, and Gujarati to Asian communities in London, Leicester, Birmingham, and elsewhere for people to tell their story to the actors, who recorded the interviews on digital video, from which transcripts were made. The actors not only used these interviews to build their characters, they learned songs, games, and skills such as making rotis (flatbread), and put some of the experiences directly into the text. It was important to honour these stories in the telling, and Tara took the productions to those communities who had provided the source material. The entrances to the various spaces in which the trilogy played were turned into an Asian bazaar, selling food and craft work and offering displays by mehndi (henna) and rangoli (sand painting) artists and presenting exhibitions by local groups and schools, who performed before the shows began and were involved in linked projects in their own neighbourhoods.

Audiences were always critical for Tara and, without adequate support from the media and funders, it was not always easy to attract them. Tara also challenged its audiences, through its treatment of conservatism in religion and patriarchal family structures and its view of pre- and post-colonial history; for some, Tara was too radical, whereas for others, not radical enough. Tara also had to contend with accusations of inauthenticity, because they did not come directly from a South Asian homeland but by way of Africa. *Journey to the West* was a culmination of an exploration of such issues. The validation of the Asian voice came through the Binglish methodology that underpins the production, both in terms of the research that informed it and the performance techniques of the multicultural cast. These were drawn from Tara's usual range of skills and employed several languages, which, at different times, would mean some audience members' getting a joke or reference while others did not – an essential part of the Binglish experience, particularly for those non-Asian language speakers used to others being marginalized. In similar Binglish spirit, the show was replete with intertextual connections, for example, in *Exodus* when Ranjit's mother, Daljeet, is told she cannot wear a sari at work for health and safety reasons. As the sari is unwound, an episode in the *Mahabharata* is evoked of the attempted disrobing of Draupadi; Krishna protects her by increasing the length of her sari so that the disrober is completely exhausted before he has reached the end of the cloth.

Without Krishna in modern Britain, as Hingorani comments, Daljeet is left standing metaphorically 'naked' in slacks and a blouse.[19]

The trilogy ranks as one of the most ambitious pieces undertaken by British diasporic theatre. Without minimizing the extent of damage and pain inflicted by colonialism, the piece celebrates not only the survival of these cultures against suppression and forced migration but their incorporation of Britain itself in their cultural practice, a historical triumph as yet only partially understood within the former imperial homelands.

Along with its children's shows and outreach work, Tara since the trilogy has continued to explore the mutual influences at work in the Asian-British relationship; sometimes the story is from the past (e.g., *A Taste for Mangoes* in 2003, telling the story of the Boston-born David Ochterlony who went to India in the late eighteenth century and embraced its culture) and sometimes the present (e.g., Hanif Kureishi's adaptation of his novel *The Black Album* in 2009, which marked the return of Tara to the National Theatre). From its inception, Tara has been at the centre of British-Asian theatre activity. It helped form the Asian Theatre Forum in 1985, was a key contributor to the Black Theatre Forum and Black Theatre Seasons, and survived several testing times, for example, when grant cuts in 1991 brought to an end the use of the studio as a programmed arts centre. The later diversity of British-Asian theatre owes a great deal to the company, which provided a productive channel for many artists, such as the writer-director team of Rukhsana Ahmad and Rita Wolf who founded the Kali Theatre Company; actors Naveen Andrews (seen in *The Buddha of Suburbia* and *The English Patient*) and Sanjeev Bhaskar (*Goodness Gracious Me* and *The Kumars at No. 42*); actor/playwright Ayub Khan-Din; director Kristine Landon-Smith and actor/playwright Sudha Buchar (the co-founders of Tamasha Theatre Company); writer/director Dominic Rai, who set up Mán Melá; composer Nitin Sawhney; and actor/writer Meera Syal.

After Tara

In the wake of Tara, a number of other British-Asian groups were formed, including Sahar Arts (1978–1981) founded by Shakila Taranum Maan, who wrote and directed several plays for the group and whose work has focused on the role and experience of women. A member of Southall Street Theatre and Lancaster Road Theatre Group, she became an award-winning film director and is co-author with Parminder Sekhon of Mehtab's *Not Just an Asian Babe* (1997–1998) and *All God's Angels* (2000). Her depiction of domestic abuse of Asian women in *The Bride* (2003) caused strong reactions. The Hounslow Arts Co-operative was established in 1981 and found realism through poetry, music, and visual arts and, according to Verma, was the only Asian group to exclude references to India in its work.[20] Pointing the way toward a multimedia future and groups such as Moti Roti was the British Asian Theatre Company, formed by Raj Patel after a film and video workshop in 1982. Shows included *Ahmed the Wonderful Oriental Gentleman* (1983) and *Anarkali* (1986), which looked at the experiences of Asian women in contemporary Britain through the story of the legendary dancer with whom a Mughal prince was infatuated. The Asian Theatre Co-operative was formed in 1983 and had a distinctive interest in language and nurturing playwrights. Its first notable production was Farrukh Dhondy's *Vigilantes* (1985) in the first Black Theatre Season. Dhondy was a key figure in diasporic culture in his writing about British Asians and African-Caribbeans and in his work on television, where he became an influential producer. Among other productions of the Co-operative were Dhondy's *Film, Film, Film* (1986); H. O. Nazareth's *Bhangra Dancer and her Man with Cancer* (1987); a comedy double bill called *Curried Chips* (1988); a devised show, *Jawaani* (Youth, 1988), which was created by Asian women as a trilingual double bill that, among other issues, explored contrasting notions of love and romance; and, in a co-production with the Half Moon, Lorca's *Blood Wedding* (1989). Taking a different tack was Madhav Sharma's company, Actors Unlimited, which in *Hedda in India* (1983) offered an early example of a diasporic group 'tradapting' the European canon by relocating Ibsen's play to post-independence India. Actors Unlimited also staged Dilip Hiro's *Apply Apply No Reply* (1983), originally seen on television and dealing with the effects of the caste system.

In the 1970s and 1980s, a new generation of writers appeared, and, like others from diasporic backgrounds who were British-born or raised in Britain, they did not want to be trapped in the black or Asian pigeon-hole. The best known is Hanif Kureishi, perhaps the writer who has done more than any other to alter perceptions of what it means to be a British Asian. A South Londoner, Kureishi's first play, *Soaking the Heat* (1976) was set among students and written while he was still at university. His father sent it to the Royal Court, where the play was seen in a Sunday evening production at the Theatre Upstairs. After finishing college, Kureishi became prolific with a string of original plays and adaptations: *The King and Me* (1980); *The Mother Country* (1980); *Tomorrow – Today!* (1981); *Outskirts* (1981); *Cinders* (1981, a version of Janusz Glowacki's play); *Borderline* (1981); Ostrovsky's *Artists and Admirers* (1982); *Birds of Passage* (1983); and Brecht's *Mother Courage and Her Children* (1984). Of these early plays, *Borderline* is the most like the type of political play previously associated with diasporic theatre from which Kureishi wished to distinguish himself. The play is based on research in Southall in the aftermath of a major clash with police in which a protester was killed at a demonstration over the National Front's being allowed to march through the area. *Borderline* was presented by the major touring company Joint Stock with a multiracial cast, a point of criticism when some Asian roles were played by white actors. Kureishi says he was writing to order like a journalist rather than an artist, and the result was 'external, sketchy'.[21] Kureishi's plays reached the mainstream – Riverside, Hampstead, Royal Court, and the RSC – and he won the prestigious George Devine new play award for *Outskirts*, in some respects a forerunner of *My Beautiful Launderette*, the 1985 film that propelled him into artistic celebrity as a film and later a book writer.

After Kureishi came the likes of Rukshana Ahmad, Harwant Bains, Parv Bancil, Sudha Buchar, Maya Chowdry, Nandita Ghose, Tanika Gupta, Raminder Kaur, Ayub Khan-Din, Jyoti Patel, Parminder Sekhon, and Meera Syal. This growth in the number of British-Asian playwrights accompanied a rise in the number and spread of groups and higher visibility of British-Asian actors and directors in a broad range of venues, from Watermans Arts Centre, Drill Hall, Oval House, and the Drum to Leicester Haymarket, Theatre Royal Stratford East, and the Birmingham Repertory. Indicative was the change in direction of a company such as Red Ladder, which had a formidable record as a (white) political theatre group. Having moved to Leeds in 1976, Red Ladder began focussing in the mid-1980s on the experiences of local young people, and, in particular, young British Asians, especially women. In 1994, Red Ladder appointed a British-Asian Artistic Director, Kully Thiarai.

Among the many groups that appeared from the late 1980s on, revealing the multiplicity of styles in British-Asian theatre, were: Tamasha; Kali; Moti Roti; Chandica Arts Company; Mán Melá; Yelele; Maya Productions; Hathi Productions (based in Leicester and known as the Asian Young People's Theatre until the mid-1980s); and Mehtab. Kali, formed in 1990 by Rita Wolf and Rukhsana Ahmad, aimed to develop new writing by South Asian women, emphasising the central role women were playing in diasporic theatre. Ahmad says Kali, which has many meanings, conjures up the idea of 'female power, regeneration, fertility and strength', all of which values have been celebrated by the company in the notable and unique achievement of its guiding ambition, from its first show on.[22] The inaugural show was Ahmad's *Song for a Sanctuary* (1990). Set mainly in a women's refuge, the play deals not only with domestic violence but the differences and tensions between the women who end up in the refuge. Other Kali productions have included plays by Azma Dar, Bettina Gracias, Joyoti Grech, Tanika Gupta, Yasmin Whittaker Khan, Anu Kumar, Bapsi Sidhwa, and Shelley Silas. Moti Roti (fat, flat bread), founded in 1991 by Ali Zaidi and Keith Khan, mixes Indian and Caribbean influences in carnivalesque, cross-discipline shows such as *Flying Costumes Floating Tombs* (1991), presented by Bristol's Arnolfini and LIFT, and *Moti Roti Puttli Chunni* (1993), co-produced with Stratford East, which captured the spirit of Bollywood on stage. Chandica (a supreme marital goddess) was founded in 1993 (folded 2000) by Raminder Kaur, who wrote several plays for the group on strong, female-oriented themes, including *Draupadi's Robes* (1993), *Bullets through the Golden Stream* (1994, 1997), *Pregnant Pauses* (1997), *Futures* (1999), and *Spirit of the Age* (1999).

The name Mán Melá (1993), founded by Dominic Rai, comes from the Hindustani for 'entertainment of the mind'. The company has a strong community focus and draws on British-Asian history and the literature of South Asian. Rai wrote and directed the first show, *Asian Voices* (1993), which came from historical stories he and Alka Prabhakar had put together earlier for *Portraits*, commissioned by Tara to celebrate the British-Asian experience. The company has promoted new writing, as with *Romeo and Ram* in 1994 by John Whitfield, which explores the love between two men, one from Shakespeare, the other from Hindu scriptures. Mán Melá has also used theatre to deal with social concerns such as HIV (*The Dangers of Common Sense*). In its *Asian Elders Theatre Campaign* (1996), the company worked with Age Concern to use theatre as a means of self-expression for older people, especially in relation to promoting mental health. *Across the Black Waters* (1998) by Gerald

Wells, presented at the National Archives in Kew, was an adaptation of part of Mulk Raj Anand's powerful anti-war novel and was accompanied by readings of Indian soldiers' letters from the Western Front. *The Cornershop* (2000), three new plays by Yasmin Khan, Ravi Mangat, and Ashok Patel, exploring British-Asian family life, was the company's most widely seen production. It was first commissioned by the Hawth, Crawley, as part of a three-year programme supported by the Arts Council of England to encourage new British-Asian theatre and to develop audiences for it.

Maya Productions was founded in 1994 by Sita Ramamurthy and Christopher Preston to encourage work by black and Asian playwrights; its first production (in 1995) was *Over Hear* by Neil Biswas. Mehtab (moon in Farsi) unusually received Arts Council support in 1995 for its first production, which was in Punjabi and not English: *Kali Salwar* is based on a short story by Saadat Hassan Manto about a prostitute whose clients are mainly British soldiers serving the Raj. The company of British Asians, founded by Parminder Sekhon, went on to produce shows in English – for example, two versions of *Not Just an Asian Babe* (short version, 1997; long, 1998); *Madhuri I Love You* (1997); *All God's Angels* (2000); *The Maharaja's Daughters* (2002); and *The Ghosts of Bhopal* (2005 – as wells as shows in Punjabi – *Atish Bazi* (1999). Parv Bancil's *Made in England* (1997), set in the milieu of the British-Asian music scene and which explores the price of success, was revived in 2003 by his Firebrand Company for a festival bearing the play's name that explored the notion of what it means to be Asian and British, and included *The Bride* by Shakila Taranum Maan.

Tamasha

Of these groups, Tamasha became the best known. Though its aim was similar to that of Tara – to 'reflect through theatre the Asian experience from British-Asian life to authentic accounts of aspects of life in the Indian subcontinent' – the means to achieve this and to be authentic were different. Tamasha's aesthetic was primarily based on 'a British Western style of acting, naturalistic and realisic'.[23] Yet, as Hingorani says of the company,

> the Asian provenance of its theatrical subjects, the methodological use of linguistically hybrid texts, its use of largely Asian casts, as well as the training it provides to new Asian writers, actors, directors and designers, demonstrates the company's insistence on placing the performance of cultural difference at the centre of the British stage.[24]

Though Tamasha can mean a sixteenth-century Indian folk performance genre, the company is closer in spirit to the word's other meanings in Urdu and Hindi of performance, revue, display, spectacle, or causing a stir.

The company was founded in 1989 to revive a production Kristine Landon-Smith had directed the year before in India, where she had been teaching at the National School of Drama in New Delhi on a British Council sponsored trip. According to Hingorani, she had intended to direct Chekov's *The Seagull* but decided to switch from this Eurocentric choice to devise a performance based on Mulk Raj Anand's novel, *Untouchable*, which, as the title suggests, deals with the predicament of that caste. Tamasha produced this story of a day in the life of a teenage latrine cleaner at Riverside Studios, playing alternate nights in Hindi and English. The attention to realistic detail won laudatory comment from critics. The production was privately financed, but the company quickly established itself around a core of artists and gained public subsidy and awards as it pursued its aims of supporting new writing, promoting intercultural theatre education, and offering professional training.[25]

Tamasha's next productions maintained a similarly realistic approach in language, gesture and design: *House of the Sun* (1991), a co-production with the Theatre Royal Stratford East, adapted by Buchar and Landon-Smith from Meira Chand's novel about the displacement after Partition of Sindhis to Bombay; two plays by Ruth Carter, *Women of the Dust* (1992), which tells of an all-female workforce on a Delhi construction site, commissioned by Oxfam in honour of its fiftieth birthday and the first of Tamasha's shows to be taken to India, and *A Yearning* (1995), Lorca's *Yerma* transposed to Birmingham's Punjabi community; and *A Shaft of Sunlight* (1994) by Abhijat Joshi, set in contemporary Gujarat, north-west India exploring communal politics and the problems of a Hindu-Muslim marriage.

Desire for authenticity pushed at the limits of realism, as Hingorani shows. In *Untouchable*, for example, the English and Hindi versions were not exact translations of each other, and, for the English to be convincing, it mixed colloquial vocabulary with Hindi phrases and rhythms. The father calls to his son: 'are uth (get up) – come on, get up ma da chodh suer ke bache. Come on – you getting up or not? Get up you bastard or I'll give you a kick up the arse.'[26] For *Women of the Dust*, Buchar, Landon-Smith, and Carter went to India to research. Buchar interviewed women in Hindi and the local dialect, and translated the interviews for Carter. When the creative team listened to the tapes, they became interested not just in the content and distinctive

FIGURE 7.2 Tamasha touring production of Ruth Carter's *Women of the Dust*, 1992 (Image by Sue Wilson. Courtesy of Tamasha)

phraseology but the way the women talked, in tone, pitch, pace, and rhythm, which also differed from urban speech. Designer Sue Mayes provided a convincing set complete with ladders, bricks, and a cement mixer, which the actors used to perform the tasks of a building site. In Britain, critics unfamiliar with the Rajasthani women who were the play's subject, once again remarked on the production's credibility – a slice of life of the Other, as Verma puts it. However, the challenge in India was greater, with a danger of stereotyping the women as unable to speak either English or Hindi 'properly'. Hingorani quotes one critic who found the production deceptive enough, and suggests the text does transcend the stereotype.[28] In Dimple Godiwala's view, the grim reality of these early Tamasha productions was designed to reassure the British-Asians that 'India, rural or metropolitan, is backward, economically and socially' and that, therefore, they had 'left behind a land of inopportunity and economic decline.'[29]

The company's next production, Ayub Khan-Din's *East is East* (1996), changed the tone, even if the 'slice of life' naturalism could be read as carrying a similar message. Developed in a writers' workshop organized by Tamasha with the Royal Court and Birmingham Repertory, *East is East* brought Tamasha to wider notice. The play moved from the Royal Court Theatre Upstairs at the Ambassadors Theatre to the Theatre Royal Stratford East and then the Royal Court Downstairs at the Duke of York's (the first British-Asian play in the West End) before being made into a successful low-budget film. A semi-autobiographical comedy, *East is East* is set in working-class Salford like *A Taste of Honey* forty years before. Khan-Din looks at issues of identity for the children of a Pakistani father and an English mother in 1970, and challenges restrictive definitions of Britishness that reject Asian or other heritages and cultural differences.

Showing British Asians not usually seen on stage, the play gained popularity with both Asian and non-Asian audiences because of the familiarity of the family situation and the laughter it stimulated; for some, acquaintance with the form would also have been a factor, as *East is East* is a recognizable social comedy whereas for others, especially British Asians, the act of representation itself would have been valued, even though there were criticisms of the portrayal of the father, the sole Asian in the play. George, or Genghis as his children call him, is conservative, patriarchal, and physical, but he is also shown at prayer, after which he embraces his eldest son, Abdul, who recognizes this as important in order 'to belong to something.'[30] In response to the criticism, Khan-Din say,s 'my Dad was like that … .[I] am not interested in what people want me to say'.[31] The children, grappling with their hybrid identity, face a tussle over finding their place in British society; one son says, 'we speak English not Urdu', whereas Abdul points out that 'no one round here thinks we're English, we're the Paki family who run the chippy'. In rejecting the compromises and humiliations of assimilation, he says: 'I don't want that out there … it's as alien to me as me dad's world is to you.'[32]

Tamasha continued to pursue a mix of styles. It used realism in productions such as *A Tainted Dawn* (1997) by Buchar and Landon-Smith, marking the fiftieth anniversary of Indian Partition with stories of displacement and disillusion, and a more flamboyant style in *Fourteen Songs, Two Weddings and a Funeral* (1998), which both cherishes and affectionately has fun with popular romantic genres in British and Asian cinema; the title evokes the British film *Four Weddings and a Funeral* whereas the plot, which revolves around matchmaking, is taken from the inspiration for the show, the Bollywood film *Hum Aapke Hain Koun*.[33] There was another British-Asian 'slice of life' comedy, *Balti Kings* (1999), which was researched among the Birmingham restaurant trade and, as Anne Fuchs says, was less private and more public.[34] More new plays also followed (Emteaz Hussain's debut play, *Sweet Cider*, in 2008, in which two Pakistani girls end up in a women's refuge, came from the company's New Writing course) and further collaborations: *A Fine Balance* (2006, with Hampstead Theatre), based on Rohinton Mistry's novel set during India's state of emergency in 1975, and Tamasha's first children's show, *Child of the Divide* (2006, with Polka Theatre), adapted by Buchar from a Bisham Sahni short story. There was also a return to Bollywood in a musical version of *Wuthering Heights* (2009). Twenty years after the company was established, this inventive diversity is summed up in Tamasha's goal 'to transform theatre to create a space where British Asian talent takes centre stage, through original writing and productions that provoke debate, ideas, passion and laughter'.[35]

Founded by women, and a company in which women play a vital and innovative part, whether as actor, director, or writer, Tamasha and groups such as Kali, Chandica, and Mehtab were symptomatic in highlighting the importance of women in the development of British-Asian theatre. The most public controversy surrounding diasporic theatre also happened to arise from the work of a female writer when some in her own community threatened her life and she had to go into hiding. British-born Sikh Gurpreet Kaur Bhatti set her play, *Behzti* (Dishonour, 2004), in a gurdwara or temple. The play, which involves rape and murder, addresses 'corruption at the heart of the community', but the issue for the Birmingham Council of Gurdwaras, which was consulted on the production, was sacrilege.[36] The Council asked for a change of location in the action of the play to avoid this but was refused. The production, directed by Janet Steel, artistic director of Kali, went ahead at the Birmingham Repertory studio theatre, which had a reputation for presenting diasporic work.[37] Protests grew, and the local police warned they could not guarantee the safety of audiences. When one of the theatre's external glass panels was broken in a crush between police and protesters, the theatre cancelled the production on health and safety grounds. This collision between art and religion, as Bhatti describes it, exposes tensions that lie behind the hybridity that is elsewhere celebrated as the dynamic of the British-South Asian aesthetic.[38]

A wider acceptance of this aesthetic was part of a social shift in which comedy and the subversion of demeaning comic stereotypes played a significant part through television shows such as *Goodness Gracious Me* and *The Kumars at No. 42* and through the theatre comedy circuit. In mainstream theatre, accommodation of a British-South Asian aesthetic meant recognition and absorption and through it intercultural renewal. This acknowledgement ranged across a broad spectrum: from the invitation to Verma to direct at the National Theatre, its staging of Salman Rushdie's *Haroun and the Sea of Stories* (1997) and the Birmingham Repertory production of *The*

Ramayana (2000) – adapted by English playwright Peter Oswald, directed by Associate Director Indhu Rubasingham, and choreographed by Piali Ray – to the West End appearance of A. R. Rahman's Bollywood spectacle, *Bombay Dreams* (2002), produced by Andrew Lloyd-Webber with script by Syal.

Bhangra bands and British-Asian fashion became chic, and British-South Asian theatre continued to draw on and help develop this rich heritage of cultural expression, whether in the mela (Asian carnival), mushaira (Urdu poetry gathering), or extravagant Bollywood satires. This wider acceptance also generated several local schemes supporting the diversity agenda. Naseem Khan, for instance, wrote the *British Asian Theatre Report* (1994) based on research in the East Midlands, and this influenced the development of the Asian Theatre Initiative, later NATAK, at Haymarket Theatre, Leicester. There remains, however, a lack of dedicated theatre/performance spaces and continuing need of greater consistency in support and audience development programmes. In response to this need, performer, teacher, and choreographer Piali Ray founded Sampad in 1990 as a national agency for the development of South Asian Arts, which is based in Birmingham.

East Asian theatre

British-Asian theatre's vibrant variety was created in the face of the homogenizing effect of racism, which cuts across ethnicity, culture, and class. Just as in India, the middle class of Asian heritage in the Caribbean and East Africa were positioned below the white strata but socialized to regard those of black African descent as inferior. In Britain, this codification was often obliterated. Briefly, Asian theatre was referred to as Black as a description of political reality and solidarity, but this apparent harmony contained tensions between those of Asian descent and those of Caribbean and African heritage and between those simply labelled Asian, a term that collapses enormous numbers of differing peoples, including the two most populous countries that together account for more than one-third of the world's estimated inhabitants. The description *South Asian* was introduced in contrast to *East Asian*, though both are still portmanteau terms concealing as much as they reveal.

Several initiatives in the 1980s confronted this presumed uniformity encoded in the label *Asian*. They included the establishment in 1986 of the Chinese Arts Centre in Manchester, home to the second largest Chinese community in Britain, and in 1988 the founding of Mu-Lan Theatre Company as a distinctively British-East Asian group with an emphasis on new writing that aimed to provide a creative voice for the British-Chinese community. The company's shows have covered many subjects: *Madame Mao's Memories* (1991) by Henry Ong tells of the actress who became more feared than her husband; *Porcelain* (1992) by Chay Yew deals with 'cottaging'; *The Magic Fundoshi* (Three Modern Kyogen, 1993) by Donald Richie, adapts in a mixture of Western and Japanese styles a comic form of theatre, Kyogen, which was developed as an alternative to the more symbolic Noh theatre – the production was taken to Singapore; *Suzy Wrong - Human Cannon* (1994), written and performed by Anna Chen, debunks the stereotypes of Chinese women; *Three Japanese Women*

(1994) by Malcolm Campbell depicts the lives of the so-called 'comfort women' in Japan after World War 2; and *Take Away* (1998) by Stephen Clark looks behind the scenes at the eponymous staple feature of every town that is normally taken for granted.

Mu-Lan presented a comedy sketch show, *Frying Circus* (1999), at London's Docklands New Year Festival and, for the millennium, produced an inter-active installation in a London park. *Take Away My Take Away* (2000) 'deconstructed' the takeaway and involved a children's kitchen takeaway orchestra with pots, woks, pans, ladles, and steamers as instruments and calligraphy on the lids of the cartons. *Romeo and Juliet* (2001) was probably the first Shakespeare production in Britain with a predominantly Anglo-Chinese cast. Matt Wilkinson's *Sun is Shining* (2004), a two-hander that crosses four countries and tells the troubled love story of a mixed heritage City trader and an artist and recovering alcoholic, was the most critically acclaimed of Mu-Lan's productions and went to New York. Paul Courtenay Hyu's *The Missing Chink* (2004) was a four part-series on television dealing with the absence of British-East Asians on television developed from a Mu-Lan idea. Despite its creativity, the company struggled to find funding and ceased doing original work in 2005.

Yellow Earth, founded in 1995 by David Tse and four other East Asian performers, at first tackled the dislocation involved in coming from Hong Kong to Britain (in *New Territories*, 1996). Relationships to China remained a key theme in both *Behind the Chinese Takeaway* (1997), a multimedia exploration of the British-Chinese diaspora during the Hong Kong handover and, at the time of the Beijing Olympics, *Running the Silk Road* (2008) by Paul Sirett, in which a group of friends run the ancient Silk Road trading route to China carrying an 'alternative' Olympic flame. Yellow Earth offered cross-media versions of *Blue Remembered Hills* (1999), the Dennis Potter TV play; *Rashomon* (2001), the story of an adolescent Filipino gang using martial arts, trance music, and digital technology and drawing on the original story and film; and *King Lear* (2006) in English and Mandarin with English surtitles. The group also staged the imagined 'prequel', *Lear's Daughters* (2003), by the Women's Theatre Group and Elaine Feinstein. In 2002, Yellow Earth launched *Typhoon*, an annual play-reading festival, and the same year staged *The Butcher's Skin*, a classic Vietnamese comedy of mistaken identity by Luu Quang Vu. Gaining Arts Council revenue funding, Yellow Earth became the flagship East Asian company in Britain, touring in Britain and abroad and combining an interest in the physical ensemble traditions of East and West with its support for new writing and multimedia presentations.

The vitality and variety of both the British East and South Asian companies are a challenge not only to the conventional theatre of Britain but to the conventional theatre of Asia. As Rustom Bharucha puts it, the 'Orient' can be manufactured in Asia itself and 'then transported abroad to validate earlier modes of "Orientalism" which are in the process of being dismantled elsewhere'.[39] In asserting a new aesthetic, British-Asian theatre offered a self-assured reply to the constraints of British naturalism and its concomitant style of subjective acting that mistrusts theory and dedicated training. The work of British-Asian theatre also formed a significant contribution to the debate on inter-culturalism amid criticism of productions such as Peter Brook's version of the *Mahabharata*, which came to Glasgow in 1988 with a multicultural cast and much acclaim. Brook was accused of a 'pick-and-mix' supermarket approach to other cultures rather than presenting a dynamic interaction between them. British-Asian theatre offered plenty of examples of encounters between East and West, between Asia and Europe, that have broken and crossed boundaries and, in so doing, have shifted them on the basis of mutual respect, relocating the former subject peoples to their rightful place.

8

'ALL A WE IS ENGLISH'[1]

Britain under Conservative rule in the 1980s and for much of the 1990s saw black and Asian theatre wax and then wane, its growth the result of earlier forces' coming to a head and its falling away a consequence of cuts allied to a state-driven cultural project that celebrated the individual over the collective and gave renewed impetus to aggressive, narrow nationalism. How to survive while simultaneously asserting the heterodox, hybrid nature of non-white theatre and its contribution to British theatre was the urgent challenge.

Within two years of the Thatcher government's election to power in 1979, Britain saw perhaps the most serious rioting of its postwar era, which led to major developments in public diversity policy, though less significant change at the level of delivery. The black community could no longer be taken for granted and was demanding its rights as British citizens. The theatre group that epitomized this new urgency and resilience and the need to adapt to survive was the Black Theatre Co-operative (BTC).[2] The group was founded by Mustapha Matura and white director Charlie Hanson in 1978 after Hanson had failed to interest any theatres in *Welcome Home Jacko*, despite Matura's standing as the leading black playwright of his generation. Under the BTC label, Hanson staged a lunchtime Matura double bill *More, More* and *Another Tuesday* at the Institute of Contemporary Arts before launching *Welcome Home Jacko* with an Arts Council project grant.[3] The production opened at the Factory in west London in May 1979 and toured to venues such as the Riverside Studios, the Sheffield Crucible, and the Theatre Royal Stratford East and also venues in the United States and continental Europe, including an appearance at the Théâtre des Nations festival in Amsterdam.

The play, set in an inner-city youth club adorned with images of Africa and Haile Selassie, focuses on the return of Jacko after five years in jail for rape, hailed as a hero for not having informed on others. He sees himself differently, however, and openly challenges the rhetoric and illusions of the young men. Though the portrayal of the young Rastafarians angered some, the play was very popular, attracting a new urban youth audience. A television producer saw the production and commissioned what became *No Problem*, one of the first black series to be broadcast at prime time. *Jacko* was given its edge in performance by actors who had helped turn Matura's language into authentic street expression, representing a texture, vocabulary, and rhythm belonging to those who were born or raised in Britain rather than the older diasporic emigrants.[4] The BTC led a reinvigoration of black theatre with its muscular, dynamic style of realism and sharp humour, which represented a shift that changed the nature of black theatre and its relationship to Britain and to heritage.

Like earlier ventures, the BTC aimed to provide opportunities in a range of skills, including those of writer, performer, director, producer, theatre technician, and administrator. Unlike earlier ventures, however, it was also able to acknowledge the existence of an indigenous black British theatre exemplified by the presence of black writers and a new generation of actors such as Brian Bovell, Burt Caesar, Gordon Case, Victor Romero Evans, Malcolm Frederick, Judith Jacob, Trevor Laird, and Chris Tummings. The BTC, which won its first Arts Council annual grant in 1984, was prolific, averaging about four shows a year in its first half decade. The BTC was at the start controlled by its pool of artists, who elected a six-strong committee to oversee the company, which offered a broad range of repertoire from new writing and revivals to opera and hip-hop performance. This repertoire included Farrukh Dhondy's *Mama Dragon* (1980), *Shapesters* (1980, which was seen at the National Theatre and the Third World Festival, Korea) and *Trojans* (1981); Matura's *One Rule* (1981); Edgar White's *Trinity* (1982), *The Nine Night* (1983), *Redemption Song* (1984), and *Ritual* (1985); a revival of Sam Shepard's *The Tooth of Crime* (1983); Steve Carter's *Nevis Mountain Dew* (1983); Frank McField's *No Place to Be Nice* (1984); Jacqueline Rudet's *Money to Live* (1984); and a revival of *A Raisin in the Sun* (1985). Yemi Ajibade's *Waiting for Hannibal* (1986) achieved one of the company's aims in having a black stage manager and assistant stage manager (both women).

The collective nature of the group was not sustained; Charlie Hanson became artistic director and, when he left to pursue his career in television, Malcolm Frederick took over and was later replaced by Joan-Ann Maynard. By this time in the early 1990s, the BTC found it could afford only one commission a year, which limited growth through a necessary commitment to planning round unknown work. The BTC, which had become Britain's (and Europe's) longest-surviving black theatre company, tried to break from this model and, in 1996, appointed Felix Cross as artistic director to carry through the transition. Cross, playwright and director but best known as a widely produced composer and lyricist of shows such as *Blues for Railton* and *Glory!*, instituted an annual beat festival and renamed the company Nitro in 1999 to begin a new phase in its life, concentrating on black British musical theatre.

The Factory, the first home of the BTC, was in many ways a west London Keskidee, a centre for the local community, in this case run by a Neighbourhood Residents Association. Founded in 1974, it was a calypso centre and housed the Paddington Print Workshop, Paddington Dark Room, Soucouyant Carnival

Club, and the Paddington Youth Steel Band, which won many of the early pan competitions in Notting Hill. The Factory was refurbished for the BTC and, in 1986, it became the Yaa Asantewaa Centre. In 1997, it began producing a season of short plays that, like its carnival programme, included international involvement. In the early years of the twenty-first century, the Yaa launched its first national and European Carnival Theatre tour and an accredited training programme for carnival artists and collaborated with Cultural Exchange Through Theatre In Education to create a new carnival theatre piece called *Dear Comrade*, based on the life and work of Carnival pioneer Claudia Jones.[5] Many similar centres around the country came and went, trying to carry out similar, under-reported activities at local level, for example, in south London, Umoja's The Base, or in Birmingham the CAVE, the Drum, the Midlands Arts Centre, and Nu Century Arts.

The theatrical achievements of the 1970s were developed in the 1980s with increased institutional backing, part of a wave of activity on many fronts – political, social, and cultural – mainly at community level, and also in other live arts and in cinema, poetry, and fiction. Non-white artists, particularly those born or raised in Britain, were going beyond the underlying notions of the previous period in exploring the meaning of difference, of being black, and trying to resolve the seemingly inescapable tension forced on black theatre between art and social work. Like their white counterparts, in a globalized, post-modern era, they wanted to discover new ways of being politically and artistically active without losing any sense of – indeed as part of finding – their distinctive identity. Many continued to wish to be considered as artists rather than as black or Asian artists. Whatever the problems with funding, which was never generous for minorities – and cuts hit them the hardest – black theatre was now recognized as a distinct phenomenon. Funders with differing degrees of persuasion and effect insisted non-diasporic clients at local, regional, or national level take diasporic theatre of colour seriously.

For diasporic theatre, the term *black* was replacing *ethnic minority* or *ethnic* and, in recognition of its political rather than literal meaning, came in the 1980s to carry an uppercase *B* to embrace all non-white theatre regardless of geography, history, or origin and to signify the common problems faced in a white culture still scarred by racism. The uppercase *B* also signified confidence and the ability of Black theatre to make demands on its own terms as it developed its own aesthetic. This was distinguished by a focused energy, whether drawing on the observations of naturalism, as writers such as Matura, Tunde Ikoli, and Caryl Phillips were doing, or non-naturalistic techniques promoted by writers such as the African-American Ntosake Shange in her choreopoem *for colored girls who have considered suicide when the rainbow is enuf*, which was seen in London in 1979, or the dub poetry of Linton Kwesi Johnson, which sounded a new note of angry resistance.

Under the Black theatre umbrella could be found an astonishing diversity – exemplified by a range of groups from the BTC, Carib Theatre, Tara, Temba, and Umoja to Black Mime Theatre, Double Edge, Options Ltd, Roots Theatre, Theatre of Black Women, and Unlock the Chains. Such groups and the many others not listed here invigorated the British theatre in the 1980s through a remarkable rise and spread in activity. This spread could be seen geographically and in range, identity, the presence of black performers and playwrights, and the number and publication of plays, not just by individual writers but as volumes of black and Asian plays.[6] Outlets such as the Africa Centre, Commonwealth Institute, and Nehru Centre (the cultural wing of the Indian High Commission), which occasionally presented plays, were supplemented by the arts centre circuit and a new diversity awareness in venues such as Contact, Derby Playhouse, Drill Hall, Hackney Empire, the ICA, Oval House, Riverside, Theatre Royal Stratford East, Tricycle, and Young Vic. Programmes were launched at venues such as the Birmingham Rep and West Yorkshire Playhouse to help develop black and Asian artists, and several were aimed at young people, as at the Theatre Centre and the Royal Court.[7]

A new feature was the higher visibility of women, who have always been important but more so until the late 1980s in the African–Caribbean rather than the Asian strand, which is dealt with in the previous chapter.[8] The pioneers were women such as Una Marson from the 1930s, then postwar, Pearl Connor and Yvonne Brewster and a core of black actors, such as Nina Baden-Semper, Nadia Cattouse, Mona Hammond, Pauline Henriques, Carmen Munroe, Ida Shepley, and Corinne Skinner-Carter. To take a few examples from the 1980s: Gloria Hamilton founded Umoja in 1983, Talawa was founded by four women in 1985, and Denise Wong, a founder member of the Black Mime Troupe, became its artistic director in 1986. With the rise of feminism came a new consciousness regarding the need not only for specifically gendered groups but for non-white ones as well, such as the Black Women's Group and Organization of Women of Asian and African Descent. This development was reflected in theatre: black theatre and white were male-dominated, and roles for women were often subsidiary and less well written than male roles. In 1982, the Theatre of Black Women (TBW) was formed, to be followed by groups such as Imani-Faith, founded by Jacqueline Rudet; Munirah; the Black Mime Women's Troupe, which initiated the Black Women's Theatre Project; the Bemarro Sisters; Siren; and Assati in Liverpool. Companies such as Sistren, a Jamaican collective of mainly former street cleaners, offered inspiration through visits and publications.[9]

The most important of these groups, the TBW, had been created when its founders, Bernadine Evaristo, Patricia Hilaire, and Paulette Randall, were at Rose Bruford working on a play called *Coping*, which concerns the lives of five different women. Directed by Yvonne Brewster, it toured to small venues and became the basis of the TBW, which, according to Lynette Goddard, was the only professional black women's company to receive public subsidy.[10] The first TBW show comprised three one-woman plays: Evaristo's *Tiger Teeth Clenched Not to Bite*, Hilaire's *Hey Brown Girl*, and Randall's *Chameleon*. In the second production, *Silhouette* (1983) by Hilaire and Evaristo, a mixed-heritage black woman meets the spirit of a black woman who had died in slavery two centuries before. The TBW followed this with Evaristo's *Pyeyucca*, (1984, with additional material by Hilaire); Jackie Kay's *Chiaroscuro* (1986); a musical *Miss Quashie and the Tiger's Tail* by Gabriela and Jean Pearse (1987); and

Ruth Harris's *The Cripple* (1987) about a woman with cerebral palsy. By the end of the decade, the company had lost its grant and folded.

A network of workshops had arisen focused on developing women's skills and aimed in particular at playwrights. The number of non-white female writers grew, from the likes of Lissele Kayla, Winsome Pinnock, and Maria Oshodi to Yazmine Judd, Jenny McLeod, Zindika and, in the twenty-first century, debbie tucker green and Bola Agbaje. They became a force in the theatrical world beyond the confines of the black and Asian groups, bringing fresh aesthetic strategies in their challenging plays. Besides offering new perspectives on history, memory, migration, generational difference, and what it means to be British, these playwrights dealt with the once taboo and still sensitive issue of lesbian sexuality in a wider exploration of identity formed in a world with many layers of hostility. In *Chiaroscuro*, for example, Kay balances poetry and naturalistic dialogue in a collage form that allows a dynamic investigation of subjectivity through the interaction of four actors, whose friendship is tested and reaffirmed in the face of racism, sexism, and anti-lesbian sentiment. In formal contrast, Rudet's *Basin* (Temba, 1987), set in a young black woman's inner-city flat, explores sisterhood and survival in a more realistic style.

It was not until 1995, however, that a black woman had a play shown at either of the national theatres. A National Theatre Mobile revival of Winsome Pinnock's *Leave Taking*, which had première at the Liverpool Playhouse in 1988, came to the Cottesloe Theatre. Also using realism to great effect, Pinnock, a major writer, looks at the tensions between a mother, who was unable to say goodbye to her mother when she left the Caribbean, and her two daughters, whom she has had to bring up in Britain alone by working as a cleaner. She raises the girls to love England but knows that in England a black woman is 'less than nuttin'.[11]

FIGURE 8.1 David Webber and Jenni George in National Theatre Mobile production of *Leave Taking* by Winsome Pinnock, 1995 (Production image © Richard Hubert Smith)

State funding

The general mushrooming of black and Asian theatre activity in the 1980s brought new ambitions to the fore and raised new demands of the state and its agencies. In response, they issued a mass of publications, at national, regional, and local level and through interest groups, inquiring into the situation of what many still called 'ethnic minority arts'. Black and Asian theatre, as part of a larger fringe and alternative movement, argued its particular case and gained much needed backing, but there was continuing unease at the compromises involved in operating within white theatre terms as against creating an autonomous theatre on one's own terms, though the two were rarely as distinct as this opposition suggests. Complicity with a discriminatory system risked loss of identity through assimilation and continued marginalization in return for subsidy and possible access to larger audiences, whereas the autonomous route offered a pure but diminishing and 'ghetto' existence that left the levers of cultural power in white hands. The point had not been reached wherein the debate could transcend perceptions of race and be undertaken primarily if not entirely in terms of art. For black and Asian artists, there was inevitably a tension with the power-brokers in British culture, who operated by narrow and constricting categories and often used this to deny or restrict access. Artists who did not wish to fit into the available slots (by telling stories from the front line, for example) often became isolated, looked abroad for work, or tried other genres.

State funding remained crucial to the expansion of black and Asian activity, but it also represented an obstacle course. Funding was at first denied or severely restricted because ethnic minority theatre was seen as amateur or community activity (community arts in urban centres remained a euphemism for African, Caribbean, or Asian arts into the 1990s). Subsequently, funding was limited because ethnic minority theatre was still deemed marginal and not professional enough, a Catch 22 parallel to that of black actors who found themselves refused work through lack of work. When funding was awarded, recipients often saw it as a method of dependency control, so that when the money was reduced or cut, they found it hard or impossible to survive. The funding system was not uniform, however. There were differences within and between national, regional, and local levels, and there were many within the system who fought to support black and Asian theatre. Yet, as a whole, the system was criticized as being designed to fail black and Asian theatre and for a general lack of trust in diasporic artists.[12] The groups mainly had to rely on short-term grants, and those were not quite enough. It was nearly impossible for the majority of groups to plan ahead and offer a consistent programme and, because most of the groups toured, the under-funding made it hard to attract the best actors, who could earn more in television and film and would not be adequately compensated for being away from the capital where such work was mostly found. Aspiration was often limited by the conditions of the grants, which frequently reflected the role the funders wanted to give black theatre, producing work the funders deemed appropriate instead of what the practitioners themselves wanted. For the funders, the representative rather than the artistic aspect of black and Asian theatre remained uppermost, a hangover from the early days when it was regarded as a quaint and exotic, if worthy, community welfare service.

Funders feared that ethnically based groups would appeal only to their own constituencies but then funded them to do just that. Paradoxically, funders and power brokers also feared the very thing they promoted, that black and Asian artists were race-obsessed and that, given more leverage, would sponsor diasporic culture to the exclusion of all else. Though some in the diasporic community confirmed the narrow expectations of the funders through an understandable mistrust of the cultural system and a desire to reflect directly and uncompromisingly the tough experience of being black in Britain, groups such as Temba that openly tried to engage with the dominant theatrical tradition were penalized. Attempts within black and Asian theatre to develop from the earlier phase that had been strongly motivated by socio-political intent and stressed anti-racism, found the ability to experiment and create a specific diasporic aesthetic severely constrained. As state funding shrank and became more competitive and other sources of funding were similarly hard to obtain, funders cut black and Asian theatre for lack of quality, poor management, and failure to gain new audiences. Nevertheless, despite manifold setbacks, black and Asian theatre continued with remarkable exuberance, displaying a buoyancy that often proved to be out of step with capacity to deliver. Strategies had to be deployed that rebutted the racism of the white system yet kept black and Asian theatre and artists supported by state agencies while at the same time finding space to follow an autonomous agenda.[13]

During the 1980s and into the 1990s and beyond, official arts policy moved slowly and inconsistently from multiculturalism toward cultural diversity, and the Conservative government began a policy of devolution as part of rolling back the state, a policy that destroyed a fair amount of Britain's theatre infrastructure and concentrated declining resources in regional buildings, the gatekeepers of which were white.[14] Cuts hit all sectors but the under-represented black and Asian theatre the hardest. In the mid-1980s, the official Arts Council approach as laid out in *The Glory of the Garden* ignored the specific needs of black and Asian theatre while supporting ethnic arts in general. At this time, the Arts Council decided to give ethnic arts a higher profile and established an Ethnic Arts Unit, which launched a two-year plan along with a monitoring committee to report upon its progress. The target was for four per cent of funding to go to ethnic arts but, despite significant gains, the absence of a coherent strategy meant there was no sustainable growth.[15] The Unit lasted until the end of the decade, when it was replaced by the Arts Access Unit and subsequently the Cultural Diversity Unit when the government asked for a review of minority arts. This has been followed by various diversity initiatives, such as the Decibel programme in 2003–2004, reinforcing the place of diversity within and across the system but also leaving the notion of diversity ill-defined and often out of kilter with particular needs.

Running through this history of engagement with diversity is an international civic agenda that supports diasporic or minority arts. *The Arts Britain Ignores*, for example, was published in the wake of the 1975 Helsinki Agreement, signed by thirty-five states in an attempt to overcome Cold War divisions, which calls for the continuation and development of ethnic minority arts. UNESCO later introduced the concept of the shared space, which was embraced by the Arts Council and, in 1997, the British Council launched 'Re-Inventing Britain', a project that looked at how very different British identities are being formed and re-formed across and between cultures. Naseem Khan, a central figure in the debate, notes that funding for black and Asian arts increased in the 1990s but the number of companies declined. Britain's record of support is admired in many European countries, yet Britain has not been able to sustain major non-white developments.[16]

The situation in the 1980s represented a classic British double act of giving with one hand while taking away with the other, familiar from the history of liberal civil rights legislation accompanying restrictive nationality and immigration laws.[17] Central government promised post-riots support but devolved implementation to the local level, confirming both the marginal status of such projects, as Floya Anthias and Nira Yuval-Davis have said, and the identification of community as a euphemism for the diaspora.[18] One result was a collision between monetarism and municipal social democracy, especially in London through the Labour-led Greater London Council (GLC), which mounted several attempts to honour a commitment to disadvantaged groups.[19] This clash was also a struggle between notions of culture, which, in terms of state structures, pitted the slow democratization of culture (top down), as advocated by the liberal elite, against cultural democracy (bottom up), as advocated by many alternative companies and artists.

Multiculturalism fostered at state level reinforced separate identities and fractured the notion of Black theatre as a unified force or movement. The cultural diversity agenda that followed lacked a central focus, and its relativism played to inherent strengths and weaknesses within the various diasporic groups. In this trajectory, there is a continuing but different interplay between the individual and the collective. Both have borne the burden of having to explain the Other to the host society, a burden created both within the diasporic communities and without. In the 1970s, there was an historic need for collective and individual diasporic identity, but the collective inevitably restricts while also empowering the individual. With the increase in British-born artists in a social context that promotes individual achievement, this interchange between the individual and the collective and between the mainstream and the grassroots shifts again. The tension is played out in the power struggles that determine British cultural and theatre politics regardless of the perceived needs of diasporic heritage and its future expression.

Key projects of the 1980s

Two projects crystallized the new diasporic ambition of the 1980s and the tensions that accompanied such ambition: the project to create a national black theatre centre at the Roundhouse and the formation of the Black Theatre Forum (BTF), which presented annual seasons of black and Asian theatre in established venues. Energy veered from the BTF to the Roundhouse and back as at first one then the other project appeared to offer the best chance of successful outcomes. The two projects ran in parallel, with one focusing on the acquisition of a building, the other on presenting a showcase within the domain of white culture. Both became possible because of the GLC, which had returned to Labour under the radical Ken Livingstone in 1981. The force that was gathering in diasporic theatre now found an audience in local government. The GLC's Arts and Recreation Committee (under future Sport and Heritage Minister Tony Banks) increased spending on the arts and, in particular, community arts, helping many groups to sustain their productivity and gain the experience necessary to win Arts Council funding. The Committee recognised and promoted the multicultural nature of London and allowed its agenda to be shaped by the communities it was serving through its Ethnic Arts Sub-Committee.

The call for a national centre was heard at the subcommittee's Ethnic Arts Consultative Conference in 1982 and, with Camden Council, a successful bid for the Roundhouse was made by the GLC. Gaining a building had remained an ambition of diasporic theatre since the 1930s. The NTW in the 1960s had hoped to secure one, as had Drum in the 1970s. Dark and Light had one briefly, and Keskidee, though aimed at a local community, acted like a national centre through ownership of its building. There were arguments, often fierce, for and against the value of a building: contending merits were scrutinized and weighed, of local versus national, permanence versus touring, autonomy versus ghettoization, and the single consumption of resources against spreading them widely. A building would be symbolic, but it could be symbolic of both good and bad. It might create an elite and narrow appeal, yet, perhaps as a single focus, it could achieve a high profile and generate more creativity among more artists. There was concern about the size of the building: if it were too small it might be manageable but it would not provide sufficient box office income for it to be sustainable; too large and it would be difficult to find a repertoire that could fill it. The main anxiety was that a national centre would prevent individual groups' acquiring their own premises and would not be able to respond to and represent the diversity of performance traditions and styles that was one of black and Asian theatre's chief features. Such disputation was not particular to diasporic culture but, in the absence of any major local, let alone national, theatre building under diasporic control, the debate was necessarily more urgent.

The building chosen was iconic for counter-culture. The Roundhouse in Camden, north London had been home to the labour movement–backed arts initiative Centre 42 in the mid-1960s, had hosted the Dialectics of Liberation conference in 1967 at which Stokely Carmichael had spoken, and had enjoyed celebrated visits at the cutting edge of theatre and culture by the likes of Peter Brook, Jean-Louis Barrault, Living Theater, Ariane Mnouchkine, and Pink Floyd. Unlike attempts in the past, such as Drum, the Roundhouse plan had the backing of the local council (to buy the building), the GLC (to cover running costs), and the Arts Council (to contribute to project costs). Architects drew up a feasibility study, a board was put in place, and there appeared to be a collective will for success.

Ambition was set high, with talk of the centre occupying the commanding heights of culture such as the National Theatre.

Thatcher's destruction of the GLC in 1986 was a major blow, which was followed by criticism of the board, the management and the scheme's director from within the African, Asian, and Caribbean artistic community and from without.[20] Local resistance, internal rows, and financial problems called the plan into doubt and, with the GLC gone, institutional backing weakened. At the end of the decade, although plans were still in place for a two-theatre centre, with an exhibition gallery, cinema, and restaurant, it was no longer to be a black arts centre but a multicultural one with a black arts trust developing diasporic arts there. At the start of the new decade, the Arts Council withheld its contribution, and the project collapsed. The Roundhouse was eventually refurbished and reopened as a performance venue in 2006 with Arts Council backing but no specific diasporic dimension.

There was a twist to the Roundhouse saga in the story of Double Edge, formed in 1984 by two former Rose Bruford students, Derrick Blackwood and Clarence Smith, who were working from their front rooms.[21] Their first show, *Johnny was a Good Man*, a portrait of heroin addiction, was included in Camden Council's drug education campaign. They moved on a temporary basis to a small space in Kentish Town, north London but needed a permanent and larger space. They approached the Roundhouse, unsuccessfully, and the Camden Council, which offered them the choice of a portakabin or, if they found their own premises, financial aid. Faced with imminent homelessness, they occupied a disused church building and faced a struggle with church authorities to avoid eviction. The group set up Camden United Theatre there to secure the building as an arts centre while the Roundhouse project was still in limbo. They organized a series of events in 1986, which included a performing arts festival, a jazz programme, the première of *The Balmyard* by Staunch Poets and Players, *Burning Embers* by the Azanaian National Theatre from the Edinburgh Festival, and Double Edge's own *Song of Songs*. The following year the company was offered the building and, in 1990, Amani Naphtali wrote and directed one of the group's outstanding shows, *Ragamuffin*, inspired by C. L. R. James's *The Black Jacobins*. Linking the Broadwater Farm revolt in Tottenham, north London to the San Domingo revolution, a rap and reggae trial of a mythological street warrior used call and response with the audience for and against the defendant in a vibrant and visceral show that captured the mood of urban protest spreading throughout black youth.

The other great mid-1980s project, the Black Theatre Forum and its annual Black Theatre seasons, was a reminder to funders that black theatre did know how to organize and administer and had an important presence that needed to be recognised not only by increased grants but with a national centre. An annual season was also a way of overcoming the short-term nature of much black theatre activity, which was a consequence of the funding system, a system the BTF hoped to alter through the success of its seasons. The first season came about after Jamaican actor and director Anton Phillips had meetings in 1983 with Parminder Vir, the GLC's Ethnic Arts Adviser, to work out a development policy for black theatre that might be adopted by the GLC.[22] Phillips, an important figure in British diasporic theatre who had studied drama in New York and at Rose Bruford, ran the Carib Theatre that he had founded with Yvonne Brewster two years before.[23] He proposed to Vir a season at the Arts Theatre, a small venue seating just more than 300 in central London and known for its innovative repertoire.[24] In his grant application to the GLC, Phillips wrote: 'Our objectives are to present plays of a high professional standard to as wide an audience as possible. Also to assert that Black Theatre has a right to be seen in the best venues.'[25] Funding was granted, but the amount awarded prevented commissioning work and only allowed groups to be invited that had shows already prepared. The season had restricted access to the Arts because the theatre was being used during the day by the resident children's theatre company. There was also a problem recruiting a press officer from the diasporic communities, so Phillips set up a traineeship.

The first season, which ran from October to December 1983, comprised four shows: from BTC, *Nevis Mountain Dew* by African American Steve Carter, directed by Rufus Collins and first produced by New York's Negro Ensemble Company; from Inventory Productions, the première of *Two Can Play* by Jamaican Trevor Rhone, which Phillips directed; from Carib Theatre, a revival of *The Outlaw* by Michael Abbensetts, directed by Robert Gillespie; and from Black Woman Time Now, *Fishing* by Paulette Randall, directed by Yvonne Brewster, which had been seen in 1982 at the Royal Court Theatre Upstairs. *Fishing*, an exploration of life as a black woman, toured London, and *Two Can Play*, a touching play set in Kingston, Jamaica about a couple's relationship changing after the wife returns with new ideas from a trip to the United States, transferred to the Theatre Royal Stratford East. The aim of the season was familiar – to offer opportunity for practising skills – but the context was different because of the venue that, though not a major West End theatre, was within the mainstream and boasted a profile with which most current black and Asian theatre had not been associated before. The season offered a selection of contrasting plays performed by leading diasporic actors and was targeted at getting diasporic audiences into the centre of the capital (and paying more than they would be used to) while attracting white audiences who might not normally see such work. As Alda Terracciano says: '…it was a case of subverting the expectations of the public as the plays neither followed in the footsteps of light comedy and musicals, as is usually the case on the West End stage, nor the "highbrow" choice of theatres like the Royal Court'.[26]

Despite spending much of the budget on advertising and the shows receiving generally favourable notices, the audience figures were poor. Nevertheless, Phillips felt emboldened to plan a second season, this time with a different publicity approach that would target community venues and areas with large black populations through the diasporic press and commercial radio. He submitted an application to the GLC in 1984 and established a company to administer it. Opening in January 1985, the second season offered only three plays: a revised version of Tunde Ikoli's *Scrape Off the Black* from Temba, directed by Alby James; Farrukh Dhondy's *Vigilantes* from the Asian Theatre Co-operative, directed by Penny Cherns; and a Carib Theatre production of

The New Hardware Store by Earl Lovelace, directed by Yvonne Brewster, dealing with post-independence Trinidad. Overall box office income doubled, and the success of *Vigilantes*, which deals with a group of young Asians trying to defend their community from racist attack, showed that young audiences could be attracted with the right material and marketing.

As the second season was opening, Phillips convened a meeting of diasporic companies to draw up a policy that could be put to the GLC's Ethnic Arts Subcommittee. This group, with representatives from the BTC (Beverly Randall); Staunch Poets and Players (Don Kinch); Talawa (Yvonne Brewster); Tara (Jatinder Verma); and Temba (Alby James) as well as Phillips from Carib Theatre and Parminder Vir from the GLC, became the core of the Black Theatre Alliance, which developed into the BTF. Subsequently, representatives joined from the Asian Theatre Co-operative (Harmage Kalirai); British Asian Theatre Company (Dhirendra); and Umoja (Gloria Hamilton), along with Joe Marcell from the Roundhouse to help coordinate the strategies of the two projects. At its height, the BTF embraced seventeen companies. Differences within the BTF were vigorously debated, and a common approach was hard to find. In 1985, the Asian Theatre Co-operative, British Asian Theatre, and Tara formed the Asian Theatre Forum, and questions continued to be raised about the dilemma of labelling: *Black* had been adopted as a political term of common resistance to common problems of discrimination, but it also had the disadvantage of evening out differences in culture and submerging identity. The BTF's plans to collaborate with the Roundhouse were dropped because of differences in artistic perspective, and the BTF made a bid to buy the Arts Theatre, which failed owing to lack of support from the GLC.

Different opinions were also expressed about the nature of the third season: should it be experimental or conventional? A proposal to move to the Royal Court was abandoned because the theatre would not relinquish its right to decide on the repertoire. The BTF agreed on a plan with the GLC to tour more and created a four-strong artistic committee with equal representation from those of Caribbean and Asian descent to run the season. With more emphasis on roots and cross-cultural influences in the choice of repertoire, a decision was taken to use greater resources in order to increase cast sizes, offer live music, enhance publicity and lower ticket prices. The season, which stayed at the Arts Theatre, comprised two Sanskrit classics: Shudraka's *The Little Clay Cart* presented by Tara under Jatinder Verma's direction; Visakhadatta's *Rākshasa's Ring*, the direction of which Anton Phillips had to take over from Rufus Collins at the last minute; and a Jamaican pantomime, *The Pirate Princess* by Barbara Gloudon, presented by Temba with new music by Felix Cross. Both *The Little Clay Cart* and *The Pirate Princess*, which was directed by Alby James and Paulette Randall and recorded the best box office income of the season, were successful reworkings of other traditions in a British theatrical context.

Tension grew within the BTF not only between the Asian and Caribbean strands but over policy: should the seasons pursue excellence as a way of raising the profile and thereby increasing opportunities for all diasporic theatre, or should they represent the diversity of groups as they existed? The BTF agreed to expand. SASS

Theatre Company, Double Edge, Afro-Sax, and L'Ouverture joined in 1987 and Theatre of Black Women, African Players, and Tenne Theatre Company in 1988. It was also agreed to hire a producer for the entire season, who would work alongside an expanded artistic committee to present all productions under the BTF banner, and to hire a director for each show. After the demise of the GLC, Greater London Arts (GLA) agreed to fund the season (£165,000) and make an annual revenue grant (of £22,000) to the BTF for the next five years.[27] In return, the BTF had to grow and make international links, coordinate a registry of black artists for outreach work, establish a centre for black artists, and set up a building centre appeal. Exchange between the BTF groups was fostered by the appointment of trainee directors, and plans were made for the publication of a journal. The quarterly *Frontseat* eventually appeared in 1995 and claimed to be Europe's only publication dedicated to black performance.

The fourth season in 1987, again at the Arts Theatre, offered two plays from the Caribbean – *Remembrance* by Derek Walcott, directed by Carmen Munroe, and *Moon Dance Night* by Edgar White, directed by Yvonne Brewster – and a modern Ethiopian play, *Tewodros*, by Tsegaye Gabre-Medhin, directed by Jatinder Verma, about the unifying nineteenth-century Emperor of that name. The season drew an audience of nearly 7,000 and box office income of £17,500.[28] Prince Edward attended a gala of the White play, organized to raise money to buy a West End theatre for the BTF. As debate continued on the direction of the BTF, an executive was agreed in 1988 that would meet monthly and report to a board of directors, and classes and seminars were arranged to meet the criticism that the BTF was remote from the community. The BTF put in a bid to run the 500-seat Shaw Theatre, Euston, but lost out, though the owners insisted the BTF had the opportunity to mount its next season there. The format for this season remained similar, but, at GLA's insistence, the season was used to help develop directors. As the Arts was having licensing problems, the season opened at the Shaw in January 1989 with Paulette Randall directing *Dog* by Dennis Scott; John Matshikiza directing Walcott's farce *Beef, No Chicken* (which proved to be the most successful of all the seasons' shows at the box office); and actor Renu Setna directing a double bill of *Lazarus and his Beloved* by Lebanese writer Kahlil Gibran and *The Song of Death* by the Egyptian writer Tawfik El-Hakim. The BTF addressed issues of under-representation by initiating the New Writer's Project, in particular to increase the number of female and British playwrights, and by developing opportunities backstage, an area where few black people were to be found.

What turned out to be the final season, in 1990 at the Riverside Studios (the Shaw was not available), was produced by Anton Phillips and opened with a new play of community interest written by a woman, Maria Oshodi's *Blood, Sweat and Fears*, followed by two revivals: Jimi Rand's *Say Hallelujah* and *Eden* by Steve Carter. A survey of this season showed that seventy per cent of the audience was African-Caribbean, twenty-four per cent European, two per cent Asian, and four per cent other; fifty-six per cent were between the ages of 22 and 35, and sixty-three per cent were professionals.[29] A gala performance of *Blood, Sweat and Fears* was held to raise money for research into sickle cell anaemia, the subject of the play and a disorder found disproportionately among those of African-Caribbean heritage. In contrast to the previous royal gala, this suggested a new direction toward community concerns, a direction taken up in a proposal put to GLA as the Roundhouse project collapsed to create an arts and media centre in Brixton named after C. L. R. James. In the process of making this submission, the BTF had not put forward proposals for the next Black Theatre season. When the bid for the centre was rejected, there were only a few days left to submit plans for the season and the BTF did not do so. GLA had already announced that the grant for the next season would have been cut back – the second time in two years, but this round of cuts was substantial – and that the considerable shortfall would have to be made up by sponsorship. When GLA was restructured to become the London Arts Board, the new body agreed to distribute the money previously allocated to the Black Theatre Season to other diasporic work, thereby ending the only regular showcase of black and Asian theatre and one under the control of the artists themselves.

The BTF's other activities continued, as it became an invaluable service to what was now a recognized sector within the arts industry. The BTF created an employment database and offered training and workshops on a range of subjects, in particular for writers and to explore the use of non-standard accents in performance. One project, 'React To', in conjunction with Crown Ten Productions, explored social exclusion and drug awareness and finished with a show at the Tricycle. The BTF ran the occasional reading, for example, of 'Biyi Bandele's *Death Catches the Hunter*, which led to a production by Wild Iris. The Forum also organized conferences, for instance, on arts administration and management and, in 1995, one called 'Future Histories'. This returned to the theme of developing a strategy for black theatre as a whole and laid the foundations for the creation of an archive of British African, Asian, and Caribbean performing arts. In 2001, a body taking the name Future Histories was established as a living repository, based on the BTF archive but initiating projects that preserved and disseminated the heritage through different media. By this point, the BTF, which the London Arts Board had wound down in the late 1990s, was closed.

Critical to the demise of both the Roundhouse and the Black Theatre seasons had been the abolition of the GLC by Thatcher's government in 1986. Though both projects survived, there was no representative body to fill the gap, and the regional funder, GLA, did not have the commitment to diasporic theatre shown by the GLC. Indeed, *In the Eye of the Needle*, a report in 1986 into GLA chaired by the director of the Institute of Race Relations Ambalavaner Sivanandan, found institutional racism and a failure to implement an effective black arts policy.[30] The momentum of black theatre in the 1980s stalled because of changes in the funding dispensation, and the absence of the GLC was critical in the closure of groups and the waning of activity. In its farewell year, however, the GLC ended on a flourish. It produced *The Black Experience*, a month-long arts programme of events, including concerts, talks, training days, a photographic exhibition, film shows, an oral history project and, most important for the future of black theatre, the first production by Talawa Theatre Company.[31]

Talawa

Yvonne Brewster, a leading figure in British black theatre, was approached in 1985 by Lord Birkett, chair of the GLC's Arts and Recreation Committee, when the fate of the parent body was known. He asked her to apply for money from the final grants that would be allocated to minority arts. The plan she submitted was to produce *The Black Jacobins* by C. L. R. James on what would be the fiftieth anniversary of its first production. With the actors Inigo Espejel, Mona Hammond, and Carmen Munroe, she founded Talawa to carry this out.

Brewster was born in Kingston, Jamaica with several cultures in her background: Jewish, Polish, Indian, and Cuban. She came to Britain in 1956 aged seventeen and soon discovered the obstacles of sexism, racism, and cultural tradition that she and others like her had to face. She studied at the Royal Academy of Music and Rose Bruford, where the principal told her she would never find work in the theatre. Brewster struggled there against the demands of Received Pronunciation, not because she could not affect it but because she thought it inappropriate.[32] She failed verse speaking one term for refusing to say the Blake line 'my soul is white'. Her first acting job came while still at college as a fairy in a pantomime at Colchester Rep. She returned to Jamaica and co-founded with Trevor Rhone the Barn Theatre. It was named after Lorca's university company, La Barraca (shack), which toured Spain, performing modern interpretations of classics, a motif that became a central part of Brewster's approach to drama and that of much diasporic theatre. She would visit England in the summers looking for plays and, in 1971, stayed to get married.

Her first production in Britain was a chastening experience. The Jamaica High Commission invited her to direct a London tour of Trevor Rhone's *Smile Orange* in 1972 to mark the tenth anniversary of Jamaican independence (an interesting choice as the play debunks the Caribbean tourist industry). The tour, which visited the Dark and Light, was probably the first such tour of a play by a black playwright with a black cast directed by a black director. Brewster says the audiences at the start of the run were miniscule but, by the end, many people who turned up were not able to get in. Their presence on the streets of what was seen as a 'white' part of London annoyed some of the local population, and the hall where the play was showing was burnt down, destroying all the props. The obvious conclusion, that the fire was arson, was officially ruled out.

After a brief return to the Caribbean in the mid-1970s, Brewster joined Bill Bryden's company at the National Theatre, became the Arts Council's first black Drama Officer (1982–1984), and picked up directing again (for example, Black Theatre Co-operative's revival of *A Raisin in the Sun* at the Tricycle, 1985). She continued directing outside Talawa after she became its artistic director. By the time she retired, besides having worked as an actor and director on TV, served on various boards, and edited three volumes of black plays, Brewster had directed more than forty stage productions in the Caribbean, Britain, the United States, and elsewhere. Among her honours, she had received the OBE in 1993. She writes in her autobiography about the 'raffia' ceiling that bars black people from progress.[33] She did as much as any other single figure in postwar British black theatre to dent that ceiling, and much of the critical contribution she made came through the work of Talawa.

The name Talawa was chosen because of a Jamaican saying:, 'Me lickle but me talawa', meaning 'I may be small but I've got guts, so look out'. Taking this notion of feistiness and resilience – like black theatre in white society and Talawa's female founders – the company saw its wider aim in terms that would be recognizable from the previous decades: to provide opportunities for black actors, to use black culture to enrich British theatre, and to enlarge theatre audiences among the black community.

Funded initially production by production, Talawa managed to make an impact in its first half-decade of existence, at the end of which it was offered a residency in London. Assisted by Carmen Munroe, Brewster directed the opening production of *The Black Jacobins* at the Riverside Studios. With a cast of some two dozen actors (nineteen of whom were black) led by Norman Beaton as Toussaint, it was an ambitious production that was made possible only because of the GLC grant. Beaton believed the production was a genuine breakthrough for black theatre, not only because of its scale but because of its quality and the predominance of black people in the creative, production and administrative teams.[34] The *Financial Times* said it was a production that, along with other projects in the GLC's *Black Experience* programme, 'lends credibility and dignity to the British black theatre movement'.[35]

Brewster followed this with the British première of Dennis Scott's *An Echo in the Bone*, set in Jamaica in 1937 in the aftermath of the murder of a white estates owner, the echo being that of slavery and the bone being that of its inheritors, both black and white. As a programme note says, the play offers a 'panoramic view of the history of black slavery and the continued economic enslavement of the worker'.[36] Through its use, and questioning, of ritual, such as consoling the spirit of the dead, the play not only shows the link between Africa and the Caribbean but raises painful questions about the meaning of, and means of achieving, emancipation. For a British audience, the play was a sharp reminder of the presence and role of history in the racism and discrimination of contemporary society.

Nearly two years later came the next production, *O Babylon!*, by Derek Walcott, with music by Galt McDermot, which deals with the complex cultural and political situation of Rastafarians living in Kingston. In the following year, 1989, came a black-cast version of Oscar Wilde's *The Importance of Being Earnest*, the company's first production as a revenue (as opposed to project) client of the Arts Council. The show was a co-production with the Tyne Theatre Company and opened in Newcastle before visiting London and Cork. According to Brewster, it did not amuse the Arts Council. Having cut Temba for, among other things, an integrated cast version of *Ghosts*, the Council now saw Talawa going one step further by tackling what is seen as a quintessentially English comedy (written, however, by an Irishman) with an all-black cast. Brewster, another 'outsider' like Wilde, saw the play as his attack on the 'barely hidden vulgarities of English snobbery', ideal, therefore, to inspire black actors who had for so long been treated condescendingly as stereotypes.[37] It won the backing of the British Council, which sent it to Ireland as part of the *Britain in Europe* Festival.

A turning point in her approach to theatre was a trip in 1989 to Nigeria, where she researched her forthcoming production of Ola Rotimi's *The Gods are Not to Blame*, a script of which she had found in the children's section of a London bookshop. Rotimi's view of the Oedipus story, or Odewale in his Yoruba version, which he had directed in London more than a decade before, presents the tragedy as Odewale's fault; he chooses to kill his father and marry his mother. In Nigeria, Brewster experienced an integrated vision of performance in contrast to the fractured European approach and, in applying this, considered her revival one of the best productions Talawa ever did.[38] It was a co-production with the Everyman Liverpool featuring Jeffrey Kissoon and was later broadcast on radio. The last two productions in this period were *The Dragon Can't Dance* by Earl Lovelace and *Antony and Cleopatra*. This latter show was another co-production with the Everyman and Talawa's – and Brewster's - first attempt at Shakespeare. Brewster – controversially for some – cast Cleopatra as a black Egyptian Queen (played by Dona Croll, whose only previous Shakespearean experience had been as maids) alongside a black Antony (Jeffrey Kissoon) and a black Octavius Caesar (Ben Thomas).[39] The production rehearsed against the backdrop of the Gulf War, and this context influenced the interpretation of the two cultures at battle in the play, which opened as the war ended. Coming just after Temba's production of *Ghosts*, one of the triggers for the company's demise, *Antony and Cleopatra* was a bold move but one that paid off.

Brewster says recognition by funders, though it brought extra resources, 'clipped her wings' because it carried with it new responsibilities to outside bodies, placing greater demands on and scrutiny of the company, particular in areas such as administration.[40] Collaborations were a key element in Talawa's survival and progress, both because funders encouraged them and because they helped artistic growth, gained new audiences, and marked a degree of acceptance and acknowledgment by the theatre establishment. The reward for this level of work was a residency at the renovated Jeanetta Cochrane Theatre, central London, which seated just more than 300. The move was announced in 1991 when the government ordered the Arts Council to review provision for minority arts, the Roundhouse project and Black Theatre seasons came to an end, Temba was cut, and Tara was forced to abandon its studio as a programmed arts centre. Talawa benefitted, and though the residency raised tension within diasporic theatre, for example, over the disparity between provision for Tara and Talawa, Talawa took on the leadership mantle of black theatre.

The company opened its residency in 1992 with (at Derek Walcott's suggestion) a revival of Soyinka's *The Road*, twenty-seven years after it had been given its world première in London, a reminder, as with Talawa's *The Black Jacobins*, of the heritage of black British theatre. Already regarded as a contemporary classic, *The Road* connects western European theatre forms with an African consciousness in its exploration of the vibrant but dangerous relationship between life and death focused on a driven professor (Ben Thomas) and his unsuspecting accomplices who operate in a nether world like existential highwaymen. The production represented a massive challenge for Talawa, and, despite its problems – the use of the Egungun mask, for instance, was not altogether successful – it made a powerful statement about the significance of the play and the company's ambition.

During the three-year residency, Talawa raised audience figures from twelve per cent to nearly sixty per cent and produced ten plays.[41] Besides a transfer from the Edinburgh Festival (Footpaul's production of *Mooi Street Moves* by Paul Slabolepszy) and Talawa's first play by a woman – a collage called *The Love Space Demands* by Ntozake Shange (1992), which had been given its première earlier that year in New York – the company presented new plays by Michael Abbensetts (*The Lion*), Tariq Ali (*Necklaces*), and 'Biyi Bandele-Thomas (*Resurrections*); an adaptation of a Jamaican musical, *Arawak Gold*, by Carmen Tipling and Ted Dwyer, which retained Jamaican and British pantomime traditions; and revivals of *Smile Orange* by Trevor Rhone, *From the Mississippi Delta* by Endesha Ida Mae Holland, and *Maskarade* by Sylvia Winter and Olive Lewin, which honoured the Jamaican street festival tradition of Jonkunnu at the heart of the piece. There was also a largely-black-cast production of *King Lear* (1994), which had been intended for Norman Beaton, who fell ill and was replaced by Ben Thomas. The production brought out the themes of generational tension, migration, social alienation, and madness and questioned ways in which authority is used to justify exclusion of those perceived as outsiders. The production opened at the NIA Centre, Manchester before coming to the Cochrane via Barnstaple and Oxford.

The residency was curtailed because, according to Brewster, the landlord, the London Institute, was not keen on Talawa's presence and restricted the available time it could be in occupation.[42] The company decided to leave altogether and pursue its long-term search for a permanent space elsewhere while, in the meantime, taking its productions to a variety of established London venues such as the Lyric, Hammersmith, Young Vic, Brixton's Shaw Theatre, the Tricycle, and Oval House and farther afield to venues such as the Bristol Old Vic. The repertoire mix continued, embracing new plays (for example, Yazmine Judd's lively comedy *Unfinished Business* in 1999 and Grant Buchanan Marshall's *The Prayer* in 2000 about domestic violence); revivals, such as Walcott's farce on cultural imperialism *Beef, No Chicken* (1996); adaptations, for instance, of Roger Mais's novel *Brother Man*, which Kwame Dawes turned into a Rastafarian musical called *One Love* (2001); and reworkings of classics, such as José Triana's *Medea in the Mirror* (1996, Euripides transported to Cuba) and *Othello* (1997). Thinking of both O. J. Simpson and Colin Powell, two leading black figures who discovered that acceptance depended on not crossing certain boundaries, Brewster adapted the Shakespeare text to help her exploration of the black general's downfall in a racist society.

Brewster wanted to leave Talawa a couple of years after the company finished at the Cochrane, but difficulties in finding a successor delayed her departure. Such difficulties continued to dog Talawa: Topher Campbell succeeded Brewster in

2001 but left immediately owing to alleged artistic differences, to be followed by African-American playwright Bonnie Greer but for only three months.[43] At this point, Talawa had great expectations of moving into a new home at the Westminster Theatre in central London, where *Toussaint Louverture* had first been seen. Other plans for the site had been proposed, including one by Anton Phillips, but Talawa's had been chosen and had the backing of grants from the Millennium Commission and the Arts Council worth £3.6 million, which had to be matched by a further £1million raised by the company itself. Director and playwright Paulette Randall took over from Greer in late 2002 and the next year showed the company still had punch with a vibrant production of *Urban Afro Saxons* by Patricia Elcock and Kofi Agyemang, which challenged notions of Britishness just as the Home Secretary stepped up plans for citizenship tests. Randall had differences with the Board and left in 2005. After a period under interim leader Ben Thomas, Jamaican playwright Pat Crumper was appointed artistic director in 2006 alongside a new chair, Joy Nichols, in an attempt to start anew.

By this time, however, the Westminster plan had fallen apart. There were internal board and management problems at Talawa, which saw several resignations at the company, and the Arts Council withdraw its support for the building project, a decision that infuriated much of the black theatre community. As with the Roundhouse, great promise – and money – had been wasted, and the Council was accused of reneging again. The possibility of gaining a national black theatre space seemed gone. Funding priorities had shifted in the years since the project was first mooted when a national centre still seemed desirable by all concerned. Diversity and integration were now being promoted by funders, as the old diasporic migration had settled and was being replaced by a white arrivals from central and eastern Europe.

In the first two decades since it was founded, Talawa had produced more than forty plays, drawing on a range of cultures and performance traditions that had been used to explore the meanings of blackness and of Britishness. The company had given a platform to many black practitioners, provided educational, outreach and skills programmes, and launched its Young People's Theatre and Black Writers Group. It had initiated an important oral history project that celebrates the pioneers of black theatre in postwar Britain. Two collections of interviews – *Blackgrounds* (recorded in 1997 and supported by Arts Council England) and *Blackstage* (recorded in 2002 and supported by the Heritage Lottery Fund) – and the company's work with the Future Histories project created an invaluable black performing arts archive as a legacy for the future.[44] Talawa also took on the administration of the Alfred Fagon Award for British playwrights of African and Caribbean descent, while, although a reduced force, it continued its various activities as Britain's major black-led theatre company.

Broader front

Retrenchment in general theatre funding in the 1980s was compounded by a shift in funding in the early 1990s away from theatre to dance and the visual arts; in the

mid-1990s, theatre had suffered a loss of profile and audience numbers. With the introduction of the National Lottery at the end of the decade came an emphasis on buildings (bastions of white theatre and white administrators), but this was followed by favourable adjustments to revenue funding and more weight being given to supporting diversity in the new millennium.[45] The sheer number of groups and initiatives that have been launched since the end of the 1980s makes it impossible to offer a meaningful survey, particularly in the absence of any focus such as the Black Theatre Forum provided. The broad range could run from the likes of Mahogany Carnival Arts (1989), a group of multi-disciplinary artists whose costumes, masks, sculptures, and puppets combine British theatre design with Asian and Caribbean performance traditions and have featured regularly at the Notting Hill Carnival, to further attempts to secure a national centre (for example, the Drum in Birmingham, opened in 1994, or the 1996 plan by Oscar Watson, BTF's co-coordinator who went on to be Talawa's administrator, for a National Black and Asian Theatre Development Centre). The range might also include the likes of Tiata Fahodzi (theatre of the emancipated), created by Femi Elufowoju in 1997 to celebrate West African heritage, or Push, set up in 2001 by Josette Bushell-Mingo and Ruth Nutter to widen the scope of black performance to include street theatre, opera, and circus, or the opening in 2003 of the Identity Drama School, said to be the first such black institution.

Many of the initiatives occurred outside London and away from the mainstream: examples include ARTBLACKLIVE events presented by the Black Arts Alliance, formed in 1985 by a group of community artists, and the longest-surviving network of diasporic artists; performances by Kuffdem in Chapeltown, Leeds; and the work in Birmingham of Barbados-born playwright and director Don Kinch.[46] The moving force behind Staunch Poets and Players in London, Kinch went to Birmingham in the late 1980s and developed the Third Dimension Theatre Company, African Peoples Theatre, which performed his *Coming Up for Air* in 1990, and Nu Century Arts (2000) as a resource for new writers, musicians, directors, and actors. Birmingham also has the Drum, built on the site of the former Aston Hippodrome variety theatre as a national centre for diasporic arts. It had a fitful beginning and was fully opened in 1998, with two auditoria, an art gallery, an exhibition space, a cafe-bar, and a multimedia production suite. As happened elsewhere, a central location was denied because the money came from a regeneration fund, thereby reinforcing the status of the project as peripheral and having welfare rather than artistic objectives.

Where diasporic companies did have buildings, they were under-resourced and mostly in culturally and economically deprived areas. Though this kept them out of the mainstream, it did keep them close to the grass roots, which, as the Black Theatre Forum found, was also important because audience remains a critical problem. This is particularly true where there is no tradition either of theatre going or of travelling outside one's own area. In overcoming such obstacles, the white media in general have not helped, whereas in the media that are aimed at diasporic communities, there have been contradictory responses: alternative or grassroots media may have been supportive, but the main outlets often took the view that its audiences were not keen on seeing on stage the problems they met daily on the streets.[47]

One strand that has managed to find a diasporic audience, however, is the commercial black theatre. Among the most popular of this sector's shows was *Black Heroes in the Hall of Fame* (1987, revived 1992), although it began in north London with a small subsidy from the local council to mark the centenary of Marcus Garvey's birth.[48] The show transferred to a central London entertainment venue (the Astoria) and then toured the United States and reappeared at the Hackney Empire. Created by Jamaican-born producer Flip Fraser, J. D. Douglas (lyrics) and Khareem Jamal (music), the show boasted a cast of some fifty performers who portrayed in a musical pageant important black figures from the worlds of history, entertainment, sport, and politics. By contrast, the major strand in commercial black theatre habitually promotes sexually and politically conservative stereotypes and generally divides the diasporic artistic community. Jamaica's popular comedian and writer, Oliver Samuels, who made his reputation through a TV series *Oliver at Large* and its theatrical spin-offs, enjoys huge support in Britain on his regular visits with bawdy Jamaican comedy, much of it in the everyday language of the islanders. Such Caribbean comedies are also promoted by Brixton Village, founded in 1988, in shows such as *BUPS, BUPS 2, The Night Before*, and *Undercover Lover*, and by Blue Mountain Theatre, founded in 1989, in shows such as *Betrayed, Affairs, Smallie, Forbidden Love, Confessions of a Black Woman*, and *Wicked Bitches* (about King Lear's daughters). Blue Mountain productions play large theatres: Leeds's City Varieties; Royal Concert Hall, Nottingham; Birmingham's Alexandria Theatre, Opera House and Palace Theatre; the Hackney Empire; and the Broadway Theatre, Catford in south London, where the company is based. They make a point of being populist in all aspects of the theatre-going experience, from production style and use of familiar language to marketing and 'good night out' environment at the venues.

The active audience rapport at such shows is the envy of the theatre world but rarely achieved outside children's theatre and pantomime. Comedies such as Ayub Khan-Din's *East is East* achieved similar responses when it played in the East End of London, and Paulette Randall reported gleefully that audiences for *The Pirate Princess* in the Black Theatre season were 'raucous,' which forced performers to adjust, to 'become an ensemble and work with one another and with the audience'.[49] Actor Brian Bovell recounts the difference he found between white and black audiences attending a black play. Of a white audience, as typified at the Royal Court, he says: '…it's a quiet night. At the end of the evening they go. Basically I believe their reactions come off of guilt'. But, the next day 'if you are doing the play for a black audience … the play becomes a different play. It is live. You are getting response and participation'.[50] Without ignoring cultural specificity, however, this is a class issue that cuts across ethnicity.

Bovell was part of a group called The Posse, whose motto was 'There's no justice, just us'.[51] With the female company Bibi Crew, groups like this chimed with the rise of a black comedy circuit. They introduced a new energized performance style into diasporic theatre in the early 1990s that was breaking away from old categories and attracting a black audience with sketch-like material, often highly political, rooted in common experience. At the same time, plays such as *Leonora's Dance* (1992) by Zindika and the involvement of diasporic artists and writers in live/performance art and performance poetry such as Patience Agbabi, Susan Lewis, Valerie Mason-John, Michael McMillan, Ronald Fraser-Munro, Sol B. River, Lemn Sissay, Dorothea Smartt, SuAndi, and Benjamin Zephaniah gave impetus to the challenge to conventional theatre. This allowed greater expression of the diversity behind being British with a renewed emphasis on non-naturalistic performance styles, striking visual imagery, and symbolic, poetic use of language and form.

Within the strategies deployed by black and Asian artists, naturalism had played a historic function of being a remedial and provocative force, offering counter images to those that confirmed marginalization and discrimination. Naturalism was powerful when any diasporic presence was made to bear the burden of being representative, but there was the concomitant trap of binary positive/negative images, neither of which are themselves 'natural'. The generation of non-white writers born or raised in Britain continued to test the criticism that naturalism confirmed the status quo and remained at the level of revelation or opposition without being able to reach beyond that to transformation. For many of them, theatre remained a prime medium for presenting the synchronicity of different time and consciousness frames through a dramaturgical approach that embraced naturalism and realism. Memory, history, and intercultural interplay – understandably major motifs of those with diasporic heritage – feature strongly in the work of the likes of Trish Cooke, Tunde Ikoli, Caryl Phillips, and Winsome Pinnock, who deal with discovery of, coming to terms with, and return to one's roots, alongside, and as a part of, exploring what it means to be British.[52]

The artists who wanted to rupture and dispense with naturalism also had historical precedent to drawn on, for instance, in the appropriation of minstrelsy to use flamboyance as a weapon of riposte. Integral to such a strategy, and to the continuing debates around developing a black aesthetic, was the African, Asian, and Caribbean heritage that did not separate drama from music and dance. The thrust of this diasporic theatre carried the potency of participatory, multi-genre forms as found in Carnival, resisting the idea of culture as a unified given and seeing it rather as a changing and interconnected set of varied practices. This diasporic approach began to alter the way state agencies perceived art, even if their pyramid of excellence was not entirely pulled down.

A slew of surveys and reports led to a number of state-supported projects focused on diasporic theatre development, such as NATAK in Leicester, BRIT (Black Regional Initiative in Theatre), and the Arts Council of England's Year of Cultural Diversity, but overall there was no consistency or coherent underlying policy.[53] The New Labour government introduced the twin approach of cultural diversity and social inclusion, which embedded an instrumental attitude toward the arts as agents of social change and collapsed together different issues of inequality. For all the effort, black and Asian theatre continued to suffer many of the problems facing white theatre, in areas such as leadership, finance, new audiences, and new plays but without the support to build mechanisms to overcome systemic difficulties. There have been initiatives to help the supply of new plays, for example, but little to help the revival of existing texts, and diasporic theatre has not yet won the 'right to fail' or to experiment. The gains were sporadic and not deep-rooted; the occasional play by a black writer or the employment of a black director could not hide the absence from the bigger picture.

A report in 2002 from Eclipse, a project that came out of the BRIT scheme and other regional initiatives, found widespread institutional racism in British theatre. The report also found that the few black people who did gain employment had to deal with race issues and were marginalized.[54] Eclipse details the lack of non-white representation among theatre staff, boards, actors, audiences and in programming, the lack of training and the lack of adequate resourcing to reach appropriate audiences.[55] Besides making recommendations, Eclipse mounted its own productions. It found it difficult to set up the first tour, of Errol John's *Moon on a Rainbow Shawl* (2003), whereas the second tour, of Brecht's *Mother Courage and Her Children* (2004), adapted by Dipo Olaboluaje to an African setting, was outsold by Nitro's basketball hip-hop musical, *Slamdunk*. Eclipse gained better audiences with *Little Sweet Thing* (2005), the Roy Williams story of a black ex-convict who tries but fails to break free from a criminal sub-culture, and Matura's *Three Sisters* (2006).

Whose Theatre…?, a report prepared in 2006 for the Arts Council of England by Lola (later Baroness) Young based on consultations in Birmingham, Bristol, Leeds, London, Manchester, and Nottingham, found that the situation had deteriorated since the mid-1980s, under-resourcing remained a critical issue, and embedded transformation had proved elusive.[56] Despite the greater access of non-white theatre workers to the generality of venues and groups, the access was uneven, and still no major non-race specific company had been non-white-led. The lack of infrastructure required for sustainability led the report to recommend the creation not of a single centre but a network of buildings, along with the professional development of leadership, more international work to be shown, and the Arts Council to overcome the habit of one-off initiatives by taking a coherent, long-term approach, recognizing the need of black and Asian theatre to own its future.

Notwithstanding the problems faced by diasporic artists, the diversity within diverse theatre has been recognized, along with the continuing struggle for self-definition and expression. This struggle is not confined to relations with white communities (whether encountering the obstacles of liberal racism or conservative bias) but involves contestation within and between the diasporic communities themselves, as the *Behzti* affair and other, less-well-publicized confrontations have revealed (involving, for example, the challenge of gay and lesbian diasporic artists).[57] Indeed, there is still a problem concerning the portrayal of fully human diasporic characters, for instance, those who may be involved in criminality or other forms of social dysfunction, for fear of feeding a stereotype.

White theatre, nevertheless, has been provoked, revivified, enriched, and changed through casting, repertoire, language, aesthetics, and important shifts in the representation of non-white people.[58] Non-white artists have frequently resisted the diasporic and race tags, but those born or raised in Britain have made the most advances because their number and history, their experiences, and their relationships both to Britain and to their diasporic heritage required different responses. This process is deepened with the changing pattern of immigration and with each subsequent post-colonial generation's becoming further removed, though not necessarily disconnected, from their diasporic roots and the colonial era. The context for this process alters rapidly in a globalized world, as do the terms of the debate about Britishness and its relationship to migration, integration, and cultural difference, a debate that the 2001 September 11 attacks in the United States and the 2005 July bombings in Britain changed radically.

Progress has been made in the theatre, however, although it is always provisional, and much remains to be done to remove the 'raffia' ceiling, despite the holes that have been made in it.[59] It took until 1987 for the West End to host an all-black, non-musical British production under black direction – *The Amen Corner* by James Baldwin, produced by the Carib Theatre and directed by Anton Phillips in a transfer from the subsidized Tricycle Theatre – but such an event proved a rarity. It was not until 2005 that a play by a black Briton, Kwame Kwei-Armah's *Elmina's Kitchen*, appeared in the West End.[60] There have been other individual breakthroughs. Venu Dhupa, for instance, was made executive director of Nottingham Playhouse in 1997 and went on to important roles at the National Endowment for Science, Technology, and the Arts and the British Council. Kully Thiarai, was appointed joint co-artistic director with Paul Kerryson of the Leicester Haymarket in 2001. The RSC presented a black Shakespearean King (David Olewayo played Henry VI in 2000), London applauded a black Hamlet (Adrian Lester in Peter Brook's 2001 visit), and pantomime discovered a remarkable black Dame (Clive Rowe first played the role at the Hackney Empire in 2004).

Midway through the first decade of the new millennium came a moment when such diversity was celebrated in the media: plays by writers Kwei-Armah, Roy Williams, and debbie tucker green were on tour round Britain, in the West End and, at the National Theatre, the RSC and Royal Court; the Globe Theatre presented a season on Islam and Shakespeare; and a production of *Twelfth Night* set in India with an all-Asian cast was seen at the Albery Theatre.[61] Before the decade had finished, Kwei-Armah had joined the board of the National Theatre and launched there the Black Theatre Archive whereas that redoubt of diverse theatre, the small Tricycle Theatre, which has presented six plays by African-American playwright August Wilson, followed its experiment with a black ensemble company staging three British premières of African-American plays by mounting in 2009 a trilogy of work by Kwei-Armah, Williams, and Bola Agbaje in a season aptly titled *Not Black and White*.[62]

None of this heralded a new dawn, but it did mark a shift and demonstrate that those with roots in Africa, Asia, and the Caribbean had made – and were to go on making – a distinctive, ineradicable theatrical contribution to multicultural, variegated, and colour-ful Britain and to the continuing debate on what it means to be human and British.

Conclusion

This complex negotiation between 'us' and 'them' runs through the entire history of black and Asian theatre in Britain and is a central strand in the wider history of British theatre. Even during the early era, dominated by the attraction of the exotic and fear of the Other, the consequent representations and changing, volatile role of colour as a sign of difference return insistently to the issue of 'who we are' and the associated question 'who are we?'

For non-white artists trying to tackle the question, the absence from – and even of – history has meant a responsibility to the pressure of history, the pressure of being representative. At first this was felt by individuals needing to demonstrate their value, but individuals alone were never going to comprise black and Asian theatre. This required the interplay of the individual and the collective. It meant – and means – not simply presence (though that was hard enough, and necessary) but a distinct approach and attitude, an intervention. It means having to balance the risks of independence against accommodation with the theatre establishment and its funders and couching one's aims in terms that allow access to resources even if that substitutes race relations for art. It means recognizing the necessary link and tension between art and community, knowing it is a link the artist has to make and a tension the artist has to embrace. It means a battle to be taken seriously as artists while operating within a white imaginary that still mistrusts the Other.

Throughout the history of black and Asian theatre in Britain, truths have been sought in an impressive range of interventions and strategies. Diasporic artists have exploited both prevailing stereotypes, which have accumulated over centuries, and the adverse expectations attached to them as well as promoting alternative systems of representation and signification. In the process of fighting for control over one's own representation, the construction of identity has been wrested bit by bit from the colonizing culture, but this struggle is not over.

Black and Asian theatre has created a network of artists and groups distinguished by their own methods, their own values, and their own body of work. Black and Asian theatre has borrowed from, added to, and changed the dominant culture. Through a new aesthetic that draws strength from but transcends racial, geographical, and artistic boundaries, the canon has been re-envisaged and revitalized while new stories and players have been introduced. By doing this from the margins and restoring the challenging meaning of being on the edge, black and Asian theatre has added its weight to the reconfiguration of what was seen as peripheral. Black and Asian theatre has thereby transformed notions not only of British theatre but also of black and Asian theatre itself and notions of a new, devolving Britain, struggling to find a new 'we' and new ways of thinking and behaving.

NOTES

Introduction

1 See, for example, Clive Barker and Maggie B. Gale (eds), *British Theatre Between the Wars, 1918–1939*, Cambridge, Cambridge UP, 2000; Michael Billington, *State of the Nation: British Theatre Since 1945*, London, Faber and Faber, 2007; Richard Eyre and Nicholas Wright, *Changing Stages: A View of British Theatre in the Twentieth Century*, London, Bloomsbury, 2000; Dominic Shellard (ed.), *British Theatre Since the War*, New Haven, CT and London, Yale UP, 1999; Aleks Sierz, *In-Yer-Face Theatre: British Drama Today*, London, Faber and Faber, 2001.

2 Kenneth Little, *Negroes in Britain: A Study of Racial Relations in English Society*, London, Kegan Paul, 1948; James Walvin, *Black Presence: A Documentary History of the Negro in England, 1555–1860*, London, Orbach and Chambers, 1971; Edward Scobie, *Black Britannia: A History of Blacks in Britain*, London, Pall Mall Press, 1972; Folarin Shyllon, *Black People in Britain 1555–1833*, London, Oxford UP, 1974; Peter Fryer, *Staying Power: The History of Black People in Britain*, London, Pluto Press, 1984.

3 Rozina Visram, *Ayahs, Lascars, and Princes: Indians in Britain 1700–1947*, London, Pluto Press, 1986; Amarjit Chandau, *Indians in Britain*, London, Oriental UP, 1986; Roger Ballard (ed.), *Desh Pardesh: The South Asian Presence in Britain*, London, Hurst, 1994; Shompa Lahiri, *Indians in Britain: Anglo-Indian Encounters, Race and Identity, 1880-1930*, London, Frank Cass, 2000.

4 Herbert Marshall and Mildred Stock, *Ira Aldridge: The Negro Tragedian*, London, Rockliff, 1958.

5 Tyrone Huggins, *The Eclipse Theatre Story*, [no publisher or date of publication given; Eclipse named on cover, and it appeared in 2006]; Raminder Kaur and Alda Terracciano, 'South Asian/BrAsian Performing Arts,' in Nasreen Ali et al. (eds), *A Postcolonial People: South Asians in Britain*, London, Hurst and Co., 2006, pp. 343–357; Bruce King, *The Internationalization of English Literature* (*The Oxford Literary History, vol. 13: 1948–2000*), Oxford, Oxford UP, 2004; Michael McMillan and SuAndi, 'Rebaptizing the World in Our Own Terms: Black Theatre and Live Arts in Britain', in Paul Carter Harrison et al. (eds), *Black Theatre: Ritual Performance in the African Diaspora*, Philadelphia, Temple UP, 2002, pp.115–127; Kwesi Owusu, *The Struggle for Black Arts in Britain: What Can We Consider Better than Freedom?* London, Comedia Publishing Group, 1986; Malcolm Page, 'West Indian Playwrights in Britain', *Canadian Drama*, vol. 6, no. 1, 1980; D. Keith

Peacock, *Thatcher's Theatre: British Theatre and Drama in the Eighties*, Santa Barbara, CA, Greenwood Press, 1999.

6 Colin Chambers, *The Story of Unity Theatre*, London, Lawrence and Wishart, 1989; Jim Pines (ed.), *Black and White in Colour: Black People in British Television Since 1936*, London, BFI Publishing, 1992 (interviewees include Michael Abbensetts, Thomas Baptiste, Norman Beaton, Pearl Connor, Farrukh Dhondy, Cy Grant, Joan Hooley, Zia Mohyeddin, Carmen Munroe, Lloyd Reckord, Cleo Sylvestre, and Rudolph Walker); Stephen Bourne, *Black in the British Frame: Black People in British Film and Television 1896–1996*, London, Cassell, 1998; Roland Rees (ed.), *Fringe First: Pioneers of Fringe Theatre on Record*, London, Oberon Books, 1992; Ruth A. Tompsett (ed.), *Black Theatre in Britain*, Harwood Academic Press, special issue of *Performing Arts International*, no. 1(2), 1996; Alison Donnell (ed.), *Companion to Contemporary Black British Culture*, London, Routledge, 2002; Geoffrey V. Davis and Anne Fuchs (eds), *Staging New Britain: Aspects of Black and South Asian British Theatre Practice*, Brussels, PIE-Peter Lang, 2006; Dimple Godiwala (ed.), *Alternatives Within the Mainstream: British Black and Asian Theatres*, Newcastle, Cambridge Scholars Press, 2006.

7 Elaine Aston, *An Introduction to Feminism and Theatre*, London, Routledge, 1995; Susan Croft, 'Black Women Playwrights in Britain', in Trevor R. Griffiths and Margaret Llewellyn-Jones (eds), *British and Irish Women Dramatists Since 1958: A Critical Handbook*, Buckingham, Open University, 1993, pp. 84–98; Mary Karen Dahl, 'Postcolonial British Theatre: Black Voices at the Center', in J. Ellen Gainor (ed.), *Imperialism and Theatre: Essays on World Theatre, Drama and Performance 1795–1995*, London and New York, Routledge, 1995, pp. 38–55; Lynette Goddard, *Staging Black Feminisms*, Basingstoke, Hants, Palgrave Macmillan, 2007; Dimple Godiwala, 'The Search for Identity and the Claim for an Ethnicity of Englishness…' (pp. 249–264) and 'Kali: Providing a Forum for British-Asian Women Playwrights' (pp. 328–346), in Godiwala, op. cit.; Lizbeth Goodman, *Contemporary Feminist Theatres: To Each Her Own*, London, Routledge, 1993; Gabrielle Griffin, *Contemporary Black and Asian Women Playwrights in Britain*, Cambridge, Cambridge UP, 2003; Valerie Kaneko Lucas, '*Shameless* – Women, sexuality and violence in British-Asian Drama', in Godiwala, op. cit., pp. 363–380; Meenakshi Ponnuswami, 'Small Island People: Black British Women Playwrights', in Elaine Aston and Janelle Reinelt (eds), *Cambridge Companion to Modern British Women Playwrights*, Cambridge, Cambridge UP, 2000, pp. 217–234; Kathleen Starck, ' "Black and Female is Some of Who I Am and I Want to Explore it": Black Women's Plays of the 1980s and 1990s', in Godiwala, op. cit., pp. 229–246.

8 Dominic Hingorani, *British Asian Theatre: Dramaturgy, Process and Performance*, Basingstoke, Hants, Palgrave Macmillan, 2010. My research for my own book was used in writing an essay, 'Images on Stage: A Historical Survey of South Asians in British Theatre before 1975', for one of the Exeter volumes: Graham Ley and Sarah Dadswell (eds), *Critical Essays on British South Asian Theatre*. The other volume (same editors) is *British South Asian Theatres – a Documented History*. Other research (for Chapter 4) was used for my essay, ' "Ours Will Be a Dynamic Contribution": the Struggle by Diasporic Artists for a Voice in British Theatre in the 1930s and 1940s', in *Key Words, A Journal of Cultural Materialism*, no. 7, 2009, pp. 38–54.

9 Mita Choudhury, *Interculturalism and Resistance in the London Theatre, 1600–1800: Identity, Performance, Empire*, London, Associated UP, 2000, p. 31.

10 A useful introduction to issues concerning researching performance in general and black and Asian performance in particular can be found in the Research Toolkit at http://www.tradingfacesonline.com.

11 The point is also made by Aparna Dharwadker, 'Diaspora, Nation, and the Failure of Home: Two Contemporary Indian Plays', *Theatre Journal*, vol. 50, no. 1, March 1998, pp. 71–94.

12 Susan Croft, with Stephen Bourne and Alda Terracciano, *Black and Asian Performance at the Theatre Museum: A Users' Guide*, Theatre Museum, London, 2003.

13 A further complication was language itself. Own-language theatre groups in Britain using Hindi, Gujarati, Marathi, or Urdu, for example, were important in the postwar years for community cohesion and identity but, in the 1970s, Tara Arts saw this trend as conservative and, instead, used English as a sign of modernity and assertion of equality. Later, as Tara developed its own aesthetic, it used a mix of English and Asian languages (see Chapter 7.) With African and Caribbean groups and writers (for whom English was the common language), the challenge was to use Creole or dialect as equally valid as standard English.

14 The 2001 British census used the following categories: white, Asian, black, Chinese, mixed, any other ethnic group.

15 *Whose Theatre…? Report on the Sustained Theatre Consultation*, London, Arts Council England, 2006, p. 13.

16 Vera Gottlieb and Colin Chambers (eds), *Theatre in a Cool Climate*, Oxford, Amber Lane Press, 1999, pp. 29–30.

17 An echo of Paul Gilroy, *There Ain't No Black in the Union Jack: The Cultural Politics of Race and Nation*, London, Routledge 2002.

1 The early era

1 The origins of Morris dancing and the meaning of the name are disputed. Though some theories suggest no link to African Moors (e.g., that Morris refers to moorland or comes from the Latin for custom), others suggest a connection by way of either the Crusades or John of Gaunt bringing captured Moors to England from Spain.

2 Anthony G. Barthelemy, *Black Face, Maligned Race: the Representation of Blacks in English Drama from Shakespeare to Southerne*, Baton Rouge, London, Louisiana State UP, 1987, p. 72.

3 See Annette Drew-Bear, *Painted Faces on the Renaissance Stage: The Moral Significance of Face-Painting Conventions*, London and Toronto, Associated UPs, 1994, pp. 33, 38–39.

4 Much more research needs to be carried out into the British theatrical practice, use, and meanings of blackface. Many factors have to be considered, such as gender (different use by men and women, related to notions of beauty which were also linked to perceived box office appeal), text, and performance style, which in turn can cover a perplexing array of factors, from choice of accompanying music to costume (the material the costume is made from, its colour and cut, use of wigs, gloves, and limb padding) and makeup (how light or dark, both in themselves and relative to the makeup of others in the play). Black did not always or exclusively signify race in plays; Romans, for instance, wore black wigs, and Spaniards might be black. For the morality and use of cosmetics and other external agents of white racial impersonation before blackface minstrelsy, see Dympna Callaghan, *Shakespeare Without Women: Representing Gender and Race on the Renaissance Stage*, London and New York, Routledge, 2000; Drew-Bear, op. cit.; Frances Dolan, 'Taking the Pencil out of God's Hand', *PMLA*, no. 108, 1993, pp. 224–239; Farah Karim-Cooper, *Cosmetics in Shakespearean and Renaissance Drama*, Edinburgh, Edinburgh UP, 2006 (who points out the close connection between cosmetics and witchcraft and their virtual synonymity in the misogyny of the time, p. 167); Virginia Mason Vaughan, *Performing Blackness on English Stages 1500–1800*, Cambridge, Cambridge UP, 2005; Tanya Pollard, *Drugs and Theatre in Early Modern England*, Oxford, Oxford UP, 2005; Ian Smith, 'White Skin, Black Masks: Racial Cross-Dressing on the Early Modern Stage', *Renaissance Drama*, no. 32, 2003, pp. 33–68; Ayanna Thompson, *Performing Race and Torture on the Early Modern Stage*, London and New York, Routledge, 2008. For blackface minstrelsy, see Chapter 2, note 55.

5 G. B. Harrison, *Shakespeare at Work*, London, Routledge, 1933, p. 310, tentatively suggests that Lucy Negro may have been the Dark Lady of Shakespeare's sonnets.

6 Thomas Dekker's 1629 mayoral pageant for the ironmongers, *London's Tempe, or the Fields of Happiness*, had an Indian youth holding a long tobacco pipe and dart (Peter Fryer,

Staying Power: the History of Black People in Britain, London, Pluto Press, 1989, p. 27). See also Richmond Barbour, *Before Orientalism: London's Theatre of the East, 1576–1626*, Cambridge, Cambridge UP, 2003; Barthelemy, op. cit; Jack D'Amico, *The Moor in English Renaissance Drama*, Tampa, FL, University of South Florida Press, 1991; Eldred D. Jones, *Othello's Countrymen: the African in English Renaissance Drama*, London, Oxford UP, 1965; Sukhdev Sandhu, *London Calling: How Black and Asian Writers Imagined a City*, London, Harper Collins, 2003, which cites Kris Collins, 'Merchants, Moors, and the Politics of Pageantry: The Representation of Africans and Indians in Civic Pageants, 1585–1682', University of Oxford, M Litt thesis, 1995; Wylie Sypher, *Guinea's Captive Kings: British Anti-slavery Literature of the XVIIIth*, New York, Octagon Books, 1969.

7   See, e.g., Kim F. Hall, 'Sexual Politics and Cultural Identity in *The Masque of Blackness*', in Sue-Ellen Case and Janelle Reinelt (eds), *The Performance of Power: Theatrical Discourse and Politics*, Iowa City, IA, University of Iowa Press, 1991, p. 3.

8   Andrea R. Stevens, ' "Assisted by a Barber": The Court Apothecary, Special Effects, and *The Gypsies Metamorphosed*', *Theatre Notebook*, vol. 61, no. 1, 2007, pp. 2–11.

9   Louis Wann, 'The Oriental in Elizabethan Drama', *Modern Philology*, vol. 12, no. 7, January 1915, pp. 423–447. Besides the titles listed in note 6, for representations of Islam see also Mohamed Hassan Abu-Baker, *Representations of Islam and Muslims in Early Modern English Drama from Marlowe to Massinger*, unpublished PhD thesis, Glasgow, Glasgow University, 1997; Barbour, op. cit.; Emily C. Bartels, *Spectacles of Strangeness: Imperialism, Alienation and Marlowe*, Philadelphia, PA, University of Pennsylvania, 1993; Brandon H. Beck, *From the Rising of the Sun: English Images of the Ottoman Empire to 1715*, New York, Peter Lang, 1987; Matthew Birchwood, *Staging Islam in England: Drama and Culture, 1640–1685* (Studies in Renaissance Literature, vol. 21), Cambridge, D. S. Brewer, 2007; Samuel Claggett Chew, *The Crescent and the Rose: Islam and England during the Renaissance*, New York, Oxford UP, 1937; Matthew Dimmock, *New Turkes: Dramatizing Islam and the Ottomans in Early Modern England*, Aldershot, Hants, and Burlington VT, Ashgate, 2005; A. J. Hoenselaars, *Images of Englishmen and Foreigners in the Drama of Shakespeare and His Contemporaries*, London and Toronto, Associated UPs, 1992; Bridget Orr, *Empire on the Stage 1660–1714*, Cambridge, Cambridge UP, 2001; Simon Shepherd, *Marlowe and the Politics of Elizabethan Theatre*, Brighton, Harvester, 1986; Daniel Vitkus, *Turning Turk: English Theater and the Multicultural Mediterranean, 1570–1630*, New York and Basingstoke, Hants, Palgrave Macmillan, 2003.

10 Christians becoming slaves (especially English sailors captured off the North African 'Barbary' coast becoming Muslims) was a topic in plays such as Thomas Heywood's *The Fair Maid of the West*; Robert Daborne's *A Christian Turned Turk* (produced in 1612, the same year twelve pirates were hanged at Wapping); a lost play, *A Turke's Too Good for Him*; and Philip Massinger's *The Renegado*. This topic resurfaced in the late 18thc/early 1800s. 'To turn Turk' was a common expression. See Chew, op. cit.; Lois Potter, 'Pirates and "Turning Turk" in Renaissance Drama', in Jean-Pierre Maquerlot and Michelle Willems (eds), *Travel and Drama in Shakespeare's Time*, Cambridge, Cambridge UP, 1996, pp 124–140.

11 See titles listed in notes 6 and 9 and Ruth Cowhig, 'Blacks in English Renaissance Drama and the Role of Shakespeare's *Othello*', pp. 1–25, in David Dabydeen (ed.), *The Black Presence in English Literature*, Manchester, Manchester UP, 1985; Elliot H. Tokson, *The Popular Image of the Black Man in English Drama, 1550–1688*, Boston, MA, G. K. Hall and Co., 1982.

12 Anthony Munday and Robert Chettle (?), *The Death of Robert, Earl of Huntingdon* (1601), Malone Society Reprints, Oxford, Oxford UP, 1967, sc. xi, line 1858; Jonathan Bate and Eric Rasmussen (eds), William Shakespeare, *Complete Works*, Basingstoke, Hants, Macmillan, 2007: *Love's Labour's Lost*, 4.3, line 254, p. 338; *Much Ado About Nothing*, 5.4, line 38, p. 302.

13 Shakespeare's *Titus Andronicus* (a.k.a. *The Most Lamentable Roman Tragedy of Titus Andronicus*, c. 1594); *Lust's Dominion, or, the Lascivious Queen* (c. 1599, though attributed to Marlowe in 1657, is thought to be a collaboration between John Marston, Thomas

Dekker, William Haughton, and John Day, or some combination of them); William Rowley's *All's Lost by Lust* (c. 1618); Aphra Behn's *Abdelazer, or, the Moor's Revenge* (c. 1676); Edward Young's *The Revenge* (1721); Matthew 'Monk' Lewis's *The Castle Spectre* (1797).

14 A drawing by Henry Peacham (1576–1643) depicting a scene or scenes from the play has been the subject of much debate. The drawing (of disputed date) shows figures from the play including one who is distinctly black, presumed to be Aaron. This might suggest the Elizabethans regarded Moors as black but does not offer any more clues to their theatrical representation. See, for example, R. A. Foakes, *Illustrations of the English Stage, 1580–1642*, Stanford, Ca., Stanford UP, 1985, pp. 48–51; Callaghan, op. cit., p. 4.

15 *Titus Andronicus* quotations, *Complete Works*, op. cit., 4.2, p. 1655, lines 74–75 and 100–101.

16 *A Midsummer Night's Dream*, *Complete Works*, op. cit., 3.2, line 260, p. 393, and line 268, p. 394.

17 Gary Taylor, *Buying Whiteness: Race, Culture, and Identity from Columbus to Hip Hop*, New York and Basingstoke, Hants, Palgrave Macmillan, 2005; Jones, op. cit.; Daryl W. Palmer, 'Merchants and Miscegenation: *The Three Ladies of London*, *The Jew of Malta*, and *The Merchant of Venice*', in Joyce Green MacDonald (ed.), *Race, Ethnicity, and Power in the Renaissance*, London, Associated UP, 1997, p. 61, says the representation of the Moors is not aimed at affirmation but erasure or negation.

18 George Peele, *The Old Wives' Tale* (1595), in *The Minor Elizabethan Drama*, vol. 2, London, J. M. Dent, 1910, p.150.

19 There is much literature on female Renaissance representation and ethnicity/race. See, for example, Callaghan, op. cit; Kim F. Hall, *Things of Darkness: Economies of Race and Gender in Early Modern England*, Ithaca, NY, and London, Cornell UP, 1995; Margo Hendricks and Patricia Parker (eds), *Women, 'Race' and Writing in Early Modern England*, London, Routledge, 1994; Ania Loomba, *Gender, Race, Renaissance Drama*, Delhi, Oxford UP,1992; Joyce Green MacDonald, 1997, op. cit., and *Women and Race in Early Modern Texts*, Cambridge, Cambridge UP, 2002; Mason Vaughan, op. cit.; Felicity A. Nussbaum, *The Limits of the Human: Fictions of Anomaly, Race, and Gender in the Long Eighteenth Century*, New York, Cambridge UP, 2003, and 'The Theatre of Empire: Racial Counterfeit, Racial Realism', in Kathleen Wilson (ed.), *A New Imperial History: Culture, Identity and Modernity in Britain and the Empire, 1660–1840*, Cambridge, Cambridge UP, 2004; Katherine M. Quinsey (ed.), *Broken Boundaries: Women and Feminism in Restoration Drama*, Lexington, KY, University of Kentucky Press, 1996.

20 There is a vast literature on ethnicity/race and *Othello* (c. 1603), which is an inescapable part of its history, whether or not the play has been over-racialized. See, for example, the titles in note 19; Catherine M. S. Alexander and Stanley Wells (eds), *Shakespeare and Race*, Cambridge, Cambridge UP, 2000; Carol Jones Carlisle, *Shakespeare from the Greenroom: Actors' Criticisms of Four Major Tragedies*, Chapel Hill, NC, North Carolina Press, 1969; Cowhig, op. cit.; Ania Loomba and Martin Orkin (eds), *Post-Colonial Shakespeares*, London, Routledge, 1998; Joyce Green MacDonald, 'Acting Black: *Othello*, *Othello* Burlesques, and the Performance of Blackness', *Theatre Journal*, vol. 46, no. 2, May 1994, pp. 231–249; Virginia Mason Vaughan, *Othello: A Contextual History*, Cambridge, Cambridge UP, 1994; Gino J. Matteo, *Shakespeare's Othello; The Study and the Stage, 1604–1904*, Salzburg, Institut für englische Sprache und Literatur, Universität Salzburg, 1974; Karen Newman, *Fashioning Femininity and English Renaissance Drama*, Chicago, IL, and London, University of Chicago Press, 1991; Edward Pechter, *Othello and Interpretive Traditions*, Iowa City, IA, University of Iowa Press, 1999; Lois Potter, *Othello*, Manchester, Manchester UP, 2002; Marvin Rosenberg, *The Masks of Othello: The Search for the Identity of Othello, Iago and Desdemona by Three Centuries of Actors and Critics*, Berkeley, CA, University of California Press, 1961.

21 There have been exceptions. Kenneth Tynan's 1950 production, for example, had a black Emilia to make Iago's jealousy more plausible, and Yvonne Brewster cast a black Cassio in 1997 to underscore Othello's jealousy. Director Jude Kelly in 1997 kept Othello a

colour different from the rest of the cast but in a 'photo negative' production: Othello (Patrick Stewart) was white and everyone else black (an experiment predated at the Baron's Court Theatre, a small west London venue, in 1992 when Othello was presented as a white mercenary serving on an island whose inhabitants were black).

22 Donald Sinden blacked up in the role for the Royal Shakespeare Company in1979; Paul Scofield for the National Theatre in 1980 – the last occasions (at time of writing) at these two national companies. For black actors, playing the part can mean confirming a stereotype. Actor Hugh Quarshie, in Ayanna Thompson (ed.), *Colorblind Shakespeare*: *New Perspectives on Race and Performance*, London and New York, Routledge, 2006, p. xv, says Othello is perhaps the one role a black actor should not play. For the RSC, Ben Kingsley, whose father was Kenyan Asian, played the role in 1985; Willard White (African American) in 1989 (at the Other Place); and the British black actor Ray Fearon in 1999. For the NT, the British black actor David Harewood played the role in 1997 (Cottesloe). Josette Simon was the first black actress to play leading Shakespearean roles in Britain (e.g. Rosaline, 1984, Isabella 1987, for the RSC).

23 *The Tempest, Complete Works*, op. cit., 1, 2, lines 423–425, p. 16.

24 Loomba, op. cit., p. 143, citing Trevor R. Griffiths, '"This Island's Mine": Caliban and colonialism', *The Yearbook of English Studies*, 13, 1983, pp. 159–180. Loomba, p.151, also cites Rob Nixon, 'Caribbean and African Appropriations of *The Tempest*', *Critical Inquiry*, 13, Spring 1987, pp. 557–77, saying the first anti-imperialist response to the play comes in 1904. See also Francis Barker and Peter Hulme, 'Nymphs and Reapers Heavily Vanish: The Discursive Con-Texts of *The Tempest*', in John Drakakis, *Alternative Shakespeares*, London, Methuen, 1985, pp. 191–205; Barbara Fuchs, 'Conquering Islands: Contextualising *The Tempest*', *Shakespeare Quarterly*, vol. 48, no. 1, Spring 1997, pp. 45–62; Helen Gilbert and Joanne Tompkins, *Post-colonial Drama*: *Theory, Practice, Politics*, London, Routledge, 1996; Heidi Hutner, *Colonial Women*: *Race and Culture in Stuart Drama*, Oxford, Oxford UP, 2001; Meredith Anne Skura, 'Discourse and the Individual: The Case of Colonialism in the *The Tempest*', *Shakespeare Quarterly*, XL, 1989, pp. 42–69; Alden T. Vaughan and Virginia Mason Vaughan, *Shakespeare's Caliban*: *A Cultural History*, Cambridge, Cambridge UP, 1991. Peter Hulme, *Colonial Encounters*: *Europe and the Native Caribbean 1492–1797*, London, Routledge, 1992, places the Prospero-Caliban story among five major accounts of European/Caribbean interchange along with Columbus and the cannibals, John Smith and Pocahontas, Robinson Crusoe and Man Friday, and Yarico and Inkle.

25 Orr, op. cit., p. 61.

26 See Ananda Lal (ed.), *Oxford Companion to Indian Theatre*, Oxford & New Delhi, Oxford UP, 2004, p. 164. *The Indian Queen* (1664) was written in collaboration with Sir John Howard. See also Nandini Bhattacharya, 'Ethnopolitical Dynamics and the Language of Gendering in Dryden's *Aureng-Zebe*', *Cultural Critique*, no. 25, Autumn 1993, pp. 153–176; Mita S. Choudhury, 'Imperial Licenses, Borderless Topographies, and the Eighteenth-Century British Theatre', in Michal Kobialka (ed.), *Of Borders and Thresholds*: *Theatre History, Practice and Theory*, Minneapolis, MN, and London, University of Minnesota Press, 1999, pp. 73–85; Binita Mehta, *Widows, Pariahs, and Bayaderes*: *India as Spectacle*, Lewisburg, PA, Bucknell UP, 2002 (who points out that in *Aureng-Zebe*, Dryden turns a Hindu princess into a Muslim).

27 See Derek Hughes, 'Restoration and Settlement: 1660–1688', in Deborah Payne Fisk (ed.), *Cambridge Companion to English Restoration Theatre*, Cambridge, Cambridge UP, 2000, pp. 127–141; Orr, op. cit., p. 16.

28 For the authenticity issue and particularly *Omai*, see Greg Dening, *Mr Bligh's Bad Language*: *Passion, Power and Theatre on the Bounty*, Cambridge, Cambridge UP, 1992, pp. 269–276; Daniel O'Quinn, *Staging Governance*: *Theatrical Imperialism in London, 1770–1800*, Baltimore, MD, Johns Hopkins UP, 2005, pp. 74–114; Laura J. Rosenthal, '"Infamous Commerce": Transracial Prostitution in the South Seas and Back', in Laura J. Rosenthal and Mita S. Choudhury (eds), *Monstrous Dreams of Reason*: *Body, Self, and Other in the Enlightenment*, London, Associated UP, 2002, pp. 189–208; Gillian Russell,

'An "Entertainment of Oddities": Fashionable Sociability and the Pacific in the 1770s', in Wilson, 2004, op. cit., pp. 48–70; Kathleen Wilson, 'Pacific Modernity: Theater, Englishness, and the Arts of Discovery, 1760–1800', in Colin Jones and Dror Wahrman (eds), *The Age of Cultural Revolutions: Britain and France, 1750–1820*, Berkeley, CA, and London, University of California Press, 2002, and *The Island Race: Englishness, Empire and Gender in the Eighteenth Century*, London, Routledge, 2003, pp. 163–170.

29 See Daniel O'Quinn, 'Mercantile Deformities: George Colman's *Inkle and Yarico* and the Racialization of Class Relations', *Theatre Journal*, vol. 54, no. 3, October 2002, pp. 14–29; 'Theatre and Empire', in Jane Moody and Daniel O'Quinn (eds), *Cambridge Companion to British Theatre, 1730–1830*, Cambridge, Cambridge UP, 2007, p 236; and O'Quinn, 2005, op. cit., p. 281. See also Mita S. Choudhury, *Interculturalism and Resistance in the London Theatre, 1600–1800: Identity, Performance, Empire*, London, Associated UP, 2000, p. 109; Nussbaum, 2003, op. cit., p. 252.

30 There are different spellings for *Sakuntala*: (e.g., *Sacontala, Sakoontala, Shakuntala*), as there are for most transliterated names. Dorothy Matilda Figueira details the appearance of different versions of *Sakuntala* in different art forms, in *Translating the Orient: The Reception of* Sakuntala *in Nineteenth- Century Europe*, New York, State University of New York Press, 1991. See also Edward Said, *Orientalism*, London, Routledge & Kegan Paul, 1978; Sue-Ellen Case, 'Eurocolonial Reception of Sanskrit Poets', in Case and Reinelt, op. cit., pp. 114–5; Ronald B. Inden, *Imagining India*, London, Hurst and Co., 2000.

31 There is much literature on this uneven process. See, for example, Douglas A. Lorimer, *Colour, Class and the Victorians: English Attitudes to the Negro in the Mid–Nineteenth Century*, Leicester, Leicester UP, 1978; Roxann Wheeler, *The Complexion of Race: Categories of Difference in Eighteenth-Century British Culture*, Philadelphia, PA, University of Pennsylvania Press, 2000, p. 4, where she cites an account from travels to Gambia in 1723 that says the translators were 'black as coal' but, being Christian, 'they account themselves White Men'; Robert Young, *Colonial Desire: Hybridity in Theory, Culture and Race*, New York, Routledge, 1995.

32 For whitening agents (p. 52) and a scholarly exposition of the representation of race on the Georgian stage and its relation to blackface, see David Worrall, *Harlequin Empire: Race, Ethnicity and the Drama of the Popular Enlightenment*, London, Pickering & Chatto, 2007, pp. 23–55. Worrall cites Leman Thomas Rede's 1827 acting guide, *The Road to the Stage; or, the Performer's Preceptor*, which describes the blacking-up process and mentions Arthur Murphy's *The Apprentice* (1756) and Colman's *Inkle and Yarico* as playing with blackface and the meaning of colour on stage.

33 Ania Loomba, 'The Color of Patriarchy: Critical Difference, Cultural Difference, and Renaissance Drama', in Hendricks and Parker (eds), op. cit., pp. 17–34.

34 See Hutner, op. cit. She argues that the Pocahontas myth was influenced by that of Malinche, who was given to Cortes by a tribe he defeated in Mexico, and that both legends influenced Stuart drama. She notes (p. 16) that women during the seventeenth century were given the negative stereotypical characteristics of native women. David Hughes, 'Race, Gender and Scholarly Practice: Aphra Behn's *Oroonoko*', *Essays in Criticism*, vol. 52, no. 1, January 2002, p. 6, contends that almost every Restoration play that depicts Europeans and non-Europeans presents love between them favourably.

35 For discussions of *Oroonoko* stage versions, see, e.g., Julie A. Carlson, 'Race and Profit in English Theatre', in Moody and O'Quinn (eds), op. cit., pp. 175–188; Choudhury, 2000, op. cit., pp. 134, 161–174; Susan B. Iwanisziw (ed.), *Troping Oroonoko from Behn to Bandele*, Aldershot, Hants, Ashgate, 2004 and its companion volume of texts, Susan B. Iwanisziw (ed.), *Oroonoko: adaptations and offshoots*, Aldershot, Hants, Ashgate, 2006; Suvir Kaul, 'Reading Literary Symptoms: Colonial Pathologies and the Oroonoko fictions of Behn, Southerne and Hawkesworth', *Eighteenth-Century Life*, vol. 18, no. 3, November 1994, pp. 80–96; MacDonald, 2002, op. cit., pp. 87–123; Nussbaum, 2003, op. cit., which lists several other titles, and Nussbaum, 2004, op. cit.; John R. Oldfield, 'The "Ties of Soft Humanity": Slavery and Race in British Drama, 1760–1800,' *Huntingdon Library Quarterly*, vol. 56, no. 1, Winter, 1993; Joseph R. Roach, *Cities of the Dead: Circum-Atlantic*

Performance, New York, Columbia UP, 1996, pp. 154–159. Discussions of *Oroonoko* often also deal with *Inkle and Yarico*.

36 The issue of actresses in blackface is under-researched. There are references (some contradictory) in the titles listed in note 19. Callaghan, op. cit., p. 82, cites Margaret W. Ferguson, 'Juggling the Categories of Race, Class, and Gender: Aphra Behn's *Oroonoko*', in Hendricks and Parker (eds), op. cit., pp. 219–20, on post-Restoration actresses' being prohibited from using blackface, though evidence is not provided. Arthur L. Little Jr, *Shakespeare Jungle Fever: National-Imperial Re-Visions of Race, Rape, and Sacrifice*, Stanford, CA, Stanford UP, 2000, p. 163, repeats Ferguson's claim. Thompson, op. cit., p. 30, also repeats the claim as if fact but cites Hutner, op. cit., p. 16. Hutner offers no reference. E-mail exchanges with Ferguson (13/14 June 2007), in which she reports on discussions with Francis Dolan and Felicity Nussbaum, suggest if not a formal prohibition then a custom of white women not blacking up until possibly the period of *Inkle and Yarico* (1787). Yet Barthelemy, op. cit., pp. 66–67, cites evidence of blackface being used for a Moorish governess, Fructifera, in a 1681 Lord Mayor's Pageant, though this does not mean the practice was widespread on the stage at the time. E-mail exchanges with period experts such as Peter Holland, Joyce MacDonald, Max Novak, and Virginia Vaughan suggest there was no ban on blackface for actresses, but the extent of its use is not known.

37 Nussbaum, 2003, op. cit., p.162. See also Sue Wiseman, 'Abolishing Romance: Representing Rape in Oroonoko', in Brycchan Carey et al. (eds), *Discourses of Slavery and Abolition: Britain and its Colonies, 1760-1838*, Basingstoke, Hants, Palgrave Macmillan, 2004, pp. 26–44. Other readings, e.g. Choudhury, 2000, op. cit., p. 171, suggest the portrayal of passion, far from avoiding reality, is a way of coping with its contradictions.

38 The Introduction in Maximillian E. Novak and David Stuart Rodes (eds), *Oroonoko* by Thomas Southerne, London, Edward Arnold, 1977, p. xxix, says the class distinction between Oroonoko and other slaves, which is evident in the text, was 'no doubt, rigorously insisted upon in the staging of the play in physical attitude as well as in dress'.

39 Srinivas Aravamudan, *Tropicopolitans: Colonialism and Agency, 1688–1804*, Durham, NC, and London, Duke UP, 1999, pp. 33-38.

40 Iwanisziw, 2006, op. cit., p. xx, says *The Sexes Mis-match'd: or a New Way to get a Husband* appears to have survived independently but only as a fairground entertainment or a theatrical afterpiece.

41 MacDonald, 2002, op. cit., p. 102.

42 David Worrall in *The Politics of Romantic Theatricality, 1787–1832*, Basingstoke, Hants, Palgrave Macmillan, 2007, pp. 68–106, contrasts the handling of slavery in this play and *Harlequin Mungo*.

43 Jeffrey N. Cox (ed.), *Slavery, Abolition and Emancipation: Writings in the British Romantic Period*, vol. 5, *Drama*, London, Pickering and Chatto, 1999, p. xiii. An Act was passed in 1833 and came into force in 1834 abolishing slavery in most of the British Empire (though not in territories ruled by the East India Company), but slaves older than six remained indentured as 'apprentices' in different categories, a system that was abolished in two stages, in 1838 and 1840. 1838 marked legal full emancipation (the reality was not as neat). Slavery in India was not abolished until 1860.

44 Herbert Marshall and Mildred Stock, *Ira Aldridge: The Negro Tragedian*, London, Rockliff, 1958, p. 57.

45 See Edward Ziter, *The Orient on the Victorian Stage*, Cambridge, Cambridge UP, 2003, pp. 58–59.

46 Mary Pix, *The False Friend, or the Fate of Disobedience*, London, 1699, Act 3, p. 28.

47 The story was published by Richard Ligon in 1657 in *A True and Exact History of the Island of Barbados*, more than a decade before Behn's *Oroonoko* appeared. The story can also be traced to Jean Mocquet's *Travels and Voyages into Africa, Asia, America, the East and West Indies* (1617). Lawrence Marsden Price, *Inkle and Yarico Album*, Berkeley, CA, University of California Press, 1937, notes forty-eight versions of the Yarico story from 1657 to 1830. Frank Felsenstein (ed.), *English Trader, Indian Maid: Representing Gender,*

Race and Slavery in the New World – An Inkle and Yarico *Reader*, Baltimore, MD, Johns Hopkins UP, 1999, shows how the story continues in America and the Caribbean. Frank Kidson, 'Some Guesses about Yankee Doodle', *The Musical Quarterly*, vol. 3, no. 1, January 1917, pp. 98–103, deals with Yarico becoming a generic name.

48 See Moira Ferguson, *Subject to Others: British Women Writers and Colonial Slavery, 1670–1834*, New York, Routledge, 1992; Nussbaum, 2003, op. cit.; O'Quinn, 2002, op. cit., pp. 389–409, and 2005, op. cit.; Swindells, op. cit., pp. 62–69. Nussbaum, p. 247, suggests the Weddell version may have been banned because the central role was a woman of colour. Cox, op. cit., p. 74, in a volume that contains the Weddell version, says that although two plays are attributed to her and possibly a third, she may not have existed.

49 According to the biographer of Jack Bannister, the leading actor of the company, he was uncomfortable with the role of Inkle and suggested the ending to show the character's repentance (cited by Felsenstein, op. cit., p. 24, and backed by archival evidence of early texts). Felsenstein, pp. 24–27, says Bannister even wrote a prologue alluding to the change, to alert the audience to the unaccustomed final twist. The ending seems to have been popular, and it is likely Bannister would have played up the comic and burlesque possibilities, which does not contradict the sentimentality that is crucial to its political impact and leverage. Bannister, however, soon swapped to the role of Trudge.

50 George Colman Jr, *Inkle and Yarico*, London, Sadler and Co., 1770?, p. 20, I.3.

51 Robert Burns wrote a poem, 'On Seeing Mrs Kemble in Yarico' (1794).

52 Uncoloured, see Rede's *The Road to the Stage* (1827), cited by Worrall, 2007, op. cit., p. 41. For Wowski's colour, see O'Quinn, 2002, op. cit., p. 405.

53 Felsenstein, op. cit., p. 19, sees racist dialogue as sardonic comment on European ineptitude in differentiating one racial group from another rather than extension of it. On the play's popularity, see Worrall, 2007, op. cit., p. 1. The play was particularly popular in the regions, and opened the Richmond Theatre in the North Riding of York in 1788.

54 *The Tempest, Or the Enchanted Isle* (1667), a precursor of *Inkle and Yarico*, has Sycorax, Caliban's sister, as 'a racial and sexual monstrosity' who later turns into Wowski, says O'Quinn, 2002, op. cit., p. 403.

55 Isaac Bickerstaff, *The Padlock*, in Cox, op. cit., I, vi, p. 87.

56 See also Hans Nathan, 'Negro Impersonation in Eighteenth Century England', *Notes* (USA Music Library, Wisconsin), vol. 2, no. 4, 1945, on Dibdin, *The Padlock* and representation of black people.

57 Isaac Bickerstaff, *Love in a City*, London, W. Lowdnes and J. Barker, 1786, 1, ii, p. 5.

58 The epilogue is reproduced at <http://www.bryccchancarey.com/slavery/padlock1.htm> (accessed 19 November, 2009) and is quoted in Sypher, op. cit., p. 237. Brycchan Carey, *British Abolitionism and the Rhetoric of Sensibility: Writing, Sentiment, and Slavery, 1760–1807*, Basingstoke, Hants, Palgrave Macmillan, 2005, pp. 178–179, says *The Morning Chronicle*, which covered the Somersett case fully, referred to Mungo as diminishing the response of Africans by relegating them to the position of actors in a sentimental comedy. Worrall, 2007, op. cit., pp. xx, notes plays such as *The Padlock*, *High Life Below Stairs*, *Robinson Crusoe*, and *Harlequin Friday*, which were performed in private houses to mock black people, like the Court masques of earlier times, used the nuance of blackface to deal with rank, authority, and sexual transgression.

59 *The Padlock* was revived in 1979 at the Old Vic, London as a curiosity to mark the bicentenary of David Garrick's death. Nickolas Grace played Mungo in blackface.

60 Julie A. Carlson, 'New Lows in Eighteenth-Century Theater: the Rise of Mungo', *European Romantic Review*, vol. 18, no. 2, April 2007, pp.139–147, in relation to the box office success of black issue plays, says 'we might pause over the oddness of this "in the black" of late-eighteenth century patent theatre, whereby black is a source of popularity in a slave-holding nation and the phrase constitutes one of the very few wholly positive associations ascribed to "black" or "blackness" in any period of Anglo-European culture'. See also Marshall and Stock, op. cit., p. 85.

61 Quoted in Gerzina Gretchen, *Black England: Life before Emancipation*, London, Allison and Busby, 1999, p.16. Nussbaum, 2004, op. cit., puts the attacks in the context of the

intermarriage of a black servant and daughter of the white master, though the play follows the tradition of reassurance through actorly blacking up that all stage black characters are really white. Hazel Waters, *Racism on the Victorian Stage: Representation of Slavery and the Black Character*, Cambridge, Cambridge UP, 2007, p. 45, says riots were caused not by the play but by comments in Bate's newspaper, *The Morning Post*.

62 Quotation taken from unpaginated online version of Carlson, April 2007, op. cit., <http://www.cla.purdue.edu/academic/engl/navsa/conferences/2006/documents/CarlsonRiseofMungo.doc> (accessed 13 May, 2008) but omitted in printed version.

63 William Dimond, *The Lady and the Devil*, Cumberland's British Theatre, vol. 45, no. 375, London, G.H. Davidson, 1849, 1.2. p.15.

64 Ibid., II, 3, p. 35.

65 Worrall, 2007, op. cit., p. 73, however, notes that Rede (1827) says Sambo was commonly a brown rather than black role for white actors.

66 Carlson, April 2007, op. cit., p.142. See also Nussbaum, 2003, op. cit., pp. 158–160; Oldfield, op. cit., p. 11; O'Quinn, 2007, op. cit., p. 235.

67 Samuel Foote, *The Cozeners*, Dublin, George Bonham, 1778, III, iv, p. 50. The incident is said to be based on a trick played on Charles James Fox MP by a matchmaker who conned him by promising him a West Indian woman with a fortune – see Jane Moody, 'Stolen Identities: Character, Mimicry and the Invention of Samuel Foote', in Mary Luckhurst and Jane Moody (eds), *Theatre and Celebrity in Britain 1660–2000*, Basingstoke, Hants, and London, Palgrave Macmillan, 2005, p. 82.

68 Quoted in John O'Brien, *Harlequin Britain: Pantomime and Entertainment, 1690–1760*, Baltimore, MD, Johns Hopkins UP, 2004, p.135.

69 Henry Louis Gates Jr, *Figures in Black: Words, Signs, and the 'Racial' Self*, Oxford, Oxford UP, 1987, pp. 51–2. For links with blackness, see also Dale Cockrell, *Demons of Disorder: Early Blackface Minstrels and Their World,* Cambridge, Cambridge UP, 1997; W.T. Lhamon, *Raising Cain: Blackface Performance from Jim Crow to Hip Hop,* Cambridge, MA., Harvard UP, 1998; Eric Lott, *Love and Theft: Blackface Minstrelsy and the American Working Class*, Oxford, Oxford UP, 1993; O'Brien, op. cit.; Worrall, 2007 and 2007a, op. cit.

70 O'Brien, op. cit., p. 137.

71 According to Human Rights Watch, 'The Security Situation Immediately after the Fall of Basra' <http://www.hrw.org> (accessed 3 June, 2008), the term *Ali Baba* is also used by American troops and, ironically, by Iraqis of foreign troops they find or suspect are looting.

72 Richard Bevis, *The Laughing Tradition: Stage Comedy in Garrick's Day*, London, George Prior Publishers, 1980. For the wider struggle against theatrical censorship, see J. S. Bratton, *New Readings in Theatre History*, Cambridge, Cambridge UP, 2003; Jane Moody, *Illegitimate Theatre in London, 1770–1840*, Cambridge, Cambridge UP, 2000; Watson Nicholson, *The Struggle for a Free Stage in London*, London, Constable, 1906; Julia Swindells, *Glorious Causes: The Grand Theatre of Political Change, 1789 to 1833*, Oxford, Oxford UP, 2001; David Worrall, *Theatric Revolution: Drama, Censorship, and Romantic Subcultures 1773–1832*, Oxford, Oxford UP, 2006.

73 See, e.g., Sypher and Cox, op. cit. In the early–seventeenth-century English theatre, the word *slave* was likely to evoke captured English.

74 Carlson, 2007, op. cit., p. 185.

75 Amal Chatterjee, *Representations of India, 1740–1840: the Creation of India in the Colonial Imagination*, Basingstoke, Hants, Macmillan, 1998, p. 113.

76 See Mehta, op. cit., p. 113. The French play (1770) is by Antoine-Marin Lemierre.

77 *The Two Farmers* was scheduled to play at Covent Garden in 1800 at a time of grain hording and related riots but was banned by the censor probably to protect the image of the English farmer. See Worrall, 2006, op. cit., pp. 169–177, and Worrall, 2007, op. cit., pp. 33–4, who points out it was not exceptional for a mainstream and topical play by a conservative playwright to feature a black worker and one being protected by the legal system. Worrall, 2007, quotes Caesar: 'Slave once, not now…No Slave here – You pay, I worke – You kick, I tell Massa Kenyon – he speak twelve men in a Box – dey take poor

Negerman's part, & you kick black man no more, I warrant, Massa.' See also Swindells, op. cit., pp. 55–56.

78 See Charles Rzepka, 'Introduction: *Obi*, Aldridge and Abolition' and Jeffrey N. Cox, 'Theatrical Forms, Ideological Conflicts, and the Staging of *Obi*', in Charles Rzepka (ed.), *Obi*, *A Romantic Circles Praxis Volume*, <http://www.rc.umd.edu/praxis/obi> (accessed 21 May, 2008). The introduction points out that *obi* also refers to the horn fetish by which *obeah* practitioners exert their powers, and these powers include conferring invisibility, like Harlequin; and Robert Hoskins, with Eileen Southern, 'Obi: or, Three-Finger'd Jack', critical introduction, *Music for London Entertainment*. Series D, vol. 4, London, Stainer and Bell, 1996. Facsimile edition of Samuel Arnold's printed piano-vocal score, published by John Longman and Muzio Clementi, 1801.

79 Both quotations, *Obi; or, Three-Finger'd Jack – A Melo-Drama in Two Acts*, in Rzepka (ed.), op. cit., II, vi. William Murray is known to have written a melodrama version for Ira Aldridge; see Chapter 2, p. 40.

80 Edward Said, quoted by Choudhury, 2000, op. cit., p. 103. For circulation of theatre, see O'Quinn, 2007, op. cit., p. 33.

81 Fryer, op. cit., p. 31.

82 See Chapter 2, notes 40 and 41 for Billy Waters.

83 W. J. Lawrence, 'First Real Negro on the Stage', *Notes and Queries*, vol. viii, July–December 1889, pp. 164–165, wrote in response to a survey 'The Negro on Stage' by Laurence Hutton, which had appeared in *Harper's New Monthly Magazine*, June 1889, pp. 131–146. Hutton, though mentioning Aldridge and the African Players, deals primarily with white American actors in blackface. Lawrence admits the 'slight difficulty' in 'determining the exact date of the occurrence' when 'a real negro first appeared upon the stage' but ventures 'there is little room for doubting that it took place within the British Isles'.

84 The reference to the black actress comes from John Jackson, *The History of the Scottish Stage*, Edinburgh, Peter Hill, 1793, pp. 349–351. It does not give a date, but the audition probably occurred in 1766 when Foote took over the Haymarket, the summer venue for the Covent Garden company. Jackson reports that Foote was seeing her for at least the roles of Lady Betty Modish in Cibber's *The Careless Husband* and Rossetta in Bickerstaff's *Love in a Village* (rather than for any specifically black roles). The person who persuaded Foote to see her is quoted by Jackson as saying: 'There is one thing, Sir, I had forgot to mention, and which you may possibly object to – THE LADY IS A BLACK'. To which Foote is reported as replying, 'Oh! No matter, we will introduce the Roman fashion: the lady shall wear a MASK'.

85 Details from John Greene, *Theatre in Dublin, 1745–1820: A Calendar of Performances*, Bethlehem, PA., Lehigh UP (forthcoming). Fryer, op. cit., p. 75. cites the same extract as Lawrence, op. cit., from Jonah Barrington, *Personal Sketches of his Own Times*, Henry Colburn, 1827–32, vol. II, p. 208. However, though Fryer and Lawrence give the date of 1770, Barrington does not, but he incorrectly states the production occurred at Smock Alley. A 'New Grand Pantomime Dance,' *The Negroes*, was performed at Smock Alley in 1757 but, according to Greene, did not include black performers (e-mail, 27 March, 2010).

86 According to one account of Soubise performing speeches from *Othello* at the spouting club based in Jacob's Well tavern at the Barbican, he was not well received – see Worrall, 2006, op. cit., p. 249. Later, after the 1819 Peterloo massacre, black leader Robert Wedderburn and another black person spoke at this tavern, a fact Worrall suggests might link this venue and radical politics. The biography of Soubise is unclear. He apparently played the violin, was an expert swordsman, and was also a sonneteer. See Vincent Carretta, Soubise entry, *Oxford Dictionary of National Biography*, Oxford, Oxford UP, 2004; Paul Edwards and David Dabydeen (eds), *Black Writers in Britain, 1760–1890*, Edinburgh, Edinburgh UP, 1991, p. 81; Paul Edwards and James Walvin, *Black Personalities in the Era of the Slave Trade*, Basingstoke, Hants, Macmillan, 1983, pp. 223–237; Nussbaum, 2003, op. cit., p. 169; O'Quinn, 2007, op. cit., pp. 234–235; Sandhu, op. cit., pp. 5–9; Keith

A. Sandiford, *Measuring the Moment: Strategies of Protest in Eighteenth Century Afro-English Writing*, Selsingrove, Susquehana UP, 1988, p. 75; Folarin Shyllon, *Black People in Britain 1555–1833*, London, Oxford UP, 1977, pp. 41–43; Worrall, 2006, op. cit., p. 247.

87 Sancho's alleged relationship with Garrick is based on a short biography, *The Life of Ignatius Sancho*, by Joseph Jekyll (1782), of which Brycchan Carey, <http://www.brycchancarey.com/sancho/life.htm> (accessed 19 November, 2009) says, 'much of it is unverifiable, and, worse still, much of it directly contradicts what Sancho himself says to people in his letters'. Several later accounts have Sancho about to play Othello and Oroonoko but not actually appearing, e.g., Hill, 1984, op. cit., p. 10, whereas a few say Sancho did appear, and his speech impediment ended his acting career, e.g. James Walvin, *Black Presence, London, Orbach and Chambers,* 1971, p. 71.

2   Aldridge and the age of minstrelsy

1 Bernth Lindfors (ed.), *Ira Aldridge: The African Roscius*, Rochester NY, University of Rochester Press, 2007, p.1.

2 For the African Theatre, see George A. Thompson Jr, *A Documentary History of the African Theatre*, Evanston, IL, Northwestern UP, 1998.

3 These appearances may have been in extracts of the plays presented by the African Theatre when it briefly decamped to Albany, north of New York on the Hudson River.

4 Bernth Lindfors, 'Ira Aldridge's London Debut', *Theatre Notebook,* vol. 60, no. 1, 2006, p. 37.

5 Ibid., p. 42.

6 Gill died in 1864, and Aldridge remarried the following year, to a Swedish concert singer, Amanda Brandt, who had already borne him two children. He had no children by Gill but fathered at least six by three other women.

7 *The Times*, 11 October, 1825; Martin Hoyles, *Ira Aldridge: Celebrated 19th Century Actor*, London and Herts, Hansib, 2008, pp. 23–24, cites the *Brighton Gazette*.

8 Lindfors, 2006, op. cit., details the changes and their possible interpretations. The Roscius label may also have linked Aldridge to slavery, as it was common to name slaves after Roman figures such as Caesar. The Northcote painting is held by the Manchester Art Gallery.

9 For Mathews, see J. S. Bratton, 'The Music Hall', in Kerry Powell (ed.), *The Cambridge Companion to Victorian and Edwardian Theatre*, Cambridge, Cambridge UP, 2004, p. 175; Heidi J. Holder, 'Other Londoners: Race and Class in Plays of Nineteenth-Century London Life', in Pamela Gilbert (ed.), *Imagined Londons*, Albany, NY, State University of New York Press, 2002, pp. 34–36; Richard L. Klepac, 'Mr Mathews At Home', London, Society for Theatre Research, 1979; Eric Lott, *Love and Theft: Blackface Minstrelsy and the American Working Class*, Oxford, Oxford UP, 1993, pp. 45–46; Jane Moody, 'Dictating to the Empire: Performance and Geography in Eighteenth-century Britain', in Jane Moody and Daniel O'Quinn (eds), *Cambridge Companion to British Theatre, 1730–1830*, Cambridge, Cambridge UP, 2007, pp. 35–78; Hazel Waters, *Racism on the Victorian Stage: Representation of Slavery and the Black Character*, Cambridge, Cambridge UP, 2007, pp. 91–94.

10 Herbert Marshall and Mildred Stock, *Ira Aldridge: The Negro Tragedian*, London, Rockliff, 1958, p.151. Nicholas M. Evans, 'Ira Aldridge: Shakespeare and Minstrelsy', in Lindfors, 2007, op. cit., p. 172, points out that by the time the Ethiopian Serenaders troupe came to Britain in 1846, reviewers compared them to Aldridge performing 'Opposum' as if his minstrelsy were the benchmark.

11 *The Black Doctor* may have been the first play to be published in Britain credited to a black author when Dicks' Standard Play series (1883?, no. 460) attributed it to Aldridge more than a decade after his death, but it is not clear whether or to what extent Aldridge was the author. Keith Byerman, 'Creating the Black Hero: Ira Aldridge's *The Black Doctor*', in Lindfors, 2007, op. cit., pp. 204–215, deals with the differences between the Dicks text and other versions. He suggests, though without incontrovertible evidence,

that Aldridge did contribute to revising the play even if he was not the sole author of the adaptation(s). Byerman believes Aldridge was responding to his racist reception in London.

12 Waters, op. cit., p. 76.

13 Jonathan Bate (ed.), Introduction to *Titus Andronicus*, London, Routledge, 1995, p. 54.

14 Marshall and Stock, op. cit., p. 215.

15 Apart from appearing in a complete *Othello* and four-act version of *The Merchant of Venice* early on, it seems Aldridge did not perform entire Shakespeare texts until he toured continental Europe, and it is not clear whether he ever played a complete *Hamlet*. See Evans in Lindfors, 2007, op. cit.

16 When Théophile Gautier saw Aldridge in Russia, he did not whiten his hands, possibly to remind audiences he was black or as a subtle reference to the fact that in minstrelsy white performers did not blacken their hands. Photographs of him as Shylock and Lear, however, show his hands whitened. See Krystyna Kujawiska Courtney, 'Ira Aldridge, Shakespeare, and Color-Consciousness Performances in Nineteenth-Century Europe', in Ayanna Thompson (ed.), *Colorblind Shakespeare: New Perspectives on Race and Performance*, London and New York, Routledge, 2006, p. 115. Thompson, p. 28, says whiteface makeup was used at the African Theatre at least on the actress playing the lead in *Pizarro*.

17 All quotations from Marshall and Stock, pp. 121–129. In reference to Aldridge 'pawing' Desdemona, Brian Roberts has pointed out ('A London Legacy of Ira Aldridge: Henry Francis Downing and the Paratheatrical Poetics of Plot and Cast(e)', forthcoming) that, according to Downing in a *Chicago Defender* article (26 April 1924), at one performance of Aldridge's Othello, a sailor in the audience was so incensed that he took out a knife and approached the stage before being bundled away.

18 Marshall and Stock, op. cit., p. 129.

19 *The Times*, 16 April, 1833. The actors came from a large company that had ready replacements. Only one other play lost a performance, the shows immediately after the missed evening went ahead, and all other scheduled appearances continued except for Aldridge's.

20 Marshall and Stock, op. cit., p. 230.

21 Ibid., p. 232.

22 Plays include David Pownall's *Black Star* (1987) and *Splendid Mummer* (1988) by Lonne Elder III. Bernth Lindfors, 'The Lives of Ira Aldridge', in Krystyna Kujawińska Courtney and Maria Łukowska (eds), *Ira Aldridge, 1807–1867: The Great Shakespearean Tragedian on the Bicentennial Anniversary of his Birth*, Frankfurt-am-Main, Peter Lang, 2009, pp.11–19, details various chronicles of Aldridge's life.

23 Bate, op. cit., p. 55, says Zanga was the second major black role in the classic repertory after Othello.

24 Marshall and Stock, op. cit., p. 83; prejudice quotation, Waters, op. cit., p. 80, and, more generally, pp. 58–88.

25 Lindfors, 2006, op. cit., p. 36.

26 Bernth Lindfors, 'The Signifying Flunkey: Ira Aldridge as Mungo,' *The Literary Griot*, vol. 5, no. 2, Fall 1993, p. 7.

27 Ibid., p. 9–10. Lindfors also argues that this 'double-voiced' discourse was not unlike the African American verbal and improvisational tradition of 'Signifyin(g)', as outlined by Henry Louis Gates, Jr, in the second chapter of *The Signifying Monkey: A Theory of African-American Literary Criticism*, Oxford, Oxford UP, 1988, pp. 44–88.

28 Marshall and Stock, op. cit., p. 75.

29 Lindfors, 1993, op. cit., p. 10.

30 Daphne A. Brooks, *Bodies in Dissent: Spectacular Performances of Race and Freedom, 1850–1910*, Durham, NC, and London, Duke UP, 2006, p. 3.

31 Edward Ziter, *The Orient on the Victorian Stage,* Cambridge, Cambridge UP, 2003, p. 10.

32 Bernth Lindfors (ed.), *Africans on Stage: Studies in Ethnological Show Business*, Bloomington, IN, Indiana UP, 1999, p. vii.

33 J. S. Bratton et al. (eds), *Acts of Supremacy: British Empire and the Stage, 1790–1930*, Manchester, Manchester UP, 1991, pp. 3–4.

34 See Brendan Gregory, 'Staging British India', in Bratton, 1991, op. cit., pp. 152–153. According to Annie E. Coombes, *Reinventing Africa, Museums, Material Culture and Popular Imagination in late Victorian and Edwardian England*, New Haven, CT, and London, Yale UP, 1994, p. 254, n. 5, Kiralfy was the central figure behind the organization of most of the major colonial exhibitions of this period.

35 See Ziter, op. cit., p. 77; Virginia Mason Vaughan, *Performing Blackness on English Stages 1500–1800*, Cambridge, Cambridge UP, 2005, pp. 147–148.

36 See Waters, op. cit., pp. 51–53.

37 British public opinion had been transformed in the 100 years since it had questioned the East India Company's imperial project in the 1750s. By the late 1850s, when the EIC collapsed and the British Crown took direct control of India, British attitudes seem generally to have become more jingoistic and supremacist.

38 David Worrall, *Harlequin Empire: Race, Ethnicity and the Drama of the Popular Enlightenment*, London, Pickering & Chatto, 2007, pp. 94–101.

39 See Michael H. Fisher, *Counterflows to Colonialism: Indian Travellers and Settlers in Britain 1600–1857*, Delhi, Permanent Books, 2004, p. 383.

40 J. C. Reid, *Bucks and Bruisers: Pierce Egan and Regency London*, London, Routledge and Kegan Paul, 1971, p. 79, notes five different stage versions of the novel in 1822 and 1823 alone. W. T. Moncrieff's adaptation, known as *Tom and Jerry*, was the most significant, introducing characters such as Billy Waters and turning characters such as African Sal, whom Egan merely mentions, into popular stage figures. Brian Maidment, *Dusty Bo: A Cultural History of Dustmen, 1780–1870*, Manchester, Manchester UP, 2007, pp. 64–72, deals with the relationship in the play between African Sal (played by a white actor in drag) and the dustman Dusty Bob, whose pas de deux of transgressive pleasure became a celebrated feature of the production. Maidment notes that Sal has a black baby, Mahogany Mary. See also David Worrall, *The Politics of Romantic Theatricality, 1787–1832*, Basingstoke, Palgrave Macmillan, 2007, pp. 190–205.

41 Holder, op. cit., p. 32. Paul Edwards and James Walvin, *Black Personalities in the Era of the Slave Trade*, Basingstoke, Hants, Macmillan, 1983, for example, say Billy Waters and African Sal appeared as themselves, but Worrall, 2007, op. cit., p. 63, says this has yet to be substantiated.

42 See Heidi J. Holder, 'The East End Theatre', in Powell op. cit., pp. 263–5; Waters, op. cit., p. 110. A possible source of interesting plays about racial discrimination was missed, probably because the plays were written in French although authored by an American. Records show that only a couple of plays by the prolific, New Orleans–born 'mulatto' playwright and actor Victor Séjour (1821–1874), who lived in France from his late teens, were seen in Britain, and these did not relate to his diasporic heritage or situation, e.g., *The Master Passion; Or, the Outlaw of the Adriatic*, adapted by Edward Falconer from the French, 1859, listed in *Victorian Plays: A Record of Significant Productions on the London Stage, 1837–1901*, compiled by Donald Mullin, Greenwood Press, New York, Westport, CT, London, 1987; *The Master Passion* also surfaced as *The Outlaw of the Adriatic; or, the Female Spy and the Chief of the Ten*, adapted by Edmund O'Rourke, published in England 1860; *The Woman in Red* adapted by Joseph Stirling Coyne, was published 1872. Séjour's plays that do deal with race include *The Fortune Teller* and *The Jew of Seville* translated by Norman R. Shapiro, Urbana, IL, University of Illinois Press, 2002. Errol G. Hill and James V. Hatch, *A History of African American Theatre*, Cambridge, Cambridge UP, 2003, p. 49, say only one of Séjour's plays ((*Le Martyre du Coeur*, 1858) includes a black character, a Jamaican. Séjour is said to be the author of the first African-American fiction, *Le Mulâtre* (1837).

43 Holder, 2002, op. cit., pp. 31–44.

44 Ibid., p. 43.

45 Black might identify type (usually bad), signal the Other generically regardless of accuracy (for example, the King of Egypt, who might historically *be* a black person, but

that was not the reason for his representation as such), or indicate an enemy (for example, the Turkish Knight, who is less likely than the King of Egypt to have been black-skinned but is still the non-white Other). See Peter Millington, 'Mystery History: The Origins of British Mummers' Plays', *American Morris Newsletter*, Nov./Dec. 1989, vol. 13, no. 3, pp. 9–16, and 'A Black and White Issue?' *English Dance and Song*, Autumn 2005, vol. 67, no. 3, pp. 31–32. As for black's being a mark of popular solidarity, that solidarity did not usually extend to people of the African or Asian diaspora, for whom the breadth of meaning associated with the colour black was absent.

46 Worrall, 2007, op. cit., pp. 134–137.

47 See Hans Nathan, 'Negro Impersonation in Eighteenth Century England', *Notes*, vol. 2, no. 4, 1945, USA Music Library, Middleton, WI, p. 248. See also note 9 for Mathews.

48 Holder, 2002, op. cit., p. 36.

49 *The Times*, 10 July, 1824.

50 See Audrey A. Fisch, 'Harriet Beecher Stowe in England', in Cindy Weinstein (ed.), *The Cambridge Companion to Harriet Beecher Stowe*, Cambridge, Cambridge UP, 2004, pp. 96–112, and *American Slaves in Victorian England: Abolitionist Politics in Popular Literature and Culture*, New York, Cambridge UP, 2000, pp. 12–13; Sarah Meer, *Uncle Tom Mania: Slavery, and Transatlantic Culture in the 1850s*, Atlanta, GA, University of Georgia Press, 2005, pp. 1–9, 13–4, 134; Waters, op. cit., pp. 155–178.

51 For example, two burlesques by William Brough: *Uncle Tom's Crib* and *Those Dear Blacks!* (1852).

52 Judie Newman, 'Staging Black Insurrection', in Weinstein, op. cit., pp 113–130.

53 Stephen Johnson, 'Blackface in the UK'. E-mail (21 March, 2010).

54 See Waters, op. cit., pp 118–125. For blackface minstrelsy and misogyny, see also titles in note 55.

55 Of the voluminous literature on blackface minstrelsy, as well as titles in notes 9 and 50, see, e.g., J. S. Bratton, 'English Ethiopians: British Audiences and Black-face Acts, 1835–1865', *Yearbook of English Studies*, 1981, pp. 127–142; Dale Cockrell, *Demons of Disorder: Early Blackface Minstrels and Their World,* Cambridge, Cambridge UP, 1997, pp. 13–20; Elizabeth Ewen and Stuart Ewen, *Typecasting: On the Arts and Sciences of Human Inequality*, New York, Seven Stories Press, 2006, pp. 361–381; Saidiya V. Hartman, *Scenes of Subjection: Terror, Slavery, and Self-Making in Nineteenth Century America*, New York, Oxford, Oxford UP, 1997; Barbara Lewis, 'An American Circus: the Lynch Victim as Clown', in David Robb (ed.), *Clowns, Fools and Picaros: Popular Forms in Theatre, Fiction and Film*, Amsterdam, New York, Rodopi, 2007, pp. 96–7, which deals with the impulses toward closeness and distance; Douglas A. Lorimer, *Colour, Class and the Victorians: English Attitudes to the Negro in the Mid-nineteenth Century*, Leicester, Leicester UP, 1978, pp. 82–90; Michael Pickering, 'White Skin, Black Masks: "Nigger" Minstrelsy in Victorian Britain', in J. S. Bratton (ed.), *Music Hall Performance and Style*, Milton Keynes, Open UP, 1986, pp. 70–91, 'Mock Blacks and Racial Mockery: The "Nigger" Minstrel and British Imperialism', in Bratton, 1991, op. cit., and 'The Blackface Clown', in Gretchen Gerzina (ed.), *Black Victorians: Black Victoriana*, New Brunswick, NJ, Rutgers UP, 2003; Felicity A. Nussbaum, 'The Theatre of Empire: Racial Counterfeit, Racial Realism' in Kathleen Wilson (ed.), *A New Imperial History: Culture, Identity and Modernity in Britain and the Empire, 1660–1840*, Cambridge, Cambridge UP, 2004; George F. Rehin, 'Harlequin Jim Crow: Continuity and Convergence in Blackface Clowning', *The Journal of Popular Culture*, vol. 9, no. 3, 1975, pp. 682–701, and 'Blackface Street Minstrels in Victorian London and its Resorts: Popular Culture and its Racial Connotations as Revealed in Polite Opinion', *The Journal of Popular Culture*, vol. 15, no. 1, 1981, pp. 19–38; *The Juba Project: Early Blackface Minstrelsy in Britain 1842–1852* <http://www.utm.utoronto.ca/~w3minstr/> (accessed 23 July, 2009).

56 For example, the Wooster Group's use of blackface to deconstruct Thornton Wilder's *Our Town* in *Route 1 & 9* (1981) and Arthur Miller's *The Crucible* in *L.S.D. (…Just the High Points…)* (1983) was controversial, and the former contributed to the group's loss of state funding.

3   After Aldridge

1 Daphne A. Brooks, *Bodies in Dissent: Spectacular Performances of Race and Freedom, 1850–1910*, Durham and London, Duke UP, 2006, p. 69.

2 Audrey A. Fisch, *American Slaves in Victorian England: Abolitionist Politics in Popular Literature and Culture*, New York, Cambridge UP, 2000, p. 95. See also Henry Box Brown, *Narrative of the Life of Henry Box Brown*, with an introduction by Richard Newman and foreword by Henry Louis Gates, Jr., New York, Oxford, Oxford UP, 2002; Samira Kawash, *Dislocating the Color Line: Identity, Hybridity, and Singularity in African-American Narrative*, Stanford, CA, Stanford UP, 1997, pp. 64–72; Jeffrey Ruggles, *The Unboxing of Henry Brown*, Richmond, VA, Library of Virginia, 2003; Suzette A. Spencer, 'Henry Box Brown, an International Fugitive: Slavery, Resistance, and Imperialism', in Katherine McKittrick and Clyde Adrian Woods (eds), *Black Geographies and the Politics of Place*, Toronto, Between the Lines, and Cambridge, MA, South End Press, 2007, pp. 115–136.

3 For Morgan Smith, see Errol G. Hill and James V. Hatch, *A History of African American Theatre*, Cambridge, Cambridge UP, 2003, pp. 63–66; Errol Hill, 'S. Morgan Smith: Successor to Ira Aldridge,' *Black American Literature Forum*, vol.16, no.4, 1982, pp. 132–135; and *Shakespeare in Sable: A History Of Black Shakespearean Actors*, Amherst, University of Michigan Press, 1984, pp. 27–38; William Norris, 'New Light on the Career of S. Morgan Smith' and 'Additional Light on S. Morgan Smith', *Black American Literature Forum*, vol. 18, no. 3, Autumn 1984, pp. 117–118, and vol. 20, no. 1/2, Spring-Summer1986, pp. 75–79, respectively.

4 Hll and Hatch, op. cit, p. 64.

5 *Era*, 24 June, 1866, says his Gravesend season finished with *My Poll and My Partner Joe*, the third act of *Othello*, *Poor Pillicoddy*, and the last act of *Richard III*, but it is not clear whether Morgan Smith appeared in all of them, though it is likely he did. The report says attendance on the final two evenings was very bad.

6 *Era*, 5 July, 1868: With 'greater physical energy', he might have taken 'a higher position in his profession than that respectable one which he already occupies'.

7 Hill and Hatch, op. cit., p. 65, but no details are given. There were other plays in existence with similar titles and/or subjects, e.g. *Chevalier de St-George*, adapted from the French of Anne Honoré Joseph Duveyrier in 1840. *Era*, 8 July, 1877, gives the title of the play in which Morgan Smith appeared as *The Bondsmen Brothers*.

8 H. Chance Newton, *Cues and Curtain Calls*, London, John Lane, 1927, p. 208 (a reference brought to my attention by Val Wilmer). Newton found Morgan Smith 'a little mannered, perhaps, but very dramatic and even natural for the most part, especially in passages of feeling and tenderness. Like the late David Garrick, "it was only when off the stage he was acting", and then our dusky tragedian used to swank a great deal.' Newton says his star part was *Othello*, yet he also received bad notices for this role (e.g. *Birmingham Daily Post*, 7 August, 1866, 'To say that Mr Smith's is the worst *Othello* we ever saw, would be perhaps going too far, but that it is one of them is quite within the mark.'). Reports suggest his Shylock was generally well received.

9 Hill, 1982, op. cit., p. 132.

10 The playbill for the benefit (26 May, 1868, Marylebone Theatre, London) in which Morgan Smith plays Gambia in *The Slave*, can be found at <http://www.westminster.gov.uk/services/libraries/archives/blackpresence/23/> (accessed 26 April, 2010). *The Musical Times and Singing Class Circular*, vol. 22, no. 458, 1 April 1881, p. 188, and vol. 22, no. 465, 1 November 1881, p, 584, record, respectively, McEwen's singing soprano solos in Van Bree's Cantata 'St Cecilia's Day' and in a miscellaneous selection at a concert by the Claremont Choral Society (21 March, 1881, Wellington Hall, Islington), and contributing two songs 'to great effect' to a concert (10 October, 1881, Mission Room of St Saviour's, Fitzroy Square).

11 'intellectual and dignified' and 'decided talent', *Freeman's Journal*, 26 September, 1868 (at Dublin's Queen's Royal Theatre, Morgan Smith swapped the roles of Othello and Iago with Harry G. Clifford); 'careful…spirited', *Era*, 5 July, 1868.

12 *Era*, 25 May, 1873.

13 Hill, 1984, op. cit., p. 37. He quotes the *Era*, 5 July, 1868.

14 The review appeared in the *Era*, 3 February, 1883, his letter, 10 February.

15 James M. Trotter, 'Paul Molyneaux', *New York Globe*, 23 April, 1883. See Hill and Hatch, op. cit., p 67.

16 Letter reproduced in Joseph A. Borome, 'Some Additional Light on Frederick Douglass', *The Journal of Negro History*, vol. 38, no. 2, April 1953, p. 223.

17 Hill, 1984, op. cit., p. 39.

18 See Sarah Meer, *Uncle Tom Mania: Slavery, and Transatlantic Culture in the 1850s*, Atlanta, University of Georgia Press, 2005, p. 159; Gary Taylor, *Buying Whiteness: Race, Culture, and Identity from Columbus to Hip Hop*, New York and Basingstoke, Hants, Palgrave Macmillan, 2005, p. 346; John Ernest, 'The Reconstruction of Whiteness: William Wells Brown's *The Escape; or, A Leap for Freedom*', *PMLA*, vol. 113, 1998, pp. 1108, 1119.

19 See Sarah Dadswell, 'Jugglers, Fakirs, and *Jaduwallahs*: Indian Magicians and the British Stage', *New Theatre Quarterly*, no. 89, vol. 23, part 1, February 2007, pp. 3–24.

20 It is possible that records have merged separate dancers, but Juba is believed to be Lane and also the dancer Dickens describes in *American Notes*. See *The Juba Project: Early Blackface Minstrelsy in Britain 1842-1852* <http://www.utm.utoronto.ca/~w3minstr/> (accessed 23 July, 2009).

21 See Paul Gilroy, *The Black Atlantic: Modernity and Double Consciousness*, Cambridge, MA, Harvard UP, 1993, pp. 87–90.

22 For an account of the creation and production of the show, see Thomas L. Riis (ed.), *The Music and Scripts of* In Dahomey, *Music of the United States of America*, vol. 5, Middleton, WI, A-R Editions, 1996.

23 Fisch, op. cit., p. 207.

24 See John Graziano, 'In Dahomey' in *Black Theatre: USA*, New York, the Free Press, 1996, p. 76; Riis, op. cit., pp. xxv–xlii, xlv–xlvi.

25 See Jeffrey Green, *Black Edwardians: Black People in Britain 1901–1914*, London, Frank Cass, 1998; Rainer Lotz, *Black People: Entertainers of African Descent in Germany and Europe*, Birgit Lotz Verlag, 1997; Rainer Lotz and Ian Pegg (eds), *Under the Imperial Carpet: Essays in Black History 1780–1950*, Crawley, W. Sussex, Rabbit Press, 1986.

26 Texts attributed in whole or in part to Aldridge were adaptations, and Séjour's plays, written in France, were published in translation. See Chapter 2, note 42. Michael McMillan, 'Going Back to My Roots', *Black Writing*, London, London Arts Board (no date, probably 1998), wrongly says that the first black play to be published (in 1907) in Britain was *The Blinkards* by Kobena Sekeye (Kobina Sekyi). It was not published in Britain until 1974. He repeats the error elsewhere, e.g. in Paul Carter Harrison et al. (eds), *Black Theatre: Ritual Performance in the African Diaspora*, Philadelphia, Temple UP, 2002, p. 116.

27 Downing's life has been pieced together from several sources. Most useful is Brian Russell Roberts, 'Lost Theatres of African American Internationalism: Diplomacy and Henry Francis Downing in Luanda and London', *African American Review*, vol. 42, no. 2, Summer 2008, pp. 269–286, to which I am indebted. It is drawn from Roberts's PhD dissertation, 'Artist Ambassadors and African American Writing at the Nation's Edge, 1893–1940', University of Virginia, Charlottesville, VA, 2008. See also: Green, op. cit., pp. 197–261 passim; Rayford W. Logan and Michael R. Winston (eds), *Dictionary of American Negro Biography*, New York, W. W. Norton and Co., 1982, pp. 188–189; Bernard L. Peterson Jr., *Early Black American Playwrights and Dramatic Writers: A Biographical Directory and Catalog of Plays, Films, and Broadcasting Scripts*, New York, Greenwood, 1990, pp. 62–64; Lawrence R. Rodgers, 'Downing, Henry F.' in William L. Andrews et al. (eds), *Concise Oxford Companion to African American Literature*, Oxford, Oxford UP, 2001, p. 116; Booker T. Washington Papers, vol. 6, p. 507, September 1902.

28 Loudin and Coleridge-Taylor also attended the first Pan-African Conference, held at Westminster Town Hall, 23–25 July 1900. Unsurprisingly, there was musical entertainment, but few details have survived. See J. R. Hooker, 'The Pan-African

Conference of 1900', *Transition* 46, 1974, Bloomington, IN, Indiana UP on behalf of W. E. B. Du Bois Institute, pp. 20–24. The Port of Spain *Mirror*, 15 August, 1900, reported that the evening session (which one is not clear) was enlivened by delegates with negro [sic] melodies and instrumental solos. Mrs Coleridge-Taylor sang.

29 London plays: 1913, published Francis Griffiths: *The Arabian Lovers; Or, The Sacred Jar* (probably earlier a.k.a. *Melic Relic*); *Human Nature; Or, The Traduced Wife, an original English Domestic Drama in Four Acts*; *Lord Eldred's Other Daughter: An Original Comedy in Four Acts*; *The Shuttlecock; Or, Israel in Russia, An Original Drama in Four Acts*. With Margarita Downing, *Placing Paul's Play: A Miniature Comedy*. 1914, publ. Griffiths: *Voodoo: A Drama in Four Acts* (earlier a.k.a. *The Exiles*), copy at the Schomburg Center for Research in Black Culture, New York; self-published: *Incentives: A Drama in Four Acts* (probably earlier a.k.a. *The Sinews of War*), copy at Schomburg; *A New Coon in Town: A Farcical Comedy Made in England* (probably earlier a.k.a. *The Statue and the Wasp*), copy at Schomburg.

30 Difficulties in tracing Downing's activities include the fact that his plays and stories reappear under different names or in different forms. Also, the Players and Playwrights Association appears to have been known as, or be related to, the Unacted Authors' Association, the Playwrights' Association and the Amateur Players' Association.

31 Roberts, op. cit., p. 273. From 1910 to 1918, the Court had no resident company. It was home to visitors and used by amateur and play-producing societies.

32 *Placing Paul's Play*, op. cit., p. 8. Brian Roberts, 'A London Legacy of Ira Aldridge: Henry Francis Downing and the Paratheatrical Poetics of Plot and Cast(e)', (forthcoming), points out that *Placing Paul's Play* echoes the Aldridge/Kean relationship: the hero's play is discovered by an actor-manager called Edmund Keen. In *Placing Paul's Play*, the playwright is working on a play called *Human Nature*, the name of one of Downing's plays, and his wife's name, Rita, is short for Margarita, the name of Downing's wife. They are members of an amateur dramatic club, as were the Downings.

33 *A New Coon in Town*, op. cit., p. 5

34 'de country whar cullud folks de equal o' anybody else', *A New Coon in Town*, op. cit., p. 14; 'nigger' p. 14 and passim; 'not exactly the correct thing', p. 64.

35 Roberts, 2008, op. cit. p. 274. Downing himself was involved briefly with a failed venture that promoted cotton raising in west Africa and encouraged black farmers to emigrate there.

36 Roberts (forthcoming), op. cit. Roberts also examines Downing's use of the racialized term *Caste* instead of *Cast* for the list of characters in two plays, *Incentives* and *Placing Paul's Play*, though it is possible it might have been in error or eccentricity.

37 Quoted by Roberts, 2008, op. cit., p. 273, from 'Unacted Plays,' *African Times and Orient Review*, July 1913, p. 43.

38 Roberts (forthcoming), op. cit.

39 Many of Ali's biographical and career details are unsubstantiated. Ian Duffield's work in the 1970s was groundbreaking and has led to further investigation by other scholars. See Ian Duffield, 'Dusé Mohamed Ali and the Development of Pan-Africanism, 1866–1945', unpublished PhD dissertation, Edinburgh University, October 1971, 'Dusé Mohamed Ali: His Purpose and His Public,' in Alistair Niven (ed.), *The Commonwealth Writer Overseas: Themes of Exile and Expatriation*, Brussels, Librarie Marcel Didier, 1976, and 'Dusé Mohamed Ali, Afro-Asian Solidarity and Pan-Africanism in Early Twentieth Century London,' in Jagdish Gundara and Ian Duffield (eds), *Essays on the History of Blacks in Britain from Roman Times to the Mid-Twentieth Century*, Aldershot, Hants, Avebury, 1992. See also Mustafa A. Abdelwahid (ed.), *The Autobiography of Dusé Mohamed Ali, 1866-1945: A Pioneer of Pan-Africanism and Afro-Asian Solidarity Movements* (forthcoming). Duffield says Ali was known as Mohamed Ali as a child and added Dusé later (around 1913/4) in honour of one of his guardians. See also Hakim Adi and Marika Sherwood, *Pan-African History; Political figures from Africa and the Diaspora since 1787*, London, Routledge, 2003, pp. 1–6; Green, op. cit., pp. 250–257; C. L. Innes, *A History of Black and Asian Writing in Britain, 1700–2000*, Cambridge, Cambridge UP, 2002. The *Stage Cyclopedia*, 1909, p. 23, lists a melodrama, *Andrew*, by Mohamed and Marlen,

performed Bournemouth, 25 February, 1895, but this is a Dr. George Mohamed, not Dusé.

40 Naoroji is often referred to as the first Indian or Asian British MP (elected 1892), but the first of Asian descent was probably David Ochterlony Dyce Sombre (elected 1841).

41 Duffield, 1971, op. cit., p. 70.

42 Ibid., p. 73.

43 *Stage*, 18 June, 1908, which gives lyrics by George Isenthal and Leo Mansfield, music by Mark Strong. By autumn 1909 (*Stage*, 30 September, 1909) lyrics are by Hinton Jones, music is by Strong and Harry M. Wellmon, with additional music by Marie Horme, and the show is by Ali and Trimmingham, who is no longer in the cast. Allardyce Nicoll, *English Drama, 1900–1930: The Beginnings of the Modern Period*, Cambridge, Cambridge UP, 1973, p. 809, gives Mohamed and Trimmingham as the authors, with music by M. Strong and H. M. Wellman.

44 *Stage*, 11 November, 1909.

45 The journal was banned by colonial administrations in India and Africa and closed in 1914. It reappeared (twice) later that decade.

46 Attitudes to performers of colour can be summed up by the following: Oscar Asche, director of and actor (as Chinese) in the long-running musical *Chu Chin Chow*, said in 1919 that 'it is just as possible for a camel to pass through the needle's eye' as it is for a black actor to portray canonical stage characters. He was quoted in *The Kinematograph and Lantern Weekly* (14 August) in an article on 'coloured artistes on the screen'. G. B. Shaw, who did not comment on 'negroes' in film, aired his views on their likely success on stage: 'He thinks negroes act very well, and that their powers of physical expression are very effective on the stage'. Actress Ivy Duke asserted that a negro character can be played only by 'the natural born black'. See Stephen Bourne, *Black in the British Frame: The Black Experience in British Film and Television*, London, Continuum, 2001, pp. 223–224.

47 See Prof. Ahmad A. Rahman, University of Michigan-Dearborn, on Abdelwahid's book <http://www.mellenpress.com/mellenpress.cfm?bookid=7877&pc=9> (accessed 6 January, 2010) and confirmed by e-mail from Prof. Rahman (25 March, 2010).

48 Stephen Bourne, op. cit., p 7. Earl Cameron, who is also Bermudan, thinks Ernest Trimmingham (sometimes spelled Trimingham) possibly took his name from a rich white Bermudan family in order to more easily find work (*Blackgrounds* interview, Theatre Collections, Victoria and Albert Museum). See also Green, op. cit., p.111.

49 *Stage*, 12 February, 1942. His shows include *The Marriage Market* (1913, Daly's); *The Old Fashioned House* (1925, The Shoreditch); *In Walked Jimmy* (1925, Q); *Sweet Aloes* (1936, New Oxford and Blackpool); *No Sleep for the Wicked* (1937, Streatham Hill); *Welcome Stranger* (1938, Saville).

50 *Stage*, 11 September, 1930.

51 James Mason, *Before I Forget: An Autobiography*, London, Sphere Books, 1982, p.79.

52 Yellowface as a term, unlike blackface, was not often used in Britain and is more associated with American stage and screen practice, mainly owing to demographic differences.

53 See Shompi Lahiri, *Indians in Britain: Anglo-Indian Encounters, Race and Identity, 1880–1930*, London, Frank Cass, 2000, p. 83. For Orientalism and music, especially *Chu Chin Chow*, see Martin Clayton and Bennett Zon (eds), *Music and Orientalism in the British Empire, 1780s–1940s: Portrayal of the East*, Aldershot, Hants, Ashgate, 2007; Brian Singleton, *Oscar Asche, Orientalism, and British Musical Comedy*, London, Praeger, 2004.

54 Lahiri, op. cit., p. 83.

55 See Kusum Pant Joshi, '1838: South Indian Dancers Tour Europe', *Hinduism Today*, January–March 2009, <http://www.hinduismtoday.com/modules/smartsection/item.php?itemid=1253> (accessed 29 April, 2010); Clayton and Zon, op. cit., pp. 61-65. *The Widow of Malabar* was based on a French play by Antoine-Marin Lemierre and became known in Britain through the version by Marina Starke.

56 See Rozina Visram, *Ayahs, Lascars, and Princes: Indians in Britain 1700–1947*, London, Pluto Press, 1986, pp. 21–23. Eleven of the troupe of eighteen came to London when

the tour collapsed and spent a night in a stable before going to the Strangers' Home for Asiatics, Africans, and South Sea Islanders. They were returned to India as a special case at the expense of the India Office, having been abandoned by the promoters, Edward and George Hanlon.

57 *The Times*, 21 December, 1885.

58 Details from William Poel, 'Hindu Drama on the English Stage', *Asiatic Quarterly Review*, vol. 1, April 1913, pp. 319–331, from which all subsequent Poel quotations are taken; and Robert Speaight, *William Poel and the Elizabethan Revival*, Heinemann, London, 1954, p. 147. Marion O'Connor (e-mail, 23 July, 2008), says Poel's retrospective account in *Notes on Some of William Poel's Productions* (1933), written when he was older than 80, records the loan of jewelled costumes for *Sakuntala* from Indian students, many of whom took part in the play (probably the 1899 production). The programme for the 1899 production says *Sakuntala* was being acted for the first time in English.' (V & A Theatre Collections).

59 *The Times*, 4 July, 1899.

60 *The Times*, 22 July, 1912, wrongly attributes the translation to a leading Sanskrit scholar, E. J. Rapson, who had been involved in the project but who wrote to Poel to complain of the association. Rapson is thanked in the programme (V & A Theatre Collections). Poel thought a French version by Bergaigne the best. A translation of this by Harinath De, head of the Imperial Library, Calcutta and noted linguist, was cut short when he died (in 1911), having completed only two of the seven acts. Poel used a large part of that, and F. W. Hubbock of Trinity translated Bergaigne's verses for the remaining acts. The prose used was modified from Sir William Jones's 1789 version, as in the 1899 production. The 1912 programme (op. cit.) says the version being performed had been copyrighted. See also William Poel Collection, Department of Special Collections, MS. 31, Kenneth Spencer Research Library, University of Kansas Libraries, Lawrence, KS.

61 H. N. Maitra, 'Indian Drama', *Westminster Gazette*, 21 May, 1913, mentions the 'rapid growth' of Indian drama in England since the King's visit. During this period, T. P. Kailasam, the bilingual actor and playwright in Kannada and English, was living in England (1908–1915) and, according to Ananda Lal (ed.), *Oxford Companion to Indian Theatre*, Oxford and New Delhi, Oxford UP, 2004, p. 122, he recited his work, but no records of any performances has been found.

62 *The Times*, 13 February, 1912. S. C. Bose is probably Sarat Chandra Bose (b. 1889) rather than his younger brother, the future independence leader Subhas Chandra Bose (b. 1897), who would have been only just fifteen at the time.

63 Ibid. *Stage*, 24 December, 1913, says it was to be performed soon by female students at Morley Memorial College. The poem was known already through recitals by the actor Frederic de Lara.

64 Also mentioned in the *Era Annual 1913*, p. 128, which suggests the cast included white British performers playing Indian roles alongside Indian performers. Maitra became an author of, among other books, *Hinduism – the World Ideal*.

65 *The Times*, 15 April, 1912, said the play was to be produced for a fortnight at the Royal Court, whereas other references – in Poel, op. cit., and *Stage*, 13 June 1912 – mention only the Whitney, where it appears to have had only one performance.

66 Poel, op. cit., pp. 327–28; *The Times*, 26 February, 1912 and 2 March, 1912. R. T. H. Griffith's verse translation of Kalidasa's *Kumarsambhava* as *The Birth of the War-God* first appeared in English in 1853. Poel says all the cast were women and children, whereas *The Times* agrees at first but, in its second reference, says 'almost entirely' instead of 'all'. The first *Times* reference also says the programme included tableaux illustrating the *Rubaiyat* of Omar Khayyam. A letter to *The Times* (28 February, 1912) from the organizers of the performance says, 'We Indian ladies have promoted it entirely ourselves' and gives the subtitle as *The Coming of the Prince*.

67 The material on Das Gupta (a.k.a. Dasgupta) is drawn from a number of sources: Kalyan Kundu, founder/chairperson, Tagore Centre UK (e-mail, 19 June, 2010), who cited Prasanta Paul (ed.), *Rabijibani* (vol.5), Kolkata, Ananda Publishers, 1990, pp. 224–225;

Ananda Lal (e-mail, 28 June, 2010) and *Rabindranath Tagore: Three Plays*, Oxford, Oxford UP, 2001 (translated, and with Introduction by, Lal); reviews of and announcements about individual productions in *The Times*, the *Stage*; J. P. Wearing, *The London Stage: A Calendar of Plays and Players, 1900–1909, 1910–1919* and *1920–1929*, Metuchin, NJ, Scarecrow Press, 1981 and 1982; *Imagining Tagore: Rabindranath and the British Press (1912–1941)*, compiled and edited by Kalyan Kundu et al., Calcutta, Sahitya Samsad, 2000; details given in the published edition of Kalidasa's *Sakuntala*, London, Macmillan, 1920; Poel, op. cit., p. 327; *New York Times*, 1 July, 1922, 7 December, 1942; Marcus Braybrooke, 'A Wider Vision: A History of the World Congress of Faiths, 1936–1996' <http://www.religion-online.org/showchapter.asp?title=3378&C=2771> (accessed 20 May, 2008). There was a tradition of 'east-west' organizations in the United Kingdom, e.g. the London Indian Society, founded in 1865 by MP Dadabhai Naoroji.

68 Quoted by Lal (e-mail), op. cit. Das Gupta graduated from Lincoln's Inn in 1911. There is no record of his being called to the bar. Presumably he turned instead to his cultural work, which he saw as integral to building world unity.

69 Printed in K. N. Das Gupta, *Consolation*, London, the Union of the East and West, 1916. Annual subscription was two guineas, which entitled members to eight stall tickets for Society performances and to membership of the Union of the East and West.

70 *The Times*, 31 July 1912.

71 *The Times*, 9 December, 1912. The item says the performance would be Thursday next, but the Albert Hall archive has no record of such a performance in December. The archive does, however, have an entry in its Gas Consumption book, 8 January, 1913, for four performances of *Sakuntala*, attributed to 'Mrs Das Gupta', and one performance, 25 January, 1913, attributed to K. N. Das Gupta. The archive has no programmes for any of the Union or Society performances. According to the *Era Annual 1914*, p. 95, *The Maharani of Arakan* was also produced by the Bushey Repertory Theatre in November 1913. The *Era Annual 1914*, p. 80, says the Cosmopolis was founded in 1910 as the Foreign Literary Society for those interested in the cultures of foreign countries and, in 1912, established a dramatic section called the Foreign Theatre Society.

72 *Chitra* was produced in London in February 1916 and, by the Garrick Society, in Stockport in March 1916, quite likely the same production.

73 *Stage*, 10 December, 1914. *The Times*, 27 July, 1936, says Holst based his opera *Savitri* on the Das Gupta play, though musical sources, such as the *New Grove Dictionary of Opera*, say Holst wrote his own libretto.

74 Das Gupta appeared in *The Gardener* and *The Maharani of Arakan*.

75 In his series of Indian plays, Francis Griffiths had published a version of *The Hero and the Nymph* by Sri Ananda Acharya in or before 1913. Other English versions had appeared since 1830, published in both India and England, but no records of productions in Britain have been found. Griffiths, who published the plays of Henry Downing (see note 29) announced in 1914 the publication of Calderon's *The Maharani of Arakan* and Das Gupta's version of *Ratnavali*, but the latter seems not to have appeared. The former appeared in 1915 with a character sketch of Tagore compiled by Das Gupta and illustrations by Clarissa Miles, one-time honorary secretary of the Union of the East and West. Kessinger Publications, a US publisher specializing in rare and out-of-print books, reissued the Calderon in 2008, with Das Gupta and Miles named as illustrators. 'Amina's Song' from *The Maharani of Arakan*, music by Katherine Ruth Heyman, was published by Composers' Music Corporation, New York in 1924.

76 *Stage*, 31 May, 1917.

77 *The Times*, 17 October, 1919. To underscore the point about cultural distance, the review reports a scene in which children act out a play. 'English children act plays about Princes and Fairies and Dragons; Indian children about Love, Life, Death, and the Hereafter. The Union of East and West…is trying to bridge this enormous gulf'.

78 The Committee was chaired by Bhupendra Nath Basu (who became vice chancellor of Calcutta University) and, with Das Gupta as honorary secretary, included the Rt. Hon. Lord Sinha KC, Sir Prabhashanka Pattani, Mr. and Mrs. Sen, and Jamnadas Dwarkadas.

79 The published version (op. cit., p. viii) makes it clear that this fragment of the original was prepared solely for presenting to an English audience. Laurence Binyon writes (p. viii): 'Fidelity to what is universal in Kalidasa has been sought for, rather than the reproduction of exotic beauties.' Das Gupta adds (p. xi): 'He [Kalidasa] is of all countries and of all ages, and his work is the inheritance of mankind.'

80 *The Times*, 15 November, 1919.

81 The Abbey Theatre had performed *The Post Office* in Dublin and London (at the Court) in 1913, directed by W. B. Yeats and Lady Gregory. The claim concerning the five short pieces is carried in *The Times*, 26 July, 1920. They were named *The Mother's Prayer*, *The Farewell Curse*, *The Deserted Mother*, *The Sinner*, and *Suttee*. They were published in 1921 in a volume called *The Fugitive*.

82 *Daily Chronicle*, 24 October, 1921 ('simple', 'delicate'); *Daily Telegraph*, 24 October, 1921.

83 *Stage*, 9 October, 1924. The play was translated by Swami Paramananda.

84 *The Times*, 25 October, 1939. Das Gupta's American activities, which seem to have included serving on the executive of the War Resisters League, led him to be dubbed a 'red' in some quarters (e.g., Elizabeth Kirkpatrick Dilling, *The Red Network*, Kenilworth, Chicago, 1935, pp. 152–153).

85 *The Times*, 30 June, 1924. Pran Nevile, *The Tribune*, Chandigarh, India, 18 September, 2010, says the group was founded by Himansunath Rai in India and then brought to London and that the production played in Manchester, Liverpool, and other UK cities before being invited to France, Italy, and Egypt. <http://www.tribuneindia.com/2010/20100918/saturday/main1.htm> (accessed 2 November, 2010).

86 *Stage*, 22 June, 1922. Indian Players published the play in London in 1925.

87 The musical selections were by Miss Meenakshi Devi, Miss Perris, Miss Kanaklakshmi Devi, and Mr Patrick (programme, V & A Theatre Collections). One copy of the Duke of York's programme held by the V & A has two inserts pasted on p. 3 saying the Indian cast of players were 'speaking in accentual English' and that 'this unique offering was afterwards placed in the evening bill at the Ambassadors' Theatre'. These inserts do not appear in any other programmes and appear to be later additions by a collector, librarian, or archivist.

88 *Era*, 21 June, 1922; *The Sunday Times*, 11 June, 1922; *The Times*, 7 June, 1922; *Stage*, op. cit. (this review picked out Himansunath Rai, Pawreen Mukherji, Rani Waller, Leela Devi, Rani Dutt, and Mohan Dutt for special mention).

89 Details of the production and the company garnered from reviews listed in the previous note, and *The Times*: 3, 20, and 31 July, and 7 August, 1922; *Stage*: 25 May and 22 June, 1922; Wearing, *1920–1929*, op. cit., pp. 283–284, 286–287.

90 See *The Times*, 30 June and 8 July, 1924; *Stage*, 26 June, 10, 24, and 31 July, 1924. *The Magic Crystal* was also known as *What a Change!* and *The Blue Bottle*.

91 See Lal (2001), op. cit., pp. 60–87 for Tagore's reception in England.

92 Ibid., p. 60.

93 Details taken from her autobiography, *India Calling-The Memories of Cornelia Sorabji*, London, Nisbet and Co., 1934, pp. 46–47.

4 Between the wars

1 Eastern influence is an enormous subject, but it is interesting to note that Gordon Craig in his periodical *The Mask*, engaged with the philosopher Ananda K. Coomaraswamy in a debate about the nature of acting and the human body and drew on his reading of Oriental theatre to justify certain of his views (e.g., why women should not be actors). Coomaraswamy, who was living in England, was a regular contributor to *The Mask*. His most important intervention was the essay, 'Notes on Indian Dramatic Technique', vol. 6, 1913, pp. 109–128, which challenged Craig's assumptions. *The Mask* was important for introducing English-speaking readers to Eastern performance ideas, which permeate the magazine, yet, as with Artaud and others, the East being reproduced is a conventional

Western construct: mysterious but wise. See Rustom Bharucha, 'A Collision of Cultures: Some Western Interpretations of the Indian Theatre', *Asian Theatre Journal*, vol. 1, no. 1, Spring 1984, pp. 1–20; Olga Taxidou (ed.), *The Mask: A Periodical Performance by Edward Gordon Craig*, London, Routledge, 1998.

2 *Stage*, 1 May, 1924.

3 Napoleon Florent, for example, who came from St. Lucia to Britain in 1907, appeared as an exotic stage extra in *Kismet* (1914) and *Chu Chin Chow* (1916) in spite of being Caribbean.

4 *Stage*, 27 July, 1922.

5 See Shompa Lahiri, 'From Empire to Decolonisation, 1901–1947', in Michael H. Fisher (ed.), *A South-Asian History of Britain*, Oxford, Greenwood World, 2007, p. 143, and Brinda, *Maharani: The Story of an Indian Princess*, New York, Henry Holt, 1953, pp. 216–217. Princess Indira became known as the 'Radio Princess' because of her BBC programme in Hindustani, which was broadcast to Indian troops in the Middle East and the Mediterranean during the war. She continued working for the BBC until 1968.

6 Ghose's volume is no.27 in a series 'Plays for a People's Theatre' published by C. W. Daniel and Co., London. The two playlets are *The Defaulters*, set after the war in an Indian town with a large number of unemployed, and *And Pippa Dances*, also set after the war, in a central European industrial town. Chattopadhyaya's plays (published by S. Fowler Wright, London) are *The Hunter*, *Pundalik*, *Saku*, and *The Proclamation* as well as *Tukaram*. An unsourced review of *Tukaram* at the Little Theatre (Theatre Collections, Victoria and Albert Museum) says eleven characters are played by Indian actors 'most of whom speak very good English'. The author played Tukaram, and Miss Coomie Dantra was Avalai.

7 *The Times*, 11 August, 1937.

8 *The Times*, 1 March, 1938.

9 Mayura (a.k.a. Mayura Vincent) was an India dancer who appeared on BBC TV in the late 1930s and at the Arts Theatre, London in 1937 in a Tibetan fairy tale, *Djroazanmo*, by Ernest Berk, presented by the Mask Theatre (with Ay Lien Tai in the cast). See *The Times*, 13 October, 1937.

10 *The Road to Dishonour* is known in the United States as *The Flame of Love*. There was also an actress, Wai Nan Wong, who appeared as a West End extra in 1931, and Diana Wong, who had minor West End roles in 1933, 1934, and 1936.

11 See Angela Woollacott, 'Rose Quong Becomes Chinese: An Australian in London and New York', *Australian Historical Studies*, vol. 38, no. 129, April 2007, pp. 16–31.

12 See Woollacott, op. cit., and Angela Woollacott, 'Quong, Rose Maud (1879–1972)', *Australian Dictionary of Biography*, Supplementary Volume, Melbourne, Melbourne UP, 2005, p. 331.

13 *The Times*, 24 June, 1944.

14 Rainer Lotz, 'Will Garland and his Negro Operetta Company', in Rainer Lotz and Ian Pegg, *Under the Imperial Carpet: Essays in Black History 1780–1950*, Crawley, W. Sussex, England, Rabbit Press, 1986, p 140, gives the example of David Leslie, assistant secretary of the Actors Association, protesting in 1922 at the Lord Chamberlain's licensing of the show *Coloured Society* (a.k.a. *All Black*), an all-black company led by an American. Leslie had also complained that cast members of *In Dahomey* had not all gone home. Lotz says foreign musicians in a dance band had to be in a minority at this time (see Jeffrey P. Green, *Edmund Thornton Jenkins: The Life and Times of an American Black Composer, 1894–1926*, Westport, CT, Greenwood Press, 1982). Deidre Osborne, 'Writing Black Back: An Overview of Black Theatre and Performance in Britain', in Dimple Godiwala (ed.), *Alternatives within the Mainstream: British Black and Asian Theatres*, Newcastle, Cambridge Scholars Press, 2006, p. 68, gives the example in 1923 of objections from the Variety Artists' Federation to a touring production of *Plantation Days*. Under the campaign slogan 'British theatres for the British', VAF chairman Albert Voyce pronounced that acting was the white person's province.

15 Payne was given a house in London's Regent's Park Road by philanthropist Lady Mary Cook, wife of rich businessman and art buff Sir Henry, whose parties were well known. He also took people to his country house to introduce them to white 'society' (artistic, social, and professional). Lady Cook sponsored a spirituals-only concert for Payne in Wigmore Hall in 1923, assisted by Lawrence Brown, who became Robeson's pianist. In 1928, she gave a Christmas party at Friends House for poor black children in London. Payne's choir appeared in such shows as *The Sun Never Sets* (Drury Lane, 1938). See Edward Scobie, *Black Britannia: A History of Blacks in Britain*, London, Pall Mall Press, 1972, p. 179; Frank C. *Taylor, Alberta Hunter: A Celebration in Blues*, New York, McGraw Hill, 1987; Leslie Thompson, *An Autobiography (as told to Jeffrey P. Green)*, Crawley, W. Sussex, England, Rabbit Press, 1985.

16 See *Kentish Mercury*, 21 December, 1934, p. 13. Payne played cannibal chieftain King Walamaloo, Hunter a cannibal princess; Billie Humphrey took the breeches part of Crusoe; Al Parkes the dame role of Mrs. Crusoe; and Buddy Lane was Man Friday (a role he reprised, for example, in Morecambe in 1938). Along with the John Payne Choir, speciality acts included Dodo Banks' Twelve Picaninnies and Dudley and his Five Chocolate Drops. See *Lewisham Borough News*, 1 January, 1935, p. 7.

17 Lotz, op. cit., p 143.

18 Thompson, op. cit., p. 95.

19 Quoted in Martin Bauml Duberman, *Paul Robeson: A Biography*, New York, Ballantine Books, 1989, p. 48.

20 Cochran had planned to bring the African-American actor Charles Gilpin to London in 1921 to reprise the role of Jones that he had created, but this fell through. When Robeson played the part to great acclaim on Broadway, O'Neil had earned renown in the West End with *Anna Christie*. Robeson appeared in London in a programme with another O'Neill play, *The Long Voyage Home*.

21 Marie Seton, *Paul Robeson*, London, Dennis Dobson, 1958, p. 38.

22 Robeson is quoted in Philip S. Foner (ed.), *Paul Robeson Speaks: Writings, Speeches, Interviews 1918–74*, London, Quartet Books, 1978, p. 513, n. 6, as saying: 'To expect the Negro artist to reject every role with which he is not ideologically in agreement', he told a journalist, 'is to expect the Negro artist under our present scheme of things to give up his work entirely'.

23 See Duberman, op. cit., pp. 133–138.

24 *Variety*, 4 June, 1930, quoted in Roy Hattersley's book, *Borrowed Time: The Story of Britain Between the Wars*, London, Abacus, 2007, p. 334.

25 James Agate, *Brief Chronicles*, London, Cape, 1943, p. 285.

26 Duberman, op. cit., p. 137.

27 John K. Hutchens 'Paul Robeson', in *Theatre Arts*, October, 1944, p. 582.

28 Ibid., p. 585.

29 In 1938, according to Visram Rozina, *Asians in Britain*, London, Pluto, 2002, pp, 259–260, a Coloured Film Artistes' Association (CFAA), and an Asian and African Film Artistes' Association, which became the Oriental and Film Artistes' Union, were founded. Robert Adams was a member of the CFAA executive committee. Sean Creighton says, in a Black and Asian Heritage in the UK paper 'Organising in the Film Industry in the Late 1930s', September 2004, the Friendly Society Registrar's files record the formation in 1939 of another body, the Eastern and Indian Film Artists' Association.

30 Seton, op. cit., p. 99. Robeson wrote in the *News Chronicle*, 30 May, 1935, that it was his aim to establish a 'Negro theatre' in London, possibly on the model of the 'Negro People's Theatre' then being formed in Harlem after the riots earlier that year. *The Keys* reported in mid 1935 (July–Sept., vol. III, no. 1, p. 13) that Robeson intended to 'open a permanent African theatre in London for the presentation of African drama, art, and music.' Its review of *Toussaint Louverture* said that when such a theatre materialized, this production 'will have first claims on it'.

31 Paul Peters and George Sklar, *Stevedore*, London, Jonathan Cape, 1935, p.123.

32 Ibid., p.137.

33 *Basalik* was written by a white American, Norma Leslie Munro, under the name Peter Garland.

34 Louverture is also spelled L'Ouverture, but the first spelling is both the one the Haitian leader himself adopted and the one used by James in the original playtext.

35 Christian Hogsbjerg, Introduction to *C. L. R. James, Toussaint Louverture; The Story of the Only Successful Slave Revolt in History*, Durham, NC, Duke UP (forthcoming), to which I am indebted and from which the play's quotations are taken. For the play's significance, see, e.g., Martin Banham et al. (eds), *Cambridge Guide to African and Caribbean Theatre*, Cambridge, Cambridge UP, 1994, pp. 148, 226–227. See also C. L. Innes, *A History of Black and Asian Writing in Britain, 1700–2000*, Cambridge, Cambridge UP, 2002, pp. 202–207.

36 C. L. R. James, 'George Padmore: Black Marxist Revolutionary,' in C.L.R. James, *At the Rendezvous of Victory; Selected Writings*, vol. 3, London, Allison and Busby, 1984, p. 263, and Bill Schwarz, 'George Padmore,' in Bill Schwarz (ed.), *West Indian Intellectuals in Britain*, Manchester, Manchester UP, p. 148, cited by Hogsbjerg.

37 Programme note, *The Black Jacobins*, Talawa Production, Riverside Studios, 1986.

38 Date of conception from author's note in the original 1936 programme of *Toussaint Louverture*, quoted by Hogsbjerg.

39 For example, in the Caribbean, Derek Walcott, *Henri Christophe* (1950); Roger Mais, *George William Gordon* (written 1940s, publ. 1976); Sistren Collective, *Nanah Yah* (1980).

40 Hogsbjerg, op. cit.

41 Ibid.

42 Ibid.

43 Norman Beaton, *Beaton but Unbowed: An Autobiography*, London, Methuen, 1986, p. xii, and Yvonne Brewster, 'Talawa Theatre Company, 1985–2002', in Geoffrey V. Davis and Anne Fuchs (eds), *Staging New Britain: Aspects of Black and Asian British Theatre Practice*, Brussels, PIE-Peter Lang, 2006, p. 88, say that the production relied on white actors blacked up. This is not supported by the number of white actors in the cast list, and no reviews mention blacking up.

44 First quotation, Paul Buhle, *C. L. R. James: The Artist as Revolutionary*, London, Verso, 1988, p. 22; second, programme note, *The Black Jacobins*, op. cit.

45 Charles Darwin, *The Times*, 17 March, 1936; GWB, *The Sunday Times*, 22 March, 1936; Ivor Brown, *Observer*, 22 March, 1936; W. A. Darlington, *Daily Telegraph*, 17 March, 1936; *New Leader*, 20 March, 1936.

46 *New York Times*, 16 March, 1936.

47 One scene, Act II, Scene 1, was published in the British journal *Life and Letters Today*, Spring 1936. Buhle (p. 57) says political differences between Robeson and James did affect the future of the play but offers no evidence. Hogsbjerg, however, quotes James's later remembering that in the context of the rising Stalinist terror against Trotskyists, though he and Robeson never quarrelled, 'the idea of doing the play automatically faded into nothing'.

48 The playscript is available in the Jock Haston Papers, [DJH/21], Brynmor Jones Library, University of Hull.

49 Hogsbjerg, op. cit.

50 Ibid.

51 Robeson, who was voted Britain's most popular radio singer in October 1937, turned down the lead in several West End shows, including at Drury Lane *The Sun Never Sets* (an adaptation that eventually starred Todd Duncan, the original Porgy; Adelaide Hall; and Robert Adams).

52 For an account of some of these organisations, see Hakim Adi, *West Africans in Britain, 1900–1960: Nationalism, Pan-Africanism and Communism*, London, Lawrence and Wishart. 1998; and *The History of the African and Caribbean Communities in Britain*, Hove, E. Sussex, Wayland, 1995; Lloyd Braithwaite, *Colonial West Indian Students in Britain*, Kingston, Jamaica, University of the West Indies Press, 2001; Peter Fryer, *Staying Power: the History of Black People in Britain*, London, Pluto Press, 1989; Philip Garigue, 'The West

African Students' Union: A Study in Culture Contact,' *Africa: Journal of the International African Institute*, vol. 23, no. 1, January 1953, pp. 55–69; Jeffrey Green with Randall Lockhart, '"A Brown Alien in a White City" – Black Students in London, 1917–1920', in Lotz and Pegg (eds), op. cit., pp. 208–216; David Killingray (ed.), *Africans in Britain*, London, Frank Cass, 1994. A play about students, *Colour Bar*, jointly written by Roland Ederisu Sawyer, a leading member of the Negro Welfare Association, and Anne M. Bagshaw, who was white, was privately published in 1939, but there is no record of its ever being performed. Written on the edge of world war, its message is that breaking down the colour bar is as important in war as in peace, and this is linked to colonial self-determination. There are fifty-two parts in what the subtitle of the published copy (available in the British Library) calls 'a novel in dialogue form'. The Foreword says, 'What started as a play turned into a cross between a novel and an essay'.

53 The Florence Mills Social Club (a.k.a. Florence Mills Social Parlour) was in Carnaby Street. Other venues mentioned, e.g., in the *News Chronicle*, 25 February, 1935, were the Grand Theatre, Croydon and the Queens Theatre, Poplar.

54 *Daily Herald*, 16 January, 1934.

55 *West Africa*, no. 886, vol. xviii, 20 January, 1934, pp. 39–40, which also cites the *Manchester Guardian* review.

56 *The Keys*, vol. 1, no. 3, January 1934, p. 43.

57 Delia Jarrett-Macauley, *The Life of Una Marson: 1905–65*, Manchester, Manchester UP, 1998, p. vii.

58 Ibid., p. 43.

59 Ibid., pp. 55, 70, 129, 133; Banham, op.cit., p. 212; Judy S. J. Stone, *Studies in West Indian Literature: Theatre*, London and Basingstoke, Hants, Macmillan, 1994, p. 21.

60 See Ferdinand Dennis and Naseem Khan (eds), *Voices of the Crossing: The Impact of Britain on Writers from Asia, the Caribbean and Africa*, London, Serpent's Tail, 2000, p. 19; Innes, op. cit., pp. 208–217; Jarrett-Macauley, op. cit., pp. 157–160; Anne Walmsley, *The Caribbean Artists Movement, 1966–1972: A Literary and Cultural History*, London, New Beacon Books, 1992, pp. 5–6, 13.

61 It was reviewed in the *Daily Worker*, 3 July, 1934, p 4, by EY under the heading 'Scottsboro' Play Goes Big' with a strap under that, 'Successful Production By Left Theatre'. The review said the show played to 'a packed and enthusiastic house' and brought home the 'real extent of the colour bar in America'. It was liked because it was about 'actual events in real life'. The review replicated a cliché while being positive: 'Praise must also be given to the Negro actors who portrayed the nine boys. The parts assigned to them were not very large, but the natural simplicity with which they played them was deeply impressive'.

62 See *The Negro Worker*, vol. 2, no. 5, February-March 1935, p. 2, for the refusal to present a benefit concert.

63 This, and subsequent quotations, from Marie Seton, 'English Theatre of the Left', *New Theatre*, December 1934, p. 21.

64 George W. Bishop, *Hampstead and St John's Wood Advertiser*, 15 November, 1934.

65 See Mohammed Elias, *Aubrey Menen (Kerala Writers in English*, vol. 7), Madras, Macmillan India, 1985; Seton, 1934, op. cit.; André van Gyseghem, 'British Theatre in the Thirties: An Autobiographical Record', in Jon Clark et al. (eds), *Culture and Crisis in Britain in the 30s*, London, Lawrence and Wishart, 1979, p. 211. Menon writes of his life, his homosexuality, and his philosophy in *The Space Within the Heart*, London, Hamish Hamilton, 1970. His book *Rama Retold*, London, Chatto and Windus, 1954, was banned in India. His novel *SheLa*, London, Hamish Hamilton, 1963, was also a play. He is mentioned in books such as Susheila Nasta, *Home Truths: Fictions about the South Asian Diaspora in Britain*, Basingstoke, Hants, Palgrave, 2001, and Ranasinha Ruvani, *South Asian Writers in Twentieth Century Britain*, Oxford, Clarendon, 2007, but only in relation to his non-theatre literature.

66 See Colin Chambers, *The Story of Unity Theatre*, London, Lawrence and Wishart, 1989, p. 236.

67 *Stage*, 21 February, 1948.

68 Quoted in Stephen Bourne, *Black in the British Frame: The Black Experience in British Film and Television*, London, Continuum, 2001, p. 75.

69 *Our Time*, vol. 3, no. 3, 1943, gives the information about the Arts Theatre (which may have been in Adams's sights as he appeared there in June 1943 in G. K. Chesterton's *The Judgment of Dr Johnson*). However, *Theatre World*, August 1943, p. 8, under a photograph of Adams and Sybil Thorndike in Russell Thorndike's *The House of Jeffreys* (Playhouse, December 1942), merely says the 'all-coloured' company will take a West End theatre in the autumn to put on *The Emperor Jones*, *All God's Chillun*, and similar productions. The article mentions the support of the British Council and says Adams is writing a book, *Caribbean Hurricane*, which will be published shortly.

70 Chambers, op. cit., p. 187, fn 19.

71 Earl Cameron, *Blackgrounds* interview, 29 May, 1997, Theatre Collections, Victoria and Albert Museum.

72 'Why Not a Negro Theatre?', Peter Noble (ed.), *British Theatre*, London, British Yearbook, 1946, pp. 61–63. Noble also refers to the group in his book *The Negro in Films*, London, Skelton Robinson, 1948, pp. 173–178, and in an article in the *Stage*, 24 August, 1944.

73 Noble, 1946, op. cit.

74 *Stage*, 26 February, 1948. Also in the cast were Frank Singuineau, Carmen Manley, Vi Thompson, and Harry Scott (son of black US variety entertainer Harry Scott).

75 Adams did not entirely give up acting but made only a brief return to the stage in Britain, in 1958 in Eugene O'Neill's *The Iceman Cometh*, and he made a number of minor television and film appearances. See Bourne, op. cit., pp. 72–76, for more on Adams's screen career.

76 Ibid., p. 75.

77 'Problems of the Negro in the Theatre', *New Theatre*, vol. 4, no. 5, November 1947, p. 11.

78 *New Theatre*, vol. 4, no. 8, February 1948, pp. 18–19.

79 Ibid., p. 20.

5 Postwar struggles 1940s–1960s

1 The nature of postwar immigration was much more complex than this. There are many books on the subject, but see, for example, titles listed in the Introduction, notes 2 and 3.

2 See Naseem Khan, *The Arts Britain Ignores: The Arts of Ethnic Minorities in Britain*, London, Community Relations Commission, 1976: Bangladeshis, pp. 13–22; Indians, pp. 53–77; Pakistanis, pp. 80–89.

3 See Jatinder Verma, 'Asian Theatre in Britain: Historical Developments and Contemporary Identity', Birmingham, Asian Theatre Conference, 2004, and 'Punjabi Theatre in Britain: Context and Challenge', Hounslow conference, 1996 <http://www.tara-arts.com> (accessed 14 May, 2009); Raminder Kaur and Alda Terracciano, 'South Asian/BrAsian Performing Arts', in Nasreen Ali et al. (eds), *A Postcolonial People: South Asians in Britain*, London, Hurst and Co., 2006, pp. 343–357.

4 *Stage*, 7 November, 1957, said the Irving revue had become an established part of that section of entertainment that seeks 'to divert the tired businessman before he homeward plods his weary way. Both in this laudable purpose and in the revelation of its feminine artists it goes further than most'. In *Stage*, 2 June, 1955, it was announced that the Irving would present Shaw's *Don Juan in Hell* by a 'coloured cast' (yet with a white Devil), but no details of this being performed have been found.

5 The Margate Theatre Royal closed in 1965 and reopened that year as a bingo hall (which it remained as until 1984).

6 The play, in a different production, was broadcast on BBC radio eight months later in November 1967. Unlike in the immediate postwar years, when radio was an occasional haven for non-white actors because they could not be seen, in this production the majority of the cast were no longer Asian but white, the female lead being Judi Dench.

7 *The Times*, 6 April, 1960.

8   Gordon Heath, *Deep are the Roots: Memoirs of a Black Expatriate*, Amherst, MA, University of Massachusetts Press, 1992, p.143. See also Stephen Bourne, *Black in the British Frame: The Black Experience in British Film and Television*, London, Continuum, 2001, pp. 99–103.

9   One contributor to the BBC was seminal Jamaican writer Roger Mais, who, according to an obituary in the *Stage* (23 June, 1955) had a play (untitled) performed in Britain in the early 1950s by the Venture group, but no record has been found of this.

10   *Checkers*, vol. 1, no. 2, October 1948, p. 9.

11   Pauline Henriques in Jim Pines (ed.), *Black and White in Colour: Black People in British Television Since 1936*, London, BFI Publishing, 1992, p. 28.

12   *Stage*, 24 June, 1948, announced the forthcoming show. Crabbe in *Checkers*, op. cit., p. 18, says it took place on Sunday 4 July. *Stage*, 15 July, 1948, reported it and said some of the cast had never appeared on stage before. Those involved were listed as Frederick O'Neal, Frank Silvera, Edric Connor, Ida Shepley, Edith Whiteman, Mako Ballo, Emmett 'Babe' Wallace, Mabel Lee, and three harmony singers: Don Fitzstanford, George Browne, and Horace Dawson. *Love from a Stranger* might be Frank Vosper's adaptation from an Agatha Christie story. Information on Evans, Stephen Bourne (e-mail, 5 March, 2009). Henriques, op. cit., p. 28, says the group did perform the Wilder play and that Errol John, who had a named part in the second run of *Anna Lucasta*, and Rita Williams were involved, but that must have been later because John was not an understudy in the first *Anna Lucasta* production. Earl Cameron (telephone interview, 25 April, 2010), also remembered the Wilder play's being performed, but it may have been performed by the NTC more than once.

13   *Checkers*, vol. 1, no. 3, November 1948, p. 17. The magazine first appeared in July 1948, carried the strap 'Britain's Premier Negro Magazine' in its second issue, and replaced it with 'A Monthly Journal in Black and White' for the November 1948 issue.

14   See Bourne, op. cit., p.72.

15   *Checkers*, vol. 1, no. 4, December 1948. In the Box play were Earl Cameron, James Clark, Daphne Segree, Carol Barro, Ida Shepley, Dorothy Rolston, Neville Crabbe, Henry Palmer, and Henry Sky. In the O'Neill, Rita Stevens played the despised wife, and in the Shaw were Pauline Henriques and James Dyer. Henriques directed the show. Rolston and Shepley were appearing that month in *Deep Are the Roots* at the Playhouse, Amersham (with white actor Haydn Jones as the black lead Brett); it was Rolston's debut.

16   See *Stage*, 15 July, 1948. Author of *An American Primitive* is not given but most likely is Thomas McEvoy Patterson, whose play of this name concerns the problems of an African-American preacher in rural Mississippi.

17   *Stage*, 15 July, 1948.

18   *Stage*, 30 October, 1952.

19   In the light of this revivifying role, it is ironic that when the *The Times* (25 May, 1948) asked what was the point of introducing West Indian calypso to a staid English comedy as mere decoration, it was only a month before the SS *Empire Windrush* landed with its iconic set of passengers who were to become the symbol of postwar black immigration. With Connor in the cast was his *Serenade in Sepia* co-star Evelyn Dove (of West African and English parentage) and the US-born Mabel Lee, who garnered the best reviews.

20   Henriques, op. cit., pp. 25–32.

21   Hill writes about his time in London, in *Shakespeare in Sable: A History of Black Shakespearean Actors*, Amherst, MA, University of Michigan Press, 1984, pp. xix–xxiii. In 1949, Barbara Assoon, another Trinidadian from Port of Spain, also won a British Council scholarship to study drama in Britain. She chose the Bristol Old Vic Theatre School. She spent the next two decades as a notable stage, radio, and screen actor but found it hard to make substantial progress and returned to Trinidad in 1968, where she became a well-known radio figure.

22   See Judy S. J. Stone, *Studies in West Indian Literature: Theatre*, London and Basingstoke, Hants, Macmillan, 1994, pp.34–38; Martin Banham et al. (eds), *Cambridge Guide to African and Caribbean Theatre*, Cambridge, Cambridge UP, 1984, pp. 235–236.

23 Errol John, *Moon on a Rainbow Shawl*, in *The Observer Plays*, London, Faber and Faber, 1958, p. 50.

24 Ibid., Preface, p. 9. Quotation cited by Bourne, 2001, op. cit., p 120.

25 Preface, op. cit., p. 9.

26 Charles Duff, *The Lost Summer: The Heyday of the West End Theatre*, London, Nick Hern Books, 1995, pp. 217–221.

27 *The Sunday Times*, 7 December, 1958; *Evening Standard*, 5 December, 1958, *The Times*, 5 December, 1958; *Observer*, 7 December, 1958; *Stage*, 11 December, 1958.

28 John, *Moon on a Rainbow Shawl*, London, Faber and Faber, 1958, p. 84. This second version changes the emphasis from Ephraim wanting to escape small town mentality and everyone knowing his business to an urge that the world holds something more for him elsewhere.

29 Bourne, op. cit., p 122.

30 Philip Hedley, 'A Theatre Director's Journey to the Obvious', in Tunde Ikoli, *Scrape Off the Black*, London, Oberon Books, 1998, p 10.

31 Tyrone Huggins, *The Eclipse Theatre Story*, Eclipse [no publisher or date; it appeared in 2006], p. 23.

32 *Independent*, 19 July, 1988.

33 Pines, op. cit., p. 41. See also Bruce King, *The Internationalization of English Literature (The Oxford Literary History, vol. 13: 1948–2000)*, Oxford, Oxford UP, 2004, p. 71; Malcolm Page, 'West Indian Playwrights in Britain', *Canadian Drama*, vol. 6, no.1, 1980, pp. 90–101.

34 Before coming to the Court, *Flesh to a Tiger* played at Southsea and Cardiff. The cast: Tamba Allen, Ena Babb, Dorothy Blondel-Francis, Berril Briggs, Nadia Cattouse, James Clarke, Franciska Francis, Lloyd Innis, Cleo Laine, Edmundo Otero, Pearl Prescod, Lloyd Reckord, Maureen Seale, Johnny Sekka, Connie Smith, and Edgar Wreford.

35 The cast included Pearl Connor in the title role, Barbara Assoon, and Lloyd Reckord. Reckord came to Britain from Jamaica in 1951 and studied at the Bristol Old Vic Theatre School, as did Assoon (see note 21). He founded the Actors' Company in Jamaica in 1956, returned to Britain as a stage and screen actor, and made two short pioneering films (*Ten Bob in Winter*, 1963; *Dream A40*, 1965), which were followed later by TV films and video dramas. Back in Jamaica in 1968, he founded the National Theatre Trust, which produced some forty productions in its first two decades. His solo show, *Beyond the Blues*, toured widely and culminated in a 1982 run at the National Theatre, London in the Cottesloe. He has acted in and/or directed around a dozen of Barry's plays.

36 Richardson was responsible for several of the Court productions that used black actors. He brought both Edric Connor and Paul Robeson to Stratford upon Avon and directed Gordon Heath in the 1955 BBC TV *Othello*.

37 *The Times*, 22 May, 1958; Molly Douglas, *Tropic*, March 1960, p. 6.

38 See Pearl Connor in Roxy Harris and Sarah White (eds), *Changing Britannia – Life Experience with Britain*, London, New Beacon Books, 1999, p. 10.

39 David Thompson, Stage Sixty director, says *The Road* was sent him by the Arts Council, probably because he was a panel member, telephone interview (1 April, 2009). Stage Sixty had written in June 1965 to the Festival organizers about mounting a production and, until August 1965, the most likely candidate was Soyinka's *The Lion and the Jewel* and possibly Obi Egbuna's *Wind versus Polygamy* (Arts Council files, ACGB/43/80, Theatre Collections, Victoria and Albert Museum).

40 *The Blood Knot* (later dropping the definite article in the title) had been seen in 1963 at the New Arts Theatre (and broadcast on TV) with Zakes Mokae, a black South African who had worked with Fugard to create the play in Johannesburg, where they first performed it in 1961. This South African performance was said to be the first time a black and a white actor had appeared together on a public stage under the apartheid regime. Mokae escaped apartheid to study at RADA and pursued an acting career in the United Kingdom and the United States. Ijinle came under the auspices of the African Drama Trust (later Africa Music and Drama Trust), to which the Arts Council gave £1,474 in

1965–1966 and £1,337 in 1966–1967, at a time when the only other recipient of funds for specific black and/or Asian theatre was the Negro Theatre Workshop (1965–1966: £300; 1966–1967: £500 – see note 65).

41 Lionel Ngakane came to Britain from South Africa in 1950 as a journalist and found work as an actor in, and adviser and assistant to the director of, the film of Alan Paton's novel, *Cry, the Beloved Country*. Ngakane continued acting and became a filmmaker (e.g. *Jemima and Johnny*, 1966).

42 Lloyd Reckord, in Pines, op. cit., p. 52.

43 Ted Willis, *Evening All: Fifty Years over a Hot Typewriter*, London, Macmillan, 1991, pp. 145–146.

44 The short-lived Concord Drama Group was set up in 1964 in north London (Chalk Farm) by Shirley Newman, a white drama tutor at the City Literary Institute. It was supported by the London Co-Operative Society, and was made up of both professional and semi-professional actors, including students from her class.

45 See Colin Chambers, *The Story of Unity Theatre*, London, Lawrence and Wishart, 1989, p. 358; Joan Clarke, 'The Negro on the "White" Stage', *Tropic*, April 1960, pp. 6–7, and July 1960, p. 36, which says the group performed the first act of *Anna Christie* at the London County Council's 1960 Drama Festival and was chosen among the four best entries.

46 See Bourne, op. cit., pp. 132–141; Pines, op. cit., pp. 56–64; Carmen Munroe, 'My Life Has Become Bigger', in Carole Woddis, *Sheer Bloody Magic – Conversations with Actresses*, London, Virago, 1991, pp. 189–199. The book also contains interviews with Cathy Tyson and Meera Syal.

47 The Ira Aldridge Players were presented by Pioneer Theatres Ltd.

48 See Bourne, op. cit., p. 182. Some sources give his year of birth as 1942, others 1940. The company's ambition is given in *Tropic*, June 1960, p.24.

49 Ibid., pp. 81–90.

50 *Horizons – The Life and Times of Edric Connor*, Kingston, Jamaica, Ian Randle Publishers, 2007. See Jeremy Taylor, 'O Pioneer', *Caribbean Review of Books*, no. 10, November 2006.

51 Archibald had a second play, *Anne-Marie*, produced in London in 1976, by L'Ouverture Theatre Players at the International Arts Centre, Newington Butts. *Stage*, 27 May, 1976, said the white characters were played by black actors at the suggestion of the poet and novelist Andrew Salkey.

52 Pearl co-authored with Joe Mogotsi, *Joe Mogotsi: Mantindane 'He Who Survives' - My Life with the Manhattan Brothers* (ed. John Patterson and Lars Rasmussen), Copenhagen, Booktrader, 2002. She took the name Connor-Mogotsi after marrying Joe.

53 Bourne, op. cit., p. 88. Papers relating to the Connors can be found in the George Padmore Institute, London; the Theatre Collections, Victoria and Albert Museum, London; the Schomburg Institute, New York; and the Main Library, University of West Indies, Trinidad and Tobago. See also Pearl Connor, 'Our Olympian Struggle', Opening Address at the 12th International Bookfair of Radical Black and Third World Books, 23 March 1995, Camden Centre, London < http://www.black-history- month.co.uk/ articles/pearl.html> (accessed 1 June, 2009); her interview in Pines, op. cit., pp. 33–41; and her *Blackgrounds* interview, Theatre Collections, Victoria and Albert Museum; entry by Stephen Bourne, *Oxford Dictionary of National Biography*, Oxford UP, Online edition, 2009 < http://www.oup.com/oxforddnb/info/online/> (accessed 3 January, 2010); Harris and White (eds), op. cit., pp. 1–18. As a tribute to the contribution her parents made, Geraldine Connor created *Carnival Messiah*, a carnival version of Handel's *Messiah*, which has a local community chorus working alongside professional performers. It premiered at the West Yorkshire Playhouse (1999) with the ambition of becoming a large-scale, sustainable production and has been restaged at Harewood House, Yorkshire and the Albert Hall. An extract was broadcast on BBC TV (2009).

54 The first mention of the subcommittee comes in the Equity annual report 1965–1966 (Martin Brown, Equity, e-mail, 18 January, 2010). In the 1966–1967 report, however, it says the committee was set up three years previously (i.e., 1964), but there is no reference to this in the relevant annual report. In the 1967–1968 annual report, it is called the

Coloured Artists' Advisory Committee. There are no more references to it until the 1973–1974 report, which says the Equity Council had revived it. The 1974–1975 report says an open meeting of 'coloured' members voted for the committee to be renamed the Afro-Asian Artists' Committee (see Chapter 6, pp. 154–6 and note 45). Pearl Connor led a fifty-strong group of actors to meet the union in 1958 to argue for the establishment of a committee to represent non-white actors.

55 <http://www.talawatheatrecompany.co.uk/> (accessed 5 January, 2009)
56 Connor, 1995, op. cit.
57 *Magnet*, 'The Voice of Britain's One Million Immigrants', no. 5, 10–23 April, 1965, p. 9, says the inaugural meeting had some eighy present, but other inaccuracies in the article raise a question about the reliability of the figure.
58 Programme for *The Prodigal Son*, George Padmore Institute.
59 Undated, George Padmore Institute, used in letter to Archbishop Michael Ramsay, the Archbishop of Canterbury, Patron of the Negro Theatre Workshop.
60 Letters, and later reference to problems with the producers, Box 3, Edric and Pearl Connor Papers, Schomburg Center.
61 Simpson's secretary June Leech acted as honorary assistant secretary of the NTW and kept the files that make up the NTW archive held at the George Padmore Institute. Simpson worked with many of the NTW core members, including the Connors, in 1959 when he filmed for television *My People and Your People*, a 'West Indian Ballad Opera' written by white producer D. G. Bridson with additional material by Andrew Salkey, which was broadcast on radio. The TV version was never transmitted. See Bourne, op. cit., pp. 117–118. Simpson used NTW members in other TV productions, such as *Job*, which won a religious television award in Monte Carlo in 1964, and *The Confession Stone* (1964), a song cycle by Owen Dodson on the life of Christ and other biblical figures. Simpson's death in 1968, the same year as Edric Connor, underscored the end of the NTW. *Bethlehem Blues* also appeared in 1966 at the Commonwealth Institute Theatre presented by Caribbean Productions – the identity of groups was more fluid then and there was much cross-over between them.
62 Arts Council files (ACGB/43/80, Theatre Collections, Victoria and Albert Museum) show that many plays were considered for the Festival, including *The Dilemma of a Ghost* by Christina Ama Ata Aidoo; *The Rose Ship* by Douglas Archibald; *Goa* by Asif Currimbhoy; *Angar* by Uptal Dutt; Obi Egbuna's *Wind versus Polygamy*; Errol Hill's *Dance Bongo*; *The Spectators* by Evan Jones (already seen at the Guildford Theatre Club); *Noises in the Night* by Bari Jonson; *A Question of Allegiance* by Louis Mahoney; Barry Reckord's *Give the Bitches Time to Love Me* (a new version of *You in Your Small Corner*); three plays by Partap Sharma; Wole Soyinka's *The Lion and the Jewel* (possibly with the author directing); and Derek Walcott's *Drums and Colours*.
63 The play was broadcast on BBC TV in 1968, and repeated in 1970 and 1971. The Pan African Players had wanted to present at the Commonwealth Arts Festival *The Black Eagle*, a play about Toussaint Louverture by Peter Munk, head of the drama society at the Commonwealth Institute where he directed productions such as *Miss Julie* with black and white casts. Munk had already directed a play about Toussaint, *Black Napoleon*, at the Irving in 1953, but *The Black Eagle* was said to be a new play. Cameron was to play Toussaint in this new version, but the Festival drama panel rejected the play (see Arts Council archive, ACGB/43/80, Theatre Collections, Victoria and Albert Museum). The panel also rejected the Pan African Players' request to perform *Osei* and *Wind versus Polygamy* on the grounds that, because companies from Trinidad and Nigeria were coming, the West Indies and the Caribbean were already well represented proportionately (ACGB/43/80).
64 The Commonwealth Arts Festival, which aimed to consolidate friendship between the old and new Commonwealth, also presented the Trinidad Theatre Company in Errol Hill's *Man Better Man* (London and Glasgow); the Duro Lapido National Theatre from Osogbo, western Nigeria performing the Yoruba opera *Oba-Koso* (London, Liverpool,

Cardiff, and Glasgow); and Eastern Nigerian Theatre Company in J. P. Clark's *Song of the Goat* and *The Masquerade* (London, Liverpool, and Glasgow).

65   Arts Council annual reports show that in 1965–1966, the Council gave the Negro Theatre Workshop £300; in 1966–1967, £300. NTW records show that the second sum received was £500, not £300. A report on *The Prodigal Son* for the Arts Council music panel (28 September, 1965) says: 'much of the performance is raw and of bare amateur standard; then, as the performers lose inhibitions and break into dance, as is the way with many coloured people, the piece changes texture and takes on an assurance and vitality that is beguiling. The acting talent shown is limited. But, as one aim is to improve standards, then if the Arts Council considers that this is an aim that it is able to support on behalf of the Commonwealth artists and would-be artists in Britain, then I believe a case can be made for offering help.' (Arts Council archive, ACGB/41/80, Victoria and Albert Museum).

66   See Marika Sherwood, *Claudia Jones: A Life in Exile*, London, Lawrence and Wishart, 1999, pp. 153–162. The event on 30 January, 1959 was directed by Edric Connor and choreographed by Stanley Jack, with stage décor by Rhoda Mills and Charles Grant. Those appearing included Fitzroy Coleman, Boscoe Holder Troupe, Cleo Laine, Mike McKenzie Trio, the Mighty Terror, Rupert Nurse and his orchestra, Pearl Prescod, Sepia Serenaders, Corinne Skinner-Carter, the Southlanders, Trinidad All-Stars and Hi-Fi steelbands, West Indian Students Dance Band. The evening included a beauty contest in celebration of black rather than white standards of attractiveness.

67   Ibid., p. 156.

68   Gary Younge, 'The politics of partying', *Guardian*, 17 August, 2002.

69   See Anne Walmsley, *The Caribbean Artists Movement, 1966–1972: A Literary and Cultural History*, London, New Beacon Books, 1992. The CAM hoped to use the Jeanetta Cochrane, which later would become the home of Talawa, as a regular venue for play-readings and play production, but this plan was not realised. The work of the CAM can be seen in the BBC2 programme *Full House* (1973), which includes extracts from *Black Blast*, a music, mime, and dance journey through Caribbean history, by eseoghene (a.k.a. Lindsay Barrett), and Mustapha Matura's *Bakerloo Line*, which explores black-white relationships at a party.

70   *Dutchman* appeared in a double bill with James Saunders's *Neighbours*. Both deal with race and sex, and both featured Calvin Lockhart and Toby Robins.

6   New beginnings in the 1970s

1   These clashes were symbolized by police harassment and attempted closure in 1970 of the Mangrove Restaurant, a vital social centre in Notting Hill. Arrests at a demonstration against the closure led to what became known as the Mangrove 9 trial, the focus of national black campaigning. The nine were acquitted by a white jury.

2   Roland Rees, *Fringe First: Pioneers of Fringe Theatre on Record*, London, Oberon Books, 1992, p. 23. The section on Black Theatre includes interviews with Norman Beaton, Claire Benedict, Pauline Black, Brian Bovell, Gordon Case, Malcolm Frederick, Tunde Ikoli, Oscar James, Stephan Kalipha, Trevor Laird, Mustapha Matura, Jimi Rand, and T-Bone Wilson.

3   Ibid., p. 23.

4   Ibid., p. 98.

5   Interviewed by Diane Abbott, *Platform*, no. 3, 1981, p. 2. See also interviews in Kwesi Owusu (ed.), *Black British Culture and Society: A Text Reader*, London and New York, Routledge, 2000, pp. 275–285; Rees, op. cit., pp. 98, 103 (where Matura says the *Black Pieces* programme omitted the 'h' in Mathura and thereafter he became Matura); Harriet Devine, *Looking Back: Playwrights at the Royal Court*, London, Faber and Faber, 2006, pp. 221–230; and <www.theatrevoice.com> (accessed 15 October, 2008). For Matura's plays, see May Joseph, 'Performing in the Postcolony: The Plays of Mustapha Matura', in

Román de la Campa et al. (eds), *Late Imperial Culture*, London, Verso, 1995; Bruce King, *The Internationalization of English Literature* (*The Oxford Literary History, vol. 13: 1948– 2000*), Oxford, Oxford UP, 2004, pp. 121–124; Malcolm Page, 'West Indian Playwrights in Britain', *Canadian Drama*, vol. 6, no.1, 1980, pp. 90–101, which also deals with John, Reckord, Abbensetts, and others; D. Keith Peacock, 'Home Thoughts from Abroad', in Mary Luckhurst (ed.), *A Companion to Modern British and Irish Drama: 1880–2005*, Oxford, Blackwell, 2006, pp. 188–197.

6   *The Times*, 26 August, 1970.

7   D. Keith Peacock, *Thatcher's Theatre: British Theatre and Drama in the Eighties*, Santa Barbara, CA, Greenwood Press, 1999, p 174.

8   Rees, op. cit., p 100.

9   For Abbensetts, see King, op. cit., pp. 121–124; Page, op. cit.; Jim Pines (ed.), *Black and White in Colour: Black People in British Television Since 1936*, London, BFI Publishing, 1992, pp. 132–136.

10 *Blackstage* interview, Theatre Collections, Victoria and Albert Museum. The company was incorporated in 1969 as a limited, non-profit company with charitable status.

11 Undated leaflet (c. 1972), Dark and Light Theatre Company files, Theatre Collections, V & A.

12 Michael McMillan, 'Rebaptizing the World in Our Terms: Black Theatre and Live Arts in Britain', in Geoffrey V. Davis, and Anne Fuchs (eds), *Staging New Britain: Aspects of Black and South Asian British Theatre Practice*, Brussels, PIE-Peter Lang, 2006, pp. 50–51, considers Dark and Light's contribution.

13 Naseem Khan, *The Arts Britain Ignores: The Arts of Ethnic Minorities in Britain*, London, Community Relations Commission, 1976, p. 114.

14 For example, *Stage*, 11 January, 1973.

15 Maddy, who had been imprisoned in Sierra Leone and applied for asylum in the UK, re-established the Gbakanda Theatre in London as a multinational company presenting African arts. He worked at the Dark and Light, Keskidee, and Africa Centre. Also involved in the Gbakanda were Gambian-born actor Louis Mahoney, who became known as an Equity activist, and Nigerian-born actor Taiwo Ajai. With journalist and writer Mike Phillips, Mahoney and Ajai formed the Black Theatre Workshop (BTW) in 1976. Taiwo Ajai-Lycett (as she became known) served on the board of the Minority Arts Advisory Service before returning to Nigeria in the late 1970s, where she ran a drama school and was successful as an actor and in promoting the arts. BTW's inaugural show was a double bill in 1976 of Bode Sewande's *Bar Beach Prelude* and Ken Saro Wiwa's *Transistor Radio*.

16 Norman Beaton, *Beaton but Unbowed: An Autobiography*, London, Methuen, 1986, p. 132.

17 A Norman Beaton Fellowship was set up in 2003 and is run by BBC Radio Drama to broaden the range of actors available to radio drama. Two winners each receive fixed-term bursary contracts with the Radio Drama Company, and up to four runners-up receive single freelance engagements in Radio Drama productions.

18 Beaton, op. cit., p. 172.

19 *Dark Days, Light Nights* was filmed as *Black Joy* (1977).

20 Arts Council figures (V & A, ACGB/41/70) show the first three programmes at Longfield Hall playing 46 performances to 2,384 people (52 people per show) with a box office income of £727.05, and 35 performances on tour playing to 4,014 people (115 per show) with an income of £2,265.80.

21 *Blackstage* interview, Theatre Collections, V & A. Figures from Arts Council annual reports show funding for Dark and Light and Black Theatre of Brixton (BTB) as follows: 1972/3 £1,350; 1973 £4,700; 1974 £6,610; 1974/5 £619; 1975/6 (BTB) £10,200; 1976/7 £18,500; 1977/8 £9,900.

22 See, for example, Kristine Landon-Smith, co-founder of Tamasha, 'I'm an Artist, Not an Audience Developer', in Heather Maitland (ed.), *Navigating Difference: Cultural Diversity and Audience Development*, London, Arts Council England, 2006, pp. 111–112.

23 See Winsome Pinnock, 'Breaking Down the Door', in Vera Gottlieb and Colin Chambers (eds), *Theatre in a Cool Climate*, Oxford, Amber Lane Press, 1999, p. 30.

24 See Keskidee Trust files, London Metropolitan Archive and Geroge Padmore Institute, London.

25 The Caribbean Artists Movement moved there in 1972, briefly, before its demise.

26 *Black Feet in the Snow* had been directed by Jimi Rand and given its name to a programme at the Commonwealth Institute in 1973, presented by Inna Circle. The programme included Ali's *Twisted Knot*, directed by Yvonne Jones, and poetry by Andrew Salkey and Linton Kwesi Johnson.

27 See Judy S. J. Stone, *Studies in West Indian Literature: Theatre*, Basingstoke, Hants, Macmillan, 1994, pp. 161–164.

28 Rees, op. cit., pp. 99–100. James went on, however, to become a noted actor on stage and television, appearing in series such as *EastEnders*, *Emmerdale Farm*, and *Casualty*.

29 Jim Hiley, *Listener*, 21 September, 1989.

30 *A Killing Passion*, Theatre Collections, V & A.

31 *City Limits* interview, quoted in Deidre Osborne, 'Writing Black Back: An Overview of Black Theatre in Performance in Britain', in Dimple Godiwala (ed.), *Alternatives Within the Mainstream: British Black and Asian Theatres*, Newcastle, Cambridge Scholars Press, 2006, pp. 76–77.

32 Sandra Carpenter, 'Black and British Temba Theatre Forges the Mainstream; An Interview with Alby James', *TDR*, vol. 34, no. 1, Spring, 1990, pp. 29–30, quoted in Derrick Cameron, ' "Better a Bad Night in Toxteth": Black British Popular Theatre', in Ros Merkin (ed), *Popular Theatres?*, Liverpool, Liverpool John Moores UP, 1996, p. 91.

33 Alby James, Temba file, Theatre Collections, V & A.

34 See, for example, quotations from BTC and Black Theatre Forum representatives, *Stage*, 3 May, 1990.

35 *Blackgrounds* interview, Theatre Collections, V & A.

36 For Grant, see *Blackgrounds* interview, Theatre Collections, V & A, and Cy Grant, *Blackness and the Dreaming Soul*, Edinburgh, Shoving Leopard, 2007. Both deal with setting up of Drum and give an account of his career.

37 *Blackgrounds* interview; Grant op. cit., p. 40.

38 A two-volume brochure for *Behind the Mask* is available at the SOAS Library archives, University of London (MS 380889), in the collection of Robert Fraser, a consultant for Drum.

39 SASS, under Francis's leadership, became a youth project in South London for training in the performing arts and associated industries.

40 Information provided by John Burgess, interview, 10 February, 2010. For the Shakespeare in dialect experiments, see John Burgess, 'Peter Gill', in John Russell Brown (ed.), *Routledge Companion to Directors' Shakespeare*, London, Routledge, 2008, pp. 101–102.

41 The consultative committee for the report consisted of Prof. Hines, Birkbeck College (chair); Taiwoo Ajai (see note 15); Peter Blackman, secretary of African performing group Agor-Mmba; Norman Beaton; Stuart Hall, director of Birmingham University Centre for Contemporary Cultural Studies; social worker and dance group leader Shantu Meher; painter Ossie Murray; and youth worker Ravi Jain.

42 Peter Lichtenfels and Lynette Hunter, 'Seeing Through the National and Global Stereotypes: British Theatre in Crisis?', in Maria M. Delgado and Caridad Svich (eds), *Theatre in Crisis?: Performance Manifestos for a New Century*, Manchester, Manchester UP, 2002, p. 44, says the report overlooked Italian, Polish, and Jewish communities, whereas it does mention Polish cultural activities.

43 MAAS archive, 1976–1995, is held as part of the Minority Arts Archive, Warwick University. See Naseem Khan, 'Choices for Black Arts in Britain over Thirty Years', in David A. Bailey et al. (eds), *Shades of Black: Assembling Black Arts in 1980s Britain*, Durham, NC, and London, Duke UP, 2005, pp. 116–7.

44 Bobby Naidoo was thought to be the first black actor elected to the Equity council (*Stage*, 13 July, 1967, the year of his election and his early death aged 40).

45 The Afro-Asian Artists' Committee continued with that name until, in 1997, the union established a single Equality Committee, comprising an Afro-Asian section, a

women's section, a disability section, and a sexuality section. In 2000, the single Equality Committee was de-merged into four separate committees, one of which was called the African Caribbean Oriental and Asian Artists' Committee. In 2007, this committee was renamed the Minority Ethnic Members' Committee.

46 Under-employment, among other things, meant non-white actors found it hard to fulfil the work requirements needed to join the union.

47 The general response of drama schools was slow and inadequate. At one, Mountview in north London, a Coloured Actors Group was formed in the late 1960s.

48 See Claire Cochrane, ' "A Local Habitation and a Name": The Development of Black and Asian Theatre in Birmingham since the 1970s', in Godiwala op. cit., p. 159. Brian Crow, 'Issues in Multicultural Theatre: Birmingham Rep and Its Audiences', in Davis and Fuchs, op. cit., p. 110, says Jacobs was the second non-white actor to appear at the Rep.

49 Khan, 1976, op. cit., pp. 159–165.

50 Quoted by Vera Lustig, 'Learning to Forget a Face', *The Listener*, 13 July, 89, pp. 29–30.

51 Mike Phillips, *New Society*, 9 March, 1978.

52 Mustapha Matura, *Play Mas*, London, Methuen, 1982, 1.1, p. 17.

7 Asian theatre: Tara Arts and beyond

1 Naseem Khan, *The Arts Britain Ignores: The Arts of Ethnic Minorities in Britain*, London, Community Relations Commission, 1976, p. 70.

2 The other founders were Sunil Saggar, Praveen Bahl, and Vijay Shaunak. For Tara, see Dominic Hingorani, 'Tara Arts and Tamasha: Producing Asian Performance – Two Approaches', in Dimple Godiwala (ed.), *Alternatives Within the Mainstream: British Black and Asian Theatres*, Newcastle, Cambridge Scholars Press, 2006, pp. 174–187; Graham Ley, 'Theatre of Migration and the Search for a Multicultural Aesthetic: Twenty Years of Tara Arts', *New Theatre Quarterly*, vol. 13, no. 52, November 1997, pp. 349–371; D. Keith Peacock, *Thatcher's Theatre: British Theatre and Drama in the Eighties*, Santa Barbara, CA, Greenwood Press, 1999, pp. 181–183.

3 Jim Hiley, 'The Moliere Wallah', *Independent*, 11 September, 1989, p 14, quoted in Peacock, op. cit., p. 182.

4 See Jatinder Verma, 'Binglishing the Stage: A Generation of Asian Theatre in England', in Richard Boon and Jane Plastow (eds), *Theatre Matters: Performance and Culture on the World Stage*, Cambridge, Cambridge UP, 1998, pp. 126–134.

5 Programme note, *Sacrifice*, 1977.

6 Kadija George (ed.), *Six Plays by Black and Asian Women Writers*, London, Aurora Metro Press, 1993, p 5.

7 'Punjabi Theatre in Britain: Context and Challenge', Hounslow Conference (1996), <http://www.tara-arts.com> (accessed 14 May, 2009).

8 Verma, e-mail (28 October, 2009).

9 See Chapter 3, pp. 83.

10 For example, BBC Radio London, 18 January, 1986; *City Limits*, 23 January, 1986; *Listener*, 23 January, 1986, cited in Dimple Godiwala, 'Genealogies, Archaeologies, Histories: the Revolutionary "Interculturalism" of Asian Theatre in Britain', in Godiwala, op. cit., p 114.

11 'The Challenge of Binglish: Analyzing Multi-cultural Productions', in Patrick Campbell (ed.), *Analyzing Performance: A Critical Reader*, Manchester, Manchester UP, 1996, p. 194.

12 Following Wole Soyinka's 1973 adaptation of Euripides's *The Bacchae*, there have been many refashionings of European classics in British diasporic theatre, such as productions of Ola Rotimi's *The Gods are Not to Blame* (*Oedipus Rex*), Steve Carter's *Pecong* (*Medea*), and Stephen Landrigan's *The Pan Beaters* (*Phaedra*).

13 Irving Wardle, *The Times*, 8 December, 1991.

14 Verma, 1998, op. cit., pp. 127–128.

15 Jatinder Verma, 'Sorry, No Saris!', in Vera Gottlieb and Colin Chambers (eds), *Theatre in a Cool Climate*, Oxford, Amber Lane Press, 1999, p.193. See also Derrick Cameron, 'Tradaptation: Cultural Exchange and Black British Theatre', in Carole-Anne Upton (ed.), *Moving Target: Theatre Translation and Cultural Relocation*, Manchester UK and Northampton, MA, St Jerome Publishing, 2000, pp. 17–24. Verma, 1998, op. cit., p. 129, traces his use of the term *tradaption* to Robert LePage. See also interview with Verma, in Maria Delgado and Paul Heritage (eds), *In Contact with the Gods: Directors Talk Theatre*, Manchester, Manchester UP, 1996, pp. 277–298. For tradaption strategy in a wider context, see Bill Ashcroft et al. (eds), *The Postcolonial Studies Reader*, London, Routledge, 2005, and Helen Gilbert and Joanne Tompkins, *Post-colonial Drama: Theory, Practice, Politics*, London, Routledge, 1996.

16 Quoted, Peacock, op. cit., p. 183.

17 *Tartuffe* and *The Little Clay Cart* were directed by Verma, but *Cyrano*, and later *The Black Album*, were Tara co-productions with the National Theatre.

18 Hingorani, op. cit., p.184.

19 Ibid., p. 187.

20 Jatinder Verma, 'Asian Theatre in Britain: Historical Developments and Contemporary Identity', Birmingham, Asian Theatre Conference, 2004, < http://www.tara-arts.com> (accessed 14 May, 2009)

21 Hanif Kureishi, Introduction to *Outskirts and Other Plays*, London, Faber and Faber, 1992, p. xix. See also Mary Karen Dahl, 'Postcolonial British Theatre: Black Voices at the Center', in J. Ellen Gainor (ed.), *Imperialism and Theatre: Essays on World theatre, drama and performance, 1795–1995*, London and New York, Routledge, 1995, pp. 43–45; Harriet Devine, *Looking Back: Playwrights at the Royal Court*, London, Faber and Faber, 2006, pp. 205–208.

22 Quoted in Dimple Godiwala, 'Kali: Providing a Forum for British-Asian Women Playwrights', in Godiwala, op. cit., p 329.

23 Quoted in Hingorani, op. cit., p.188. This may also help explain why several of the company's productions were also broadcast on radio. For Tamasha, see Elaine Aston, *Feminist Views on the English Stage: Women Playwrights, 1990–2000*, Cambridge, Cambridge UP, 2003, pp. 136–146; Anne Fuchs, 'Looking at New British Heritage: Tamasha Theatre Company', in Geoffrey V. Davis and Anne Fuchs (eds), *Staging New Britain: Aspects of Black and South Asian British Theatre Practice*, Brussels, PIE-Peter Lang, 2006, pp. 127–139; Hingorani, op. cit., pp. 187–197.

24 Hingorani, op. cit., p.188.

25 Fuchs, op. cit., p.132–133.

26 Hingorani, op. cit., p.190.

27 Verma, 1998, op. cit., p 132.

28 Arti Vaish, *Economic Times*, Delhi, 5 February, 1994.

29 Godiwala ('Genealogies') in Godiwala, op. cit., p 112.

30 Ayub Khan-Din, *East is East*, London, Nick Hern Books, 1996, p. 49. For an analysis of *East is East,* see Anne Fuchs, 'Un exemple de théâtre interculturel: la Tamasha Theatre Company', in Richard Corballis and André Viola (eds), *Postcolonial Knitting: The Art of Jacqueline Bardolph*, Nice, France, CRÉLA and Massey, New Zealand, Massey University, 2000, pp. 54–60.

31 Quoted, Hingorani, op. cit., p. 196

32 Khan-Din, op. cit., pp. 40, 39, 49.

33 See Jen Harvie, *Staging the UK*, Manchester, Manchester UP, 2005, pp. 156–191.

34 Fuchs, 2006, op. cit., p. 136.

35 <www.tamasha.org.uk> (accessed 20 June, 2009).

36 Anthony Frost, 'Drama in the Age of Kalyug: Behzti and Sikh Self-censorship', in Godiwala, op. cit., p. 204. See also Valerie Kaneko Lucas, '*Shameless* – Women, Sexuality and Violence in British-Asian Drama', in Godiwala, op. cit., pp. 371–375; Janet Steel, 'Shame in Birmingham', *Index on Censorship*, vol. 34, no. 2, May 2005, pp. 121–123.

37 David Edgar, 'Saying the Unsayable', in *At the Turning of the Tide*, London, Commission for Racial Equality, 2006, an anthology marking thirty years of the CRE, details the programme the Rep had already announced at the time of *Behzti*. It included plays on African-Caribbean gun crime, Muslim brothels, terrorism, communalism, and teenage sex. During their runs, the theatre kept a rough head-count, by ethnicity, of audiences for all its shows. In the studio, Asma Dar's *Chaos* (set in a Muslim home, concerned with careerism, communalism, and terrorism) gained a forty per cent, largely Asian audience, about the same as Yasmin Whittaker Khan's *Bells*, the play about Muslim brothels. A revival of Kwame Kwei-Armah's *Elmina's Kitchen* (in Birmingham en route to London's West End) achieved the largest black audience of its pre-London tour (nearly one-third) in the Rep's 900-seat main house. More than sixty per cent of the audience for a short run of Roy Williams' *Little Sweet Thing* (the Eclipse tour) were non-white. Before *Behzti*, the Rep studio had presented more than twenty plays by black or Asian writers, from Ayub Khan-Din's *East is East*, via Charles Mulekwa's *A Time of Fire* and Sudha Bhuchar's *Balti Kings*, to Amber Lone's *Paradise*. In the same period, the main house hosted twelve shows with predominantly non-white casts. Claire Cochrane, '"A Local Habitation and a Name": the Development of Black and Asian Theatre in Birmingham since the 1970s', in Godiwala, op. cit., pp. 165–170, looks at the Rep from the 1980s and notes that in the 1990s, black actors such as Jeffrey Kissoon and Rakie Ayola became familiar in the classical repertoire beyond the obviously racialized repertoire but that audience figures were poor across the board. See also Brian Crow, 'Issues in Multicultural Theatre: Birmingham Rep and its Audiences', in Davis and Fuchs, op. cit., pp. 107–126.

38 Frost, op. cit., p. 203. *Behzti* has had further performances in France and Belgium but not (at time of writing) in Britain. Bhatti has since written a fictional account of the affair called *Behud* (Beyond Belief), which was produced in Coventry and London in 2010.

39 Rustom Bharucha, 'Somebody's Other: Disorientations in the Cultural Politics of our Time', in Patrick Pavis (ed.), *The Intercultural Performance Reader*, London, Routledge, 1996, p. 210.

8   'All a we is English'

1 Mustapha Matura, *Play Mas*, London, Methuen, 1982, 1.1, p. 17.

2 Issue no. 3, 1981, of the left-wing theatre magazine *Platform* that carried an interview with Mustapha Matura (see Chapter 6, note 5), went to press the week after the 'Brixton Rebellion' and devoted much of its space to black theatre: Mike Phillips explored 'Black Theatre in Britain', pp. 3–6; there was a discussion including Matura, Caz Phillips, Hanif Kureishi, and H. O. Nazareth on the neglected status of black playwrights, pp. 7–14; an interview with black playwright Michael McMillan, p. 15.

3 *More, More* was also seen at the National's Lyttleton Theatre as a Platform Performance and at the Royal Court Theatre Upstairs paired with Matura's *Black Slaves, White Chains*. *More More* had been rehearsed under the auspices of Temba for a tour that was cancelled before Charlie Hanson presented it independently.

4 See Roland Rees, *Fringe First: Pioneers of Fringe Theatre on Record*, London, Oberon Books, 1992, pp. 126–128.

5 Winsome Pinnock also wrote a play about Jones, *A Rock in Water* (1989), and Jones was commemorated by a stamp in 2008 in the Royal Mail's 'Women of Distinction' series.

6 For example, Yvonne Brewster (ed.), *Black Plays*, London, Methuen, 1987, *Black Plays Two* (1989) and *Three* (1995); and Kadija George (ed.), *Six Plays by Black and Asian Women Writers*, London, Aurora Metro Press, 1993.

7 Mark Heath, for example, was Theatre Programme Organiser at the Africa Centre in the mid-1970s, and under Alistair Niven (1978–1984), the Centre presented a wide range of performances. Oval House, to take another example, presented *Mid Way* by Alphi Pritchart at the Black Theatre Festival, New York in 1980 and, in the 1990s (unusually for the time) had a black female programmer in Karena Johnson. For an example of regional initiatives,

see Brian Crow, 'Issues in Multicultural Theatre: Birmingham Rep and Its Audiences', in Geoffrey V. Davis and Anne Fuchs (eds), *Staging New Britain: Aspects of Black and South Asian British Theatre Practice*, Brussels, PIE-Peter Lang, 2006, pp. 107–126.

8　See titles listed in the Introduction, note 7.

9　See Helen Gilbert and Joanne Tompkins, *Post-Colonial Drama: Theory, Practice, Politics*, London, Routledge, 1996, pp. 78–100; Lizbeth Goodman, *Contemporary Feminist Theatres: To Each Her Own*, London, Routledge, 1993, pp. 163–166; Karina Smith, 'Narratives of Success, Narratives of Failure: The Creation and Collapse of Sistren's "Aesthetic Space"', *Modern Drama*, vol. 51, no. 2, Summer 2008, pp. 234–258. Sistren issued a magazine of the same name as the group, and also available were their videos and *Lionheart Gal*, London, Women's Press, 1986, a biography of the group's members (Elean Thomas, 'Lionhearted Women: Sistren Women's Theatre Collective', *Spare Rib*, no. 172, November 1986, pp. 14–19).

10　Lynette Goddard, *Staging Black Feminisms*, Basingstoke, Hants, Palgrave Macmillan, 2007, p. 26. See also Goodman, op. cit., pp. 153–155.

11　Winsome Pinnock, *Leave Taking*, in Kate Harwood (ed.), *First Run: New Plays by New Writers*, London, Nick Hern Books, 1989, p. 148. For Pinnock, see Elaine Aston, *Feminist Views on the English Stage: Women Playwrights, 1990–2000*, Cambridge, Cambridge UP, 2003, pp. 125–136, 130–133; Goddard, op. cit., pp. 57–81; Gabriele Griffin, *Contemporary Black and Asian Women Playwrights in Britain*, Cambridge, Cambridge UP, 2003, pp. 37–63, 62–74, 78–87, 125–131, 213–223, and 'The Remains of Empire: the Plays of Winsome Pinnock', in Mary Luckhurst (ed.), *A Companion to Modern British and Irish Drama: 1880–2005*, Oxford, Blackwell, 2006, pp. 198–210; D. Keith Peacock, 'Black British Drama and the Politics of Identity', in Nadine Holdsworth and Mary Luckhurst (eds), *A Concise Companion to Contemporary British and Irish Drama*, Oxford, Blackwell, 2008, pp. 49–53; Meenakshi Ponnuswami, 'Alienation and Alienation Effects in Winsome Pinnock's *Talking in Tongues*', in R. Victoria Arana (ed.), *"Black" British Aesthetics Today*, Newcastle upon Tyne, Cambridge Scholars Publishing, 2007, pp. 206–221; Heidi Stephenson and Natasha Longridge, *Rage and Reason: Women Playwrights on Playwriting*, London, Methuen, 1997, pp. 45–53 (this book also has interviews with Tanika Gupta and Jenny McLeod).

12　See, for example, Ian Brown, Rob Brannen, and Douglas Brown, 'The Arts Council Touring Franchise and English Political Theatre after 1986', *New Theatre Quarterly*, vol. 16, no. 4, November 2000, pp. 379–387, which says the 1987–1988 settlement freed money from the national companies to fund the likes of Tara on an annual revenue basis. The authors argue that other strategies, such as the introduction of staggered three-year franchises for middle- and small-scale touring companies, helped too. See also Ian Brown, 'The Road through Woodstock: Counter-Thatcherite Strategies in ACGB's Drama Development between 1984–1994', *Contemporary Theatre Review*, vol. 17, no. 2, 2007, pp. 218–229. See note 17.

13　An example of attempting to walk this tightrope can be found in the work of Karim Alrawi, born of an Egyptian father and British mother, who came to Britain when he was fourteen. He had a radio play produced and two short pieces in fringe theatres before the full-length *Migrations* was seen in 1982 at the Theatre Royal Stratford East where he became writer in residence. *Migrations*, a snapshot of society depicted through the prism of an adventure playground project, won the esteemed John Whiting award. For Joint Stock, a leading and innovative touring company, Alrawi wrote *Fire in the Lake* (1985), which explores interracial tension in the shadow of nuclear tragedy. However, he found the company in serious administrative and financial difficulty, and Alrawi's play became the first by this feted group not to be seen in London, though it did win a Fringe First at the Edinburgh Festival. After writing for the Royal Court *A Colder Climate* (1986), looking at the far-right in Britain, he returned to Joint Stock, drawn by its collective ethos. The company policy of having half its policy committee female and half its project participants non-white caused differences within the group and with the Arts Council, which preferred the usual model of a group led by a single authority. Alrawi became one of three artistic directors alongside actor Souad Faress (born in Ghana to Syrian and Irish parents) and (white) director Nick Broadhurst. Alrawi wrote *Child in the Heart* (1987), which deals with racial difference and Western charity, and *Promised Land* (1988), which tackles the Palestinian issue, for Joint Stock before returning to Egypt. By this point, the Arts Council had reduced the company's grant by ten per cent and, in 1989, it was cut altogether. See Susan Carlson, 'Collaboration, Identity, and Cultural Difference: Karim Alrawi's Theatre of Engagement', *Theatre Journal*, vol. 45, no. 2, May 1993, pp. 155–173.

14 The shift in terminology can be seen in the 1989 Arts Council report called *Towards Cultural Diversity*. By the time of the Council's 1997 report, *The Landscape of Fact*, cultural diversity had become synonymous with non-white, especially black and Asian.

15 See Naseem Khan, 'Choices for Black Arts in Britain over Thirty Years,' in David A. Bailey et al. (eds), *Shades of Black: Assembling Black Arts in 1980s Britain*, Durham NC, and London, Duke University Press, 2005, pp. 119–120.

16 Naseem Khan article, *British Council News*, April 1997, <http://www.britishcouncil.org/ > (accessed 4 January, 2009), and 'Arts Council England and Diversity: Striving for Change', in Heather Maitland (ed.), *Navigating Difference: Cultural Diversity and Audience Development*, London, Arts Council of England, 2006. Samantha Harding, 'We'll not fail in our search for a new home', *Stage*, 11 April 1976, says there were 86 black companies in 1991 and five years later only 21.

17 There were many layers of contestation (see note 12). For example, after *The Glory of the Garden* (1984) and similar reports for Scotland and Wales, the Cork Report (1986) was expected in certain quarters to deliver a Thatcherite message but instead supported the idea that theatre is for all. It advocated a holistic approach and additional funding and called for the national companies to increase non-white participation. This added pressure on the National Theatre, which contributed to its decision to stage shows such as August Wilson's *Ma Rainey's Black Bottom* and invite Jatinder Verma to direct there. See Ian Brown and Rob Brannen, 'When Theatre Was for All: The Cork Report after Ten Years', *New Theatre Quarterly*, vol. 12, no. 48, November 1996, pp. 367–383.

18 Floya Anthias and Nira Yural-Davis, *Racialized Boundaries: Race, Nation, Gender, Colour and Class and the Anti-racist Struggle*, London and New York, Routledge, 1996, p. 181.

19 Similar experiences can be found elsewhere, e.g., in Manchester and Sheffield.

20 The history of the Roundhouse project is complex and disputed. There were many flashpoints, including the disbanding in 1985 of a steering committee of professional artists to make way for a trust, a decision that GLC money could not be paid after its abolition, a much-criticised first festival, *Twelve Days at the Roundhouse* (1986), the handling of dismissals (1987), and poor communication by the project with the funders.

21 See Adeola Solanke, 'Creative Space: Double Edge Versus the Church of England', in Kwesi Owusu (ed.), *Storms of the Heart: An Anthology of Black Arts and Culture*, London, Camden Press, 1988, pp. 61–72.

22 See Alda Terracciano, 'Mainstreaming African, Asian and Caribbean Theatre: The Experiments of the Black Theatre Forum', in Dimple Godiwala (ed.) *Alternatives Within the Mainstream: British Black and Asian Theatres*, Newcastle upon Tyne, Cambridge Scholars Press, 2006, pp. 22–60, and 'Crossing Lines: An Analysis of Integration and Separatism within Black Theatre in Britain', unpublished PhD dissertation, History of Theatre, Istituto Universitario Orientale, Naples, 2002.

23 Among Carib's productions were Derek Walcott's *Remembrance* (1980), Michael Abbensetts's *The Outlaw* (1983), Earl Lovelace's *The New Hardware Store* (1985), Peggy Bennette-Hume's *The Girl who Wished* (1985), James Baldwin's *The Amen Corner* (1987) and many school shows.

24 The Arts was noted among other things as being the venue of the English-language première of Samuel Becket's *Waiting for Godot* and for the premières of Harold Pinter's *The Caretaker* and Joe Orton's *Entertaining Mr Sloane*. Since the 1970s, the theatre had been known as a transfer house and for the work of the resident children's company, the Unicorn.

25 Quoted in Terracciano, 2006, op. cit., p. 25.

26 Ibid., p 25.
27 Ibid., p. 43.
28 Ibid., p. 44.
29 Ibid., p. 47.
30 See *Race and Class*, vol. 28, no. 1, 1986, pp. 73–79.
31 One aim of *Black Experience* was to establish in Britain an annual Black History Month as
    occurred every February in Canada and the United States. October became the month
    in Britain.
32 For her biography, see Yvonne Brewster, *The Undertaker's Daughter: The Colourful Life of
    a Theatre Director*, Black Amber Books, London, 2004, and for Talawa: Yvonne Brewster,
    'Talawa Theatre Company 1985–2002', in Davis and Fuchs, op. cit., pp. 87–105;
    Blackstage interview, Theatre Collections, Victoria and Albert Museum; and, 'Drawing
    the Black and White Line: Defining Black Women's Theatre', an interview with Lizbeth
    Goodman, *New Theatre Quarterly*, vol. 7, no. 28, November 1991, pp. 361–368. For
    Talawa, see also Goodman, 1993, op. cit., pp. 155–163; David Vivian Johnson, 'The
    History, Theatrical Performance Work and Achievements of Talawa Theatre Company
    1986–2001', unpublished PhD dissertation, University of Warwick, Centre for British
    and Comparative Cultural Studies, 2001; Victor Ukaegbu, 'Talawa Theatre Company:
    The "Likkle" Matter of Black Creativity and Representation on the British Stage', in
    Godiwala, op. cit., pp. 123–152.
33 Brewster, 2004, op. cit., p. 47.
34 Norman Beaton, *Beaton but Unbowed: An Autobiography*, London, Methuen, 1986, p. xi.
35 *Financial Times*, 27 February, 1986. Reviews, however, were mixed. *The Times*, 5 March,
    1986, for instance, found the play 'diffuse, at times dull to the point of vapidity', and
    Brewster's production 'intermittently vigorous'.
36 Programme held in Talawa Archive, Theatre Collections, V & A. For the play, see Gilbert
    and Tompkins, op. cit., pp. 69–71; John Thieme, 'Repossessing the Slave Past: Caribbean
    Historiography and Dennis Scott's *An Echo in the Bone*', in Michael Walling (ed.), *Theatre
    and Slavery: Ghosts at the Crossroads*, Enfield, Border Crossings, 2007, pp. 42–51.
37 Brewster, 2004, op. cit., p. 125.
38 Ibid., p. 140.
39 See 'Shakespeare and Black Theatre' file, Theatre Collections, V & A, for Brewster's
    struggle to have Cleopatra accepted as black.
40 Brewster, 2004, op. cit., p. 227.
41 Audience figures from *Blackstage* interview. A list of Talawa productions from 1986 to
    2005 can be found in Ukaegbu, op. cit., pp. 149–150.
42 *Blackstage* interview, op. cit; Brewster, 2006, op. cit., pp. 92–93.
43 As is often the way in such matters, different parties to the events claim different versions,
    and confusion still surrounds the succession of these artistic directors.
44 The video archive interviews and transcripts cover: *Blackgrounds* – Earl Cameron, Pearl
    Connor, Cy Grant, Barry Reckord, Alaknanda Samarth; *Blackstage* – Michael Abbensetts,
    Thomas Baptiste, Yvonne Brewster, Frank Cousins, Mona Hammond, Ram Jam Holder,
    Naseem Khan, Carmen Munroe, Corinne Skinner-Carter, and Rudolph Walker. The
    transcripts are unedited and contain several uncorrected factual errors.
45 Statistics can be notoriously tricky, but Arts Council figures show in 1984–1985 that
    black and Asian arts accounted for 13.9% of the total art forms budget, with Music
    0.01%, Dance 0.03% and Drama 0.08%, whereas ten years later in 1984–1985, the non-
    white diasporic total had dropped to 0.8%, with Music 1.4%, Dance 5.91% and Drama
    2.5%. Reports such as that produced by Peter Boyden (2000) continued the approach
    taken by the Cork Report (1986) in recognising non-white under-representation and
    calling for increased provision. *The Future of Multi-Ethnic Britain* (chair, Bhikhu Parekh),
    London, Runnymede Trust, 2000, examined the under-funding of culturally diverse
    arts. The Lottery-funded Arts Capital Programme in 2001 did finance 23 black and
    Asian building-based projects (according to Jude Bloomfield, 'Crossing the Rainbow:

National Differences and International Convergences in Multicultural Performing Arts in Europe', Informal European Theatre Meeting, 2003).

46 Barnaby King, 'Landscapes of Fact and Fiction: Asian Theatre Arts in Britain' and 'The Afro-Caribbean Identity and the English Stage', *New Theatre Quarterly*, vol. 16, part 1, no. 61, February 2000, pp. 26–33, and part 2, no. 62, May 2000, pp. 131–136 respectively, look at developments outside London in terms of the interaction between black and Asian community and professional theatre and its relationship to mainstream theatre and arts funding.

47 Alda Terracciano, 'Together We Stand!', in Maitland, op. cit., explores why the press ignores much non-white theatre.

48 The Shaw Theatre, with a modest grant from Camden Council.

49 Terracciano, in Godiwala, op. cit., p 41.

50 Quoted in Rees, op. cit., p. 122.

51 Quoted in Derrick Cameron, '"Better a Bad Night in Toxteth": Black British Popular Theatre', in Ros Merkin (ed.), *Popular Theatres?*, Liverpool, Liverpool John Moores UP, 1996, p. 92.

52 Though white writers such as David Edgar, Trevor Griffiths, Michael Hastings, and Stephen Poliakoff have dealt with racism and right-wing presence in Britain, and Barrie Keeffe's *Sus* (1979) was a key play of its period on state racism, there is little in mainstream white writing that deals with non-white characters outside the race/politics paradigm.

53 Tyrone Huggins, *The Eclipse Theatre Story* [no publisher or date but it appeared in 2006], p. 9, cites Mel Jennings, who in 1998 audited for the Arts Council 55 reports compiled 1985–1997 on audiences for black and Asian work. Venu Dhupa, 'Diversity – Is It Colourless?', in Maitland, op. cit., p. 61, notes that 30 years on from *The Arts Britain Ignores*, there were 83 publications in the ACE library under the category 'Cultural Diversity'. BRIT began in 1994 with three theatres: Nottingham Playhouse, West Yorkshire Playhouse, and Leicester Haymarket. It expanded later to include Derby Playhouse, Hudawi Cultural Centre, and Lawrence Batley Theatre (Huddersfield); Green Room (Manchester); Kuumba and Old Vic (Bristol); Wolsey (Ipswich); and Oval House (London). To take one example of initiatives that were launched, West Yorkshire Playhouse staged two black theatre seasons (in 1996 and '97) but, with box office poor, discontinued them.

54 *Eclipse: Developing Strategies to Combat Racism in Theatre*, London, Arts Council of England, 2002, was based on a conference held at Nottingham Playhouse, 12–13 June, 2001. The notion of institutional racism is taken from the Macpherson Report (1999) into the murder of Stephen Lawrence and is defined as the 'collective failure of an organisation to provide appropriate and professional service to people because of their colour, culture or ethnic origin. It can be seen or detected in processes, attitudes, and behaviour which amount to discrimination through unwitting prejudice, ignorance, thoughtlessness and racist stereotyping which disadvantage minority ethnic people.' The Macpherson Inquiry hearings were dramatized by Richard Norton-Taylor as *The Colour of Justice* (1999). Naseem Khan, 'The Arts in Transition', *Reinventing Britain: Cultural Diversity up Front and on Show*, Guardian publication in association with Decibel, 2003, cites the Independent Theatre Council's *Glass Ceiling* report (2000) that says eighty-six per cent of the sixty-five black and Asian administrators interviewed had personally encountered racism working in the mainstream performing arts.

55 *Eclipse*, op. cit., p. 9, reported that only four per cent of staff in English theatre and three-and-a-half per cent of board members on English producing theatres were African, Asian or Caribbean. See also Rita Kottasz, 'Resistance to Identity Change in UK Theatres', in Maitland, op. cit..

56 Lola Young, *Whose Theatre…?*, Report on the Sustained Theatre consultation, London, Arts Council England, 2006, p. 5.

57 For example, the problems Pomo Afro Homos (Post-Modern African-American Homosexuals) found when they tried to tour *Dark Fruit* in 1991, though Hanif Kureishi's

film *My Beautiful Launderette* had been adapted for the stage the year before. Writers such as Paul Boakye in *Boy with Beer* (1992), however, have tackled black homosexuality and AIDS, which remained a sensitive subject.

58 For instance, Winsome Pinnock, 'Breaking Down the Door', in Vera Gottlieb and Colin Chambers (eds), *Theatre in a Cool Climate*, Oxford, Amber Lane Press, 1999, p. 29, says black rhythms of speech, a kind of street argot, have become the benchmark for all youth culture and gives examples of Rebecca Prichard's *Yard Gal*, Che Walker's *Been So Long* and David Eldridge's *Serving It Up*.

59 The provisional nature of progress can be seen in the example of the National Theatre. Several 'firsts' – first non-white director (Jatinder Verma), first female non-white director (Decima Francis, then Yvonne Brewster), first play by a non-white female playwright (Winsome Pinnock) – were associated with mobile, educational, or Studio productions and seen in the smallest auditorium (Cottesloe). Drawing on her experience at the NT, Pinnock, op. cit., p. 32, notes that 'When a so-called "black" play is produced at a theatre, the marketing department will call on its list of black institutions and invite them. The message is that they are only invited to see plays by black artists and are not otherwise welcome'.

60 Kwei-Armah was born in Hillingdon, London as Ian Roberts to Grenadian parents and changed his name after a visit to Ghana tracing his roots.

61 Roy Williams, 'Black Theatre's Big Breakout', *Guardian*, 28 September, 2009, counted twenty-eight writers of colour produced in the previous two years by Britain's leading theatres: Zawe Ashton, Oladipo Agboluaje, Kwame Kwei-Armah, Bola Agbaje, Michael Bhim, Levi David Addai, Linda Brogan, Trevor Williams, Winsome Pinnock, Ashmeed Sohoye, Neil D'Souza, Paven Virk, Amy Evans, Jennifer Farmer, Lydia Adetunji, debbie tucker green, Rex Obano, Tanika Gupta, Atiha Gupta, Paula B. Stanic, Marcia Layne, Mark Norfolk, Lorna French, Sheila White, Amber Lone, Rikki Beadle-Blair, Femi Oguns, and Grant Buchanan Marshall. For Williams, see Elizabeth Barry and William Boles, 'Beyond Victimhood: Agency and Identity in the Theatre of Roy Williams,' in Godiwala, op, cit., pp. 297–313; Peacock, op. cit., pp. 57–59; and Aleks Sierz, '"Two Worlds Fighting Each Other": Roy Williams and Contemporary Black British Theatre', in Davis and Fuchs, op. cit., pp. 177–188. For Kwei-Armah, see Samuel Kasule, 'Aspects of Madness and Theatricality in Kwame Kwei-Armah's Drama', in Godiwala, op. cit., pp. 314–328; interview in Davis and Fuchs, op. cit., pp. 239–251, and ' "Know Whence You Came": Dramatic Art and Black British Identity', *New Theatre Quarterly*, vol. 23, no. 3, August 2007, pp. 253–263; and Peacock, op. cit., pp. 53–58. For debbie green tucker, see Goddard, op. cit., pp. 181–192, Deidre Osborne, 'Not "In-Yer-Face" But What Lies Beneath: Experiential and Aesthetic Inroads in the Drama of debbie tucker green and Dona Daley', in Arana (ed.), op. cit., pp. 222–242, and Peacock, op. cit., pp. 59–64.

62 The archive, which is limited to black British plays, was launched in 2009 and is funded by the Arts Council of England in partnership with the National Theatre Studio and Sustained Theatre, an artist-led initiative that came out of the *Whose Theatre..?* report, op. cit. The African-American plays presented in 2005–2006 by the ensemble were *Walk Hard* by Abram Hill, *Gem of the Ocean* by August Wilson, and *Fabulation* by Lynn Nottage. The plays in the *Not Black and White* season were *Seize the Day* by Kwame Kwei-Armah; *Category B* by Roy Williams; and *Detaining Justice* by Bola Agbaje, whose first produced play, *Gone Too Far!* (Royal Court, 2007), won a Laurence Oliver Award for Outstanding Achievement in an Affiliated Theatre.

SELECT BIBLIOGRAPHY

Abdelwahid, Mustafa A., (ed.), *The Autobiography of Dusé Mohamed Ali, 1866–1945: A Pioneer of Pan-Africanism and Afro-Asian Solidarity Movements* (forthcoming).

Abu-Baker, Mohamed Hassan, *Representations of Islam and Muslims in Early Modern English Drama from Marlowe to Massinger*, unpublished thesis, Glasgow, Glasgow University, 1997.

Adi, Hakim, *The History of the African and Caribbean Communities in Britain*, Hove, East Sussex, Wayland, 1995.

Adi, Hakim, *West Africans in Britain, 1900–1960: Nationalism, Pan-Africanism and Communism*, London, Lawrence and Wishart, 1998.

Adi, Hakim, and Sherwood, Marika, *Pan-African History; Political Figures from Africa and the Diaspora since 1787*, London, Routledge, 2003.

Agate, James, *Brief Chronicles*, London, Cape, 1943.

Alexander, Catherine M. S., and Wells, Stanley (eds), *Shakespeare and Race*, Cambridge, Cambridge UP, 2000.

Ali, Nasreen, et al. (eds), *A Postcolonial People: South Asians in Britain*, London, Hurst and Co., 2006.

Altick, Richard D., *The Shows of London*, Cambridge, MA, Belknap Press, 1978.

Andrews, William L., et al. (eds), *Concise Oxford Companion to African American Literature*, Oxford, Oxford UP, 2001.

Anthias, Floya, and Yural-Davis, Nira, *Racialized Boundaries: Race, Nation, Gender, Colour and Class and the Anti-racist Struggle*, London and New York, Routledge, 1996.

Arana, R. Victoria (ed.), *"Black" British Aesthetics Today*, Newcastle upon Tyne, Cambridge Scholars Publishing, 2007.

Aravamudan, Srinivas, *Tropicopolitans: Colonialism and Agency, 1688–1804*, Durham, NC, and London, Duke UP, 1999.

Ashcroft, Bill, et al., *The Empire Writes Back*, London, Routledge, 1989.

Ashcroft, Bill, et al. (eds), *The Post-Colonial Studies Reader*, London, Routledge, 2005.

Aston, Elaine, *An Introduction to Feminism and Theatre*, London, Routledge, 1995.

Aston, Elaine, *Feminist Views on the English Stage: Women Playwrights, 1990–2000*, Cambridge, Cambridge UP, 2003.

Aston, Elaine, and Reinelt, Janelle (eds), *Cambridge Companion to Modern British Women Playwrights*, Cambridge, Cambridge UP, 2000.

Bailey, David A., et al. (eds), *Shades of Black: Assembling Black Arts in 1980s Britain*, Durham, NC, and London, Duke UP, 2005.

Balibar, Etienne, and Wallerstein, Immanuel (eds), *Race, Nation, Class: Ambiguous Identities*, London, Verso, 1991.

Ballard, Roger (ed.), *Desh Pardesh: The South Asian Presence in Britain*, London, Hurst, 1994.

Banham, Martin, et al. (eds), *Cambridge Guide to African and Caribbean Theatre*, Cambridge, Cambridge UP, 1984.

Barbour, Richmond, *Before Orientalism: London's Theatre of the East, 1576–1626*, Cambridge, Cambridge UP, 2003.

Barker, Francis, and Hulme, Peter, 'Nymphs and Reapers Heavily Vanish; the Discursive Con-Texts of *The Tempest*', in Drakakis, *Alternative Shakespeares*, 1985.

Barrington, Jonah, *Personal Sketches of his Own Times*, London, H. Coburn & R. Bentley, 1827.

Barry, Elizabeth, and Boles, William, 'Beyond Victimhood: Agency and Identity in the Theatre of Roy Williams,' in Godiwala (ed.), *Alternatives Within the Mainstream*, 2006.

Bartels, Emily C., *Spectacles of Strangeness: Imperialism, Alienation and Marlowe*, Philadelphia, PA, University of Pennsylvania, 1993.

Barthelemy, Anthony G., *Black Face, Maligned Race: The Representation of Blacks in English Drama from Shakespeare to Southerne*, Baton Rouge, LA, and London, Louisiana State UP, 1987.

Bate, Jonathan (ed.), Introduction to *Titus Andronicus*, London, Routledge, 1995.

Bhattacharya, Nandini, *Slavery, Colonialism and Connoisseurship: Gender and Eighteenth-Century Literary Transnationalism*, Aldershot, Hants, Ashgate, 2006.

Beaton, Norman, *Beaton but Unbowed: An Autobiography*, London, Methuen, 1986.

Beck, Brandon H., *From the Rising of the Sun: English Images of the Ottoman Empire to 1715*, New York, Peter Lang, 1987.

Bevis, Richard, *The Laughing Tradition: Stage Comedy in Garrick's Day*, London, George Prior Publishers, 1980.

Bhabha, Homi K., *The Location of Culture*, London, Routledge, 1994.

Bhabha, Homi K., 'Re-inventing Britain', *British Studies Now*, no. 9, April 1997.

Bharucha, Rustom, 'A Collision of Cultures: Some Western Interpretations of the Indian Theatre', *Asian Theatre Journal*, vol. 1, no. 1, Spring 1984.

Bharucha, Rustom, *Theatre and the World: Performance and the Politics of Culture*, London, Routledge, 1993.

Bharucha, Rustom, 'Under the Sign of the Onion: Intracultural Negotiations in Theatre', *New Theatre Quarterly*, vol. XII, no. 46, May 1996.

Bharucha, Rustom 'Somebody's Other: Disorientations in the Cultural Politics of Our Time', in Pavis (ed.), *The Intercultural Performance Reader*, 1996.

Bhattacharya, Nandini, 'Ethnopolitical Dynamics and the Language of Gendering in Dryden's *Aureng-Zebe*', *Cultural Critique*, no. 25, Autumn 1993.

Birchwood, Matthew, *Staging Islam in England: Drama and Culture, 1640–1685* (*Studies in Renaissance Literature*, vol. 21), Cambridge, D. S. Brewer, 2007.

Bolaffi, Guido, et al. (eds), *Dictionary of Race, Ethnicity and Culture*, London, Sage Publications, 2003.

Boon, Richard, and Plastow, Jane, *Theatre Matters: Performance and Culture on the World Stage*, Cambridge, Cambridge UP, 1998.

Booth, Michael, *Prefaces to English Nineteenth-Century Theatre*, Manchester, Manchester UP, 1980.

Borome, Joseph A., 'Some Additional Light on Frederick Douglass', *The Journal of Negro History*, vol. 38, no. 2, April 1953.

Bourne, Stephen, *Black in the British Frame: The Black Experience in British Film and Television*, London, Continuum, 2001 (updated).

Bovilsky, Lara, *Barbarous Play: Race on the English Renaissance Stage*, Minneapolis, MN, University of Minnesota Press, 2008.

Boyle, Sheila Tully, and Bunie, Andrew, *Paul Robeson: The Years of Promise and Achievement*, Amherst, MA, University of Massachusetts Press, 2001.

Bradby, David, et al. (eds), *Performance and Politics in Popular Drama: Aspects of Popular Entertainment in Theatre, Film and Television 1800–1976*, Cambridge, Cambridge UP, 1980.

Bragg, Melvyn, *The Adventure of English: The Biography of a Language*, London, Sceptre, 2004.

Brah, A. K., *Cartographies of Diaspora: Contesting Identities*, London, Routledge, 1996.

Braithwaite, Lloyd, *Colonial West Indian Students in Britain*, Kingston, Jamaica, University of the West Indies Press, 2001.

Bratton, J. S., 'English Ethiopians: British Audiences and Black-face Acts, 1835–1865', *Yearbook of English Studies*, 1981.

Bratton, J. S., *New Readings in Theatre History*, Cambridge, Cambridge UP, 2003.

Bratton, J. S., 'The Music Hall', in Powell (ed.), *Cambridge Companion to Victorian and Edwardian Theatre*, 2004.

Bratton, J. S. (ed.), *Music Performance and Style*, Milton Keynes, Open UP, 1986.

Bratton, J. S., et al. (eds), *Acts of Supremacy: British Empire and the Stage, 1790–1930*, Manchester, Manchester UP, 1991.

Brewster, Yvonne, 'Drawing the Black and White Line: Defining Black Women's Theatre', an interview with Lizbeth Goodman, *New Theatre Quarterly*, vol. 7, no. 28, November 1991.

Brewster, Yvonne, *The Undertaker's Daughter: The Colourful Life of a Theatre Director*, London, Black Amber Books, 2004.

Brewster, Yvonne, 'Talawa Theatre Company 1985–2002', in Davis and Fuchs (eds), *Staging New Britain*, 2006.

Brinda, *Maharani: The Story of an Indian Princess*, New York, Henry Holt, 1953.

Brooks, Daphne A., *Bodies in Dissent: Spectacular Performances of Race and Freedom, 1850–1910*, Durham, NC, and London, Duke UP, 2006.

Brown, Ian, 'The Road through Woodstock: Counter-Thatcherite Strategies in ACGB's Drama Development between 1984–1994', *Contemporary Theatre Review*, vol. 17, no. 2, 2007.

Brown, Ian, and Brannen, Rob, 'When Theatre Was for All: The Cork Report after Ten Years', *New Theatre Quarterly*, vol. 12, no. 48, November 1996.

Brown, Ian, Brannen, Rob, and Brown, Douglas, 'The Arts Council Touring Franchise and English Political Theatre after 1986', *New Theatre Quarterly*, vol. 16, no. 4, November 2000.

Buhle, Paul, *C. L. R. James: The Artist as Revolutionary*, London, Verso, 1988.

Butler, Martin, *Theatre and Crisis 1632–1642*, Cambridge, Cambridge UP, 1984.

Byerman, Keith, 'Creating the Black Hero: Ira Aldridge's *The Black Doctor*', in Lindfors (ed.), *Ira Aldridge: The African Roscius*, 2007.

Callaghan, Dympna, *Shakespeare Without Women: Representing Gender and Race on the Renaissance Stage*, London and New York, Routledge, 2000.

Cameron, Derrick, ' "Better a Bad Night in Toxteth": Black British Popular Theatre', in Merkin (ed), *Popular Theatres?*, 1996.

Cameron, Derrick, 'Tradaptation: Cultural Exchange and Black British Theatre', in Upton (ed.), *Moving Target*, 2000.

Campbell, Patrick (ed.), *Analyzing Performance: A Critical Reader*, Manchester, Manchester UP, 1996.

Canfield, Douglas, and Payne, Deborah (eds), *Cultural Readings of Restoration and Eighteenth Century English Theater*, Athens, GA, University of Georgia Press, 1995.

Carey, Brycchan, *British Abolitionism and the Rhetoric of Sensibility: Writing, Sentiment, and Slavery, 1760–1807*, Basingstoke, Hants, Palgrave Macmillan, 2005.

Carey, Brycchan, Ellis, Markman, and Salih, Sara (eds), *Discourses of Slavery and Abolition: Britain and its Colonies, 1760–1838*, Basingstoke, Hants, Palgrave Macmillan, 2004.

Carlisle, Carol Jones, *Shakespeare from the Greenroom: Actors' Criticisms of Four Major Tragedies*, Chapel Hill, NC, North Carolina Press, 1969.

Carlson, Julie A., 'New Lows in Eighteenth-Century Theater: The Rise of Mungo', *European Romantic Review*, vol. 18, no. 2, April 2007.

Carlson, Julie A., 'Race and Profit in English Theatre', in Moody and O'Quinn (eds), *Cambridge Companion to British Theatre, 1730–1830*, 2007.

Carlson, Susan, 'Collaboration, Identity, and Cultural Difference: Karim Alrawi's Theatre of Engagement', *Theatre Journal*, vol. 45, no. 2, May 1993.

Carpenter, Sandra, 'Black and British Temba Theatre Forges the Mainstream; an interview with Alby James', *TDR*, vol. 34, no. 1, Spring, 1990.

Case, Sue-Ellen, 'Eurocolonial Reception of Sanskrit Poets', in Case and Reinelt (eds), *The Performance of Power*, 1991.

Case, Sue-Ellen, and Reinelt, Janelle (eds), *The Performance of Power: Theatrical Discourse and Politics,* Iowa City, IA, University of Iowa Press, 1991.

Chambers, Colin, *The Story of Unity Theatre*, London, Lawrence and Wishart, 1989.

Chambers, Colin, '"Ours Will Be a Dynamic Contribution": the Struggle by Diasporic Artists for a Voice in British Theatre in the 1930s and 1940s', *Key Words, A Journal of Cultural Materialism*, no. 7, 2009.

Chambers, Colin, 'Images on Stage: A Historical Survey of South Asians in British Theatre before 1975', in Graham Ley and Sarah Dadswell (eds), *Critical Essays on British South Asian Theatre*, University of Exeter Press (forthcoming).

Chandau, Amarjit, *Indians in Britain*, London, Oriental UP, 1986.

Chatterjee, Amal, *Representations of India, 1740–1840: the Creation of India in the Colonial Imagination*, Basingstoke, Hants, Macmillan, 1998.

Chew, Samuel Claggett, *The Crescent and the Rose: Islam and England during the Renaissance,* New York, Oxford UP, 1937.

Childs, Peter, and Storry, Mike, *Encyclopedia of Contemporary British Culture*, London, Routledge, 1999.

Choudhury, Mita S., 'Imperial Licenses, Borderless Topographies, and the Eighteenth-Century British Theatre', in Michal Kobialka (ed.), *Of Borders and Thresholds: Theatre History, Practice and Theory*, 1999.

Choudhury, Mita S., *Interculturalism and Resistance in the London Theatre, 1600–1800: Identity, Performance, Empire*, London, Associated UP, 2000.

Clarence, R., *'The Stage' Cyclopaedia*, London, The Stage, 1909.

Clark, Jon, et al., *Culture and Crisis in Britain in the Thirties*, London, Lawrence and Wishart, 1979.

Clayton, Martin, and Zon, Bennett (eds), *Music and Orientalism in the British Empire, 1780s–1940s: Portrayal of the East*, Aldershot, Hants, Ashgate, 2007.

Cochrane, Claire, '"A Local Habitation and a Name": the Development of Black and Asian Theatre in Birmingham since the 1970s', in Godiwala (ed.), *Alternatives within the Mainstream*, 2006.

Cockrell, Dale, *Demons of Disorder: Early Blackface Minstrels and Their World,* Cambridge, Cambridge UP, 1997.

Coomaraswamy, Ananda K., 'Notes on Indian Dramatic Technique', *The Mask*, vol. 6, 1913.

Coombes, Annie E., *Reinventing Africa, Museums, Material Culture and Popular Imagination in Late Victorian and Edwardian England*, New Haven, CT, and London, Yale UP, 1994.

Corballis, Richard, and Viola, André (eds), *Postcolonial Knitting: The Art of Jacqueline Bardolph*, Nice, France, CRÉLA and Massey, New Zealand, Massey University, 2000.

Costello, Ray, *Black Liverpool: The Early Years of Britain's Oldest Black Community 1730–1918*, Liverpool, Picton Press, 2001.

Courtney, Krystyna Kujawińska, 'Ira Aldridge, Shakespeare, and Color-Consciousness Performances in Nineteenth-Century Europe', in Thompson (ed.), *Colorblind Shakespeare*, 2006.

Courtney, Krystyna Kujawińska, and Łukowska, Maria (eds), *Ira Aldridge, 1807–1867: The Great Shakespearean Tragedian on the Bicentennial Anniversary of His Birth*, Frankfurt-am-Main, Peter Lang, 2009.

Cowhig, Ruth, 'Blacks in English Renaissance Drama and the Role of Shakespeare's *Othello*', in Dabydeen (ed.), *The Black Presence in English Literature*, 1985.

Cox, Jeffrey N. (ed.), *Slavery, Abolition and Emancipation: Writings in the British Romantic Period, vol. 5: Drama*, London, Pickering and Chatto, 1999.

Craig, Sandy (ed.), *Dreams and Deconstructions: Alternative Theatre in Britain*, Oxford, Amber Lane Press, 1980.

Croft, Susan, 'Black Women Playwrights in Britain', in Griffiths and Llewellyn-Jones (eds), *British and Irish Women Dramatists Since 1958*, 1993.

Croft, Susan, *She Also Wrote Plays: An International Reference Guide to Women Playwrights from the 11th to the 21st Century*, London, Faber and Faber, 2001.

Croft, Susan, with Bourne, Stephen, and Terracciano, Alda, *Black and Asian Performance at the Theatre Museum: A Users' Guide*, Theatre Museum, London, 2003.

Crow, Brian, 'Issues in Multicultural Theatre: Birmingham Rep and Its Audiences', in Davis and Fuchs (eds), *Staging New Britain*, 2006.

Dabydeen, David (ed.), *The Black Presence in English Literature*, Manchester, Manchester UP, 1985.

Dabydeen, David, and Wilson-Tagoe, Nana, with additional material by Floraine Eastelow, *A Reader's Guide to Westindian and Black Literature*, London, Hansib Publications, 1997.

Dadswell, Sarah, 'Jugglers, Fakirs, and *Jaduwallahs*: Indian Magicians and the British Stage', *New Theatre Quarterly*, no. 89, vol. 23, part 1, February 2007.

Dahl, Mary Karen, 'Postcolonial British Theatre: Black Voices at the Center', in J. Ellen Gainor (ed.), *Imperialism and Theatre*, 1995.

D'Amico, Jack, *The Moor in English Renaissance Drama*, Tampa, FL, University of South Florida Press, 1991.

Davis, Geoffrey V., and Fuchs, Anne (eds), *Staging New Britain: Aspects of Black and South Asian British Theatre Practice*, Brussels, PIE-Peter Lang, 2006.

De la Campa, Román, et al. (eds), *Late Imperial Culture*, London, Verso, 1995.

Delgado, Maria M., and Heritage, Paul (eds), *In Contact with the Gods: Directors Talk Theatre*, Manchester, Manchester UP, 1996.

Delgado, Maria M., and Svich, Caridad (eds), *Theatre in Crisis?: Performance Manifestos for a New Century*, Manchester, Manchester UP, 2002.

Dening, Greg, *Mr Bligh's Bad Language: Passion, Power and Theatre on The Bounty*, Cambridge, Cambridge UP, 1992.

Dennis, Ferdinand, and Khan, Naseem (eds), *Voices of the Crossing: The Impact of Britain on Writers from Asia, the Caribbean and Africa*, London, Serpent's Tail, 2000.

Devine, Harriet, *Looking Back: Playwrights at the Royal Court*, London, Faber and Faber, 2006.

Dharwadker, Aparna, 'Diaspora, Nation, and the Failure of Home: Two Contemporary Indian Plays', *Theatre Journal*, vol. 50, no. 1, March 1998.

Dhupa, Venu, 'Diversity - Is It Colourless?', in Maitland (ed.), *Navigating Difference*, 2006.

Dimmock, Matthew, *New Turkes: Dramatizing Islam and the Ottomans in Early Modern England*, Aldershot, Hants, and Burlington VT, Ashgate, 2005.

Dolan, Frances, 'Taking the Pencil out of God's Hand', *PMLA*, no. 108, 1993.

Donnell, Alison (ed.), *Companion to Contemporary Black British Culture*, London, Routledge, 2002.

Drakakis, John, *Alternative Shakespeares*, London, Methuen, 1985.

Drew-Bear, Annette, *Painted Faces on the Renaissance Stage: The Moral Significance of Face-Painting Conventions*, London and Toronto, Associated UPs, 1994.

Duberman, Martin Bauml, *Paul Robeson: A Biography*, New York, Ballantine Books, 1989.

Duff, Charles, *The Lost Summer: The Heyday of the West End Theatre*, London, Nick Hern Books, 1995.

Duffield, Ian, 'Dusé Mohamed Ali and the Development of Pan-Africanism, 1866–1945', unpublished PhD dissertation, Edinburgh University, October 1971.

Duffield, Ian, 'Dusé Mohamed Ali: His Purpose and His Public', in Niven (ed.), *The Commonwealth Writer Overseas*, 1976.

Duffield, Ian, 'Dusé Mohamed Ali, Afro-Asian Solidarity and Pan-Africanism in Early Twentieth Century London,' in Gundara, and Duffield (eds), *Essays on the History of Blacks in Britain from Roman Times to the Mid-twentieth Century*, 1992.

Edgar, David, 'Saying the Unsayable', in *At the Turning of the Tide*, London, Commission for Racial Equality, 2006.

Edwards, Paul, *The Early African Presence in the British Isles*, Edinburgh, Centre of African Studies, 1990.

Edwards, Paul, and Dabydeen, David (eds), *Black Writers in Britain, 1760–1890*, Edinburgh, Edinburgh UP, 1991.

Edwards, Paul, and Walvin, James, *Black Personalities in the Era of the Slave Trade*, Basingstoke, Hants, Macmillan, 1983.

Elias, Mohammed, *Aubrey Menen* (*Kerala Writers in English*, vol. 7), Madras, Macmillan India, 1985.

Ernest, John, 'The Reconstruction of Whiteness: William Wells Brown's *The Escape; or, A Leap for Freedom*', *PMLA*, no. 113, 1998.

Evans, Nicholas M., 'Ira Aldridge: Shakespeare and Minstrelsy', in Lindfors (ed.), *Ira Aldridge: The African Roscius*, 2007.

Ewen, Elizabeth, and Ewen, Stuart, *Typecasting: On the Arts and Sciences of Human Inequality*, New York, Seven Stories Press, 2006.

Fanon, Frantz, *The Wretched of the Earth*, Harmondsworth, Middx, Penguin, 1967.

Fanon, Frantz, *Black Skin, White Masks*, New York, Grove Press, 1967.

Felsenstein, Frank (ed.), *English Trader, Indian Maid: Representing Gender, Race and Slavery in the New World – An* Inkle and Yarico *Reader*, Baltimore, MD, Johns Hopkins UP, 1999.

Ferguson, Margaret W., 'Juggling the Categories of Race, Class, and Gender: Aphra Behn's *Oroonoko*', in Hendricks and Parker (eds), *Women, 'Race' and Writing in Early Modern England*, 1994.

Ferguson, Moira, *Subject to Others: British Women Writers and Colonial Slavery, 1670–1834*, New York, Routledge, 1992.

Ferguson, Russell, et al., *Out There: Marginalization and Contemporary Cultures*, New York, New Museum of Contemporary Art, 1990.

Figueira, Dorothy Matilda, *Translating the Orient: The Reception of Śākuntala in Nineteenth-Century Europe*, New York, State University of New York Press, 1991.

Fisch, Audrey A., *American Slaves in Victorian England: Abolitionist Politics in Popular Literature and Culture*, New York, Cambridge University Press, 2000.

Fisch, Audrey A., 'Harriet Beecher Stowe in England', in Weinstein (ed.), *Cambridge Companion to Harriet Beecher Stowe*, 2004.

Fischer-Lichte, Erika, et al. (eds), *The Dramatic Touch of Difference: Theatre, Own and Foreign*, Tubingen, Gunter, 1990.

Fisher, Michael H., *Counterflows to Colonialism: Indian Travellers and Settlers in Britain 1600–1857*, Delhi, Permanent Black, 2004.

Fisher, Michael H., et al., *A South-Asian History of Britain: Four Centuries of Peoples from the Indian Sub-continent*, Oxford, Greenwood World, 2007.

Fisk, Deborah Payne (ed.), *Cambridge Companion to English Restoration Theatre*, Cambridge, Cambridge UP, 2000.

Foakes, R. A., *Illustrations of the English Stage, 1580–1642*, Stanford, CA, Stanford UP, 1985.

Foner, Philip S. (ed.), *Paul Robeson Speaks: Writings, Speeches, Interviews 1918–74*, London, Quartet Books, 1978.

Frost, Anthony, 'Drama in the Age of Kalyug: Behzti and Sikh Self-censorship', in Godiwala (ed.), *Alternatives within the Mainstream*, 2006,.

Fryer, Peter, *Black people in the British Empire: An Introduction*, London, Pluto Press, 1988.

Fryer, Peter, *Staying Power: The History of Black People in Britain*, London, Pluto Press, 1989 (4th edition).

Fuchs, Anne, 'Un exemple de théâtre interculturel: la Tamasha Theatre Company', in Corballis and Viola (eds), *Postcolonial Knitting*, 2000.

Fuchs, Anne, 'Looking at New British Heritage: Tamasha Theatre Company', in Davis and Fuchs (eds), *Staging New Britain*, 2006.

Fuchs, Barbara, 'Conquering Islands: Contextualising *The Tempest*', *Shakespeare Quarterly*, vol. 48, no. 1, Spring 1997.

Gainor, J. Ellen (ed.), *Imperialism and Theatre: Essays on World Theatre, Drama and Performance 1795–1995*, London and New York, Routledge, 1995.

Gale, Maggie, and Stokes, John (eds), *Cambridge Companion to the Actress*, Cambridge, Cambridge UP, 2007.

Garigue, Philip, 'The West African Students' Union: A Study in Culture Contact,' *Africa: Journal of the International African Institute*, vol. 23, no. 1, January 1953.

Gates, Henry Louis Jr, *Figures in Black: Words, Signs, and the 'Racial' Self*, Oxford, Oxford UP, 1987.

Gates, Henry Louis Jr, *The Signifying Monkey: A Theory of African-American Literary Criticism*, Oxford, Oxford UP, 1988.

George, Kadija (ed.), *Six Plays by Black and Asian Women Writers*, London, Aurora Metro Press, 1993, with essays by George, Valerie Small, Sita Ramamurthy, Bernadine Evaristo, and Stella Oni.

Gerzina, Gretchen, *Black England: Life before Emancipation*, London, Allison and Busby, 1999.

Gerzina, Gretchen (ed.), *Black Victorians: Black Victoriana*, New Brunswick, NJ, Rutgers UP, 2003.

Gilbert, Helen, and Tompkins, Joanne, *Post-Colonial Drama: Theory, Practice, Politics*, London, Routledge, 1996.

Gilbert, Pamela K. (ed.), *Imagined Londons*, Albany, State University of New York Press, 2002.

Gilliat-Ray, Sophie, *Muslims in Britain: An Introduction*, Cambridge, Cambridge UP, 2010.

Gilroy, Paul, *The Black Atlantic: Modernity and Double Consciousness*, Cambridge, MA, Harvard UP, 1993.

Gilroy, Paul, *There Ain't No Black in the Union Jack: The Cultural Politics of Race and Nation*, London, Routledge, 2002.

Goddard, Lynette, *Staging Black Feminisms*, Basingstoke, Hants, Palgrave Macmillan, 2007.

Godiwala, Dimple, 'The Search for Identity and the Claim for an Ethnicity of Englishness…' and 'Kali: Providing a Forum for British–Asian Women Playwrights' in Godiwala (ed.), *Alternatives within the Mainstream*, 2006.

Godiwala, Dimple (ed.), *Alternatives within the Mainstream: British Black and Asian Theatres*, Newcastle upon Tyne, Cambridge Scholars Press, 2006.

Goodman, Lizbeth, *Contemporary Feminist Theatres: To Each Her Own*, London, Routledge, 1993.

Gottlieb, Vera, and Chambers, Colin (eds), *Theatre in a Cool Climate*, Oxford, Amber Lane Press, 1999.

Grant, Cy, *Blackness and the Dreaming Soul*, Edinburgh, Shoving Leopard, 2007.

Graziano, John, 'In Dahomey', *Black Theatre: USA*, New York, Free Press, 1996.

Green, Jeffrey P., *Edmund Thornton Jenkins: The Life and Times of an American Black Composer, 1894–1926*, Westport Ct, Greenwood Press, 1982.

Green, Jeffrey, with Lockhart, Randall, ' "A Brown Alien in a White City" – Black Students in London, 1917–1920', in Lotz and Pegg (eds), *Under the Imperial Carpet*, 1986.

Green, Jeffrey, *Black Edwardians: Black People in Britain 1901–1914*, London, Frank Cass, 1998.

Greene, John, *Theatre in Dublin, 1745–1820: A Calendar of Performances*, Bethlehem, PA, Lehigh UP (forthcoming).

Gregory, Brendan, 'Staging British India', in Bratton et al. (eds), *Acts of Supremacy* 1991.

Griffin, Gabriele, *Contemporary Black and Asian Women Playwrights in Britain*, Cambridge, Cambridge UP, 2003.

Griffiths, Trevor R., and Llewellyn-Jones, Margaret (eds), *British and Irish Women Dramatists since 1958: A Critical Handbook*, Buckingham, Open University, 1993.

Gundara, Jagdish, and Duffield, Ian (eds), *Essays on the History of Blacks in Britain from Roman Times to the Mid-twentieth Century*, Aldershot, Hants, Avebury, 1992.

Hall, Catherine, *Civilising Subjects: Metropole and Colony in the English Imagination, 1830–1867*, Oxford, Polity, 2002.

Hall, Catherine (ed.), *Cultures of Empire: Colonisers in Britain and the Empire in the Nineteenth and Twentieth Centuries*, Manchester, Manchester UP, 2000.

Hall, Kim F., 'Sexual Politics and Cultural Identity in *The Masque of Blackness*', in Case and Reinelt, (eds), *The Performance of Power*, 1991.

Hall, Kim F., *Things of Darkness: Economies of Race and Gender in Early Modern England*, Ithaca, NY, and London, Cornell UP, 1995.

Hall, Stuart (ed.), *Representation: Cultural Representations and Signifying Practices*, London, Sage, in association with the Open University, 1997.

Harris, Roxy, and White, Sarah (eds), *Changing Britannia – Life Experience with Britain*, London, New Beacon Books/George Padmore Institute, 1999.

Harrison, G. B., *Shakespeare at Work*, London, Routledge, 1933.

Harrison, Paul Carter, et al. (eds), *Black Theatre: Ritual Performance in the African Diaspora*, Philadelphia, PA, Temple UP, 2002.

Hartman, Saidiya V., *Scenes of Subjection: Terror, Slavery, and Self-Making in Nineteenth Century America*, New York and Oxford, Oxford UP, 1997.

Harvie, Jen, *Staging the UK*, Manchester, Manchester UP, 2005.

Harwood, Kate (ed.), *First Run: New Plays by New Writers*, London, Nick Hern Books, 1989.

Hattersley, Roy, *Borrowed Time: The Story of Britain Between the Wars*, London, Abacus, 2007.

Heath, Gordon, *Deep are the Roots: Memoirs of a Black Expatriate*, Amherst, MA., University of Massachusetts Press, 1992.

Hedley, Philip, 'A Theatre Director's Journey to the Obvious', in Tunde Ikoli, *Scrape Off the Black*, London, Oberon Books, 1998.

Hendricks, Margo, and Parker, Patricia (eds), *Women, 'Race' and Writing in Early Modern England*, London, Routledge, 1994.

Herbert, Ian (ed.), *Theatre Record* (formerly *London Theatre Record*), Middx and London, I. Herbert, annually from 1981.

Highfill, Philip H., et al. (eds), *A Biographical Dictionary of Actors, Actresses, Musicians, Dancers, Managers and Other Stage Personnel in London, 1660–1800*, 16 vols., Carbondale, IL, South Illinois Press, 1973-93.

Hill, Errol, 'S. Morgan Smith: Successor to Ira Aldridge', *Black American Literature Forum*, vol. 16, no. 4, 1982.

Hill, Errol, *Shakespeare in sable: a history of black Shakespearean actors*, Amherst, University of Michigan Press, 1984.

Hill, Errol G., and Hatch, James V., *A History of African American Theatre*, Cambridge, Cambridge UP, 2003.

Hingorani, Dominic, 'Tara Arts and Tamasha: Producing Asian Performance – Two Approaches', in Godiwala (ed.), *Alternatives within the Mainstream*, 2006.

Hingorani, Dominic, *British Asian Theatre: Dramaturgy, Process and Performance*, Basingstoke, Hants, Palgrave Macmillan, 2010.

Hodges, Graham Russell Gao, *Anna May Wong: From Laundryman's Daughter to Hollywood Legend*, New York and Basingstoke, Hants, Palgrave Macmillan, 2004.

Hoenselaars, A. J., *Images of Englishmen and Foreigners in the Drama of Shakespeare and His Contemporaries*, London and Toronto, Associated UPs, 1992.

Hogsbjerg, Christian (Introduction), *C. L. R. James, Toussaint Louverture; The story of the Only Successful Slave Revolt in History*, Durham, NC, Duke UP (forthcoming).

Holder, Heidi J., 'Other Londoners: Race and Class in Plays of Nineteenth-Century London Life', in Gilbert (ed.), *Imagined Londons*, 2002.

Holder, Heidi J., 'The East End Theatre', in Powell (ed.), *Cambridge Companion to Victorian and Edwardian Theatre*, 2004.

Holdsworth, Nadine, and Luckhurst, Mary (eds), *A Concise Companion to Contemporary British and Irish Drama*, Oxford, Blackwell, 2008.

Hooker, J. R., 'The Pan-African Conference of 1900', *Transition* 46, 1974.

Hoskins, Robert, with Southern, Eileen, 'Obi: or, Three-Finger'd Jack', critical introduction, *Music for London Entertainment*. Series D, vol. 4, London, Stainer and Bell, 1996.

Howe, Elizabeth, *The First English Actresses: Women and Drama 1660–1700*, Cambridge, Cambridge UP, 1992.

Hoyles, Martin, *Ira Aldridge: Celebrated 19th Century Actor*, London and Herts, Hansib, 2008.

Huggins, Tyrone, *The Eclipse Theatre Story*, [no publisher or date of publication; Eclipse named on cover; it appeared in 2006].

Hughes, Derek, 'Restoration and Settlement: 1660–1688', in Fisk (ed.), *Cambridge Companion to English Restoration Theatre*, 2000.

Hughes, Derek, 'Race, Gender and Scholarly Practice: Aphra Behn's *Oroonoko*', *Essays in Criticism*, vol. 52, no. 1, January 2002.

Hulme, Peter, *Colonial Encounters: Europe and the Native Caribbean 1492–1797*, London, Routledge, 1992.

Hutchens, John K., 'Paul Robeson', *Theatre Arts*, October 1944.

Hutner, Heidi, *Colonial Women: Race and Culture in Stuart Drama*, Oxford, Oxford UP, 2001.

Hutton, Laurence, 'The Negro on Stage', *Harper's New Monthly Magazine*, June 1889.

Inden, Ronald B., *Imagining India*, London, Hurst and Co., 2000.

Innes, C. L., *A History of Black and Asian Writing in Britain, 1700–2000*, Cambridge, Cambridge UP, 2002.

Itzin, Catherine, *Stages in the Revolution: Political Theatre in Britain since 1968*, London, Eyre Methuen, 1980.

Itzin, Catherine, et al. (eds), *British Alternative Theatre Directory*, 1979–1993/4, Eastbourne, E. Sussex, John Offord, 1979–1994.

Iwanisziw, Susan B. (ed.), *Troping Oroonoko from Behn to Bandele*, Aldershot, Hants, Ashgate, 2004.

Iwanisziw, Susan B. (ed.), *Oroonoko: Adaptations and Offshoots*, Aldershot, Hants, Ashgate, 2006.

Jackson, John, *The History of the Scottish Stage*, Edinburgh, Peter Hill, 1793.

James, Winston, and Harris, Clive (eds), *Inside Babylon: The Caribbean Diaspora in Britain*, London, Verso, 1993.

Jarrett-Macauley, Delia, *The Life of Una Marson: 1905–65*, Manchester, Manchester UP, 1998.

Jones, Colin, and Wahrman, Dror (eds), *The Age of Cultural Revolutions: Britain and France, 1750–1820*, Berkeley, CA, and London, University of California Press, 2002.

Jones, Eldred D., *Othello's Countrymen: The African in English Renaissance Drama*, London, Oxford UP, 1965.

Joseph, May, 'Performing in the Postcolony: The Plays of Mustapha Matura', in de la Campa et al. (eds), *Late Imperial Culture*, 1995.

Joseph, May, 'Bodies outside the State: Black British Women Playwrights and the Limits of Citizenship', in Phelan and Lane (eds), *The Ends of Performance*, 1998.

Karim-Cooper, Farah, *Cosmetics in Shakespearean and Renaissance Drama*, Edinburgh, Edinburgh UP, 2006.

Kasule, Samuel, 'Aspects of Madness and Theatricality in Kwame Kwei-Armah's Drama', in Godiwala (ed.), *Alternatives within the Mainstream*, 2006.

Kaul, Suvir, 'Reading Literary Symptoms: Colonial Pathologies and the Oroonoko fictions of Behn, Southerne and Hawkesworth', *Eighteenth-Century Life*, vol. 18, no. 3, November 1994.

Kaur, Raminder, and Terracciano, Alda, 'South Asian/BrAsian Performing Arts', in Ali et al. (eds), *A Postcolonial People: South Asians in Britain*, 2006.

Kawash, Samira, *Dislocating the Color Line: Identity, Hybridity, and Singularity in African-American Narrative*, Stanford, CA, Stanford UP, 1997.

Kershaw, Baz (ed.), *The Cambridge History of British Theatre, vol. 3: Since 1895*, Cambridge, Cambridge UP, 2004.

Khan, Naseem, 'The Public-going Theatre: Community and "Ethnic" Theatre', in Craig (ed.), *Dreams and Deconstructions*, 1980.

Khan, Naseem, 'Choices for Black Arts in Britain over Thirty Years', in Bailey et al. (eds), *Shades of Black*, 2005.

Kidson, Frank, 'Some Guesses about Yankee Doodle', *The Musical Quarterly*, vol. 3, no. 1, January 1917.

Killingray, David (ed.), *Africans in Britain*, London, Frank Cass, 1994.

King, Barnaby, 'Landscapes of Fact and Fiction: Asian Theatre Arts in Britain', *New Theatre Quarterly*, vol. 16, part 1, no. 61, Feb. 2000.

King, Barnaby, 'The Afro-Caribbean Identity and the English Stage', *New Theatre Quarterly*, vol. 16, part 2, no. 62, May 2000.

King, Bruce, *The Internationalization of English Literature* (*The Oxford Literary History, vol. 13: 1948–2000*), Oxford, Oxford UP, 2004.

Kishi, Tetsuo, Pringle, Roger, and Wells, Stanley (eds), *Shakespeare and Cultural Traditions*, Newark, DE, University of Delaware Press, 1994 .

Klepac, Richard L., 'Mr Mathews At Home', London, Society for Theatre Research, 1979.

Kobialka, Michal (ed), *Of Borders and Thresholds: Theatre History, Practice and Theory*, Minneapolis, MN, and London, University of Minnesota Press, 1999.

Kottasz, Rita, 'Resistance to Identity Change in UK Theatres', in Maitland (ed.), *Navigating Difference*, 2006.

Kundu, Kalyan, et al. (eds), *Imagining Tagore: Rabindranath and the British Press (1912–1941)*, Calcutta, Sahitya Samsad, 2000.

Kureishi, Hanif, Introduction to *Outskirts and Other Plays*, London, Faber and Faber, 1992.

Kwei-Armah, Kwame, interview in Davis and Fuchs (ed.), *Staging New Britain*, 2006.

Kwei-Armah, Kwame, '"Know Whence You Came": Dramatic Art and Black British Identity', *New Theatre Quarterly*, vol. 23, no. 3, August 2007.

Lahiri, Shompa, *Indians in Britain: Anglo-Indian Encounters, Race and Identity, 1880–1930*, London, Frank Cass, 2000.

Lahiri, Shompa, 'From Empire to Decolonisation, 1901–1947', in Fisher (ed.), *A South-Asian History of Britain*, 2007.

Lal, Ananda (translator and Introduction by), *Rabindranath Tagore: Three Plays*, Oxford, Oxford UP, 2001.

Lal, Ananda (ed.), *Oxford Companion to Indian Theatre*, Oxford and New Delhi, Oxford UP, 2004.

Landon-Smith, Kristine, 'I'm an Artist, Not an Audience Developer', in Maitland (ed.), *Navigating Difference*, 2006.

Lawrence, W.J., 'First Real Negro on the Stage', *Notes and Queries*, vol. viii, July-December 1889.

Lennep, William van, et al. (eds), *The London Stage 1660–1800* (5 vols. plus index), Carbondale, IL, 1960–1968.

Lewis, Barbara, 'An American Circus: The Lynch Victim as Clown', in Robb (ed.), *Clowns, Fools and Picaros*, 2007.

Ley, Graham, 'Theatre of Migration and the Search for a Multicultural Aesthetic: Twenty Years of Tara Arts', *New Theatre Quarterly*, vol. 13, no. 52, November 1997.

Lhamon, W.T., *Raising Cain: Blackface Performance from Jim Crow to Hip Hop*. Cambridge, MA, Harvard UP, 1998.

Lichtenfels, Peter, and Hunter, Lynette, 'Seeing through the National and Global Stereotypes: British Theatre in Crisis?', in Delgado and Svich (eds), *Theatre in Crisis?*, 2002.

Lindfors, Bernth, 'The Signifying Flunkey: Ira Aldridge as Mungo', *The Literary Griot*, vol. 5, no. 2, Fall 1993.

Lindfors, Bernth, '"Nothing extenuate, nor set down aught in malice": New Biographical Information on Ira Aldridge', *African American Review*, vol. 28, no. 3, Fall 1994.

Lindfors, Bernth, '"Mislike me not for my complexion…": Ira Aldridge in Whiteface,' *African American Review*, vol. 33, no. 2, Summer 1999.

Lindfors, Bernth, 'Ira Aldridge's London Debut', *Theatre Notebook,* vol. 60, no. 1, 2006.

Lindfors, Bernth, 'Ira Aldridge at Covent Garden, April 1833', *Theatre Notebook*, vol. 61, no. 3, 2007.

Lindfors, Bernth, 'Ira Aldridge's Life in New York City', *Afro-Americans in New York Life and History*, January 2008.

Lindfors, Bernth, 'The Lives of Ira Aldridge', in Courtney and Łukowska (eds), *Ira Aldridge, 1807–1867*, 2009.

Lindfors, Bernth (ed.), *Africans on Stage: Studies in Ethnological Show Business*, Bloomington, IN, Indiana UP, 1999.

Lindfors, Bernth (ed), *Ira Aldridge: The African Roscius*, Rochester NY, University of Rochester Press, 2007.

Lindfors, Bernth, and Sander, Reinhard (eds), *Twentieth-Century Caribbean and Black African Writers,* in series *The Dictionary of Literary Biography,* vols. 117 (1992), 125 (1996), and 157 (1996), Detroit, MI, and London, Gale Research Inc.

Little, Arthur L., Jr, *Shakespeare Jungle Fever: National-Imperial Re-Visions of Race, Rape, and Sacrifice*, Stanford, CA, Stanford UP, 2000.

Little, Kenneth, *Negroes in Britain: A Study of Racial Relations in English Society*, London, Kegan Paul, 1948.

Lock, Gloria, *Caribbeans in Wandsworth*, London, Department of Technical Services, Wandsworth Borough Council, 1992.

Loftis, John, *The Politics of Drama in Augustan England*, Oxford, Oxford UP, 1963.

Logan, Rayford W., and Winston, Michael R. (eds), *Dictionary of American Negro Biography*, New York, W. W. Norton and Co., 1982.

Loomba, Ania, *Gender, Race, Renaissance Drama*, Delhi, Oxford UP, 1992.

Loomba, Ania, 'The Color of Patriarchy: Critical Difference, Cultural Difference, and Renaissance Drama', in Hendricks and Parker (eds), *Women, 'Race' and Writing in Early Modern England*, 1994.

Loomba, Ania, and Orkin, Martin (eds), *Post-Colonial Shakespeares*, London, Routledge, 1998.

Lorimer, Douglas A., *Colour, Class and the Victorians: English Attitudes to the Negro in the Mid-nineteenth Century*, Leicester, Leicester UP, 1978.

Lott, Eric, *Love and Theft: Blackface Minstrelsy and the American Working Class*, Oxford, Oxford UP, 1993.

Lotz, Rainer, 'Will Garland and his Negro Operetta Company', in Lotz and Pegg, *Under the Imperial Carpet*, 1986.

Lotz, Rainer, *Black People: Entertainers of African Descent in Germany and Europe*, Bonn, Birgit Lotz Verlag, 1997.

Lotz, Rainer, and Pegg, Ian (eds), *Under the Imperial Carpet: Essays in Black History 1780-1950*, Crawley, W. Sussex, Rabbit Press, 1986.

Lucas, Valerie Kaneko, '*Shameless* – Women, Sexuality and Violence in British-Asian Drama', in Godiwala (ed.), *Alternatives within the Mainstream*, 2006.

Luckhurst, Mary (ed.), *A Companion to Modern British and Irish Drama: 1880–2005*, Oxford, Blackwell, 2006.

Luckhurst, Mary, and Moody, Jane (eds), *Theatre and Celebrity in Britain 1660–2000*, Basingstoke, Hants, and London, Palgrave Macmillan, 2005.

MacDonald, Joyce Green, 'Acting Black: *Othello*, *Othello* Burlesques, and the Performance of Blackness', *Theatre Journal*, vol. 46, no. 2, May 1994.

MacDonald, Joyce Green, *Women and Race in Early Modern Texts*, Cambridge, Cambridge UP, 2002.

MacDonald, Joyce Green (ed.), *Race, Ethnicity, and Power in the Renaissance*, London, Associated UP, 1997.

Macdonald Roderick, J. (introductory essay), *The Keys: The Official Organ of the League of Coloured Peoples*, Millwood, NY, Kraus-Thomson Organization Ltd, 1976.

MacKenzie, John M., *Propaganda and Empire: The Manipulation of British Public Opinion, 1880–1960*, Manchester, Manchester UP, 1984.

MacKenzie, John M. (ed.), *Imperialism and Popular Culture*, Manchester, Manchester UP, 1986.

McMillan, Michael, and SuAndi, 'Rebaptizing the World in Our Own Terms: Black Theatre and Live Arts in Britain', in Paul Carter Harrison et al. (eds), *Black Theatre*, 2002. [Also in Davis and Fuchs (eds), *Staging New Britain*, 2006, under McMillan's name.]

Maidment, Brian, *Dusty Bo: A Cultural History of Dustmen, 1780–1870*, Manchester, Manchester UP, 2007.

Maitland, Heather (ed.), *Navigating Difference: Cultural Diversity and Audience Development*, London, Arts Council England, 2006.

Maquerlot, Jean-Pierre, and Willems, Michelle (eds), *Travel and Drama in Shakespeare's Time*, Cambridge, Cambridge UP, 1996.

Marshall, Herbert, and Stock, Mildred, *Ira Aldridge: The Negro Tragedian*, London, Rockliff, 1958.

Mason, James, *Before I Forget: An Autobiography*, London, Sphere Books, 1982.

Mason Vaughan, Virginia, *Othello: A Contextual History*, Cambridge, Cambridge UP, 1994.

Mason Vaughan, Virginia, *Performing Blackness on English Stages 1500–1800*, Cambridge, Cambridge UP, 2005.

Matar, Nabil, *Islam in Britain, 1558–1685*, Cambridge, Cambridge UP, 1998.

Matteo, Gino J., *Shakespeare's Othello; The Study and the Stage, 1604–1904*, Salzburg, Institut für englische Sprache und Literatur, Universität Salzburg, 1974.

Matthew, H. C. G., and Harrison, Brian (eds), *Oxford Dictionary of National Biography*, Oxford UP, 2004.

McClintock, Annie, *Imperial Leather: Race, Gender and Sexuality in the Colonial Context*, New York and London, Routledge, 1995.

McKenzie-Mavinga, Isha, and Perkins, Thelma, *In Search of Mr McKenzie*, London, Women's Press, 1991.

McKittrick, Katherine, and Woods, Clyde Adrian (eds), *Black Geographies and the Politics of Place*, Toronto, Between the Lines, and Cambridge, MA, South End Press, 2007.

Meer, Sarah, *Uncle Tom Mania: Slavery, and Transatlantic Culture in the 1850s*, Atlanta, GA, University of Georgia Press, 2005.

Mehta, Binita, *Widows, Pariahs, and Bayaderes: India as Spectacle*, Lewisburg, PA, Bucknell UP, 2002.

Menen, Aubrey, *The Space within the Heart*, London, Hamish Hamilton, 1970.

Merkin, Ros (ed.), *Popular Theatres?*, Liverpool, Liverpool John Moores UP, 1996.

Millington, Peter, 'Mystery History: The Origins of British Mummers' Plays', *American Morris Newsletter*, vol. 13, no. 3, November/December 1989.

Millington, Peter, 'A Black and White Issue?', *English Dance and Song*, vol. 67, no. 3, Autumn 2005.

Moody, Jane, *Illegitimate Theatre in London, 1770–1840*, Cambridge, Cambridge UP, 2000.

Moody, Jane, 'Dictating to the Empire: Performance and Geography in Eighteenth-century Britain', in Moody and O'Quinn, *Cambridge Companion to British Theatre, 1730–1830*, 2007.

Moody, Jane, and O'Quinn, Daniel (eds), *Cambridge Companion to British Theatre, 1730–1830*, Cambridge, Cambridge UP, 2007.

Mortimer, Owen, *Speak of Me as I Am: The Story of Ira Aldridge*, Wangaratta, Australia, 1995.

Mullaney, Steven, *The Place of the Stage: License, Play, and Power in Renaissance England*, Chicago, IL, University of Chicago Press, 1988.

Mullin, Donald, *Victorian Plays: A Record of Significant Productions on the London Stage, 1837–1901*, New York, Westport, CT, London, Greenwood Press, 1987.

Myers, Norma, *Reconstructing the Black Past: Blacks in Britain, 1780–1830*, London and Portland, OR, Frank Cass, 1996.

Nasta, Susheila, *Home Truths: Fictions about the South Asian Diaspora in Britain*, Basingstoke, Hants, Palgrave Macmillan, 2001.

Nathan, Hans, 'Negro Impersonation in Eighteenth Century England', *Notes*, Middleton, WI, USA Music Library, vol. 2, no. 4, 1945.

Newman, Judie, 'Staging Black Insurrection', in Weinstein (ed.), *Cambridge Companion to Harriet Beecher Stowe*, 2004.

Newman, Karen, *Fashioning Femininity and English Renaissance Drama*, Chicago, IL, and London, University of Chicago Press, 1991.

Newman, Richard (Introduction), *Henry Box Brown, Narrative of the Life of Henry Box Brown*, New York and Oxford, Oxford UP, 2002.

Newton, H. Chance, *Cues and Curtain Calls*, London, John Lane, 1927.

Nicholson, Watson, *The Struggle for a Free Stage in London*, London, Constable, 1906.

Nicoll, Allardyce, *A History of English Drama, 1660–1900* (6 vols), Cambridge, Cambridge UP, 1952–1965.

Nicoll, Allardyce, *English Drama, 1900–1930: The Beginnings of the Modern Period*, Cambridge, Cambridge UP, 1973.

Niven, Alistair (ed.), *The Commonwealth Writer Overseas: Themes of Exile and Expatriation*, Brussels, Librarie Marcel Didier, 1976.

Noble, Peter (ed.), *British Theatre*, London, British Yearbook, 1946.

Noble, Peter (ed.), *The Negro in Films*, London, Skelton Robinson, 1948.

Norris, William, 'New Light on the Career of S. Morgan Smith', *Black American Literature Forum*, vol. 18, no. 3, Autumn 1984.

Norris, William, 'Additional Light on S. Morgan Smith', *Black American Literature Forum*, vol. 20, no. 1/2, Spring-Summer, 1986.

Norwood, Janice, *The Britannia Theatre, Hoxton (1841–1899): The Creation and Consumption of Popular Culture in an East End Community*, unpublished PhD thesis, University of Leicester, 2006.

Novak, Maximillian E., and Rodes, David Stuart (eds), *Oroonoko* by Thomas Southerne, London, Edward Arnold, 1977.

Nussbaum, Felicity A., *The Limits of the Human: Fictions of Anomaly, Race, and Gender in the Long Eighteenth Century*, New York, Cambridge UP, 2003.

Nussbaum, Felicity A., 'The Theatre of Empire: Racial Counterfeit, Racial Realism' in Wilson (ed.), *A New Imperial History*, 2004.

Nussbaum, Felicity A., and Brown, Laura (eds), *The New Eighteenth Century: Theory, Politics, English Literature*, London and New York, Methuen, 1987.

O'Brien, John, *Harlequin Britain: Pantomime and Entertainment, 1690–1760*, Baltimore, MD, Johns Hopkins UP, 2004.

Okokon, Susan, *Black Londoners, 1880–1990*, Stroud, Sutton, 1998.

Oldfield, John R., 'The "Ties of Soft Humanity": Slavery and Race in British Drama, 1760–1800', *Huntingdon Library Quarterly*, vol. 56, no. 1, Winter 1993.

Oldfield, John R., *Popular Politics and British Anti-slavery: The Mobilisation of Public Opinion against the Slave Trade, 1787–1807*, London, Frank Cass, 1998.

O'Quinn, Daniel, 'Mercantile Deformities: George Colman's *Inkle and Yarico* and the Racialization of Class Relations', *Theatre Journal*, vol. 54, no. 3, October 2002, Baltimore, MD, Johns Hopkins UP.

O'Quinn, Daniel, *Staging Governance: Theatrical Imperialism in London, 1770–1800*, Baltimore, MD, and London, Johns Hopkins UP, 2005.

O'Quinn, Daniel, 'Theatre and Empire', in Moody and O'Quinn (eds), *Cambridge Companion to British Theatre, 1730–1830*, 2007.

Orr, Bridget, *Empire on the Stage 1660–1714*, Cambridge, Cambridge UP, 2001.

Osborne, Deidre, 'Writing Black Back: An Overview of Black Theatre and Performance in Britain', in Godiwala (ed.), *Alternatives within the Mainstream*, 2006.

Osborne, Deidre 'Not "In-Yer-Face" But What Lies Beneath: Experiential and Aesthetic Inroads in the Drama of debbie tucker green and Dona Daley', in Arana (ed.), *"Black" British Aesthetics Today*, 2007.

Owusu, Kwesi, *The Struggle for Black Arts in Britain: What Can We Consider Better than Freedom?* London, Comedia Publishing Group, 1986.

Owusu, Kwesi (ed.), *Storms of the Heart: An Anthology of Black Arts and Culture*, London, Camden Press, 1988.

Owusu, Kwesi (ed.), *Black British Culture and Society: A Text Reader*, London and New York, Routledge, 2000.

Page, Malcolm, 'West Indian Playwrights in Britain', *Canadian Drama*, vol. 6, no. 1, 1980.

Palmer, Daryl W., 'Merchants and Miscegenation: *The Three Ladies of London, The Jew of Malta, and The Merchant of Venice*', in MacDonald (ed.), *Race, Ethnicity, and Power in the Renaissance*, 1997.

Panayi, Panikos, *An Immigration History of Britain: Multicultural Racism since 1800*, Harlow, Essex, Longman, 2010.

Parker, John, et. al. (eds), *Who's Who in the Theatre, 1912–1976* (16 editions), London, Pitman, 1912–1978.

Pavis, Patrick (ed.), *The Intercultural Performance Reader*, London, Routledge, 1996.

Peacock, D. Keith, *Thatcher's Theatre: British Theatre and Drama in the Eighties*, Santa Barbara, CA, Greenwood Press, 1999.

Peacock, D. Keith, 'Black British Drama and the Politics of Identity', in Holdsworth and Luckhurst (eds), *A Concise Companion to Contemporary British and Irish Drama*, 2008.

Pearson, Jacqueline, 'Blacker Than Hell Creates: Pix Rewrites *Othello*', in Quinsey (ed.), *Broken Boundaries*, 1996.

Pechter, Edward, *Othello and Interpretive Traditions*, Iowa City, IA, University of Iowa Press, 1999.

Peterson, Bernard L. Jr, *Early Black American Playwrights and Dramatic Writers: A Biographical Directory and Catalog of Plays, Films, and Broadcasting Scripts*, New York, Greenwood, 1990.

Phelan, Peggy, and Lane, Jill (eds), *The Ends of Performance*, New York and London, New York UP, 1998.

Phillips, Mike, *London Crossings: A Biography of Black Britain*, London, Continuum, 2001.

Pickering, Michael, 'White Skin, Black Masks: "Nigger" Minstrelsy in Victorian Britain', in Bratton (ed.), *Music Hall Performance and Style*, 1986.

Pickering, Michael, 'Mock Blacks and Racial Mockery: The "Nigger" Minstrel and British Imperialism', in Bratton et al., *Acts of Supremacy*, 1991.

Pickering, Michael, 'The Blackface Clown', in Gerzina (ed.), *Black Victorians*, 2003.

Pines, Jim (ed.), *Black and White in Colour: Black People in British Television Since 1936*, London, BFI Publishing, 1992.

Pinnock, Winsome, 'Breaking Down the Door', in Gottlieb and Chambers (eds), *Theatre in a Cool Climate*, 1999.

Poel, William, 'Hindu Drama on the English Stage', *Asiatic Quarterly Review*, vol. 1, April 1913.

Pollard, Tanya, *Drugs and Theatre in Early Modern England*, Oxford, Oxford UP, 2005.

Ponnuswami, Meenakshi, 'Small Island People: Black British Women Playwrights,' in Aston and Reinelt (eds), *Cambridge Companion to Modern British Women Playwrights*, 2000.

Ponnuswami, Meenakshi, 'Alienation and Alienation Effects in Winsome Pinnock's *Talking in Tongues*', in Arana (ed.), *"Black" British Aesthetics Today*, 2007.

Potter, Lois, 'Pirates and "Turning Turk" in Renaissance Drama', in Maquerlot and Willems (eds), *Travel and Drama in Shakespeare's Time*, 1996.

Potter, Lois, *Othello*, Manchester, Manchester UP, 2002.

Powell, Kerry (ed.), *Cambridge Companion to Victorian and Edwardian Theatre*, Cambridge, Cambridge UP, 2004.

Price, Lawrence Marsden, *Inkle and Yarico Album*, Berkeley, CA, University of California Press, 1937.

Quinsey, Katherine M. (ed.), *Broken Boundaries: Women and Feminism in Restoration Drama*, Lexington, KY University of Kentucky Press, 1996.

Rees, Roland, *Fringe First: Pioneers of Fringe Theatre on Record*, London, Oberon Books, 1992.

Rehin, George F., 'Harlequin Jim Crow: Continuity and Convergence in Blackface Clowning', *The Journal of Popular Culture*, vol. 9, no. 3, 1975.

Rehin, George F., 'Blackface Street Minstrels in Victorian London and its Resorts: Popular Culture and its Racial Connotations As Revealed in Polite Opinion', *The Journal of Popular Culture*, vol. 15, no. 1, 1981.

Reid, J.C., *Bucks and Bruisers: Pierce Egan and Regency London*, London, Routledge and Kegan Paul, 1971.

Reynolds, Harry, *Minstrel Memories: The Story of Burnt Cork Minstrelsy in Great Britain from 1836 to 1927*, London, Alston Rivers, 1928.

Richardson, Tony, *Long Distance Runner: A Memoir*, London, Faber and Faber, 1993.

Riis, Thomas L. (ed.), *The Music and Scripts of* In Dahomey (*Music of the United States of America*, vol. 5), Middleton, WI, A-R Editions, 1996.

Roach, Joseph R., *Cities of the Dead: Circum-Atlantic Performance*, New York, Columbia UP, 1996.

Robb, David (ed.), *Clowns, Fools and Picaros: Popular Forms in Theatre, Fiction and Film*, Amsterdam and New York, Rodopi, 2007.

Roberts, Brian Russell, 'Lost Theatres of African American Internationalism: Diplomacy and Henry Francis Downing in Luanda and London', *African American Review*, Summer 2008.

Roberts, Brian Russell, 'A London Legacy of Ira Aldridge: Henry Francis Downing and the Paratheatrical Poetics of Plot and Cast(e)', (forthcoming).

Roberts, Diane, *The Myth of Aunt Jemima: Representations of Race and Region*, London and New York, Routledge, 1994.

Rosenberg, Marvin, *The Masks of Othello: the Search for the Identity of Othello, Iago and Desdemona by Three Centuries of Actors and Critics*, Berkeley, CA, University of California Press, 1961.

Rosenthal, Laura J., 'Juba's Roman Soul: Addison's *Cato* and Enlightenment Cosmopolitanism', *Studies in the Literary Imagination*, vol. 32, Fall 1999.

Rosenthal, Laura J., ' "Infamous Commerce": Transracial Prostitution in the South Seas and Back', in Rosenthal and Choudhury (eds), *Monstrous Dreams of Reason*, 2002.

Rosenthal, Laura J., and Choudhury, Mita S. (eds), *Monstrous Dreams of Reason: Body, Self, and Other in the Enlightenment*, London, Associated UPs, 2002.

Ruggles, Jeffrey, *The Unboxing of Henry Brown*, Richmond, VA, Library of Virginia, 2003.

Russell, Gillian, 'An "Entertainment of Oddities": Fashionable Sociability and the Pacific in the 1770s', in Wilson (ed.), *A New Imperial History,* 2004.

Ruvani, Ranasinha, *South Asian Writers in Twentieth-Century Britain*, Oxford, Clarendon, 2007.

Said, Edward, *Orientalism*, London, Routledge and Kegan Paul, 1978.

Sandhu, Sukhdev, *London Calling: How Black and Asian Writers Imagined a City*, London, Harper Collins, 2003.

Sandiford, Keith A., *Measuring the Moment: Strategies of Protest in Eighteenth Century Afro-English Writing*, Selsingrove, PA, Susquehana UP, 1988.

Schueller, Malini Johar, 'Performing Whiteness, Performing Blackness: Dorr's Cultural Capital and the Critique of Slavery', *Criticism*, vol. 41, Spring 1999.

Scobie, Edward, *Black Britannia: A History of Blacks in Britain*, London, Pall Mall Press, 1972.

Seton, Marie, 'English Theatre of the Left', *New Theatre*, December 1934.

Seton, Marie, *Paul Robeson*, London, Dennis Dobson, 1958.

Shepherd, Simon, *Marlowe and the Politics of Elizabethan Theatre*, Brighton, Harvester, 1986.

Sherwood, Marika, *Claudia Jones: A Life in Exile*, London, Lawrence and Wishart, 1999.

Shyllon, Folarin, *Black People in Britain 1555–1833*, London, Oxford UP, 1977.

Sierz, Aleks, ' "Two Worlds Fighting Each Other": Roy Williams and Contemporary Black British Theatre', in Davis and Fuchs (ed.), *Staging New Britain*, 2006.

Singleton, Brian, *Oscar Ashe, Orientalism, and British Musical Comedy*, London, Praeger, 2004.

Sivanandan, Ambalavaner, *From Resistance to Rebellion*, London, Institute of Race Relations, 1986.

Skura, Meredith Anne, 'Discourse and the Individual: The Case of Colonialism in *The Tempest*', *Shakespeare Quarterly*, XL, 1989.

Smith, Ian, 'White Skin, Black Masks: Racial Cross-Dressing on the Early Modern Stage', *Renaissance Drama*, no. 32, 2003.

Smith, Karina, 'Narratives of Success, Narratives of Failure: The Creation and Collapse of Sistren's "Aesthetic Space" ', *Modern Drama*, vol. 51, no. 2, Summer 2008.

Solanke, Adeola, 'Creative Space: Double Edge Versus the Church of England', in Owusu (ed.), *Storms of the Heart*, 1988.

Sorabji, Cornelia, *India Calling: The Memories of Cornelia Sorabji*, London, Nisbet, 1934.

Southern, Eileen, *Biographical Dictionary of Afro-American and African Musicians*, Westport, CT, Greenwood Press, 1982.

Speaight, Robert. *William Poel and the Elizabethan Revival*, London, Heinemann, 1954.

Spencer, Suzette A., 'Henry Box Brown, An International Fugitive: Slavery, Resistance, and Imperialism', in McKittrick and Woods (eds), *Black Geographies and the Politics of Place*, 2007.

Stanbrook, T. W., 'The Black Presence in London Theatre, 1974–1979', *Western Journal of Black Studies*, vol. 7, no. 2, Summer 1983.

Starck, Kathleen, ' "Black and Female Is Some of Who I Am and I Want to Explore It": Black Women's Plays of the 1980s and 1990s', in Godiwala (ed.), *Alternatives Within the Mainstream*, 2006.

Steel, Janet, 'Shame in Birmingham', *Index on Censorship*, vol. 34, no. 2, May 2005.

Stephenson, Heidi, and Langridge, Natasha, *Rage and Reason: Women Playwrights on Playwriting*, London, Methuen, 1997.

Stevens, Andrea R., ' "Assisted by a Barber": The Court Apothecary, Special Effects, and *The Gypsies Metamorphosed*', *Theatre Notebook*, vol. 61, no. 1, 2007.

Stone, Judy S.J., *Studies in West Indian Literature: Theatre*, London and Basingstoke, Hants, Macmillan, 1994.

Swindells, Julia, *Glorious Causes: The Grand Theatre of Political Change, 1789 to 1833*, Oxford, Oxford UP, 2001.

Sypher, Wylie, *Guinea's Captive Kings: British Anti-slavery Literature of the XVIIIth*, New York, Octagon Books, 1969.

Taxidou, Olga (ed.), *The Mask: A Periodical Performance by Edward Gordon Craig*, London, Routledge, 1998.

Taylor, Frank C., *Alberta Hunter: A Celebration in Blues*, New York, McGraw Hill, 1987.

Taylor, Gary, *Buying Whiteness: Race, Culture, and Identity from Columbus to Hip Hop*, New York and Basingstoke, Hants, Palgrave Macmillan, 2005.

Terracciano, Alda, 'Mainstreaming African, Asian and Caribbean Theatre: The Experiments of the Black Theatre Forum', in Godiwala (ed.), *Alternatives within the Mainstream*, 2006.

Terracciano, Alda, 'Together We Stand!', in Maitland (ed.), *Navigating Difference*, 2006.

Thieme, John, 'Repossessing the Slave Past: Caribbean Historiography and Dennis Scott's *An Echo in the Bone*', in Walling (ed.), *Theatre and Slavery*, 2007.

Thompson, Ayanna, *Performing Race and Torture on the Early Modern Stage*, London and New York, Routledge, 2008.

Thompson, Ayanna (ed.), *Colorblind Shakespeare: New Perspectives on Race and Performance*, London and New York, Routledge, 2006.

Thompson, George A. Jr, *A Documentary History of the African Theatre*, Evanston, IL, Northwestern UP, 1998.

Thompson, Leslie, *An Autobiography (as told to Jeffrey P. Green)*, Crawley, W. Sussex, Rabbit Press, 1985.

Tokson, Elliot H., *The Popular Image of the Black Man in English Drama, 1550–1688*, Boston, MA., G. K. Hall and Co., 1982.

Tompsett, Ruth A. (ed.), *Black Theatre in Britain*, Harwood Academic Press; special issue of *Performing Arts International*, no. 1(2), 1996.

Turner, John M., 'Pablo Fanque, Black Circus Performer', in Gerzina (ed.), *Black Victorians*, 2003.

Ugwu, Catherine (ed.), *Let's Get It On: The Politics of Black Performance*, London, ICA, 1995.

Ukaegbu, Victor, 'Talawa Theatre Company: The "Likkle" Matter of Black Creativity and Representation on the British Stage', in Godiwala (ed.), *Alternatives within the Mainstream*, 2006.

Uno, Roberta, with Burns, Lucy Mae San Pablo (eds), *The Color of Theater: Race, Culture and Contemporary Performance*, London, Continuum, 2002.

Upton, Carole-Anne (ed.), *Moving Target: Theatre Translation and Cultural Relocation*, Manchester and Northampton, MA, St. Jerome Publishing, 2000.

van Gyseghem, André, 'British Theatre in the Thirties: An Autobiographical Record', in Clark et al. (eds), *Culture and Crisis in Britain in the 30s*, 1979.

Vaughan, Alden T., and Mason Vaughan, Virginia, *Shakespeare's Caliban: A Cultural History*, Cambridge, Cambridge UP, 1991.

Verma, Jatinder, interview in Delgado and Heritage (eds), *In Contact with the Gods?*, Manchester, Manchester UP, 1996.

Verma, Jatinder, 'The Challenge of Binglish: Analyzing Multi-cultural Productions', in Campbell (ed.), *Analyzing Performance*, 1996.

Verma, Jatinder, '"Binglishing" the Stage: A Generation of Asian Theatre in England', in Boon and Plastow (eds), *Theatre Matters*, 1998.

Verma, Jatinder, 'Sorry, No Saris!', in Gottlieb and Chambers (eds), *Theatre in a Cool Climate*, 1999.

Visram, Rozina, *Ayahs, Lascars, and Princes: Indians in Britain 1700–1947*, London, Pluto Press, 1986.

Visram, Rozina, *Asians in Britain: 400 Years of History*, London, Pluto Press, 2002.

Vitkus, Daniel, *Turning Turk: English Theater and the Multicultural Mediterranean, 1570–1630*, New York and Basingstoke, Hants, Palgrave Macmillan, 2003.

Walling, Michael (ed.), *Theatre and Slavery: Ghosts at the Crossroads*, Enfield, Border Crossings, 2007.

Walmsley, Anne, *The Caribbean Artists Movement, 1966–1972: A Literary and Cultural History*, London, New Beacon Books, 1992.

Walvin, James, *Black Presence: A Documentary History of the Negro in England, 1555–1860*, London, Orbach and Chambers, 1971.

Walvin, James, *Black and White: The Negro and English Society 1551–1945*, London, Allen Lane, 1973.

Wann, Louis, 'The Oriental in Elizabethan Drama', *Modern Philology*, vol. 12, no. 7, January 1915.

Waters, Hazel, *Racism on the Victorian Stage: Representation of Slavery and the Black Character*, Cambridge, Cambridge UP, 2007.

Wearing, J. P., *The London Stage: A Calendar of Plays and Players, 1890–1959* (6 vols), Metuchen, NJ, The Scarecrow Press, 1976–1993.

Weinstein, Cindy (ed.), *Cambridge Companion to Harriet Beecher Stowe*, Cambridge, Cambridge UP, 2004.

Wheeler, Roxann, *The Complexion of Race: Categories of Difference in Eighteenth-Century British Culture*, Philadelphia, PA, University of Pennsylvania Press, 2000.

Willis, Ted, *Evening All: Fifty Years over a Hot Typewriter*, London, Macmillan, 1991.

Wilson, Kathleen, 'Pacific Modernity: Theater, Englishness, and the Arts of Discovery, 1760–1800', in Jones and Wahrman (eds), *The Age of Cultural Revolutions*, 2002.

Wilson, Kathleen, *The Island Race: Englishness, Empire and Gender in the Eighteenth Century*, London, Routledge, 2003.

Wilson, Kathleen (ed.), *A New Imperial History: Culture, Identity and Modernity in Britain and the Empire, 1660–1840*, Cambridge, Cambridge UP, 2004.

Wiseman, Sue, 'Abolishing Romance: Representing Rape in Oroonoko', in Brycchan Carey et al. (eds), *Discourses of Slavery and Abolition*, 2004.

Woddis, Carole, *Sheer Bloody Magic – Conversations with Actresses*, London, Virago, 1991.

Wood, Marcus, *Blind Memory: Visual Representations of Slavery in England and America, 1780–1865*, Manchester, Manchester UP, 2000.

Woollacott, Angela, 'Rose Quong Becomes Chinese: An Australian in London and New York', *Australian Historical Studies*, vol. 38, no. 129, April 2007.

Worrall, David, *Theatric Revolution: Drama, Censorship, and Romantic Subcultures 1773–1832*, Oxford, Oxford UP, 2006.

Worrall, David, *The Politics of Romantic Theatricality, 1787–1832*, Basingstoke, Hants, Palgrave Macmillan, 2007.

Worrall, David, *Harlequin Empire: Race, Ethnicity and the Drama of the Popular Enlightenment*, London, Pickering and Chatto, 2007.

Yang, Chi-ming, 'Virtue's Vogues: Eastern Authenticity and the Commodification of Chinese-ness on the 18th-century Stage', *Comparative Literature Studies*, vol. 39, no. 4, 2002.

Young, Robert J. C., *Colonial Desire: Hybridity in Theory, Culture and Race*, New York, Routledge, 1995.

Ziter, Edward, *The Orient on the Victorian Stage*, Cambridge, Cambridge UP, 2003.

Plays quoted

Bate, Henry, *The Black-a-moor Wash'd White*, in Gretchen Gerzina, *Black England: Life before Emancipation*, London, Allison and Busby, 1999.

Bate, Jonathan, and Rasmussen, Eric (eds), William Shakespeare, *Complete Works*, Basingstoke, Hants, Macmillan, 2007 [*A Midsummer Night's Dream*, *Love's Labour's Lost*, *Much Ado About Nothing*, *Othello*, *The Tempest*, *Titus Andronicus*].

Bickerstaff, Isaac, *Love in a City*, London, W. Lowdnes and J. Barker, 1786.

Bickerstaff, Isaac, *The Padlock*, in Jeffrey N. Cox (ed.), *Slavery, Abolition and Emancipation: Writings in the British Romantic Period*, vol. 5, *Drama*, London, Pickering and Chatto, 1999; The Epilogue, <www.brycchancarey.com/slavery/padlock1.htm>.

Colman, George Jr, *Inkle and Yarico*, London, Sadler and Co., 1770?

Dibdin, Charles, *The Mirror; Or Harlequin Every-where*, < www.cla.purdue.edu/academic/engl/navsa/conferences/2006/documents/CarlsonRiseofMungo.doc>.

Dimond, William, *The Lady and the Devil*, Cumberland's British Theatre, vol. 45, no. 375, London, G. H. Davidson, 1849.

Downing, Henry Francis, with Margarita Downing, *Placing Paul's Play*, London, Francis Griffiths, 1914.

Downing, Henry Francis, *A New Coon in Town*, self-published, copy held at Schomburg Center for Research in Black Culture, New York.

Foote, Samuel, *The Cozeners*, Dublin, George Bonham, 1778.

Garrick, David, *Harlequin Invasion*, in John O'Brien, *Harlequin Britain: Pantomime and Entertainment, 1690-1760*, Baltimore, MD, Johns Hopkins UP, 2004.

James, C.L.R., *Toussaint Louverture; The story of the only successful slave revolt in history*, Durham, NC, Duke UP (forthcoming.

John, Errol, *Moon on a Rainbow Shawl*, in *The Observer Plays*, London, Faber and Faber, 1958, and revised, *Moon on a Rainbow Shawl*, London, Faber and Faber, 1958.

Khan-Din, Ayub, *East is East*, London, Nick Hern Books, 1996.

Matura, Mustapha, *Play Mas*, London, Methuen, 1982.

Munday, Anthony, and Chettle, Robert (?), *The Death of Robert, Earl of Huntingdon* (1601), Malone Society Reprints, Oxford, Oxford UP, 1967.

Murray, William (?), *Obi; or, Three-Finger'd Jack – A Melo-Drama in Two Acts*, <www. rc.umd. edu/praxis/obi>.

Peele, George, *The Old Wives' Tale* (1595), in *The Minor Elizabethan Drama*, vol. 2, London, J. M. Dent, 1910.

Peters, Peters, and Sklar, George, *Stevedore*, London, Jonathan Cape, 1935.

Pinnock, Winsome, *Leave Taking*, in Kate Harwood (ed.), *First Run: New Plays by New Writers*, London, Nick Hern Books, 1989.

Reports

Baker, Walter V., *The Arts of Ethnic Minorities: Status and Funding – A Research Report*, London, Commission for Racial Equality, 1985.

Black Writing, a Guide for Black Writers, London, London Arts Board, no date but probably 1998.

Bloomfield, Jude, *Crossing the Rainbow: National Differences and International Convergences in Multicultural Performing Arts in Europe* (Report for Informal European Theatre Meeting), London, IETM, 2003.

Boyden Associates, Peter, *Roles and Functions of the English Regional Producing Theatres*, London, Arts Council of England, 2000.

Cork, Kenneth (chair), *Theatre Is for All*, Report of the Inquiry into Professional Theatre in England, London, Arts Council of Great Britain, 1986.

Decibel Evaluation: Key Findings, London, Arts Council England, 2005.

Eclipse Report: Developing Strategies to Combat Racism in Theatre, London, Arts Council of England, 2002.

Equal Opportunities: The Glass Ceiling Report, London, Independent Theatre Council, 2002.

Focus on Cultural Diversity: The Arts in England: Attendance, Participation and Attitudes, London, Arts Council of England, 2003.

Going Black Under the Skin, London, London Arts Board/ New Playwrights Trust, [no date; c1995/6].

Harding, F., *Report on the Arts of the Ethnic Minorities in Scotland*, London, Commission for Racial Equality and Scottish Arts Council, 1982.

Jennings, Mel, ARTS, *Audit of Research into Audiences for Black and Asian Work*, London, Arts Council of England, 1998.

Jermyn, Helen, and Desai, Philly, *Arts – What's in a Word? Ethnic Minorities and the Arts*, London, Arts Council of England, 2000.

Khan, Naseem, *The Arts Britain Ignores: The Arts of Ethnic Minorities in Britain*, London, Community Relations Commission, 1976.

Khan, Naseem, *British Asian Theatre Report*, London, Arts Council of Great Britain (for East Midlands Regional Arts Board), 1994.

Khan, Naseem, 'Towards a greater diversity: results and legacy of the Arts Council of England's cultural diversity action plan', London, Arts Council of England, 2002.

Khan, Naseem, 'The Arts in Transition', *Reinventing Britain: Cultural Diversity up front and on show*, London, Guardian publication in association with Decibel, 2003.

National Policy for Theatre in England, London, Arts Council of England, 2000.

Parekh, Bhikhu (chair), *The Future of Multi-Ethnic Britain*, London, Runnymede Trust, 2000.

Ross, Jacob, and Small, Valery, mpr ltd, *Archiving the Arts of England's Culturally Diverse Communities*, London, Arts Council of England, 1999.

Sivanandan, Ambalavaner (chair), *In the Eye of the Needle*, London, Institute of Race Relations, 1986.

The Arts of Ethnic Minorities: An Arts Council Reading Guide, London, Arts Council of Great Britain, 1986.

The Arts of Ethnic Minorities: A Role for the CRE, London, Commission for Racial Equality, 1979.

The Glory of the Garden: The Development of the Arts in England – A Strategy for a Decade, London, Arts Council of Great Britain, 1984.

The Landscape of Fact: Towards a Policy for Cultural Diversity for the English Funding System, London, Arts Council of England, 1997.

The Theatre Commission: A Report on Subsidised Theatre in the UK, London, British Actors' Equity Association, 1996.

Towards Cultural Diversity, London, Arts Council of Great Britain, 1989.

Young, Lola, *Whose Theatre…? Report on the Sustained Theatre Consultation*, London, Arts Council England, 2006.

Other media

Blackgrounds interviews (recorded in 1997 and supported by Arts Council England, Talawa Archive, Theatre Museum): Earl Cameron, Pearl Connor, Cy Grant, Barry Reckord, Alaknanda Samarth.

Blackstage interviews (recorded in 2002 and supported by the Heritage Lottery Fund, Talawa Archive, Theatre Museum): Michael Abbensetts, Thomas Baptiste, Yvonne Brewster, Frank Cousins, Mona Hammond, Ram Jam Holder, Naseem Khan, Corinne Skinner Carter, and Rudolph Walker [an interview with Carmen Munroe is listed but did not take place).

TheatreVOICE interviews/ discussions (theatrevoice.com): Jimmy Akingbola, Oladipo Agboluaje, Pat Crump and Deborah Sawyer, Mustapha Matura and Nicholas Kent; discussions/debates: 'The State of Black Theatre', 'Writing from Reality', *Sing Yer Heart Out for the Lads*.

Online

www.bcaheritage.org.uk

www.artscouncil.org.uk

www.backstage.ac.uk

www.black-history-month.co.uk

www.britishcouncil.org

www.brycchancarey.com

www.casbah.ac.uk

www.cla.purdue.edu/academic/engl/navsa/conferences/2006/documents/ CarlsonRiseofMungo.doc

www.edumfa.com/index.htm

www.everygeneration.co.uk

www.futurehistories.org.uk
www.hinduismtoday.com/modules/smartsection/item.php?itemid=1253
www.hrw.org
www.mellenpress.com/mellenpress.cfm?bookid=7877&pc=9
www.movinghere.org.uk
www.open.ac.uk/makingbritain
www.oup.com/oxforddnb/info/online
www.rc.umd.edu [Charles Rzepka (ed.), *Obi, A Romantic Circles Praxis Volume*]
www.religion-online.org/showchapter.asp?title=3378&C=2771
www.salidaa.com/salidaa/site/Home (for South Asian Diaspora)
www.talawatheatrecompany.co.uk
www.tamasha.org.uk
www.tara-arts.com
www.theatrevoice.com
www.tradingfacesonline.com
www.tribuneindia.com/2010/20100918/saturday/main1.htm
www.utm.utoronto.ca/~w3minstr/
www.westminster.gov.uk/services/libraries/archives/blackpresence/23

INDEX